Advances in Spatial Science

For further volumes:
http://www.springer.com/series/3302

Stilianos Alexiadis

Convergence Clubs and Spatial Externalities

Models and Applications of Regional Convergence in Europe

 Springer

Dr. Stilianos Alexiadis
Ministry of Rural Development and Foods
Athens
Greece

ISSN 1430-9602
ISBN 978-3-642-31625-8   ISBN 978-3-642-31626-5 (eBook)
DOI 10.1007/978-3-642-31626-5
Springer Heidelberg New York Dordrecht London

Library of Congress Control Number: 2012948988

Printed on acid-free paper

Springer is part of Springer Science+Business Media (www.springer.com)

Preface

A major concern for regional scientists is whether regional per capita incomes tend to converge or diverge over the long run, and whether such trends apply to all or only limited groups. This latter phenomenon is known as 'club convergence'. Notwithstanding the vast theoretical and empirical literature, a textbook devoted exclusively to regional convergence does not exist. Standard textbooks on economic growth devote a few sections to the issue of convergence, usually without a regional dimension and ignoring the possibility of club convergence.

This book is concerned with whether levels of labour productivity across the regions of an enlarged Europe converge or diverge. In particular, it is argued that the EU-27 regions follow a pattern of club convergence. In the early chapters the neoclassical model is extended by several elements from Endogenous Growth and New Economic Geography models, as a theoretical framework. It is argued that club or local convergence is attributed to differences in technology creation and adoption and agglomeration externalities across regions. This argument is developed in an explicitly spatial context, taking into account interaction and spillovers from technology creation across geographical areas. To support this argument, a theoretical model is developed, which attributes club convergence to existing differences with respect to the degree of technology adoption across regions. This model postulates that convergence amongst regions is feasible only if they share similar structural characteristics, regarding the creation and adoption of technology. A range of convergence tests are examined and applied. In the first instance, empirical results suggest that in terms of absolute and conditional convergence, the NUTS-2 regions of the EU-27 converge at a very slow rate. Further tests, however, indicate that convergence is restricted to a specific subset of regions, suggesting that the European regions have followed a pattern of convergence that can be characterised as club convergence over the period 1995–2006. These tests also show a geographical pattern to the convergence club. Such conclusions are tested further, using an alternative model of club convergence, which incorporates the impact of spatial interaction, agglomeration externalities and technology. This shows that the convergence club in Europe follows a certain geographical pattern and members share similar characteristics regarding technology creation and adoption and agglomeration externalities.

Writing a book devoted exclusively to regional convergence dates back to 2006 when I was a PhD Student at Manchester Metropolitan University. With this volume I hope to present a textbook tailored to the needs of students and working professionals in economics. This textbook can be used by lectures and students at undergraduate and postgraduate levels in a wide range of areas, including Economics, European Studies, Regional Economics, and Economic Geography. At postgraduate level, especially, this book would be useful for students in Regional Economics, and Economic Geography given that there are very few (if any) textbooks devoted exclusively to regional convergence. PhD students of regional convergence can use the present volume as a reference book to review the theoretical and empirical literature on regional convergence in an easy, comprehensive and quick way. Economists dealing with practical and applied issues will also find this volume an efficient and easy-to-use textbook. Planners, policy-makers and regional development institutions in the EU, especially in the new member states, will find this book particularly useful, given that the models/methods can be applied easily to conduct policy experiments/simulations.

I am now in the pleasant duty of thanking the people who contributed to its preparation and final realization of this book. I am truly indebted to Mrs. Judith Tomkins for her helpful comments, suggestions and creative discussions, without which it would have been almost impossible to realize this book. Therefore, I would like to express my profound appreciation for her unfailing help and guidance and being able to resolve every obstacle that I encountered. I would like to express my appreciation to Prof. Derek Leslie for his guidance and support. Special thanks to Dr. Dimitrios Tsagdis for his support and encouragement. I would like to thank Dr. Konstantinos Eleftheriou for his help. I am grateful to Professor Athanasios Argiris who introduced me to the exiting world of regional economics and 'lit my fire' for research when I was a student at the Department of Economics at the University of Thessaloniki. Also, I would like to thank Mr. P. Pezaros and Mr. S. Kokkidis, of the Department of Agricultural Policy & Documentation of the Ministry of Rural Development & Foods of Greece, for their unreserved support. The findings, interpretations and conclusions are entirely those of the authors and, do not necessarily represent the official position, policies or views of the Ministry of Rural Development & Foods and/or the Greek Government. I am grateful to Springer Publications, especially to Barbara Fess and Marion Kreisel, who have been involved in the publication of this book.

I feel I am particularly indebted to Eleanor and David MacKay for their help. A very special person I wish to thank is my wife Helen for her understanding and patience. A very special mention, finally, is to my parents, Simeon and Chrisaugi and my sister Despoina. Apart from the immense gratitude I feel towards them, I would like to mention their presence, love and encouragement were a catalyst in realizing this book.

Athens, May 2012   Stilianos Alexiadis

Contents

List of Figures

List of Tables

Chapter 1
Introduction

1.1 The Overall Context

A major concern for regional economists is whether regional per-capita incomes tend to converge or diverge over the long-run, and whether such trends apply to all or only limited groups of economies. This latter possibility is known as 'club convergence' and provides a realistic and detailed picture about regional growth (Fischer and Stirböck 2006). The notion of club convergence was originally introduced by Baumol (1986) in recognition of convergence within a subset of national economies. As Baumol and Wolff (1988, p. 1159) subsequently noted, however, "just how countries achieve membership in the convergence club, and on what basis they are sometimes ejected" is a difficult question to answer.

1.2 Major Aims of this Study

An essential aim of this study is to contribute to an understanding of convergence and specifically of club convergence, using the regions of the European Union (hereafter EU) as an empirical context. Europe is characterised by considerable regional disparities that constrain future development. Regional convergence is justified on the ground that 'imbalances do not just imply a poorer quality of life for the most disadvantaged regions and the lack of life-chances open to their citizens, but indicate an under-utilisation of human potential and the failure to take advantage of economic opportunities which benefit the Union as a whole' (European Commission 1996, p. 13). A central question is therefore whether regional disparities constrain the extent of convergence across all the regions of Europe, that is whether or not there exist particular groups of regions that exhibit different tendencies in their patterns of growth and convergence.

The main focus of this study involves the examination of differences in labour productivity, expressed as output per-worker. However, it has been pointed out that regional disparities in Europe are reflected not only in terms of labour productivity

S. Alexiadis, *Convergence Clubs and Spatial Externalities*,
Advances in Spatial Science, DOI 10.1007/978-3-642-31626-5_1,
© Springer-Verlag Berlin Heidelberg 2013

but also in terms of several aspects of economic and social activity, such as levels of technology, research activity, degrees of urbanisation and so forth. Such disparities are of critical significance and therefore it is also an aim of this study to provide a theoretical and an empirical assessment of such key factors in determining the pattern of convergence across Europe.

Regional convergence or 'cohesion' is one of the primary targets in the context of the EU. Indeed, the question of regional convergence, expressed in terms of economic and social cohesion, is mentioned in the Preamble of the Treaty of Rome and is formulated in the Single European Act (title XIV, currently title XVII, Articles 2 and 4), signed in 1986. According to Article 158 of the Rome Treaty 'reducing disparities between the levels of development of the various regions and the backwardness of the least favoured regions or islands, including rural areas' is one of the primary objectives of EU development policies. The objective of regional cohesion includes also provision of basic services such as health, education and housing. Regional cohesion also implies an effective counteracting of concentration of economic activities in 'central' or 'core' regions and the 'centripetal' effects of European integration. The treaties of Maastricht and Amsterdam, signed in 1992 and 1997, respectively emphasise the unequal effects of the integration process in progress at territorial level.

According to the third report of the European Commission (2004) on social cohesion, regional convergence is seen as vital to the success of several other key policy objectives, such as the single market, monetary union, and EU competitiveness. This is formulated in the design of Strategic Guidelines on Cohesion 2007–2013, which in a background of increasing globalisation and a 'second industrial revolution', due to information technology, marks the cohesion policy as the main road to success of the EU's ambitions. The strategy 'Europe 2020' aims to make the EU more attractive for investment and employment, an area of high growth, competitiveness, innovation, full employment with higher productivity and more and better jobs (European Commission, 2006a,b; 2007a,b). As a result, the EU has implemented a range of development policies to achieve regional convergence (and continues to do so), such as the direction of funds towards less-advanced areas of Europe from sources, such as Structural Fund Support, the European Regional Development Fund, the European Social Fund and implementation of projects, such as the Mediterranean Integrated Programs. In budgetary terms, from a marginal importance up to the mid-1970s, Regional Cohesion Policy has become one of the most important policies, together with the Common Agricultural Policy (CAP). However, to what extent such policy measures help the poor regions of the EU to catch up? Although it has been suggested that about one third of the reduction in regional disparities is due to development policies, nevertheless, a precise answer to this question requires, according to Fagerberg and Verspagen (1996), knowledge about what determines differences in regional economic performance.

The EU is not a static entity, as Button and Pentecost (1999) aptly note. In 1957 six countries (Belgium, France, West Germany, Italy, Luxemburg and the Netherlands) signed the Treaty of Rome, constituting the European Economic Community. Ever since there have been several process of enlargement carried out simultaneously with an integration process. In particular, the UK, Ireland and Denmark were joined in 1973, followed by Greece in 1981, Portugal and Spain in 1986; countries with substantial internal regional disparities. The EU was enlarged to 15 members in 1995 by Austria, Finland and Sweden while in 2004 and 2007 several countries of Eastern Europe were included, leading to the EU-27. This last enlargement brought several regions located in the eastern periphery of Europe. This constitutes a great challenge for the EU due to three key reasons (Mancha-Novarro and Garrido-Yserte 2008). First, the New Member-States have substantial difficulties in adopting European political and institutional structures; a political perspective. Second, the New Member-States have a very limited contribution capacity; a financial, perspective. Third, and most importantly, the economic conditions prevailing in the regions of the New Member-States differ substantially with those in the 'central' Member-States of the EU-15 (e.g. the UK, France, Germany, the Benelux countries) although they are more close to the 'peripheral' countries of the EU-15, such as Greece and Portugal, countries characterized by wide socio-economic gaps. The enlargement of the EU to Central and Eastern countries as well as to Cyprus and Malta has resulted in a 21% increase in the geographical area of Europe and a 19% increase in population. However, the accession of new countries has brought an increase to EU's GDP only by 10% accompanied with a decrease in GDP per-capita by 8% (European Commission 2003, 2004). These changes, led to what Ertur and Koch (2005) have aptly called 'a shifting from the historical North/South dualism to the North-west/East income disparities in terms of per capita GDP' (p. 10). Consequently, convergence across all the regions of the EU-27 appears to be questionable while club convergence emerges as a distinct possibility.

   This study, therefore, aims to inform policy intervention in the context of the EU-27, by seeking to identify the existence of a convergence club and, therefore, those specific geographical areas excluded from this club where regional economic policy might be concentrated to encourage regional convergence. In addition to an examination of the extent of club convergence in an enlarged Europe, this study also seeks to provide an explanation of regional growth trends by developing a model that contributes to an understanding of the differential economic performance between regions. Such evidence may help to guide the focus of policy and assist in promoting overall regional convergence.

1.3   Major Themes and Theoretical Context

This study contributes to the literature on economic convergence by developing and testing a model that focuses upon a series of factors that may lead some regions to converge while others do not. These factors can be grouped in two broad categories: a) those related to differences in levels of technology and b) those related to spatial agglomeration externalities.

   Differences in levels of technology concern both the creation of new technology and its adoption. Creation of technology promotes regional growth, since advances in technology are transformed into higher rates of productivity. However, not all regions are able to innovate and for those regions which lag behind, the alternative is the adoption of technological improvements developed by technologically leading regions. Thus, there is a possibility that these regions may converge or at least catch-up to some degree. To be more concrete, if such regions are able to adopt the latest technological advancements, then they will exhibit a relatively faster rate of growth, ceteris paribus, and thereby experience a technological catch-up effect.

This possibility of technological catch-up has received comparatively little attention in the relevant literature, especially at the empirical level. Indeed, Bernard and Jones (1996a) argue that empirical analyses of convergence have over-emphasised the role of capital accumulation in generating convergence at the expense of the process of technological diffusion:

> To the extent that the *adoption* and *accumulation* of *technologies* is important for convergence, the empirical convergence literature is misguided. (p. 1037) [Emphasis added]

Nevertheless, the catch-up effect is not a simple and automatic process. A necessary condition for technological catch-up is that technologically lagging economies have an infrastructure and appropriate conditions that will allow the effective adoption of new technology. Abramovitz (1986), for example, stresses the importance of infrastructure conditions in determining patterns of convergence:

> Countries that are technologically backward have a potentiality for generating growth more rapid than that of more advanced countries, provided their *social capabilities are sufficiently developed* to permit successful *exploitation* of technologies already employed by the technological leaders (p. 225) [Emphasis added]

Following this argument, an alternative model of club convergence is developed in this study in which club convergence is attributed to differences in the absorptive abilities of regions.

In seeking to explain why some regional economies converge or diverge, attention is also often directed towards the spatial patterns of interaction between regions, and how these contribute to internal growth processes. The mechanisms underlying convergent growth paths are complex and hinge upon a variety of factors such as the extent of factor mobility, price and wage flexibility and the diffusion of technology and innovation, as noted above. In general terms, all of these convergence mechanisms are likely to be enhanced, rather than inhibited, by spatial proximity, since distance remains a friction or barrier to many forms of economic, social and cultural interaction, even in the face of rapid developments in information and communication technology. Proximity facilitates economic interaction in a variety of forms beyond simply trade relations, such as in the areas of knowledge exchange and technology diffusion.

Finally, another set of factors concerns the operation of spatial agglomeration externalities. Hence, the impact of specialisation and diversity in the business environment upon regional growth is examined. In this context, spatial agglomeration externalities are conceived in their dynamic nature, by considering their effects on determining future rates of regional growth and, subsequently, shaping patterns of regional convergence.

The direction of this study is such as to move towards the empirical application of a model so as to address some critical questions concerning regional convergence in Europe. Do dynamic externalities, in the form of technology creation, adoption and spatial agglomeration shape the pattern of regional convergence? Is convergence restricted to a group of regions that share similar characteristics with respect to technology creation and adoption, and which form a convergence club? If so, is there spatial dependence between the region-members of the convergence club? These questions are simple and straightforward; the answers less so.

Existing empirical studies on club convergence in Europe do not include the role of technology creation and adoption nor dynamic externalities. In this study an attempt is made to remedy the lack of empirical studies by examining the possibility of club convergence and shedding some light on the factors that determine the pattern of club convergence in Europe. Therefore, the primary contribution of the present study is not only to augment the empirical literature which tests for the existence of convergence or convergence clubs, but also to examine, in the context of Europe, the impact of technology, dynamic externalities and spatial effects in shaping regional convergence clubs.

1.4   Structure of the Study

A major focus of this study is to develop and test a suitably extended neoclassical model of club convergence, emphasising the joint interaction of technology and spatial agglomeration externalities. However, working towards this, several other empirical approaches to the issue of regional convergence are taken into consideration. In particular, the issue of regional convergence in Europe is examined using two commonly applied notions of convergence, namely absolute and conditional convergence with particular emphasis on spatial interaction. Nevertheless, examination of club convergence is an issue that receives the primary focus of this study, and is examined using a variety of econometric models, deploying cross-section data. The study unfolds over the next nine chapters in the following manner.

The general theoretical framework upon which the empirical analysis is based is articulated in three chapters. Chapter 2 outlines two traditional approaches to regional growth, as put forward by the neoclassical and post-Keynesian schools of thought. Starting with the former, several theoretical growth models rooted in the neoclassical tradition predict that convergence in regional per-capita incomes in the long-run is an inevitable outcome of the free and unrestricted operation of market mechanisms. The neoclassical theory is a useful starting point, since the predictions of this theory carry important implications for the regional convergence debate. Indeed, most of the conceptual definitions of regional convergence used in empirical studies derive directly from the neoclassical model. A series of models that extend the standard neoclassical model, such as the two-sector neoclassical model and the augmented Solow's model, are therefore examined in Chap. 2.

Contrary to the neoclassical predictions of overall convergence, models following the Post-Keynesian tradition argue that regional per-capita incomes are unlikely to converge due to forces that perpetuate established differences among regions. These alternative models of cumulative and divergent growth are also examined in Chap. 2. According to these, the cumulative nature of regional growth is due to the operation of spatial agglomeration externalities. These externalities appear in two forms, localisation and urbanisation externalities, and are examined in detail, with particular emphasis on their effects in promoting knowledge creation across regions.

Endogenous Growth and New Economic Geography models emphasise to a greater degree some of the key features present in the earlier neoclassical and Post-Keynesian approaches and can predict club convergence due to technological factors, such as the intentional creation and diffusion of technology, and to geographical factors, such as spatial proximity and externalities from the concentration of activities in space. Chapter 3, therefore, provides a review of these models. For example, endogenous growth models, in which technology creation is modelled explicitly through the introduction of intentionally produced knowledge and innovation, are examined in this chapter. Such elements, in conjunction with spatial agglomeration externalities are seen to imply a clustering of regions, leading to a club convergence pattern. Likewise, the framework of New Economic Geography is also able to predict a process of regional clustering with different clusters converging towards different equilibria. Chapter 3, therefore, concludes with a brief review of the New Economic Geography approach.

Chapter 4 completes the theoretical background of this research by focusing specifically on the development of an appropriate theoretical framework for club convergence. Club convergence initially emerged as an empirical outcome and as a result, several different empirical approaches to club convergence have been put forward in the relevant literature, each emphasising different factors and employing different methods to test this phenomenon; examples include Chatterji 1992; Durlauf and Johnson 1995; Corrado et al. 2005; Fischer and Stirböck 2006, to name but a few. Nevertheless, club convergence also emerges from two theoretical models that predict multiple equilibria, developed by Azariadis and Drazen (1990) and de la Fuente (2000), with the former focusing on differences in human capital and the latter on technological capital. These models are examined in Chap. 4 in some detail.

Of particular importance for the purposes of this study is the model by de la Fuente (2000). Here convergence is attributed to the ability of economies (countries or regions) to adopt technological innovations which allow poor economies to grow faster than rich ones, ceteris paribus. Chapter 4 offers an extension to the model of de la Fuente (2000) by introducing differences in the degree of technology absorption. Thus, regions with high degrees of technology absorption, attributed to better infrastructure conditions, form a convergence club with the technologically leading regions, while regions with a low ability to absorb technology diverge.

The first three substantive chapters are thus focused upon the theoretical framework. Given that the issue of convergence is, to a great extent, an empirical one, Chap. 5 aims to act as bridge between theory and empirical evidence. Recent years have seen an increasing interest in assessing regional convergence, particularly since Baumol (1986) and Barro and Sala-i-Martin (1992) in their seminal papers adduced the inverse relation between the growth rate and the initial level of income as evidence of convergence among economies. As Rey and Montouri (1999) state:

YBP Library Services

ALEXIADIS, STILIANOS.

CONVERGENCE CLUBS AND SPATIAL EXTERNALITIES:
MODELS AND APPLICATIONS OF REGIONAL CONVERGENCE
IN EUROPE.   Cloth   244 P.
HEIDELBERG: SPRINGER, 2013
SER: ADVANCES IN SPATIAL SCIENCE.

TEXTBOOK--GRAD. CONSIDERS WHETHER LEVELS OF LABOR
PRODUCTIVITY ACROSS EU CONVERGE OR DIVERGE.
LCCN 2012-948988
  ISBN 3642316255   **Library PO#** GENERAL APPROVAL

	List	179.00	USD
5461 UNIV OF TEXAS/SAN ANTONIO	**Disc**	17.0%	
App. Date 1/02/13 GRG.APR 6108-11	**Net**	148.57	USD

SUBJ: 1. CONVERGENCE (ECONOMICS) 2. REGIONAL
ECONOMICS--MATH. MODELS.

CLASS HB3722   DEWEY# 338.9   LEVEL ADV-AC

YBP Library Services

ALEXIADIS, STILIANOS.

CONVERGENCE CLUBS AND SPATIAL EXTERNALITIES:
MODELS AND APPLICATIONS OF REGIONAL CONVERGENCE
IN EUROPE.   Cloth   244 P.
HEIDELBERG: SPRINGER, 2013
SER: ADVANCES IN SPATIAL SCIENCE.

TEXTBOOK--GRAD. CONSIDERS WHETHER LEVELS OF LABOR
PRODUCTIVITY ACROSS EU CONVERGE OR DIVERGE.
  LCCN 2012-948988
  ISBN 3642316255   **Library PO#** GENERAL APPROVAL

	List	179.00	USD
5461 UNIV OF TEXAS/SAN ANTONIO	**Disc**	17.0%	
App. Date 1/02/13 GRG.APR 6108-11	**Net**	148.57	USD

SUBJ: 1. CONVERGENCE (ECONOMICS) 2. REGIONAL
ECONOMICS--MATH. MODELS.

CLASS HB3722   DEWEY# 338.9   LEVEL ADV-AC

The recent explosion of interest in regional growth and convergence has not followed a uniform path. Instead, several distinct types of convergence have been suggested in the literature, each being analysed by distinct groups of scholars employing different methods. (p. 144)

It is the purpose of this chapter to provide an overview of the main approaches and methodologies used in testing for regional convergence and hence to provide a background context for the subsequent empirical work. This chapter, therefore, examines the most common measures of absolute and club convergence and a series of econometric techniques that are of particular importance to the aims of this study. In particular, three econometric models, which are able to provide an empirical approximation of the effects of spatial interaction, are discussed.

The empirical assessment of regional convergence in Europe is undertaken in Chaps. 6 and 7. Chapter 6 presents an assessment of convergence in Europe between 1995 and 2006, including an explanation of club convergence and using a variety of techniques discussed in Chap. 5. Chapter 7 proceeds to develop and test the particular model outlined earlier, which combines the impact of technology and agglomeration externalities into a club convergence framework. In the first instance, regional convergence in Europe is assessed by two of the most frequently used concepts of convergence, namely σ and β convergence. σ-convergence occurs if the dispersion of income per-capita displays a declining trend. On the other hand, Barro and Sala-i-Martin (1992a, 1995) suggest that β-convergence occurs when poor regions tend to grow faster than rich regions, such that the poor regions catch up. As will be shown, the application of these two concepts in the context of European regions reveals the presence of σ-convergence while tests of absolute β-convergence imply that European regions converge at a relatively slow rate. This brings the notion of club convergence into consideration. Compared to the traditional convergence analysis, club convergence offers a more realistic approach to the convergence performance of regions, as Fischer and Stirböck (2006) point out. Preliminary tests of club convergence seem to verify this argument across the regions of an enlarged Europe.

The analysis of club convergence is taken further in Chap. 7 by examining this phenomenon in a way which takes account of factors related to the creation and diffusion of technology across regions, in conjunction with the effects of regional agglomeration and spatial interaction. In essence, this chapter is devoted to an empirical application of the model developed in Chap. 4, in the context of the European regions. This is a 'multiple equilibria' model, an area in which, as Gruber and Soci (2010) note, systematic empirical research is still absent.

In the first instance, the results of three formal spatial econometric models are presented, to provide evidence of spatial interaction in regional convergence in Europe. The next step is the identification of the factors that also contribute to this performance. Thus, in summary, the main contribution of this chapter is the introduction of an econometric model that examines club convergence in the context of spatial interaction, technology creation and adoption in conjunction with the impact of spatial agglomeration in the form of localisation and diversification effects. This chapter considers the methodology employed and the data used to test the model, followed by discussion of the econometric results.

As will be shown, application of this model provides further support to the argument of Chap. 6 that the European regions exhibit club convergence. Econometric results clearly suggest that spatial interaction, technology creation and adoption together with spatial agglomeration effects all play a role in determining the pattern of regional growth. A closer inspection of the econometric results shows that adoption of technology is a significant factor in regional growth and convergence. In addition, the results imply also that diversity in economic activity is more significant than regional specialisation. Chapter 7 concludes by examining the implications of excluding the leading regions from the convergence club. A more detailed analysis of the members of a convergence club also shows that regions in a club are likely to share similar structural characteristics.

Chapter 8, finally, presents a conclusion, by providing an overall summary of the study and an assessment of the implications for the debate concerning the pattern of regional economic activity in Europe.

Chapter 2
Neoclassical and Post-Keynesian Theories of Regional Growth and Convergence/Divergence

2.1 Introduction

The study of regional growth has been dominated by two broad and contrasting theoretical approaches regarding regional convergence. According to the first, market forces will lead to a general convergence of per-capita incomes across an integrated space economy over time. This approach is labelled as 'neoclassical regional growth theory' and its premises are based upon the standard growth model, as outlined by the pioneering work of Solow (1956) and Swan (1956). Using a general equilibrium framework these models predict that disparities in per-capita incomes across regions are unlikely to occur or, at least, to be persistent, thus creating a pattern of convergence towards a unique level of per-capita income. By contrast, there is a large body of theoretical and empirical work, known as the 'post-Keynesian approach', which supports the argument that regional disparities in per-capita incomes are permanent and self-perpetuating and therefore divergence in per-capita incomes is the most likely outcome. Representative models can be found in the work of Myrdal (1957), Perroux (1950, 1955) and Kaldor (1967, 1970 and 1972). This chapter outlines the major approaches to regional growth, as put forward by the neoclassical and post-Keynesian schools of thought. Throughout this and subsequent chapters more emphasis is placed upon the neoclassical model, for two reasons. First, the neoclassical model offers both a theoretical explanation and testable predictions concerning the possibility of convergence in per-capita incomes across regions. Indeed, most of the conceptual definitions of regional convergence used in empirical studies derive directly from the neoclassical model. Second, the vast majority of empirical literature has in fact tested the neoclassical model rather than alternative models.

The remainder of this chapter is organised as follows. Section 2.2 provides a summary of the neoclassical model of regional growth. Section 2.3 examines two main extensions of the 'standard' neoclassical model: the 'two-sector' model and the 'augmented Solow model', as proposed by Mankiw et al. (1992). Section 2.4 outlines an alternative approach to regional growth, namely models of cumulative

S. Alexiadis, *Convergence Clubs and Spatial Externalities*,
Advances in Spatial Science, DOI 10.1007/978-3-642-31626-5_2,
© Springer-Verlag Berlin Heidelberg 2013

and divergent growth, as proposed by Myrdal (1957) and Kaldor (1970, 1972). Particular emphasis is placed upon the impacts of agglomeration externalities, localisation and urbanisation effects, in producing divergent regional growth. Finally, a summary is provided in Sect. 2.5.

2.2   The Neoclassical Approach to Regional Growth

The 'standard' neoclassical model of economic growth was formulated in the late 1950s by the pioneering work of Solow (1956, 1957) and independently by Swan (1956), Kendrick (1956) and Abramovitz (1956). These authors[1] applied the neoclassical structure of thought to explain the mechanisms by which an economy grows in the long-run. Thus, capital accumulation and labour growth explain some proportion of the growth in output per-worker (labour productivity),[2] while the residual is attributed to exogenous technological progress.

These initial contributions offer no theory of a spatial pattern to growth and do not include any explicit spatial features. The analysis is focused on 'aggregate' growth, i.e. the growth of an economy as a whole. However, the Solow (1956) and Swan (1956) formulation is widely accepted in theoretical and empirical work, since it is considered to have substantial power to explain economic growth across economies. A number of authors, including Borts (1960), Borts and Stein (1964), Romans (1965), Carlberg (1981) and more recently Barro and Sala-i-Martin (1992a, 1995), Barro et al. (1995), King and Rebelo (1990, 1993) and Knight et al. (1993), have therefore expanded the Solow (1956) and Swan (1956) model in order to apply its concepts within the context of geographical regions. According to Richardson (1978a) the adaptation of neoclassical theory to regional growth is one of the major contributions of mainstream economics to regional economics.

Neoclassical analysis has dominated the theoretical and empirical literature on growth at both national and regional level. This may be ascribed to a number of factors. Firstly, the elements of the neoclassical model can be applied at both the aggregate and regional level of analysis. Secondly, such models simultaneously offer explanations of endogenous system growth and of interregional factor flows. Thirdly, the general structure of the standard neoclassical model is such that a range of factors influencing growth may be incorporated, notably, various forms of capital (e.g. human and 'technological' capital) and spatial and agglomeration effects. Richardson (1978a) describes the flexibility property of the neoclassical model as follows:

---

[1] Meade (1961), Cass (1965) and Koopmans (1965), based on Ramsey (1928), extend Solow's model with refinements on optimal growth.

[2] Income and output are used interchangeably. Nevertheless, throughout this and subsequent chapters output instead of income is used. Moreover, the hypothesis of regional convergence in a neoclassical context is related to output per-worker rather than income per-capita.

> There is little doubt that the neoclassical regional growth model is sufficiently flexible to absorb some *features* of *alternative* models, thereby enriching and strengthening the neoclassical approach. (p. 141) [Emphasis added]

This section therefore proceeds by providing an outline of the overall structure of the neoclassical model, with particular attention placed upon two issues. The first is the issue of regional convergence to a single 'steady-state' equilibrium and the second concerns the contribution of interregional factor flows to the process of convergence between regions.

2.2.1   The Microeconomic Framework

The neoclassical contribution to an understanding of economic growth is based within the framework of microeconomics and, hence upon the working of the market mechanism. The interaction of supply and demand determines equilibrium prices with firms maximising profits, given a production function, and consumers maximising utility. Any disturbance to the system will cause a new equilibrium to be established, following the assumption that markets for the factors of production and for goods respond to market signals.

The economy as portrayed by the neoclassical model consists of a large (or indeterminate) number of firms, which are considered to be price takers following the structure of perfect competition. Firms, assumed profit-maximisers, will hire labour until the marginal product of labour is equal to the wage and will rent capital until the marginal product of capital is equal to the rental price.

An underlying assumption of critical importance is that perfect competition prevails in all markets, for products and for factors of production. When this approach is used in the context of explaining regional growth, it leads to the conclusion that regional economies will exhibit both allocative and productive efficiency, in the long-run and there is therefore full and efficient utilisation of a given volume of resources. Total output is determined by the supply of the factors of production. From this perspective, the neoclassical process of regional growth is, essentially, supply-driven in the sense that the long-run rate of regional growth is determined by the rate of growth of labour and capital over time and the speed at which technological change occurs. Thus, as will be explained below, different growth rates and levels of output per-worker between regions arise, at any point in time, through differences in one or more of these factors. In essence, however, the neoclassical model of regional growth is a model of 'regional convergence'. Bearing in mind the above framework, the next step forward is to describe the mechanisms by which the growth of regional output is determined.

2.2.2   Regional Growth in the 'One-Sector' Neoclassical Model

The simplest version of the neoclassical model is encapsulated in the 'one sector' model of regional growth. An assumption of the model is that each region produces a single and uniform product, which can be either consumed or saved for future consumption, using a combination of the factors of production, capital and labour, which are assumed to be homogenous. It is also assumed that production functions are identical across regions and exhibit diminishing marginal products and constant returns to scale. In the absence of any technological progress output is determined exclusively by inputs of capital and labour. In general terms:

$$Y_{i,t} = F(K_{i,t}, L_{i,t})$$ (2.1)

where $Y_{i,t}, K_{i,t}$ and $L_{i,t}$ are output, the stock of physical capital and the labour force, respectively, in region i at time t.

Expressed in terms of output per-worker, this gives

$$y_{i,t} = f(k_{i,t})$$ (2.2)

where $k_{i,t} = \frac{K_{i,t}}{L_{i,t}}$.

In the simplest case, it is assumed that regions are 'closed' economies. In other words, there are no interregional flows of factors or products and any 'steady-state' equilibrium is generated through mechanisms internal to each region. Growth in output per-worker is proportional to the growth in capital per worker, i.e. capital deepening. Due to the diminishing marginal product of capital the process of capital deepening cannot continue indefinitely, however, and there is a limit to the capital-labour ratio. Assuming zero labour growth, as the marginal product of capital approaches zero, then net investment will also tend towards zero, i.e. there is no further capital deepening. The capital-labour ratio it will be at its long-run equilibrium level, which corresponds to an equilibrium level of the output-labour ratio.

2.2.3 Inputs to Production in the Neoclassical Model

The simplified 'one-sector' neoclassical model shows the growth of output in a regional economy to be dependent on the growth in labour and capital inputs. The labour force varies over time because of three reasons. These are population growth, changes in employment participation rates and shifts in the time worked by the typical worker. In turn, the growth of population reflects fertility, mortality and migration rates (Barro and Sala-i-Martin, 1995). Although many of these factors are endogenous, particularly in the long-run, the supply of labour is often assumed to be exogenously determined.[3] Solow (1956), for example, assumes labour to grow at a constant proportional rate, excluding migration. Thus:

---

[3] Nevertheless, this is valid only in the short-run, since reproduction can and does change in the long-run in response to changes in income levels. However, the neoclassical model does not include a theory of population change. See also McCombie (1988a).

$$L_{i,t} = L_0 e^{nt} \quad \text{with} \quad n \geq 0 \quad \text{and} \quad \frac{\dot{L}_{i,t}}{L_{i,t}} = n \tag{2.3}$$

which implies that labour force is growing at a constant proportional rate, n, from an initial level of L_0 at time t_0. The assumption of full employment yields the condition that labour supply is always equal to labour demand.[4]

Turning to the second source of growth in this simple version of the neoclassical model, which is the accumulation of physical capital, then this occurs over time through investment expenditures (I). However, in the neoclassical model there is no explicit function as such, to describe investment behaviour. Instead it is assumed that all savings (S) are automatically invested (i.e. $S \equiv I$).[5] Assuming perfect capital markets, the mechanism for equating investment with savings[6] at the full employment level is the rate of interest and regional aggregate savings $S_{i,t}$ are assumed to be a constant proportion of regional output, that is:

$$S_{i,t} = sY_{i,t} \quad \text{with} \quad 0 \leq s \leq 1 \tag{2.4}$$

where s is the propensity to save. This is assumed to be spatially invariant, that is, the same for all regions.

Aggregate savings $S_{i,t}$ in a region will, therefore, finance gross regional investment, given that savings are automatically invested and there are no capital inflows (or outflows) in this simple model. Hence, the net increase in the stock of physical capital ($\dot{K}_{i,t}$) is given by the following equation:

$$\dot{K}_{i,t} = I_{i,t} - \delta K_{i,t} \quad \text{with} \quad \delta > 0 \tag{2.5}$$

where $I_{i,t}$ is gross investment and δ is a constant and spatially invariant rate of depreciation.

Given the assumption that investment is equal to savings and the general production function in Eqs. 2.2, 2.5 can be written as follows (Barro and Sala-i-Martin, 1995):

$$\dot{K}_{i,t} = sL_{i,t}f(k_{i,t}) - \delta K_{i,t} \tag{2.6}$$

---

[4] A dot over a variable indicates its rate of change with respect to time.

[5] For a more detailed analysis of savings behaviour in the neoclassical model, see Cesaratto (1999).

[6] In a closed economy, saving equal investment, namely the only use of investment is to accumulate physical capital. This assumption might be considered as unrealistic in a regional context, where regions are by definitions open economies. Feldstein and Horioka (1980), however, have shown that the coincidence of investments and savings is empirically valid across regions.

Dividing both sides of Eq. 2.6 by $L_{i,t}$ yields:

$$\frac{\dot{K}_{i,t}}{L_{i,t}} = sf(k_{i,t}) - \delta k_{i,t} \tag{2.7}$$

The next step forward is to describe the determination of a 'steady-state' equilibrium. In particular, it is of critical importance to describe the behaviour of the capital-labour ratio (or capital per-worker).

2.2.4 Steady-state Equilibrium in the Neoclassical Model

Steady-state equilibrium is analysed by deriving an expression for the evolution of capital per worker over time. In the absence of technological change, since $\frac{\dot{L}_{i,t}}{L_{i,t}} = n$ and $\frac{\dot{k}_{i,t}}{k_{i,t}} = \frac{\dot{K}_{i,t}}{K_{i,t}} - \frac{\dot{L}_{i,t}}{L_{i,t}}$ the evolution of the capital-labour ratio can be written as follows:

$$\dot{k}_{i,t} \equiv \frac{\dot{K}_{i,t}}{L_{i,t}} - nk_{i,t} \tag{2.8}$$

Substituting Eq. 2.7 into Eq. 2.8 yields the following expression:

$$\dot{k}_{i,t} = sf(k_{i,t}) - (n+\delta)k_{i,t} \tag{2.9}$$

This is the fundamental differential equation of the Solow (1956) model, which describes the dynamic behaviour of the capital-labour ratio over time, given an initial level $(k_{i,0})$. The term $(n+\delta)$ is described as the effective depreciation rate of the capital-labour ratio in that, if the saving rate was zero, then the capital-labour ratio would decline due to capital depreciation and growth of the labour force. For there to be a steady-state $\dot{k}_{i,t} = 0$ and therefore the equilibrium capital-labour ratio (k^*) must satisfy the following condition:

$$sf(k^*) = (n+\delta)k^* \tag{2.10}$$

This system and its equilibrium can be represented by the 'basic Solow diagram' shown in Figure 2.1 (Barro and Sala-i-Martin, 1995, p. 18):

Thus, given an initial capital-labour ratio of $k_{i,0}$, the distance ab represents per capita consumption and gross investment per-capita is equal to the distance $bk_{i,0}$. The vertical distance bc between gross investment and effective depreciation therefore shows positive net investment and hence growth in the capital-labour ratio. This process continues until the growth of the capital-labour ratio is zero at point e where gross investment is just equal to the effective depreciation rate. The economy has reached its 'steady-state equilibrium' in which the per capita variables $(y_i$ and $k_i)$ are constant.

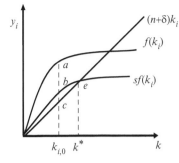

Fig. 2.1 Steady-state equilibrium in the neoclassical model

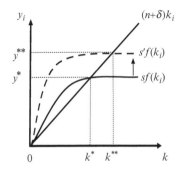

Fig. 2.2 A higher savings ratio

A similar process takes place when the initial capital-labour ratio exceeds its equilibrium value. In this case gross investment per unit of labour provided by the economy is less than the amount required to sustain a constant capital-labour ratio. Hence, the capital-labour ratio declines until it reaches its 'steady-state' level once again.

If this model is applied to a group of regional economies, then it is clear that the only way in which all of these economies would converge to the same steady-state would be if all were characterised by identical production functions and preferences regarding savings. Even if initial levels of k were different, provided that each economy were characterised exactly by Figure 2.1, each would end up in the same equilibrium point.

The explanation for convergence to different steady-states is, therefore, to be found in innate structural 'steady-state' differences. The co-existence of both 'rich' and 'poor' regions is illustrated in Figures 2.2 and 2.3. It is clear that regions that have high savings/investment rates will have a higher equilibrium level of output per-worker, ceteris paribus, as shown by Figure 2.2.

An alternative scenario is represented in Figure 2.3, which shows the effects of an increase in the labour force growth rate.

This rise in the effective depreciation shifts the curve $(n + \delta)k_i$ upwards so that at the initial level of k^*, savings and hence investment per-worker is no longer enough

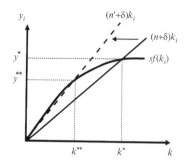

Fig. 2.3 An increase in labour force growth

to maintain a constant capital-labour ratio in the face of the rising labour force. Thus, gross investment is not sufficient to offset depreciation, and declines towards a new equilibrium. At this point the new capital-labour ratio k^{**} corresponds to a lower level of output per-worker y^{**}. Hence, 'poor' regions have low a capital-labour ratio whilst 'rich' regions are characterised by a high capital-labour ratio. These differences between regions are, however, due to different structural characteristics embodied in the savings propensity s and rate of population growth n.

In the framework outlined thus far, the prediction of regional convergence to the same equilibrium depends on the condition that all regions have the same structural characteristics. However, a crucial question remains as to how 'poor' regions catch up to 'rich' regions even if there are no differences in structural characteristics. This leads to the issue of the transitional dynamics of the neoclassical model.

2.2.5 Transitional Dynamics of the Neoclassical Model

The concept of 'transitional dynamics' is used to describe the process by which a region's output per-worker converges to its own steady-state value and to the output per-worker of other regions. In the present context, the primary driving force is movements in the capital-labour ratio. Here, in order to examine this, Eq. 2.9 is transformed by dividing both sides by $k_{i,t}$:

$$\kappa = \frac{sf(k_{i,t})}{k_{i,t}} - (n + \delta) \qquad (2.11)$$

where $\kappa = \frac{\dot{k}_{i,t}}{k_{i,t}}$ is the growth rate of the capital-labour ratio.

This process is illustrated in Figure 2.4, which plots κ for different levels of k.

The function representing 'average' savings has a negative slope due to the assumption of diminishing marginal productivity of capital. Equilibrium occurs when the growth rate for the capital-labour ratio becomes zero at point e where average savings $(sf(k_i)/k_i)$ equals effective depreciation $(n + \delta)$. If a region is not in

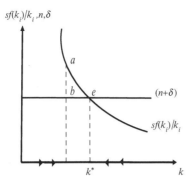

Fig. 2.4 Transitional dynamics in the neoclassical model (Jones, 1998, p. 32)

equilibrium with a capital-labour ratio below k^*, the vertical distance (ab) represents the growth rate for the capital-labour ratio (κ) and this approximates the growth rate of output per-worker. Savings exceed depreciation and net investment is positive. Furthermore, as can also be seen from Figure 2.4, the growth rate is initially high but gradually decreases over time as the economy moves towards its steady-state position. The reverse holds for a region with a capital-labour ratio in excess of its steady-state level. Initially growth is negative, approaching zero as the capital-labour ratio falls towards k^*. This process of transitional dynamics can be used to compare progress towards convergence experienced by different regions. Of particular importance is the difference between 'rich' and 'poor' regions. Suppose that the economy is divided into two regions, denoted by i and j and that these regions differ in their initial factor endowments, with the initial capital-labour ratio ($k_{i,0}$) of region i exceeding that of region j($k_{j,0}$). Thus, region i may be considered to be the 'rich' region initially, but neither region is at its steady-state position. It is assumed that the growth of labour and the rate of depreciation are identical across the two regions, as are preferences concerning saving and consumption. However, the growth rate of these two regions, as determined by the underlying parameters, is not the same at any point in time as each moves towards an equilibrium position. This process is depicted in Figure 2.5.

The key to this lies in the assumption of diminishing returns to capital. Additional investment in physical capital is not as profitable in the 'rich' region (i) as each addition to the capital stock in region i generates smaller additions to output in comparison to region j. The 'poor' region will grow faster than the 'rich' region, or more specifically, the region with the lower capital-labour ratio will grow at a faster rate, as both regions move towards the same steady-state level of k^*.

Although highly restrictive in terms of assumptions, the neoclassical model nevertheless provides significant insights into how a 'poor' region might catch up with a 'rich' one. In conclusion, therefore, the predictions of this model for regional convergence are unambiguous. If regions are assumed to be identical with respect to production functions and preferences, but differ in their initial capital stocks, then poor regions, defined to be those with low initial values of the capital-labour

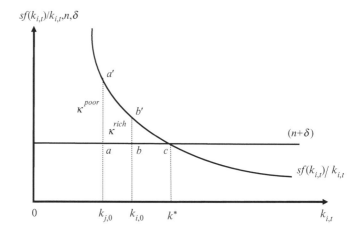

Fig. 2.5 Catching up of a 'poor' with a 'rich' region (Sala-i-Martin, 1996a, p. 1343)

ratio, will grow faster and will catch up the richer regions, during the process of convergence to the steady-state. Differences in growth rates are a disequilibrium phenomenon and will be eliminated in the long-run provided that regional economies are similar. According to Jones (1998) this prediction is the 'principle of transitional dynamics' which states that:

> The further an economy is 'below' its steady-state, the faster the economy should grow. The further an economy is 'above' its steady-state, the slower the economy should grow. (p. 62)

The prediction that a group of economies will converge in the manner described above to the same steady-state, is referred to in the literature as absolute convergence. The catching-up process, embodied in differential growth rates, is referred to as β-convergence. As will be seen in Chap. 5 both concepts form the basis of much empirical work on international and regional convergence. However, in the present context, the next step is to extend the simple neoclassical model, by incorporating technological progress into the production function.

2.2.6   Steady-state Equilibrium with Technological Progress

The simple 'one-sector' model described above has excluded the effects of improvements in technology, such that attainment of steady-state equilibrium is the end of the growth process. However, exogenous productivity gains, such as those arising from improvements in technology, can preserve the incentive for new investments leading to a new steady-state with a higher capital-labour ratio. In addition to such shifts in technology, the introduction of technological progress on a continuing basis into the Solow (1956) and Swan (1956) model can therefore also generate sustained growth in output per-worker.

The impact of technological change may be modelled in a number of ways. Following Solow (1956) advances in technology can be treated simply as another input in the production function.[7] Hence, the rate of output growth is driven by three separate sources (Richardson, 1973b): capital accumulation, an increase in labour supply and a residual, which may be called technical progress, and which includes everything that improves the efficiency of a given stock of resources. In the neoclassical model technological progress may also be incorporated into the production function in a 'labour-augmented' form. Labour-augmenting technological progress implies that with the same amount of capital, less labour is required to produce the same amount of output.

In Solow's (1956) model technological progress is not explained, but considered to be exogenous. Thus the equation:

$$A_t = A_0 e^{gt} \qquad (2.12)$$

represents technological progress over time, with a constant and exogenously determined growth rate of g. Of particular importance is the impact of technological progress in the transitional dynamics of the neoclassical model. Introducing the, exogenously determined, growth of technology modifies the expression for the evolution of the capital-labour ratio as follows:[8]

$$\dot{k} = sf(\hat{k}_{i,t}) - (n + g + \delta)\hat{k}_{i,t} \qquad (2.13)$$

---

[7] Solow (1957) suggested that gross output per man hour in the US manufacturing doubled between 1909 and 1949. However, only 12.5 % of this trend is attributable to increases in capital per worker while the remaining 87.5 % was the outcome of improvements in technology. Solow's model implies that in the absence of any improvements in technology, output per worker in the long-run will be constant while total output increases at the same rate as the growth of population.

[8] The properties of the neoclassical model can be shown using the theory of optimal control (Novales et al., 2010). Consider the production function: $y_{i,t} = f(k_{i,t})$, where $y_{i,t} = Y_{i,t}/A_{i,t}L_{i,t}$ and $k_{i,t} = K_{i,t}/A_{i,t}L_{i,t}$. Let $L_{i,t} = L_{i,0}e^{nt}$, $A_{i,t} = A_{i,0}e^{gt}$, $\dot{L}_{i,t}/L_{i,t} = n$ and $\dot{A}_{i,t}/A_{i,t} = g$, then $A\dot{L}_{i,t}/AL_{i,t} = n + g$. Given that $Y_{i,t} = C_{i,t} + S_{i,t} \Rightarrow S_{i,t} = Y_{i,t} - C_{i,t}$, $\dot{K}_{i,t} = I_{i,t} - \delta K_{i,t}$, where $I_{i,t}$ is net investment, and $S_{i,t} = s Y_{i,t}, S_{i,t} \equiv I_{i,t}$, then $\dot{K}_{i,t} = S_{i,t} - \delta K_{i,t} \Rightarrow \dot{K}_{i,t} = Y_{i,t} - C_{i,t} - \delta K_{i,t}$. Dividing by $A_{i,t}L_{i,t}$ yields: $\dot{K}_{i,t}/A_{i,t}L_{i,t} = y_{i,t} - c_{i,t} - \delta k_{i,t} \Rightarrow \dot{K}_{i,t}/A_{i,t}L_{i,t} = f(k_{i,t}) - c_{i,t} - \delta k$, where $c_{i,t} = C_{i,t}/A_{i,t}L_{i,t}$ and $\dot{k}_{i,t}/k_{i,t} = \dot{K}_{i,t}/K_{i,t} - A\dot{L}_{i,t}/AL_{i,t}$. Therefore, $\dot{k}_{i,t} = \dot{K}_{i,t}/AL_{i,t} - (n + g)k_{i,t}$ or $\dot{k}_{i,t} = f(k_{i,t}) - c_{i,t} - (n + g + \delta) k_{i,t}$. The representative household is assumed to maximize total utility, which in each period is weighted by the size of population and the rate of time preferences, ρ, thus, $Max \int_0^T e^{-\rho t}u(c)dt$, subject to $\dot{k}_i = f(k_i) - c_i - (n + g + \delta)k_i$, with $k_i(0) = k_{i,0}, k_i(T) = k_{i,T}$. The Hamiltonian associated with the problem is: $H = e^{-\rho t}u(c) + \mu[f(k_i) - c_i - (n + g + \delta)k_i]$, with the necessary conditions $\partial H/\partial c_i = 0 \Rightarrow e^{-\rho t}u'_{c_i} - \mu = 0$ and $\partial H/\partial k_i = -\dot{\mu} \Rightarrow -\mu[f(k_i) - (n + g + \delta)]$. Given that $\mu = e^{-\rho t}u'_{c_i}$, the shadow price of capital equals the present value of the marginal utility of consumption. This condition must hold at all time t: $\dot{\mu} = -\rho e^{-\rho t}u'_{c_i} + e^{-\rho t}u''_{c_i c_i}\dot{c}$. The equation of motion for $\dot{c}_i$ is $\dot{c}_i = (\rho + n + g + \delta - f'_{k_i})(u'_{c_i}/u''_{c_i c_i})$. Given that $u_{c_i} > 0$, then $\dot{c}_i = 0$ only when $f_{k_i} = \rho + n + g + \delta$. Under the neoclassical conditions for the marginal productivity of k_i ($f_{k_i} > 0$, $f_{k_i k_i} < 0$ and $f'(0) \to \infty$) there is a unique value of capital per-worker ($\hat{k}_i$), such that $f_{k_i}(\hat{k}_i) = \rho + n + g + \delta$.

Equation 2.13 is similar to Eq. 2.9, only this time the critical variable is expressed in terms of per effective unit of labour,[9] i.e. $\hat{k}_{i,t} = \frac{K_{i,t}}{A_{i,t}L_{i,t}}$. In the steady-state equilibrium $\hat{k}_{i,t} = 0$ and the equilibrium capital-labour ratio $(\hat{k}_{i,t}^*)$ satisfies the following condition:

$$sf(\hat{k}_{i,t}) = (n + g + \delta)\hat{k}_{i,t}^* \tag{2.14}$$

From a regional perspective the implications of the above are that growth disparities across regions occur not only because of differences in the growth of capital relative to labour (or the capital-labour ratio) but also because of the possibilities of different rates of technological progress. Furthermore, persistent variations in rates of technological progress have the potential to accentuate or reduce the extent to which regions converge to each other, depending upon which particular regions experience higher or lower rates of progress. Thus, technology and technological change are fundamental to the question of convergence, or non-convergence, between regions, and more detailed discussion of these issues is therefore provided in Chaps. 3 and 4.

At this juncture, in the context of the one-sector neoclassical model, it may be argued that rates of technological progress will tend to be the same across different regions, for the following reasons. When the neoclassical model is applied to a system of regional economies, (exogenous) technology is assumed to be a public good characterised by two features, namely non-rivalry in consumption and non-excludability. The former characteristic indicates that consumption by one agent does not affect its availability to be consumed by any other, while the latter feature means that there is no feasible way of preventing anyone from benefiting from the consumption of this good. Under the assumption of perfect competition it may be argued that technology has such characteristics and is, as Borts and Stein (1964) argue 'available to all' (p.8).

Technology is therefore assumed to be a spatially invariant public good such that the production of a region's output by a given technology does not preclude other regions from adopting the same technology, even simultaneously. Thus, all regions have access to the same technology validating the assumption of identical production functions, and leading to common levels of technological growth across regions, which is consistent with a convergence process. The notion that regions 'share' a common technology, and the rate of progress, contains within it an acknowledgement of a type of regional interaction in the form of technology/knowledge transfer. This is considered in more depth in Chap. 4, whilst the impact of other regional interactions on convergence are analysed in Sect. 2.2.8. Prior to this, however, the concept of the speed of convergence is introduced.

---

[9] Sometimes referred to as the 'output-technology' ratio since technological progress is assumed to be of the labour-augmented form, i.e. labour becomes more productive when the level of technology is higher, and AL is the 'effective' amount of labour used in production. For a more detailed discussion see Hahn and Matthews (1964).

2.2.7   The Speed of Convergence

Assuming that convergence to a 'steady-state' is taking place an obvious question arises concerning the speed at which this process is occurring.[10] Following Islam (2003) the evolution of the effective capital-labour ratio is proportional to the gap between its actual value at any point in time $(\hat{k}_{i,t})$ and its steady-state value $(\hat{k}_{i,t}^*)$ and can be written as follows:

$$\dot{\hat{k}}_{i,t} = [sf'(\hat{k}_{i,t}^*) - (n + g + \delta)](\hat{k}_{i,t} - \hat{k}_{i,t}^*) \tag{2.15}$$

where $f'(k_{i,t})$ is the marginal product of capital.[11]

From Eq. 2.14 it follows that the propensity to save can be written as follows:

$$s = \frac{(n + g + \delta)\hat{k}_{i,t}^*}{f(\hat{k}_{i,t}^*)} \tag{2.16}$$

Substituting Eq. 2.16 into Eq. 2.15 yields the following expression for the growth of the effective capital-labour ratio:

$$\dot{\hat{k}}_{i,t} = \left(\frac{f'(\hat{k}_{i,t}^*)k_{i,t}^*}{f(\hat{k}_{i,t}^*)} - 1\right)(n + g + \delta)(\hat{k}_{i,t} - \hat{k}_{i,t}^*) \tag{2.17}$$

The structure of the neoclassical model implies that capital earns its marginal product, which is equal to the share of capital in output. Substituting the share of capital (α) into Eq. 2.17 it is possible to derive an expression for the speed at which the effective capital-labour ratio approaches its steady-state value:

$$\dot{\hat{k}} = \beta(\hat{k}_{i,t}^* - \hat{k}_{i,t}) \tag{2.18}$$

where $\beta = (1 - a)(n + g + \delta)$.

In Eq. 2.18 the coefficient β gives the speed at which the gap between the steady state level of the effective capital-labour ratio and its current level is closed and measure the rate or the speed of convergence. Assuming that $0 < \alpha < 1$, then a value of $\beta > 0$ indicates convergence.[12]

---

[10] For a more detailed analysis see Appendix I.

[11] Equation (2.15) can be derived by taking a first order Taylor expansion of the right hand side of equation (2.13) around the steady-state value of the effective capital-labour ratio.

[12] If $a = 1$, then the property of convergence is not apparent. This is an outcome implied by the various models of Endogenous Growth Theory, which will be examined in more detailed in Chapter 3.

2.2.8   Regional Convergence and Interregional Factor Movements

Up to this point the neoclassical model of regional growth has been restricted to a 'closed economy' framework in which regions are assumed to be identical, but with differing initial factor endowments, and without any explicit 'links' or interaction between them, apart from technological linkages, based on technology as a public good. Thus, the assumption of 'closed' regional economies[13] provides an overview of the internal mechanisms by which regions reach 'steady-state' equilibrium. Despite the restrictive conditions of the analysis two important conclusions can be drawn. First, despite their independence from each other regions will converge towards a common 'steady-state' if the growth rate of technology, rate of investment and rate of growth of the labour force are identical across regions. Differences in the growth of technical progress, labour force and capital stock are, therefore, possible reasons for the emergence of persistent regional disparities in output per-worker. Second, the further a region is 'below' its 'steady-state', the faster this region should grow, which leads to the more general prediction that poorer regions will grow faster than richer regions.

Romer (1996) focusing on this latter prediction identifies three possible reasons to explain this. The first two are rooted in the structure of the neoclassical model which predicts that economies converge to a 'steady-state' level of output per-worker. Therefore, to the extent that differences in output per-worker arise from economies being at different stages relative to their balanced growth paths, one would expect the poorer economies to catch up to the richer. Second, as previously noted, the rate of return on capital is lower in economies with more capital per-worker. Additional capital investment will be less profitable, due to diminishing marginal productivity of capital. This provides an 'incentive' for capital to 'flow' from rich to poor economies while labour will flow in the opposite direction, i.e. from poor to rich economies. This will generate tendencies to convergence. Third, if there are lags in the diffusion of knowledge, differences in output per-worker might emerge due to the fact that some economies are not yet employing the best available technologies. As poor economies obtain access to new technologies, income gaps between poor and rich economies will tend to narrow.

In these last two cases, interaction between regions has, in fact, been explicitly acknowledged in the form of inter-regional factor movements and diffusion of technology. Such interactions are introduced to the neoclassical spatial model via the assumption of factor mobility, whilst retaining the standard neoclassical assumptions of perfect competition, zero transportation costs, full employment, a single homogenous product and constant returns to scale production functions, which are identical across regions. Given the conditions of perfect competition factors are paid the value of their marginal products. Hence, the wage (equal to

---

[13] Richardson (1973c) notes that it is often permissible, if incomplete, to treat a national economy as closed. This assumption, however, can never be made for regional economies.

marginal product of labour) is a direct function of the capital-labour ratio and the marginal product of capital (return to capital) is an inverse function of the capital-labour ratio.

Within the model, movements of factors between regions are induced by differences in the returns to factors of production. The assumption of diminishing marginal productivity of capital ensures that regions with a high (low) capital-labour ratio will exhibit low (high) marginal product of capital. Similarly, regions with a high (low) capital-labour ratio offer high (low) wages. In such circumstances it is argued that labour will have a propensity to migrate away from low wage regions towards high wage regions while capital will move in the opposite direction, away from the more prosperous regions where its marginal product is low, towards lagging regions where additional capital investment is more profitable. These factor flows will boost growth in output per-worker in lagging regions. Thus, capital and labour migrate in response to interregional differences in factor returns and these factor movements will continue until factor returns are equalised in each region. Migration from low-wage to high-wage regions but also from high-inequality to low-inequality regions will decline spatial disparities and, in the long run, regions will move towards an economically optimum equilibrium (Pike et al., 2006).

The overall outcome is, therefore, one in which an interlocking and mutually–reinforcing set of processes (i.e. diminishing returns, labour migration, capital mobility and access to the same level of technology) erode regional economic disparities;[14] a process described by Camangi and Capello (2010) as a sort of 'entropic trend' towards spatial homogeneity.

It is reasonable to assume that labour and capital can more easily migrate between regions rather than across nations. It might be argued, therefore, that a network of regional economies provides an appropriate 'laboratory' for testing the neoclassical predictions of convergence. Barro and Sala-i-Martin (1992, 1995), note that convergence is more likely to occur between regions rather than national economies for precisely this reason. Although recognising the existence of some structural differences between regions they argue that these differences are likely to be small or even insignificant, compared to differences between nations. Their argument runs as follows:

> Firms and households of different regions within a single country tend to have access to similar technologies and have roughly similar tastes and cultures. Furthermore, the regions share a common government and, therefore, have similar institutional set-ups and legal systems. This relative homogeneity means that absolute convergence is more likely to apply across regions within countries than across countries. Legal, cultural, linguistic and institutional barriers to factor movements tend to be smaller across regions within a country than across countries. (Barro and Sala-i-Martin 1995, pp. 382–383)

In concluding this description of the neoclassical model, two major contributions of this model to an understanding of the process of regional growth and convergence

---

[14] Tselios (2009) examines empirically the relation between income convergence and regional inequalities across the European regions.

can be identified. First, as Armstrong and Taylor (2000) point out, the neoclassical framework draws attention to the importance of supply factors in the growth process, namely the growth of the labour force, the growth of the capital stock and technical progress. In addition, the model explains the interregional mobility of factors of production and analyses their effect upon the patterns of regional convergence. Second, as presented thus far, the neoclassical approach to regional growth leads to the absolute convergence hypothesis, which states that, in the long-run, regional economies converge to the same 'steady-state' level of output per unit of labour irrespective of initial conditions. This is embodied in the testable prediction that poor regions grow faster than rich regions, i.e. the growth rate of per-capita output is inversely related to the initial level of output per-worker.

Clearly, however, the model contains assumptions which are unrealistic, such as identical production functions and identical preferences with respect to saving and consumption across regions. Recognition of this has led to alternative formulations of the 'standard' neoclassical model. Broadly speaking, two extensions of the 'standard' neoclassical model have been proposed, namely a 'two-sector' model and an 'augmented' Solow model, both of which shed further light on the issues of regional growth and convergence. The following section provides an overview of these approaches.

2.3 Alternative Formulations of the Neoclassical Model

As is evident from the previous section, the dominant prediction of the neoclassical regional growth model is convergence in regional economic performance. Any tendencies to diverge are seen as transitory in nature, which will vanish gradually through the impact of diminishing marginal product of capital, factor migration[15] and diffusion of technologies across regions. As is also evident, the main focus is upon the supply side of the economy. However, it is possible to assign a role to demand factors in the context of a 'two-sector' neoclassical model. This version, although retaining the same basic assumptions, nevertheless leads to quite different predictions about regional growth and convergence.

2.3.1 Regional Growth in the 'Two-sector' Neoclassical Model

In the 'two-sector' model[16] a regional economy is divided into two output sectors, which differ in terms of labour productivity. Assume that the sector with higher labour productivity produces output for export to other regions. This might apply,

---

[15] Muth (1965), Rowthorn (2008, 2009) developed formal models of regional migration while some empirical evidence is provided by Faini et al. (1997), Faini (1999), Kirdar and Saracoğlu (2008), Hierro and Maza (2010).

[16] For a more detailed description of the 'two-sector' neoclassical model see Uzawa (1962, 1963).

for example, to a region during the process of industrialisation, where the low productivity sector consists of agricultural activities and the high productivity sector corresponds to manufacturing. Assume, further, that labour is homogenous and can move freely not only from one region to another, but also between sectors within the same region in response to any wage differentials. Growth of regional output can therefore occur due to a shift of labour from low productivity (agricultural) activities to high-productivity (manufacturing) activities. Such intraregional movements of the labour force can therefore account for a part of a region's output growth. However, what is of crucial importance is the performance of the high-productivity sector, which is normally viewed as the export sector.[17] If the demand for the region's exports increases, what will be the impact on regional growth?

An increase in the demand for a region's exports will increase the demand for capital, leading to capital growth in the export sector, not only as a result of indigenous investment but also from a net inflow of capital from other regions. This process will continue until the marginal cost of capital becomes identical with the marginal product of capital. However, the demand for labour also rises when export demand expands. Higher wages in the export (high-productivity) sector will attract workers from the low productivity sector until inter-sectoral wage equality is once again established. Moreover, this expansion of the exporting sector can lead to a net inflow of workers from other regions, the process continuing until regional wages are equalised. The low-productivity sector is further affected by the export stimulus since the increase in regional income raises the demand for the output of the low-productivity sector hence increasing the demand for labour in this sector also. A cycle of expansion and growth is, thus, apparent. The distinctive feature of the 'two-sector' model is that both labour and capital may flow in the same direction towards regions experiencing a demand stimulus. This is in sharp contrast to the 'one-sector' model in which the factors move in opposite directions in a disequilibrium situation. Furthermore, the possibility of interregional differences in technical progress emerges from the fact that regions are specialising in particular kinds of export activities. Armstrong and Taylor (1985) emphasise this point as follows:

> To the extent that technical progress varies between industries, differences in the industrial base of regions may help to account for regional differences in growth. (p. 63)

Thus, by introducing demand factors into the model, via an export sector, two further explanations of regional growth differences can be derived; the movement of both capital and labour into successful regions, and differential rates of technological progress due to differences in the export/industrial base of regions.

Nevertheless, despite its greater realism the 'two-sector' model has received less attention from regional economists than might be expected. Theoretical and empirical literature, in particular, has paid greater attention to another extension of the neoclassical model, proposed by Mankiw et al. (1992) in the context of the 'augmented Solow model'.

---

[17] North (1955) initially articulated the idea of regional growth propelled by exports. See also Tiebout (1956a).

2.3.2 Growth in the 'Augmented' Solow's Model

Mankiw et al. (1992) rekindled interest in Solow's model and its potential to provide a plausible account of the persisting disparities across economies by recognising that differences across economies might be attributed to differences in the educational skill levels of the labour force, i.e. differences in human capital.[18] As Chisholm (1991) notes:

> [...] national and regional fortunes are attributable in large measure to the qualities and abilities of the people, individually and collectively, rather than to some 'permanent' conditions either of location and resource, or to the quantity of capital and labour inherited from a previous generation. (p. 17)

Mankiw et al. (1992) assume that the output of an economy is produced by a combination of physical capital and skilled labour, and the accumulation of human capital occurs in the same way as the accumulation of physical capital. To be more precise, the production function in the 'augmented' Solow model takes the following form:

$$Y_{i,t} = K_{i,t}^{\alpha} H_{i,t}^{\beta} (A_{i,t} L_{i,t})^{1-\alpha-\beta} \tag{2.19}$$

where H is the stock of human capital, with $\alpha, \beta > 0$ and $\alpha, \beta < 1$ while $A_{i,t} = A_0 e^{gt}$.

An important condition imposed by Mankiw et al. (1992) is that $\alpha + \beta < 1$. This condition implies that there are diminishing returns to broad capital.[19] According to Crafts (1996) the introduction of human capital has two important implications. Diminishing returns to broad capital are less severe than to physical capital alone in the Solow (1956) and Swan (1956) model, and the transitory effects of increased investment, in both kinds of capital, on growth will last for longer.

A key assumption of the 'augmented' Solow model is that human capital accumulates as individuals devote time acquiring new skills instead of working. The skilled labour of an economy is taken to be a fraction of the total labour force, L, and assuming that individuals devote a certain time, u, for acquiring skills, human capital can be expressed in the following relation:

$$H_{i,t} = e^{\psi u} L_{i,t} \quad \text{with} \quad \psi > 0 \tag{2.20}$$

Equation 2.20 states that unskilled labour, learning skills for time u, generates skilled labour equal to the amount of H. If $u = 0$, then this indicates that all labour is unskilled while a small increase in u increases the human capital of an economy by

---

[18] The concept of 'human capital' developed initially by Becker (1964) and Schultz (1961, 1981), embodies education, skills and the on-the-job training of workers. This is the feature that distinguishes skilled labour from unskilled or crude labour.

[19] The concept of 'broad capital' includes both physical and human capital, following the intuition proposed by Knight (1921, 1944). This concept forms the basis for several models of the 'New-Endogenous Growth Theory', as will be seen in Chapter 3.

the percentage ψ. As Mankiw et al. (1992) show, the evolution of an economy is determined by the following two relations:

$$\dot{\hat{k}}_i = s_k \hat{y}_i - (n + g + \delta)\hat{k}_i \tag{2.21}$$

$$\dot{\hat{h}}_i = s_h \hat{y}_i - (n + g + \delta)\hat{h}_i \tag{2.22}$$

where $\hat{y}_i = \frac{Y_i}{AL_i}$, $\hat{k}_i = \frac{K_i}{AL_i}$ and $\hat{h}_i = \frac{H_i}{AL_i}$. The parameters s_k and s_h denote the portions of output invested in physical and human capital, respectively.

As can be seen from the above, the human capital per effective unit of labour evolves over time in a manner identical to that of physical capital. This is in fact unsurprising, since the incorporation of the human capital input does not change the structure of the production function. Mankiw et al. (1992) prove that the economy converges to 'steady-state' equilibrium, defined as a situation in which output per-worker grows at a constant rate. The 'steady-state' is determined by the values of physical and human capital:

$$\hat{k}_i^* = \left(\frac{s_k^{1-\beta} s_h^{\beta}}{n + g + \delta}\right)^{\frac{1}{1-\alpha-\beta}} \quad \text{and} \quad \hat{h}_i^* = \left(\frac{s_k^{\alpha} s_h^{1-\alpha}}{n + g + \delta}\right)^{\frac{1}{1-\alpha-\beta}} \tag{2.23}$$

Equation 2.23 implies that in the 'augmented' neoclassical model differences across economies (countries or regions), which occur in equilibrium (i.e. different steady-states), can be explained not only by differences in the rates of investment in physical capital (s_k) and in technology growth (g), but also in differences in the formation of human capital (s_h).[20] Higher rates of human capital accumulation and higher rates of growth are found in those economies in which individuals devote a larger fraction of time to learning and acquiring new skills.

The 'augmented' neoclassical model implies that economies (countries or regions) with different proportions of income invested in physical and human capital, or different rates of population growth, depreciation and technological progress have different levels of output per-worker in equilibrium.[21] In other words, there is a component of output differences that persists over time.

---

[20] Given that $\ln \frac{Y_{i,t}}{A_{i,t}L_{i,t}} = \ln \frac{Y_{i,t}}{L_{i,t}} - \ln A_{i,t}$ and $A_{i,t} = A_0 e^{gt} \Rightarrow \ln A_{i,t} = \ln A_0 + gt$, then substituting equation (2.19) into (2.19) yields:

$$\ln\left[\frac{Y_{i,t}}{L_{i,t}}\right] = \ln A_0 + gt - \frac{\alpha + \beta}{1 - \alpha - \beta} \ln(n + g + \delta) + \frac{\alpha}{1 - \alpha - \beta} \ln(s_k) + \frac{\beta}{1 - \alpha - \beta} \ln(s_h).$$

[21] It is not uncommon, however, in most empirical studies for the rates of depreciation and technological progress to be considered as being constant for all the economies included. Indeed several authors (e.g. Yao, 1999; Zhang and Yao, 2001; Fingleton and Fischer. 2010) assume that $(g + \delta) = 0.05$.

While the 'standard' model predicts absolute convergence, in the 'augmented' model, economies do not necessarily converge to the same 'steady-state' irrespective of their initial conditions. In this light, the 'augmented' neoclassical model introduces a new notion of convergence, conditional convergence. Sala-i-Martin (1996a) claims that the concept of conditional convergence is encapsulated in the prediction of the neoclassical model that the growth rate of an economy will be positively related to the distance that separates it from its own steady-state. Generalising across a group of regional economies, the simple proposition that poor economies catch-up with rich economies no longer holds true. The latter prediction relies on the presence of common steady-state, so that initially poor economies which are further away from this steady-state will grow faster. It follows, therefore that, conditional convergence coincides with absolute convergence only if all the economies have the same steady-state.

Both forms of convergence, however, represent movements towards an equilibrium or 'steady-state' position. In order to examine the possibilities for non-convergence across regions, it is necessary to either assume certain conditions in the models do not hold, such as factors are not perfectly mobile, or to turn to alternative approaches to the analysis of regional growth, which do not rely on the concept of equilibrium. The following section provides an overview of one such approach.

2.4   Post-Keynesian Regional Growth

An alternative framework for the analysis of regional growth, the post-Keynesian view, emphasises the role of demand factors. Kaldor (1970, 1972) is the most prominent economist in the post-Keynesian tradition. His work had great influence on several authors including Thirlwall (1983a, b), McCombie and Thirlwall (1994; 1997). Thirlwall (1980a) states that:

> Regional growth is demand-determined for the obvious reason that no region's growth rate can be constrained by supply when factors of production are freely mobile. For a region in which capital and labour are highly mobile in and out, growth must be demand-determined. If the demand for a region's output is strong, labour and capital will migrate to the region to the benefit of that region and to the detriment of others. Supply adjusts to demand. We cannot return to the pre-Keynesian view that demand adjusts to supply. If we could, the solution to any region's lagging growth rate would be for it to save more and breed more! (p. 420)

Furthermore, post-Keynesian economists argue that, at the regional level convergence is unlikely to take place. Instead, unbalanced regional growth or divergence is the more likely outcome due to the operation of cumulative causation processes, drawing on the work of Myrdal (1957), who argued that once regional income disparities occur, there is a strong tendency for these inequalities to be reinforced.[22] Kaldor took up this theme of cumulative causation in a series of influential papers (1967, 1972 and 1975):

> To explain why certain regions have become highly industrialised, while others have not we must introduce quite *different* kinds of considerations – what Myrdal called the principle of 'circular and cumulative causation. (Kaldor 1970, p. 315). [Emphasis added]

Thus, Kaldor (1970) not only challenged the standard neoclassical convergence view, but also provided the basis for a more interventionist regional policy, based on the development of a more formal analysis of the processes underpinning divergent regional growth.

2.4.1   An Overview of the Concept of Cumulative Causation

The essence of circular or cumulative causation, originally developed by Myrdal (1957) in a period of economic crisis[23] and extended by Kaldor (1970), is that a fast rate of output growth in certain regions will provide them with a productive advantage (lower costs), which in turn, leads to further output growth, which may be at the expense of other regions. Thus, prosperous regions will be able to sustain a productive advantage, reinforcing the existing gap with poor regions.[24] Aggregate growth is related to the rate of expansion in the sector with the most favourable characteristics, as indicated by the degree of increasing returns to scale. Typically, increasing returns are associated with manufacturing industry, whilst activities such as mining and agriculture are subject to decreasing returns (McCombie and Thirlwall, 1994). Thus, regions specialising in activities with increasing returns are likely to grow faster than those specialising in activities of the primary sector. This process is cumulative and shapes the spatial distribution of economic activity. Cumulative causation and its spatial consequences share many common characteristics with the ideas and concepts of Perroux (1950, 1955) and Hirschman (1957, 1958).[25] Nevertheless, the most influential contribution to the development of cumulative causation models are Perroux's concepts of 'propulsive industry', and 'growth poles'.

---

[22] A cumulative process in can be generated by the demand–supply interaction on the markets for goods and labour in advanced-core regions. Investment in core regions causes further expansion, increasing in-migration and local demand, which in turn brings new investment and further development.

[23] The concept of cumulative causation was first introduced in Myrdal's book: *An American Dilemma* (1944). See Streeten (1998) for further details.

[24] Prebisch (1962) and Seers (1962) argue that a similar mechanism operates across the world's economies. An initial advantage, even a small one, can be compounded several times by the free play of market forces.

[25] Friedmann (1969, 1972) provides a broader version of the cumulative causation model by introducing 'core-periphery' relations in the context of a 'colonial' system.

2.4.2   'Growth Poles'

According to Perroux (1950), economic development is imbalanced or polarised, in the sense that there are several forces at work which result in the concentration of economic activity into certain poles in 'abstract economic space', defined as a set of existing economic relations among economic agents, rather than geographical space or a 'field of forces' (Plummer and Taylor, 2001a). A 'growth pole'[26] is defined as a set of industries capable of generating dynamic growth in an economy and strongly interrelated to each other via input–output linkages around a leading (propulsive) industry.[27] These 'propulsive industries', or 'the instruments of prosperity', as Perroux (1950, p. 103) calls them, are seen as having a set of distinctive characteristics and development effects. These include a high degree of concentration, high income elasticity of demand for their products, strong multiplier and polarisation effects through input linkages, advanced technology and managerial expertise promoting local diffusion through demonstration effects, promotion of a highly developed local infrastructure. This industry and its interdependent sectors grow faster than the rest of economy (Plummer and Taylor, 2001a). Richardson (1978) claims that this tendency for faster growth is attributed to factors such as a high degree of concentration, use of advanced technology, high innovation rates, spillovers and multiplier effects[28] on the other segments of the economy. Similarly, Hirschman (1958) uses the notion of input–output linkages to describe the development of an economy. Hirschman (1958) stresses the importance of technical complementarities between industries at different stages of production ('vertical' linkages). Although, Hirschman (1958) did not include an explicit spatial dimension, the existence of strong linkage effects in certain sectors of the economy implies the concentration of these sectors in certain points in space. Hirschman (1958) implies that rapid economic growth requires a concentration of diverse, though interrelated, activities in a few large centres, which then become attractive locations for new firms. This sectoral and geographical concentration leads to a situation similar to the 'growth poles' described by Perroux (1950). This theory shares similarities with Schumpeter's discussion (1934) of direct and indirect effects of a radical innovation. According to Schumpeter (1934) a set of dynamic industries (the 'propulsive' industries) might be spatially clustered. Agglomeration effects occur as a result of this clustering, together with spillover effects on the surrounding

---

[26] Perroux's theory of growth poles has been used extensively in regional economics and economic geography (Hayter, 1997). However, the transmission of the 'growth pole' concept into geographical rather than abstract economic space is attributed to Boudeville (1966) who has defined a regional 'growth pole' as 'a set of expanding industries located in an urban area and inducing further development of economic activity throughout its zone of influence' (p. 11). For a more detailed review on the concept of 'growth poles' see Lasuen (1969), Parr (1999a,b).

[27] Similar is the theory of 'development blocks' elaborated by Dahmén (1950), developed in order to describe the Swedish industries prior to World War II. See also Dahmén (1988).

[28] For a conceptual discussion of the regional multipliers see Weiss and Gooding (1968), Richardson (1985) and Mulligan (2008).

hinterland. These effects can take the form of 'spread' and 'backwash' effects, stressed by Myrdal (1957), or 'trickling down' and 'polarisation' effects,[29] implied by Hirschman (1958) which are the favourable and unfavourable impacts of growth at the pole on its hinterland. An impulsive growth process begins with an initial stimulus such as that provided by the establishment in a location of a sizeable firm exporting goods or services from a region.

Linkage and multiplier processes are then argued to stimulate other firms to locate in the region and thereby increase regional output; a process similar to the Keynesian multiplier mechanism but with a spatial dimension.

However, a 'growth pole' implies more than just a spatial concentration of activity. It induces considerable expansion in the surrounding area and for this particular effect, features such as a highly developed infrastructure, are more critical than inter-industry linkages. Thus, income will be maximised in the growth area as a whole by concentrating development at growth points rather than spreading it over the region as a whole. This implies a structural imbalance in regional economic activity, such that beyond the boundary of the zone of influence of the pole income levels may stagnate and areas decline. Successful areas grow cumulatively, at the expense of other areas.

2.4.3 Cumulative Causation: Internal and External Economies

In seeking to explain the underlying mechanisms of cumulative growth, attention is often directed at internal and external (agglomeration) economies of scale. Such increasing returns are a direct challenge to static equilibrium theory, as Thirlwall (1983a) argues:

> The existence of increasing returns not only undermines the concept of a competitive equilibrium but makes the whole growth and development process a cumulative one in favoured 'regions' relative to others. Trade and factor mobility between 'regions' become disequilibrating rather than equilibrating as far as income, employment opportunity and other indices of welfare are concerned. (p. 342)

Internal economies exist when long-run average cost falls as the scale of production expands, thus reducing competition, in terms of the number of firms needed to supply a given total demand. Moreover, internal economies of scale may take two forms, static and dynamic. Static economies of scale relate to the size and scale of production units whereas dynamic economies refer to effects such as increasing returns brought about by 'induced' technical progress and learning-by-doing. These arguments are almost identical to increasing returns to scale proposed by the early arguments of Adam Smith (1776) and Alfred Marshall (1890). Following the standard microeconomic structure, economies of scale can be analysed in a 'production function' framework (e.g. Schaefer, 1977, 1978; Shefer, 1973;

---

[29] For a more detailed discussion see Richardson (1976) and Gaile (1980).

Sveikauskas, 1975, 1979; Moomaw, 1982, 1983). Each firm in each industry faces a production function, which essentially describes the maximum output that is obtainable with a given technology and quantities of inputs. With given the factor costs (or quantities of inputs) and the available technology there is an optimum size of plant, which if operated at full capacity would result in the lowest average (or per unit) cost of production.

In one of the earliest studies on scale economies at the spatial level, Guthrie (1955), points out that the optimum size of plant in each industry can be considered as the result of technical, managerial, marketing and finance factors. A large firm may be able to operate at lower levels of average cost by combining the scale of operation of each factor. As the size of plant and the scale of operation reach higher levels economies of scale come into operation attributed to the division and specialisation of labour. According to Richardson (1978a), these economies account for the 'one-company' towns. External economies, on the other hand, are beyond the influence of an individual firm and can arise, for example, from the geographical concentration of activities, which permits services and other facilities to be shared in common (Chisholm 1991, p.72). Theoretical[30] and empirical research[31] in urban and regional economics makes extensive use of spatial externalities. Fingleton and McCombie (1998) point out, that:

> [...] it is almost an article of faith of regional economics that production is characterised by substantial internal and *external* economies of scale from the *agglomeration* of economic activities. (p. 90) [Emphasis added]

Spatial externalities can be categorised and analysed in several ways. Just as an example, early analysis by Robinson (1931) divides externalities into mobile and immobile economies, where the former include effects that are unrelated to the size of the industry in a given location but which depend on the size of industry in the

---

[30] Spatial externalities is one of the earliest concepts and is extensively used in economics and economic geography, e.g. Weber (1929), Lösch (1938, 1954), Harris (1954), Lampard (1955), Leser (1948), Isard (1954, 1956), Nicholson (1956), Moses (1958), Tiebout (1961), Winnick (1961), Marcus (1965), Moses and Williamson (1967), Alonso (1968), Webber (1972), Henderson (1974, 1982), Richardson (1969), Mulligan (1984), Weiss (1972), Carlton (1983), Dicken and Lloyd (1990), Phelps (1992). More recently theoretical aspect of agglomeration are suggested by Glaeser (1999), Netzer (1992), Crampton and Evans (1992), McCann (1995), Dekle and Eaton (1999), Quigley (1998).

[31] Empirical studies on spatial externalities are extensive and usually pay attention to industry-specific models without considering regional growth and convergence explicitly. The majority of empirical literature is concentrated on the US experience, e.g. Duffy (1987), Henderson (1994, 2003), Henderson et al. (1995), Ellison and Glaeser (1997, 1999), Pascal and McCall (1980), Carlino and Voith (1992), Desmet and Fafchamps (2005) while similar studies were conducted for Sweden (Åberg, 1973; Braunerhjelm and Borgman, 2004), Germany (Gross, 1997), Japan (Kawashima, 1975; Nakamura, 1985), Malaysia (Bhattacharya, 2002), Nepal (Fafchamps and Shilpi, 2005), Canada (Soroka, 1994; Baldwin et al., 2008), Korea (Henderson et al., 2001a); Poland (Bivand, 1999), India (Mitra, 1999), Italy (Mion, 2004), the UK (Graham, 2001), Spain (Viladecans-Marsal, 2004; Alonso-Villar et al., 2004), Mexico (Hanson, 1996), Holland (de Vor and de Groot, 2010) and Finland (Mukkala, 2004).

entire economy. On the other hand, immobile economies affect the firms concentrated in a particular location and hence are spatially defined. However, of more relevance to the regional context are the concepts introduced by Hoover (1936, 1948), who distinguishes external economies according to their differential impacts. Hoover (1936, 1948), drawing on Ohlin (1933),[32] suggests that spatial effects are realised either at firm level, i.e. large-scale internal economies or at regional-local level, i.e. localisation and urbanisation economies. As Button (1976) claims, where agglomeration effects accrue to a number of separate firms in the same industry congregating in a particular location, these are said to be external to each individual firm but internal to the industry as a whole. Such localisation economies occur when a firm benefits from proximity to other local firms in the same industry, which impacts upon the growth of total industrial output. Thus, the region becomes specialised in that industry, providing further scale economies for firms located in that region, as well as incentives to attract similar firms to the region. Thus, at a specific location, scale economies are realised within a single plant, as well as from localisation economies, which apply to all plants within a single industry. Geographical concentration of a specific industry in a particular area tends to encourage the establishment of complementary industries to meet its demands for imports and to provide facilities to market and transport the final product. Spatial concentration of an industry permits development of highly specialised factors of production, such as skilled labour, which are shared by many firms in the industry.[33] For example, new research-oriented industries show a tendency to cluster near universities and other research establishments.

While localisation economies are external to the firm, but internal to the industry to which the firm belongs, there is another type of effect, which is external to the specific industry. These externalities are known as urbanisation economies and derive from the scale of total economic activity in a region, allowing a firm to benefit from overall local scale and diversity. Chinitz (1961) argues that agglomeration economies, industrial diversification and competitiveness are positively related.[34] Indeed, urbanisation economies emerge when the range and quality of services provided to all industries increases with the size of an urban area (Collins and Walker, 1975). External economies arise not only in production but also in consumption through the concentration of many types of activity. Firms in many different sectors benefit from the larger market for their output, as well as access to large and well-

---

[32] The Heckscher-Ohlin (factor endowment) theory predicts that an economy with abundance in skilled labour relative to unskilled labour will expand production and exports of goods that are relatively skill-intensive in their production, when trade between economies is allowed. Increased specialisation in the comparative advantages sectors would eventually become an increased agglomeration through space. Indeed, '[. . .] international trade theory cannot be understood except in relation to and as a part of the general location theory' (Ohlin, 1993, p. 97).

[33] This leads to formation of 'clusters'; a notion that emphasises synergy, a creative milieu, innovation and quality of life and urban environment for attracting highly skilled labour.

[34] For a more detailed review see Evans (1986), Norton (1992).

organised labour markets, specialist commercial facilities and improved transport. For people generally, a large urban area can provide specialised leisure and recreational amenities and can offer a wide range of job opportunities, shopping outlets and educational, medical and recreational opportunities (Harvey, 1992). In the case of urbanisation economies, it is the size of the area rather than its industrial composition which matters. As Henderson (1983) notes:

> If scale effects are ones of localisation, then for a given city size and associated cost of living, scale effects and hence incomes are maximised by concentrating local export employment all in one industry, rather than dissipating the scale effects by spreading employment over many industries. However, if scale effects are ones of urbanisation, then this specialisation may not matter since it is the general level of economic activity rather than its industry specific *concentration* which enhances productivity. (p. 165) [Emphasis added]

The overall conclusion, therefore, is that internal and external economies of scale contribute to a geographical concentration of economic activities and thus, in the spatial economy, this is a potential source of dynamic change leading to local growth. Economists belonging to the Keynesian tradition attribute the cumulative nature of growth to the existence of substantial increasing returns:

> Once, however, we allow for increasing returns, the forces making for continuous change are endogenous - 'they are engendered from within the economic system'- and the actual state of the economy during any one 'period' cannot be predicted except as the result of the sequence of events in the previous periods which led up to it. (Kaldor, 1972, p.1244)

The most prominent model in the post-Keynesian school is developed by Kaldor (1970).

2.4.4 A (post)-Keynesian Approach to Regional Growth

Kaldor (1970) incorporated the concept of cumulative causation within a formal economic model, postulating that the speed at which a region's per-capita output grows is determined by the extent to which regions are able to take advantage of internal scale economies and thus attain the benefits that accrue from greater specialisation. If the manufacturing sector exhibits substantially greater economies of scale than primary or land-based activities, then regions specialising in manufacturing activities are likely to grow faster than regions that rely heavily on land-based activities.

This could be described as the 'sectoral' approach to growth. Indeed, Kaldor (1970) claims that it is impossible to understand the growth process without taking a sectoral approach. It might be argued that Kaldor's sectoral approach shares similar characteristics with the two-sector neoclassical model, discussed in Sect. 2.3, particularly regarding the impact of exporting activities in generating regional growth disparities. Similar features are included in the early 'export-base' models (e.g. Tiebout, 1956a,b; Williamson, 1975) which take as their premise that regional income is determined by the region's exports. Although Kaldor (1967, 1970) puts emphasis on specialisation in exporting activities, there are two significant differences in comparison to the two-sector model. First, there is far greater emphasis on the demand side of the economy. According to Kaldor (1970) the share of 'autonomous' demand which a region captures depends on its costs of production relative to costs of production elsewhere. Production costs can be viewed as the outcome of productivity and factor prices, with the former influenced by the rate of technical change and growth of the capital-labour ratio. These, in turn, depend partly on output growth, which itself is determined to a large extent by the growth of the export sector. A reinforcing feedback mechanism is apparent. Export growth affects output growth in a region, which then further enhances productivity and competitiveness in the export sector. Second, unlike the 'two-sector' neoclassical model, Kaldor (1970) argues that the process of cumulative causation does not promote convergence between regions, but instead perpetuates the tendencies for divergent regional growth rates through the positive link between growth and competitiveness of a region's export sector.[35] The mechanism by which the circular process of cumulative causation operates is captured in the relation between employment and output growth, known as Verdoorn's Law (Verdoorn, 1949).

Factor movements in this model appear similar in direction to those predicted by the two-sector neoclassical model. However, they do not operate to promote convergence. Although workers move out of regions where employment opportunities are poor and move into regions where employment opportunities are good and wages are higher, there is now recognition that the consequences over the long-run are likely to be harmful to the origin regions. This is due to the fact that migration tends to be age and skill selective with younger and more skilled or educated workers exhibiting greater mobility, thereby diminishing workforce quality in the origin region and making it less attractive to potential employers. Likewise, capital will flow into successful regions. However, the implications of this may also be complex. In an advanced economy, it is reasonable to assume that as capital accumulation takes place new production facilities will embody more advanced technology. Recently installed plant may lead to lower unit costs compared to older equipment, and/or higher quality output is possible at any given cost. It follows that, if the average age of capital stock in one region is lower than elsewhere then cheaper or better commodities and services can be produced. This applies both to private capital and to public capital such as transport infrastructure, utilities and education/training facilities, and so forth. This particular feedback process, embodied within Verdoorn's Law,[36] describes technological progress in an economy.[37] In the simple (conventional) neoclassical model, despite the significance of technical progress, no sufficient explanation is provided for its

---

[35] Nevertheless, Setterfield (1997) argues that it is possible to extend Kaldor's model to allow for the limits to increasing returns, the dynamic of structural change, growth reversal and relative decline. This argument has caused a considerable debate (e.g. Toner, 2001; Argyrous, 2001; Setterfield, 1998, 2001) while Alexiadis and Tsagdis (2010) attempt to examine it empirically.

[36] There is a considerable debate regarding Verdoorn's Law. See Kaldor (1975), Wolfe (1968), Rowthorn (1975a,b), Vaciago (1975), Boulier (1984), Cornwall (1976), Parikh (1978), McCombie (1981) and Thirlwall (1980b). For a more detailed review see McCombie (1982a,b, 1983, 1985, 1986), Bairam (1987).

[37] However, it should be noted that Verdoorn's Law is only one facet or form of Kaldor's (1957) model of growth. See also Black (1962) and McCombie (1988b).

emergence. In summary, the process of cumulative causation embodied in Verdoorn's Law implies that leading regions grow at the expense of others, and regional inequalities are re-enforced, rather that reduced by factor movements. Regional disparities are perpetuated across regions through the existence of disequilibrating mechanisms and initial differences between regions tend to persist or expand, in contrast to the predictions of convergence more typically associated with neoclassical models.

Several attempts have been made to formalise the concept of cumulative causation outlined by Myrdal (1957) and Kaldor (1970) in order to allow for empirical verification. For example, Baumol (1967), and to a certain extent, Oates et al. (1971), attempt a formulation of cumulative causation, but with emphasis upon urban unbalanced growth and cumulative deterioration. In the context of regional cumulative growth Dixon and Thirlwall's (1975)[38] model is the most prominent. According to Dixon and Thirlwall (1975), regional growth is a function of the demand for a region's exports. A faster growth of output leads to an increase in productivity growth (the Verdoorn effect) which leads to an increase in a region's price competitiveness.[39] This, in turn, generates a faster growth of the region's exports which, through the 'dynamic super-multiplier', increases the overall rate of growth. To be more specific, firm chose their location due to labour cost or 'efficiency wages' (wages/productivity). In advanced regions, a high productivity generated by a substantial industrial base, efficient services and infrastructure might out-weight the disadvantages of higher wages increasing thus competitiveness. This model may be applied to a group of regions, in order to consider the question 'what causes regional growth rates to differ?' According to Dixon and Thirlwall (1975) the 'Verdoorn effect' is a source of regional growth rates differences only to the extent that the Verdoorn coefficient[40] varies between regions.[41]

---

[38] Richardson (1978a,b) attempts a formulation of cumulative causation in more narrow terms; it does not include an explicit demand function for exports nor any kind of balance of payment conditions.

[39] Thirlwall (1980a) expressed this relationship in almost identical terms, namely that regional growth rates in balance of payments equilibrium approximates to the growth of regional exports divided by the regional income elasticity of demand for imports ('Thirlwall's Law). See Gibson and Thirlwall (1993).

[40] In algebraic terms Verdoorn's Law is specified as follows: $\dot{e}_i = a_i + \lambda \dot{q}_i$, where $\dot{e}_i$ is the rate of employment growth in a region, a_i is the rate of autonomous productivity growth, $\dot{q}_i$ is the rate of output growth and λ is the Verdoorn coefficient.

[41] Verdoorn's Law has been tested across a number of countries, e.g. for the UK (Stoneman, 1979), Australia (Whiteman, 1987), Holland (Fase and van den Heuvel, 1988; Fase and Winder, 1999), Turkey (Bairam, 1991), Greece, (Drakopoulos and Theodossiou, 1991) the US (McCombie, 1983; 1985, Atesoglu, 1993); Japan (Wulwick, 1991); China (Hansen and Zhang, 1996), Eastern Europe (Gomulka, 1983), Columbia (Rivas, 2008) and in various regional contexts, e.g. for the USA states (Casetti, 1984; Casetti and Jones, 1987; McCombie and deRidder, 1983; 1984, the EU regions (Fingelton and McCombie, 1998; Dall'erba et al., 2008; Alexiadis and Tsagdis, 2010), the UK regions (Hildreth, 1989), the regions of Japan (Casetti and Tanaka, 1992), the Greek regions (Alexiadis and Tsagdis, 2006b). In general, the majority of the empirical literature seems to confirm the validity of this relation both across countries and regions.

This variation tends to exaggerate the effects of these differences. As McCombie and Thirlwall (1997) argue

> [...] the dependence of productivity growth on the growth rate per se is not sufficient to cause differences in regional growth rates unless the Verdoorn coefficient varies between regions or growth rates would diverge for other reasons anyway. (p. 460)

It is the 'Verdoorn effect' which makes the model circular and cumulative, and as Dixon and Thirlwall (1975) point out 'the Verdoorn coefficient gives rise to the possibility that once a region obtains a growth advantage, it will keep it' (p. 205). In other words, the Verdoorn relation acts as a sustaining factor in the persistence of regional growth differences once they have arisen due to initial differences in the parameters of the model. Furthermore, if a region gains an initial competitive advantage in the production of goods with a high income elasticity of demand, it will then be difficult (if not impossible) for other regions to establish the same activities. This is the essence of Kaldor's view on cumulative causation and the divergence between 'centre' (industrialised regions) and 'periphery' (agricultural regions).

In summary, the process of cumulative causation, as outlined in this section, is an essential element in Kaldor's view of regional growth disparities. 'Verdoorn's Law' encapsulates the cumulative growth process within the export-led model of regional growth, and the underlying rationale is based on the operation of increasing returns to scale. In this context increasing returns to scale are conceived in a broader sense, as to include both internal and external scale economics.

2.5 Conclusions

This chapter has provided, in essence, two competing perspectives on regional growth, and on the potential for convergence or divergence in economic performance within a group of regional economies. The neoclassical model has been shown as essentially supply driven and reliant on price and wage flexibility, factor mobility and the operation of competitive markets. The model leads to predictions of absolute or conditional convergence. However, a major criticism is that the 'spatial economy' is not addressed explicitly in the neoclassical context. Space and distance, in reality, impose constraints on competitive forces. Furthermore, perfect competition is incompatible with increasing returns to scale and yet many regional economists argue that production is characterised by substantial increasing returns to scale, due to the agglomeration of economic activity in space. As stated by Richardson (1973a):

> Perfect competition cannot be assumed in regional economic analysis since space itself and the existence of transport costs limits competition; oligopoly, pure monopoly or monopolistic competition, are much more appropriate market structures. (p. 22)

The approach to regional growth outlined by post-Keynesian economists places more emphasis on demand factors and, by focusing to internal and external economies, implicitly acknowledges spatial factors at the regional level. In Kaldor's original approach the principle of cumulative causation depends, inter alia, upon increasing (internal) returns to scale in manufacturing. However, increasing returns to scale may be defined in a wider sense to include both internal and external (agglomeration) economies. Thus, as Richardson (1973a) states:

> [...] reliance on a simple Verdoorn Law relationship is too *aggregative* for the regional economist since it says very little about the complex role played by agglomeration economies, external economies and indivisibilities in the spatial concentration ('polarisation') of economic activity. (p. 33). [Emphasis added]

Although another contribution of post-Keynesian models is to highlight the fact that different sectors possess different growth characteristics which may contribute to divergence in regional growth, in such models the supply side is generally passive. Moreover, the process of technology diffusion or adoption is not clearly articulated. Productivity gains are represented in the context of Verdoorn's Law, which embodies the effects of economies of scale and technological progress but explains little about technical advances in backward regions and provides no explanation of the link between output growth and technological change in leading regions (Button and Pentecost, 1999). It is evident that the two approaches lead to very different predictions regarding regional performance. In particular, the neoclassical model argues that differences in growth rates across regions, with poor regions growing faster than rich regions, will be eliminated as all regions move towards a unique level of output per-worker. This outcome, absolute convergence, is based on the assumption that the only difference across regions lies in their initial levels of output per-worker. However, if regions differ in several other structural parameters, then there will be different 'steady-states' and the argument of absolute convergence will not hold. Thus, the prediction of convergence holds only when account is taken of structural differences across regions, which represent the different steady-states (conditional convergence). In general, however, the neoclassical model predicts that differences will diminish as regions move towards 'steady-state' equilibrium. On the other hand, the post-Keynesian approach predicts that differences will perpetuate and even grow further. However, further developments have led to models that lie between these two extreme perspectives in the sense that they can encompass both possibilities. Thus, 'Endogenous Growth Theory' and 'New Economic Geography' are the subject of the next chapter.

Chapter 3
'Endogenous Growth Theory' and 'New Economic Geography'

3.1 Introduction

The 1980s and 1990s have seen the earlier neoclassical and Post-Keynesian models augmented by a new generation of growth theories, notably Endogenous Growth Theory in which technical progress develops within the economic system. Hammond and Rodriguez-Clare (1995) summarise the contribution of the endogenous growth models as follows:

> Progress in economic science often takes the form of explaining what was previously inexplicable. That is, variables, which had earlier been treated as exogenous, become *endogenized*. Their values become determined, at least in principle, *within* an economic model. (as quoted in Fine 2000) [Emphasis added]

Specifically, technology is no longer an exogenous variable, but it is explained within the new growth models. Endogenous growth models are able to generate positive growth rates in the main economic variables because growth is related positively to the deliberate production of knowledge and technology and to external effects arising from broad capital formation. Thus, long-run growth in per-capita output depends on investment decisions, which are generated within the growth process rather than unexplained or exogenous improvements in technology. Regarding the contribution of endogenous growth theory to an understanding of regional growth, Armstrong and Taylor (2001) note that this theory has given a

> [...] welcome fillip to what had become a rather sterile debate between supporters of neoclassical and post-Keynesian views of regional growth (p. xii).

Elements of endogenous growth mechanisms can be found in models of the post-Keynesian tradition. For example, the Verdoorn relationship, discussed in Chap. 2, provides a feedback mechanism to incorporate the interactions between output growth, increasing returns to scale and technology. However, recent models of endogenous growth theory incorporate technology explicitly by focusing upon human capital formation (as introduced in Sect. 2.3.2) and the existence of sectors that deliberately produce technological innovations. Furthermore, the adaptation of

S. Alexiadis, *Convergence Clubs and Spatial Externalities*,
Advances in Spatial Science, DOI 10.1007/978-3-642-31626-5_3,
© Springer-Verlag Berlin Heidelberg 2013

endogenous growth models to a regional context, which acknowledges the importance of spatial features, such as the spatial distribution of economic activity and localised dynamic externalities, leads to the conclusion that it may be too simplistic to view regional growth patterns as either convergent or divergent. Endogenous growth models that explicitly incorporate the spatial dimension constitute a new tradition in regional research, known as 'New Economic Geography'. The aim of this chapter is, therefore, to summarise the main models of endogenous growth theory and their application to spatial analysis.

Divided into six sections, the two main categories of endogenous growth models are discussed first in Sect. 3.2, including the AK or endogenous broad capital models and those that generate endogenous growth through the workings of externalities. The concept of 'externalities' in mainstream economic analysis is outlined in this section, followed by a closer examination of externalities in a spatial context, with particular emphasis upon the dynamic effects of spatial externalities and the significance of knowledge spillovers. Section 3.3 outlines the basic elements of 'New Economic Geography', emphasising in particular the 'path-dependence' mechanism which 'locks-in' regions into certain 'clusters'. While the neoclassical model suggests the regional disparities will disappear, in the various models of 'New Economic Geography' agglomeration forces will result in specialisation patterns and regional 'clustering'. These sections conclude with the 'two-sector' models of endogenous growth theory in which technology creation is modelled explicitly through the introduction of intentionally produced knowledge and innovation. The implications for regional convergence arising from endogenous growth are discussed in Sect. 3.4. Finally, Sect. 3.5 concludes.

3.2 'One-Sector' Models of Endogenous Growth

This section outlines two types of models in endogenous growth theory or 'New Growth Theory', as sometimes is called.[1] First, models that emphasise the contribution of 'broad' capital to growth, such as the simple 'AK' model, are explained. This is followed by a discussion of models that attribute economic growth to the working of externalities.

3.2.1 'AK' Models of Endogenous Growth

The simplest model that generates endogenous growth is a reformulation of the standard neoclassical model of Solow (1956) and Swan (1956) in which a constant

---

[1] For a more detailed review see Boltho and Holtham (1992), Pack (1994), Solow (1994), Andersen and Moene (1995), Jones and Manuelli (1990b), Aghion et al. (1999), Temple (1999), Fine (2000), Brinkman and Brinkman (2001), Nijkamp and Abreu (2009).

proportional relationship between output and capital is assumed. The new element to this model is that capital includes human as well as physical capital. Following the intuition developed initially by Knight (1944), a definition of capital in such terms does not restrict this factor to exhibiting diminishing returns. A production function without diminishing returns can be written as follows (Barro and Sala-i-Martin 1995):

$$Y_i = AK_i \tag{3.1}$$

where the subscript i represents a region.

In this 'one-sector' model, referred to as the 'AK' model the parameter A indicates the level of technology.[2] Equation 3.1 can be expressed in per worker terms as follows:

$$y_i = Ak_i \tag{3.2}$$

As shown in Chap. 2 in the neoclassical model of Solow (1956) and Swan (1956) the growth rate of output per-worker is a function of the capital-labour ratio, as follows:

$$\frac{\dot{k}_i}{k_i} = \frac{sf(k_i)}{k_i} - (\delta + n) \tag{3.3}$$

where s is the propensity to save, δ is the rate of depreciation of physical capital and n the growth rate of labour.

The particular form of $f(k_i)$ is given by Eq. 3.2, so that substitution of $A = f(k_i)/k_i$ into Eq. 3.3 yields:

$$\frac{\dot{k}_i}{k_i} = sA - (\delta + n) \tag{3.4}$$

Equation 3.4 shows that in the absence of diminishing returns it is now the case that a higher savings rate generates higher growth in the capital-labour ratio and, hence, higher output per-capita. Following Barro and Sala-i-Martin (1995, p. 39), long-run growth in the AK model can be depicted by Fig. 3.1:

The distance between sA and $(n + \delta)$ represents the constant growth rate for the capital-labour ratio (k_i), which is positive provided, of course, that $sA > (n + \delta)$. For each level of the capital-labour ratio perpetual growth of the capital-labour ratio occurs. The message, consequently, from this simple version of the AK model is

---

[2] Barro and Sala-i-Martin (1995) claim that Von Neumann (1945) first introduced the AK style model. Frankel (1962) also developed a similar along those lines. Nevertheless, 'AK' style models were developed recently by King and Rebelo (1990), Jones and Manuelli (1990a) and Rebelo (1991) while Jones (1995a), Kocherlakota and Yi (1995, 1996, 1997) conducted empirical tests of AK models.

Fig. 3.1 Sustainable long-run growth in the AK model

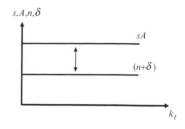

clear. Endogenous growth in output per-worker occurs due to the absence of diminishing returns to capital in the long-run and technological progress is embodied in the accumulation of physical and human capital. However, this model and its conclusions are subject to several criticisms. In particular, Blomstrom et al. (1996) argue that accumulation of capital appears to follow rather than precede rapid growth. In other words, a higher rate of capital accumulation is a symptom rather than a cause of growth. Additionally, technological progress is considered to be a simple 'side effect'. Romer (1994) and subsequently Crafts (1995a, b and 1996) argue that improvements in technology are the result of deliberate activities or choices by economic agents. This has led to models that pay particular attention to the intentional creation of technology and expansion in broad capital through activities relating to research and education, for example, an issue which is examined in Sect. 3.4.1. Another important aspect of endogenous growth analysis involves modification of the traditional neoclassical production function in such a way as to include externalities to investment in broad capital. Prior to an examination of this approach, however, it is essential to provide an overview of those aspects of externalities, which are relevant in the context of this discussion of growth and convergence.

3.2.2 Externalities

Marshall (1890, 1920) deployed the concept of 'external economies' or 'externalities'[3] to refer to sources of productivity growth that lie outside individual firms, such as labour market pooling, the availability of specialist suppliers and the presence of technological spillovers. Thus, producers derive external benefits by sharing the fixed costs of common resources, such as infrastructure and services, and by having access to skilled labour pools, specialised suppliers and a common knowledge base.[4] As pointed out in Sect. 2.4.3 in Chap. 2, Marshall (1890, 1892) puts primary emphasis on externalities as determinants of firm concentration within

---

[3] For a more detailed analysis see Meade (1952), Mishan (1971), Chipman (1970), among others.

[4] Drucker (1989) provides a useful definition of 'knowledge', which is conceived as information that changes something or somebody, either by becoming grounds for action or by making an individual or an institution capable of different or more action.

a limited number of regions, arguing that any one firm enjoys external economies by locating close to other firms. To be more precise, Marshall (1890) notes that

> [...] external economies arise from the general development of an industry and especially from the *concentration* of many businesses of a similar character in particular localities or, as is commonly said, from the Location of Industry (p. 150). [Emphasis added]

Firms can, through spatial concentration, benefit from the division of labour,[5] the exchange of inputs, expertise and information. These self-reinforcing mechanisms are able to generate increasing returns, especially in the process of knowledge creation and transfer, and further influence the spatial distribution of economic activity. Moreover, it is possible that the external advantages of certain locations may dwarf other economies resulting from high production levels, i.e. internal economies of scale. According to Marshall (1890):

> Those internal economies which each establishment has to arrange for itself are frequently very small as compared to those external economies which result from the general progress of the industrial environment; the situation of a business nearly always plays a great part in determining the extent to which it can avail itself of external economies; and the situation value which a site derives from the growth of a rich and active population close to it, or from the opening up of railways and other good means of communication with existing markets, is the most striking of all the influences which changes in the industrial environment exert on cost of production. (pp. 365–366)

The Marshallian concept of externalities has been widely applied within the domain of economic geography (e.g. Chapman and Walker 1988; Harrington and Barney 1995) to explain, for example, national competitive advantage (Porter 1990, 1994; Storper 1992) or the rise and success of new industrial districts (e.g. Hall 1982; Harrison 1992). This approach usually involves examination of specific regional case studies, which allows for a detailed analysis of the complex interacting forces, economic, social and cultural, that determine the evolution of a local system (e.g. Storper 1993; Scott 1988; Markusen 1985; 1996). Scitovsky (1954) offers another dimension to externalities by distinguishing between 'pecuniary' and 'technological' externalities, where the former include the external price effects arising from market conditions. Thus, the effects arising from market-size are important elements in the formation of pecuniary external economies. To be more specific, the larger the market is, ceteris paribus, the more an individual firm can increase its output without having to decrease prices. On the other hand, 'technological externalities' arise where there are inter-dependencies in production functions, that is, spillovers from the production function of one firm to another. The diffusion of innovation by various means such as imitation may be described as an externality of this type. A distinction between these two kinds of externalities is that influences from pecuniary externalities are spread widely throughout the

---

[5] Stigler (1951) considers the externalities arising from the division of labour as a fundamental principle of economic organisation, while Young (1928) emphasises the externalities from the division of labour as the primary reason driving the progress of the economy. See also Blitch (1983) and Scott (1990, 1992).

market via the price mechanism while the same is not necessarily true in the case of technological externalities. Finally, another conceptualisation of externality is provided by Arrow (1962), extended subsequently by Romer (1986; 1990a, b).[6] Here, the creation and accumulation of knowledge is seen as an inevitable consequence of production and investment.[7] According to this view, improvements in productivity occur without any evident innovation in the production process or as a result of deliberate effort; knowledge accumulation is a side effect of conventional economic activity, i.e. a form of 'learning-by-doing'. In Arrow's model (1962), technical progress is embodied in the latest vintage of capital. Thus:

> [...] the very act of increasing the capital stock through investment by the firm raises the *level of knowledge elsewhere*. The economy *as a whole*, therefore, is operating subject to increasing returns (Shaw 1992, p. 613–614) [Emphasis added].

In Arrow's vintage model technological progress is endogenized as 'learning-by-doing'. New vintages of capital goods embody improvements based on the experiences with the previous vintage. In this way progress in technology is interpreted as an externality. From the various concepts of externality outlined above, those derived from Arrow (1962) are a key feature of modern growth theory. Indeed, Romer (1986; 1987a) argues that 'learning by doing' and 'spillovers' of knowledge, as put forward by Arrow (1962) and arising from investment in capital stock, make the progress of technology endogenous to the growth process.[8] It is these externalities that give technology some of the characteristics of a 'public good'. Thus, technological progress is not only generated within the system as an outcome of the growth process, but it spreads beyond its initial source.

3.2.3   Endogenous Growth with Spillover Effects

An example of how externalities can be included in models of endogenous growth is given by Crafts (1996), who employs the following production function:

$$Y_i = K_i^{\alpha+\varepsilon} L_i^{\beta} \text{ with } \alpha + \varepsilon = 1 \tag{3.5}$$

This formulation contains no exogenous productivity growth but does include the parameter ε to represent externalities which enhance the productivity of capital (for example, through additional experience or further training and education of

---

[6] Early attempts to extend Arrow's concept include Levhari (1966a, b).

[7] Unlike simple information, knowledge involves action and is a function of a particular stance (Nonaka and Takeuchi 1995).

[8] Arrow (1962) and to a certain extent Kaldor (1957), are considered to be, as McCombie and Thirlwall (1997) claim, the 'progenitors' of endogenous growth theory. Several elements highlighted by endogenous growth theory can be found in Rosenstein-Rodan (1943) Scott (1989), Skott and Auerbach (1995) emphasise a similar mechanism of knowledge spillovers that makes the progress of technology endogenous.

workers) and which accrue to the economy as whole. Such 'social returns' are in addition to the private returns to individual investors. The model in Eq. 3.5, which excludes diminishing returns to capital (as in the simple AK model outlined previously), implies that an increase in the growth of the capital stock from additional investment will permanently increase the growth rate of output per-worker. In this formulation there is no distinction between the externalities arising from physical and human capital (Crafts 1996). There is a case for the separate inclusion of human capital, since it is, arguably, investment in human capital which generates the spillover effects that increase the productivity of both physical capital and labour. As stated by Martin and Sunley (1998):

> It is assumed that human capital is acquired *intentionally* by individuals because it leads to higher wages and that each generation of workers assimilates ideas passed on by the preceding generation so that there are no diminishing returns. (p. 209) [Emphasis added]

Therefore, an 'intentional' human capital model of endogenous growth[9] could be written as follows (Crafts 1996):

$$Y_i = K_i^{\alpha} L_i^{\beta} H_i^{\tau} \text{ with } \alpha + \tau = 1 \tag{3.6}$$

where H represents human capital and broad capital.

In essence, such models incorporate technological progress as a consequence of the accumulation of human capital through research and education and also 'learning-by-doing'. Implied in the 'intentional' human capital model is the argument that the accumulation of capital (physical or human) by a firm contributes indirectly to the enhancement of capital productivity held by other firms. In particular, investment in human capital generates spillover effects that increase the productivity of both physical capital and the wider labour force. Capolupo (1998) points out that if spillovers are strong enough, even if individual investments face diminishing returns, growth can be sustained by the continuing accumulation of inputs that generate

---

[9] The European Commission (2006a) has highlighted investment in human capital as the most effective way to compensate for the negative impact of ageing polulation on productivity. In the mid 1990s, regional policy in the European Commission (EC) was operating along those lines. In particular, first Community Support Framework (CSF) Programmes (EC Regulation 2052/88, *On the Tasks of the Structural Funds*), activated during the period 1989–1993, were associated with structural development of the productive sector (industry, services and agriculture), upgrading infrastructure (mainly in transportation and telecommunication) and labour market measures for long-run and young unemployment. Yet, several insufficiencies were identified in these programmes (e.g. inefficient administration abilities of the member states to implement the programmes, inappropriate control mechanisms of the EC to ensure a correct and efficient use of financial resources, unstable national macroeconomic policies, absence of an explicit focus to the regional development requirements, etc.). On the other hand, the second CSF Programmes (Regulation 2081/93, *On the Tasks of the Structural Funds* and Regulation 1164/94, *On the Cohesion Fund*), operated from 1994 until 1999, were concentrated in schemes in improving training, education, health and communal services (e.g. waste treatment), etc. This aspect is analysed extensively by Tondl (1998). For a more detailed discussion of regional policy in the EU see Cappelen et al. (2003), Tondl (1999), among others.

positive externalities. In a similar context, Lucas (1988), drawing on the work of Uzawa (1965), shows human capital growing at an endogenous rate, depending upon the time spent by individuals in the accumulation of skills and the effectiveness at which new skills are acquired.[10] A further necessary condition for endogenous growth is that the incentive to invest in human capital does not decrease over time (Capolupo 1998) which is represented by the assumption of constant returns to the accumulation of human capital. What distinguishes human capital from the conventional form of capital is its ability to create more favourable conditions for long-run growth in the absence of exogenous technical progress. Thus, economies with relatively more human capital can generate more innovations and, thus, relatively higher growth rates in per-capita income, i.e. the level of human capital is positively associated with per-capita income growth. Several empirical studies support this conclusion at the international level (e.g. Barro 1991, 1997; Barro et al. 1995; Brezis et al. 1993; Hansen and Knowles 1998) and also at the regional level (e.g. Ke and Bergman 1995; Stokey 1991; Coulombe and Tremblay 2001; Bradley and Taylor 1996; Bennett et al. 1995; Goetz and Hu 1996; Qiu and Hudson 2010).

Overall, this literature particularly that focused on regional economies relies excessively on cases studies and emphasises the dynamic spillover effects of externalities, but also the significance of the concentration of human capital or innovative and technologically intense activities, across regions. Rauch, (1993), for example, argues that technical progress increases with the regional concentration of highly skilled and educated workers (the level of local average human capital) due to externalities created by the exchange of ideas. Regions that already have a large stock of R&D and experience-based knowledge, a specialised labour force or infrastructure are often in better position to make further breakthroughs which add to their existing stock o knowledge than regions which have limited initial endowments of such factors (Maskell and Malmberg 1999). The geographical concentration of economic activities and knowledge exchange/spillover are mutually reinforcing, and provide a dynamic aspect to the operation of externalities with critical implications for regional growth (e.g. Benabou 1993; Lawson and Lorenz 1999; Das and Finne 2008). Hence, it is important to examine the dynamic aspect of externalities at the spatial level in some detail.

3.2.4 Dynamic Spatial Externalities

In Chap. 2 the separation of spatial externalities into two categories was discussed. Regions characterised by significant localisation economies will tend to specialise in order to enhance their 'own industry' agglomeration, while if urbanisation economies dominate firms will seek more diversified, larger locations (Henderson

---

[10] The Lucas-Uzawa model is, in fact, a two-sector model of endogenous growth. Given that the combined share of physical and human capital is one, accumulation of capital is not subject to diminishing returns, and positive growth can be maintained in the long-run (Klenow and Rodriguez-Clare 1997).

et al. 2001a). The agglomeration of industries is inevitably linked to the incidence of spillover effects of all kinds and may also be associated specifically with knowledge spillovers. Agglomeration in a given location may be a rational strategy adopted by firms to ease the exchange of information and expertise (Acs and Audretsch 1987; Acs et al. 1994; Gertler 2003). Since the local collective learning[11] process is based mainly on the local stock of knowledge, this can form an important part of the competitive advantage of a location.

Regional economists, until recently, have considered localisation and urbanisation economies in terms of their static nature, i.e. their impact on levels of output at a particular point in time (e.g. Mills 1967; Carlino, 1979, 1985; Calem and Carlino 1991). The feature that distinguishes static from dynamic externalities is that the latter are concerned with the impact of knowledge accumulation on local or regional growth, in conjunction with the role of the past or history of the area in question, i.e. the 'initial conditions' (Henderson 1997). Such externalities are, as Armstrong and Taylor (2000) note, a 'web of additional external economies' (p. 137) arising from information spillovers and Henderson et al. (2001a) describe dynamic externalities as a 'stock of local trade secrets'. Past industrial conditions in an area affect productivity in the present in terms of their contribution to knowledge accumulation. Conversely, areas lacking an industrial tradition are disadvantaged due to the absence of an accumulated body of knowledge for new plants to draw upon.

It is possible to make a distinction between two categories of dynamic externality, one relating to specialisation and the other to diversity. The first category derives from Marshall (1890), Arrow (1962) and Romer (1990a) (hereafter MAR externalities), while the second follows the perspective of Jacobs (1964, 1969, 1984, 1993).[12] MAR externalities involve the mechanisms that generate a local and cumulative process of knowledge creation and the intra-industry transmission of innovation, due to geographical proximity.[13] The effect of knowledge and information spillovers between spatially concentrated firms in the same industry is to facilitate local growth.[14] Such knowledge is acquired at no monetary cost and

---

[11] Keeble et al. (1999) see regional collective learning as 'the emergence of basic common knowledge and procedures across a set of geographically proximate firms which facilitates co-operation and solutions to problems' through establishing a common language, trust, shared technological knowledge, as well as tacit codes of conduct. This links in turn with the concepts of the 'learning region' and 'regional innovation systems'.

[12] De Vor and de Groot (2010) identify a third category, that of competition externalities, which combine elements from specialization and diversity externalities.

[13] According to Ford et al. (2009) MAR externalities exist due to cross-fertilisation of ideas, leading to agglomeration. See Beaudry and Schiffauerova (2010) for a thoughtful review on MAR and Jacobs externalities.

[14] Glaeser et al. (1992) find that employment grows faster in diversified than specialised cities, which may be seen as some empirical support for linkages over localised information spillovers as the primary force in agglomeration. Dekle (2002) supports the view by Glaeser et al. (1992) and argues that MAR externalities are present for many retailers due to the density of full-time, human capital labour employed by the industry.

hence constitutes a positive externality. Knowledge externalities are so important and forceful that there is no reason to believe that regional borders will prevent knowledge from spilling over[15] (Audretsch and Feldman 2004). The concentration of an industry in a location increases the potential for knowledge spillovers between firms and, hence, industries that are regionally specialised should grow faster. Thus, regions with MAR externalities are likely to specialise in just a few industries, which represents the main exporting activity of the specific location.

The second category of dynamic externality relates to diversity and hence the spread of new knowledge across different sectors. According to Jacobs (1969, 1984) the variety of local activities acts as a catalyst in the innovation process for a local economy. It follows that diversity externalities, or 'communication externalities', as Thisse (2000) calls them, are more likely to operate within large urban areas, encompassing a variety of activities where the incentives to innovate are greater (Glaeser et al. 1992; Henderson et al. 1995). Thus, Jacobs (1964, 1969, 1984) claims that innovation and acceleration of local growth are more connected to the variety and diversity of geographically proximate industries, than to the degree of local specialisation. Dynamic urbanisation effects also derive from a build-up of knowledge and ideas associated with historical diversity (Henderson et al. 2001a). This implies that growth in a local area is enhanced if there is a history and tradition of economic and social interaction among diverse sectors as is likely to be the case in urban areas.[16] In general terms, gains from specialisation in one or more closely interrelated industries, i.e. MAR externalities, are more likely to have positive effects on the growth of output rather than on the growth of overall knowledge and technology. Localisation effects may affect only the particular industry in which a region is specialised and are unlikely to create an appropriate environment for 'technology creation' or 'adoption of technology' (combination of ideas from totally unrelated contexts), more generally.[17] An appropriate environment for overall 'knowledge creation' or 'technology adoption' is more likely to be related to Jacobs's externalities. From this perspective, reproducing such an environment or conditions in lagging regions will result to a fast rate of growth. Several theoretical models (e.g. Black and Henderson 1999; Davis and Henderson 2003; Bertinelli and Black 2004; Oerlemans and Meeus 2005) and empirical studies (e.g. Henderson, 1996, 1997, 2003a, b; Henderson et al. 2001b; Rosenthal and Strange 2001) stress the importance not just of a simple concentration of activities in a region but also the degree of diversity of those activities in creating an

---

[15] As Feldman (1994) notes 'knowledge crosses corridors and streets more easily than oceans and continents' (p. 2).

[16] Urban growth is a spatial manifestation of increasing returns to scale and external economies (Lampard 1963).

[17] This has led to the development of 'evolutionary economic geography'. See also Boschma (2005), Boschma and Frenken (2006), Boschma and Lambooy (2002), Boschma and Wenting (2007). Kelly and Hageman (1999) have shown that externalities are more important for innovation than for production.

appropriate environment for 'knowledge and innovation creation' through interaction of agents and activities.[18] In summary, this section has examined the key characteristics of 'one-sector' endogenous growth models in which technical change is embodied within the process of physical and human capital accumulation. Particular attention has been paid to the role of dynamic externalities because of their significance for firms and industries that are spatially concentrated, and for regional growth. A new generation of regional models that put strong emphasis on spatial externalities has emerged. The next section of this chapter considers further such spatial issues by focusing on literature which has become known as 'New Economic Geography'.

3.3 'New Economic Geography'

A fundamental element of 'New Economic Geography' is the argument that externalities associated with agglomeration are key factors in explanations of economic phenomena, ranging from international trade to patterns of local development, including regional growth, which is generally specified as endogenous, and convergence (Krugman 1991a, b, c; Arthur 1989, 1990, 1994; Puga and Venables 1999; Venables 1996a,b; Fujita and Tabuchi 1997; Pinch and Henry 1999; Pinch et al. 2003; Fujita et al. 1999a, b; Ottaviano and Puga 1998; Robert-Nicoud 2005; Markusen and Venables 1999; Drifflied 2006).

New Economic Geography is, as Fingleton and Fischer (2010) argue, particularly appealing given that increasing returns are fundamental to a proper understanding of regional disparities in economic development. This section provides a brief overview of New Economic Geography[19] and how this contributes to an understanding of regional growth and convergence. The analysis of New Economic Geography explores the interaction between increasing returns at plant level, market size, imperfect competition[20] and geographical distance. In the presence of increasing returns and significant transportation costs, firms will seek to establish themselves in large markets. Many manufacturing industries, for example, exhibit increasing returns to scale and produce many differentiated products and will thus

---

[18] Early attempts to highlight the importance of diversity in regional growth include Rogers (1955) and Bergsman et al. (1972).

[19] For a more detailed review see Martin and Sunley (1996), Martin (1999), Schmutzler (1999), Neary (2001), Krugman and Venables (1995a, b), Ottaviano and Thisse (2001) Brakman and Garretsen (2003) and Gruber and Soci (2010).

[20] The various models of New Economic Geography reject the hypothesis of perfect competition since increasing returns are not compatible with the assumptions of perfect competition. Instead they use the models of imperfect competition proposed by Knight (1921) and subsequently by Dixit and Stiglitz (1977) and Ethier (1982). The associated production function is that of constant elasticity of substitution with increasing returns at the firm level. For example, Thisse (2000) using a model of monopolistic competition develops a model of spatial cluster formation, which produces divergence between clusters.

benefit from easy access to a large market. In some analyses (e.g. Davis and Weinstein 1999; Rice and Venables 2003), market access is no longer regarded as exogenously determined. Instead, regions with a head start find their market size advantage is enhanced further as market-size externalities and input-output linkages produce self-reinforcing agglomeration processes (Brulhart 1998).

The outcome is a spatial 'centre-periphery' structure, i.e. a spatial 'polarisation' of regions. As Henderson et al. (2001a) point out 'development and underdevelopment are simply manifestations of agglomeration' (p. 85). Their argument runs as follows:

> Demand for manufacturing comes not just from final consumers but also from intermediate demand, so a location with a lot of firms will have high demand for intermediates, making it an attractive location for intermediate products. This in turn makes it an attractive location for firms that use these intermediate goods, as they can economise on transport costs on inputs. There is thus, a *positive feedback* between location decisions of upstream and downstream firms, tending to draw both types of firms together in the same location, so leading to *agglomeration*. (p. 83) [Emphasis Added]

Venables (1996a) also stresses the importance of 'forward' and 'backward' linkages. In particular, he demonstrates that vertical linkages between upstream and downstream industries, when both of them are imperfectly competitive, can play a role in determining the size of the market in different regions.[21] There are, thus, many different factors contributing to spatial polarisation. In addition to increasing returns, market size and 'forward-backward' linkages, Krugman (1991a) shows that the interaction of labour migration across regions with increasing returns and trade costs creates a tendency for firms and workers to cluster together as regional economies become more open, to exploit gains from specialisation. Moreover, if technology spillovers decline with distance, neighbours to rich and innovative regions should benefit more from technological spillovers than distant regions (Martin and Ottaviano 1999). In a similar vein, Porter (2003) argues that the performance of regional economies is strongly influenced by the strength of local clusters and the vitality and plurality of innovative activities.

The implications of 'New Economic Geography' for regional growth and convergence are significant. Krugman (1991b, 1996a, b, 1998) stresses the importance of the internal geography of a nation, i.e. the spatial distribution of economic activity, in determining the trading performance of that nation's industries.[22]

Furthermore, Krugman (1995) argues that, as international trade grows, economies become less constrained by national frontiers and this leads them to become more geographically specialised. Similarly, Hanson (1996, 2001) claims that there is a growing tendency to identify regions, rather than nations, as the locus of industrial competitiveness. Thus, it is essential to understand the processes leading to the concentration of economic activity both at a local and regional scale. For Krugman (1991a, b) agglomeration is a central element of regional

---

[21] Barde (2010) develops a model along similar lines.

[22] This has led to the formation of the 'New Trade Theory' or 'New Economics of Comparative Advantage' and the 'Strategic Trade Theory' (Krugman 1979, 1980, 1981).

growth and can take place in a certain location simply because everyone expects this to happen, so that this shared belief is responsible for the cumulative causation that eventually confirms the original expectation.[23] Krugman (1991a) also argues that growth is endogenously determined due to the presence of a range of scale economies, internal and external to the firm. It is also demonstrated that in an economy with a backward and an advanced sector, characterised by substantial scale economies, two possible equilibria exist depending on the output concentration in each sector. If output is concentrated in the advanced sector the first equilibrium is a high-level equilibrium, while concentration of output in the less advanced sector implies a low-level equilibrium. Assuming, further, that activities subject to increasing returns to scale are concentrated at certain points in space then this will 'lock in' such central regions into a situation of continuous growth, at the expense of regions with less favourable initial conditions ('peripheral' regions), usually rural regions having a share of agricultural employment (a contribution to output) above (below) the average.[24]

This type of analysis introduces the idea of regional economic activity as path dependent with the initial conditions established by history and accident:[25] an accident to start with but with strong indigenous institutionalized capacities to continue. For example, leading regions with an established differentiated production structure will be considered a more attractive location for new industry and the leading position will be maintained. This inertia is again reinforced by the favourable infrastructure position such regions usually possess (Martin and Sunley 2006). Once available in a region, such an infrastructure will remain of importance for subsequent stages. This leads to a pattern of path dependence, in that economic forces will tend to reinforce initial advantages or disadvantages. Martin and Sunley (1998) describe this process as follows:

> Temporary conditions, and shocks, as well as historical 'accidents', may have *permanent* effects as patterns of specialisation, of economic success or economic backwardness, become '*locked in*' through *external* and self-reinforcing effects (p. 211). [Emphasis added]

In summary, the New Economic Geography approach developed by Krugman suggests that increased regional industrial concentration and specialisation accentuated by dynamic externalities leads to regional instability over the

---

[23] Martin and Ottaviano (2001) support Krugman's view by constructing a model in which economic growth is related positively with agglomeration economies. In this model agglomeration and growth reinforces each other in a circular and cumulative way. Similarly, Ferguson et al. (2007) find a strong positive correlation with population growth in urban and rural areas.

[24] Perfect competition and constant returns to scale characterise the agricultural sector. The primary role of this sector in the models of New Economic Geography is to serve as a numeraire sector and 'peripheral' (rural) regions supply the 'core' regions with agricultural products. The demand for manufacturing products is covered by imports from the 'core' regions.

[25] Krugman calls the association between economic geography and 'path dependence' as 'the economics of QWERTY', initially proposed by David (1985, 1994). This term refers to the top line letters on typewriter keyboards, which although designed for in the nineteenth century, still appear as the norm on modern computer keyboards.

long-run. Regional disparities are intensified and the most probable outcome is divergent growth paths. Thus far, this chapter has outlined some of the most indicative models of Endogenous Growth and New Economic Geography. By placing particular emphasis on specific elements, such as externalities and spatial agglomerations, these models imply that regions will not necessarily follow a process of absolute convergence. In contrast to the neoclassical model where technology is assumed to spread across regions via knowledge spillovers contributing, thus, to the process of regional convergence, endogenous growth theory models argue that if knowledge-creation and high technological activities are concentrated in rich regions, then regional divergence is the most probable outcome. The next section, therefore, extends this analysis further by examining models that attribute the endogeneity of technology to the existence of a separate sector that intentionally produces knowledge and technological innovations.

3.4 'Two-sector' Endogenous Growth

According to Martin and Sunley (1998), traditional neoclassical and one-sector models of endogenous growth fail to provide an explanation for technological progress. 'Two-sector' models of endogenous growth, or models of endogenous innovation, attempt to overcome this deficiency by emphasising the existence of a sector that deliberately produces technological innovations. Furthermore, these models, drawing on Schumpeter (1934), suggest the possibility of perpetual growth in capitalist economies due to entrepreneurial innovations. Schumpeter (1934) envisaged firms coming into existence as a result of an innovative idea. If an innovation consists of a radical departure from existing products or technologies it would create a new market and the innovating firm will earn abnormal or monopoly profits. Other firms leave the market, since they cannot compete with the innovative firms; a process known as 'creative destruction' (Andersen 1996). Hence, the market structure loses its competitive nature and moves towards a rather more imperfect structure, such as monopolistic competition or oligopoly and innovative firms earn 'abnormal' or monopolistic profits. These profits are the main incentive for firms to devote substantial resources to Research and Development (R&D) investment. 'Two-sector' models of endogenous growth attempt to formalise the process of endogenous innovation in an economy (Grossman and Helpman 1991a, b, c; Aghion and Howitt 1992; Jones 1995a).[26] The R&D sector combines human capital together with the existing stock of knowledge to produce new knowledge. Furthermore, new knowledge enhances productivity and is available to other sectors of the economy at virtually zero marginal cost (Stern 1991). Assume that a firm develops a new product, which is positioned higher up the

---

[26] The notion of 'knowledge-driven economy' is drawing on the models of endogenous innovation. For a more detailed review see Simmie (2005).

'quality ladder'. Such a firm can capture some of the profits of the producers of previous generations of the product. In this way knowledge and innovation is a factor of production contributing to profit and growth and, hence, the overall rate of growth is influenced by innovations. This process is known as 'innovation-driven' growth.[27] Romer (1986, 1990a, b, 1993) developed the most instructive model in this category. A central tenet is that firms can patent inventions and innovations, which gives them the exclusive right to produce new goods (private knowledge). However, in turn, these products create new 'general' knowledge, which is freely available to all firms (public knowledge). Following Armstrong and Taylor (2000), the mechanism leading to endogenous growth in Romer's model (1986, 1990a) can be described as follows. As in the standard neoclassical model, a region's output is a function of the capital stock, the labour force and technological knowledge available in a region. Unlike Solow's model, Romer (1986, 1990a) assumes that technological knowledge is attached to the labour force. In other words, the labour force is assumed to be 'knowledge adjusted'. The relevant production function, in terms of output per-worker, takes the familiar Cobb-Douglas form, i.e. $y = k^\alpha A^{1-\alpha}$ while the growth rate of output per-worker is expressed in terms of the following equation:

$$\frac{dy}{y} = \alpha \frac{dk}{k} + (1 - \alpha) \frac{dA}{A} \tag{3.7}$$

where dy/y, dk/k and dA/A are the growth rate of output per-worker, of capital per-worker and of technical knowledge.

In the long-run equilibrium, output and capital per-worker grow at the same rate, i.e. the capital-output ratio is constant. Given that $\frac{dy}{y} = \frac{dk}{k}$ then $\frac{dy}{y} = \frac{dk}{k} = \frac{dA}{A}$ implying that output per-worker must be growing at the same rate as technological knowledge, which is growing due to the 'natural desire for profit by entrepreneurs in the knowledge-producing industry' (Armstrong and Taylor 2000, p. 77). The critical question, however, refers to the factors that determine the rate of growth of technological knowledge. The change in the technological knowledge (dA) is determined as follows:

$$dA = \delta L_A^\lambda A^\phi \tag{3.8}$$

---

[27] This view has led to the development of the 'regional innovation and network systems' literature. Cooke (2008) suggests that 'regional innovation systems' consist of interacting knowledge generation and exploitation of sub-systems linked to global, national and other regional systems stressing the importance of both regionally internal and external linkages. Such a system is characterised by interaction among firms and institutions from both public and private sector, such as firms, universities, research laboratories and business support technology transfer agencies. Malecki (2004) describes the process of increasing the innovativeness of firms, and promoting the development and enhancement of knowledge networks and regional innovation systems as the 'high road' to regional competition. This approach, however, does not include an explicit legal dimension (Taylor 2009).

In Eq. 3.8 L_A denotes the number of labour units in the knowledge-producing sectors of the economy and $0<\lambda, \phi<1$, δ are the parameters of this knowledge-production function with δ implying the rate at which new ideas are discovered. Thus, the change in knowledge in an economy is a function of the number of workers employed in the innovative sector and the existing 'stock' of knowledge, A. The amount of new ideas created during any point in time is influenced by the existing stock of knowledge. Romer (1990a) assumes that 'anyone engaged on research has free access to knowledge' (p. S83). The values of parameters λ and ϕ indicate the possibility of diminishing returns to the labour force in the knowledge-producing sector and the existing 'stock' of knowledge, due to the possibility of duplication of new ideas as more people become involved. For given values of λ and ϕ, the rate of growth in knowledge is proportional to the growth of labour employed in the innovation-producing sector. The faster the labour employed in this sector grows, the faster will new ideas be produced and, hence, the faster will output per-worker grow. Thus, technology and subsequently output growth are determined within the economic system, i.e. endogenously.

Romer's ideas were incorporated into a generation of models that put primary focus on the level of knowledge in an economy as a principal factor in growth (e.g. Lever and Bailly 1996). Such 'knowledge-based' models also found application in a regional context (e.g. Davelaar and Nijkamp 1989, 1997; Frenkel and Shefer 1997).[28] Shefer and Rietveld (1999) state that:

> [...] regional development, *as a location where technological innovation* takes place, is usually accompanied by new economic activities, market expansion and technological adaptation. (p. 260) [Emphasis added]

Thus, if activity in the knowledge producing sector is spatially concentrated within a region, then this will constitute a source of further growth through the operation of dynamic externalities (Feldman and Kutay 1997; Bartelsman et al. 1994). The spatial distribution of innovative sectors, as will be shown in the next section, is therefore a crucial element in the process of regional growth. This recognition that knowledge creation is crucial for regional development also produces a shift in perspective (Audretsch and Vivarelli 1996; Marquis and Reffett 1995; Skott 1999; Lawson 1999; Miguélez et al. 2011). From this perspective, spatially proximate knowledge networks are considered a key factor underlying the success of the most advanced and successful regions. As stated by Maskell and Malmberg (1999):

> The region, the territory, or 'space, is not seen merely as a 'container', in which attractive location factors may (or may not) happen to exist, but rather as a milieu for *collective learning* through intense interaction between a broadly composed set of actors. (p. 174) [Emphasis added]

---

[28] The notion of the 'knowledge-based economy' can be traced to the work of Machlup (1962). A 'knowledge-based economy' is characterised by three elements: a growing importance of economic transactions focused on knowledge itself; rapid changes in goods and services; and incorporation of the creation and implementation of change itself into the mission of economic agents (Carter, 1990).

Thus, a region is a 'created space' that is both a result of and a precondition for learning – 'an active resource rather than a passive surface' (Coffey and Bailly 1996; as quoted in Lawson 1999). Thus, the 'knowledge economy' model which derives from innovation driven endogenous growth theory, sees regions as competing economies

[...] that try to obtain an economic advantage through developing or adopting technologically advanced products or processes (Button and Pentecost 1999 p. 57).

Given this perspective, an important question in the present context concerns the implications of such endogenous growth mechanisms for regional convergence. This is addressed in the following section.

3.5 Endogenous Growth Models: Convergence or Divergence?

From the discussion in Sects. 3.3 and 3.4 it is evident that there are several approaches to modelling endogenous growth. It is important, however, to consider now whether endogenous growth is consistent with a prediction of convergence amongst regions. As will be demonstrated in this section, although the concept of endogenous growth would tend to suggest divergent trends there are circumstances in which convergence remains a possibility.

3.5.1 Convergence in the 'One-sector' Endogenous Growth Models

The analysis of regional growth and convergence, within the AK model framework, presented in Sect. 3.2.1, suggests that regions will diverge in growth rates and levels of output per-worker. This can be shown in figure 3.2.

Assume that the economy is divided into two regions i and j, which differ in their initial conditions, with the capital-labour ratio of region j ($k_{j,0}$), exceeding that of region i, ($k_{i,0}$) but which exhibit the same growth rates for labour, savings and depreciation (n, s and δ, respectively) and the same level of technology, A. The equilibrium growth rate of capital per worker is the same in the two regions and is given by the distances aa' and bb'. In the standard neoclassical model it has been demonstrated that poor regions grow faster than rich regions. However, in the 'one-sector' endogenous growth model there is no such convergence mechanism because of the absence of diminishing returns to capital. Since the marginal product of capital is constant there is also no incentive for capital to flow from the rich to the poor regions. This model is, in essence, a Cobb-Douglas model with a unit capital share (Barro and Sala-i-Martin 1995). As shown in Chap. 1, the speed of convergence in the standard neoclassical model is given by the product $\beta = (1 - a)(n + g + \delta)$.

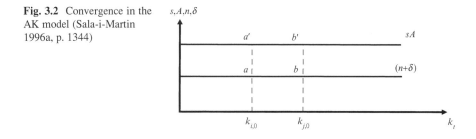

Fig. 3.2 Convergence in the AK model (Sala-i-Martin 1996a, p. 1344)

A unit capital share($a = 1$) gives a zero value for β implying that growth rates do not exhibit the convergence property. The outcome is that if regions have the same parameters with respect to preferences and technology, but differ in their initial capital stock, poor regions will always be poorer (in levels of output per-worker) and rich regions will be richer, since they all will grow at the same constant rate.

This conclusion, however, does not apply in general to all models which embody endogenous growth. Examination of 'two-sector' models, and in particular the 'Technological Gap' model which incorporates the role of technology the purposeful pursuit of innovation, technology diffusion and knowledge spillovers between regions, means that it is possible to generate predictions of convergence.

3.5.2 The 'Technological Gap' Model

A major contribution in this context is provided by the early work of Nelson (1956, 1960) and Nelson and Phelps (1966), in which the rate of technological progress in an economy is assumed to be a function of the gap between its level of technology and technology in the leading economy. It is possible to express this model in terms of the following equation (Armstrong and Taylor 2000, p. 79):

$$\frac{dA_i}{A_i} = \lambda(A^* - A_i) \text{ with } \lambda > 0 \qquad (3.9)$$

where A_i and A^* denote the technological level in any region and the most advanced region, respectively. According to this formulation the further away a region's technology is from the most advanced region, i.e. the greater the technological gap, the faster will be its technological progress. Armstrong and Taylor (2000) describe the economics of this argument as follows. Those regions which are already employing state-of-art technology will need to invest in new knowledge, which is likely to be more expensive than copying existing techniques of production. Regions which lag behind should be able to adopt new technology fairly cheaply (technology transfer) and hence will have a fast rate of technological progress provided that other conditions, such as social and political infrastructures, are favourable. Technical progress is then not an automatic outcome, but requires an appropriate institutional environment, which is conductive to the adoption and assimilation of new ideas into the production system. Armstrong and Taylor (2000) put the argument as follows:

> Regional disparities therefore occur in technical progress because the *institutional environment varies* between regions. In other words, some regions are more capable of using production technical progress than others (p. 86) [Emphasis added].

Therefore, if lagging regions are able to adopt technology from rich regions, then this will enhance their growth rates leading to the possibility of convergence in levels of output per-worker. The larger the 'technological gap' compared to the leading region, the faster will be the rate of technological progress and, thus, the faster the growth in output per-worker. Consequently, the diffusion of technological progress across regions is the means by which convergence may occur in the context of endogenous growth.

According to economic historians, such as Rostow (1960), Gerschenkron (1962), Gomulka (1971), Kuznets (1964) and Abramovitz (1986, 1993, 1994) technological progress is dependent on the specific historic and national characteristics of the environment for firms in which innovation takes place. In this context, a distinction is made between the potential of an economy to innovate and its ability to adopt new technologies developed by advanced economies. Theoretical and empirical work suggests that the degree of technology adoption is not identical across economies and, therefore, the growth rates will differ across economies, depending systematically on the way in which economies are able to absorb, apply and adopt the latest technological innovations. Several empirical studies have shown that growth is a function of the 'technological distance' between a country and the world leader (Dowrick 1992; Dosi et al. 1988, 1990; Verspagen 1991, 1999; Fagerberg 1987, 1988, 1994, 1996). A parallel set of arguments about the 'technological-gap' is found specifically within regional economics. Several empirical studies[29] suggest that activities related to advanced technology are not distributed evenly in space and tend to cluster in 'key' locations due to the presence of pools of skilled labour and the proximity of universities and R&D establishments. Other studies (e.g. Guerrero and Seró 1997; Piergiovanni and Santarelli 2001) suggest that technological innovations diffuse slowly across regions. Thus, it may be argued that the localisation of high-technology together with the slow diffusion of technological innovations creates considerable technological gaps across regions. In some cases, specific factors are highlighted, such as localised externalities (e.g. Arauzo-Carod 2009), the relative diversity of activities and the degree of urbanisation in each region (e.g. Shefer and Frenkel 1999; Alexiadis and Tsagdis, 2006a), technological spillovers amongst neighbouring regions (e.g. Paci and Usai 2000a),

---

[29] See for example Shanks (1967), Schaefer (1977) and Malecki (1983, 1991). Hagerstrand (1966, 1667), Mansfield (1968) and Griliches (1957) argue that the spatial diffusion of technological innovations begins in the largest urban areas and then tends to be transmitted down along the urban hierarchy. See also McCombie (1982a), Oakey (1984), Oakey et al. (1980), Andonelli (1990), Audretsch (1998).

university-industry collaboration (Ponds et al. 2010), cultural diversity (e.g. Ottaviano and Peri 2005; 2006; Bellini et al. 2008) and so forth. However, these studies do not, on the whole, address the issue of regional convergence directly; do technological spillovers and variation of technology across space imply a pattern of regional convergence or divergence?

A critical question concerns the specific pattern of convergence that is implied by endogenous growth models. If the rate of technological progress is determined endogenously by private decisions to invest in physical or human capital and if there are benefits from the spatial concentration of innovative activity, permanent differences in growth rates across economies may arise. As Capolupo (1998) claims, even when the rate of technological change is not endogenous, if the marginal productivity of capital does not decline with increasing GDP per-capita, convergence does not necessarily occur and the accumulation of capital can sustain growth indefinitely. These are clearly significant aspects of the endogenous growth framework which undermine the prediction of convergence. However, the capacity of regional economies to adapt, or at least to imitate, innovations and advanced technology works in the opposite direction. Differences in this capacity may lead to convergence for some regions and divergence for others. Empirical evidence tends to support the view that regions do differ in this respect. Martin and Sunley (1998) argue that if imitation is cheaper than innovation, then a process of convergence will occur only between interdependent economies as discoveries occur in the 'leading edge' economy and then are imitated, relatively quickly, in the 'follower' economies.

Therefore, to the extent that technology innovation is localised, spatial spillovers are geographically limited and technology diffusion is slow, poor regions will not necessarily catch up with rich regions. Moreover, if human capital is spatially concentrated in the richer regions, this generates yet further localised externalities and increasing returns to reinforce then the 'gap' between rich and poor regions.

Convergence to a common level of output per-worker, as the neoclassical model predicts, is no longer possible under these conditions.[30] Regions form different groups or sets, depending on the specific characteristics of each region. In this light, convergence is identified only amongst regions that share similar characteristics and initial conditions, and which therefore form a convergence club. If there are two sets of economies identified as 'central' (or 'core') and 'peripheral' regions, convergence may exist within the set of 'central' regions, and within each set, but with little or no convergence between these two sets. Two clusters could, therefore, be said to exist. The divergence between these two sets is attributed to the 'lock in' of regions into certain growth paths. The particular growth path that each set follows depends, among other things, on creation and diffusion of technology. This pattern of 'club convergence' points towards the rejection of any tendencies

---

[30] Martin (1999) notes that 'the slow rate of convergence, and the doubt cast on the validity of the neoclassical model of long-run regional growth, clearly provide a link to the increasing returns and spatial agglomeration' (p. 72).

for overall convergence. Instead, due to the existing gaps in technology and innovation, economies (countries or regions) form different clubs and convergence is identified rather within the members of the club. There need be no convergence among these clubs, and hence the broad inequalities among the different club sets may persist or even increase, so that income distribution becomes polarised.[31] However, the 'technological gap' model, and the notion of 'club convergence' in general, will be discussed more fully in Chap. 4.

3.6 Conclusions

Chapters 2 and 3 together present a summary of regional growth models of relevance to the present study. By necessity, this overview cannot provide full details of the range of models to be found in the literature. Nevertheless, from this brief review, some important conclusions emerge.

The early neoclassical and post-Keynesian models generate completely opposite predictions about regional growth. The former predicts convergence in regional output per-worker while the latter implies perpetuation of regional disparities. A 'new generation' of regional models of Endogenous Growth and New Economic Geography, has provided an alternative view on the process of regional growth and convergence.

This chapter has outlined key features of Endogenous Growth Theory and New Economic Geography. More precisely, this chapter has progressed from an examination of a simple model of Endogenous Growth, the 'AK' model in which the absence of diminishing returns to capital generates endogenous growth. Due to this, there is no incentive for capital to flow from the rich to the poor regions and resulting to divergence across regions. Particular attention is placed on models that emphasise the contribution of knowledge/technology creation and diffusion to the process of regional convergence.

The importance of externalities that arise from knowledge and technology creation, spatial interaction and the dynamic aspect of spatial externalities stemming from the history of a region are also highlighted, within the models of New Economic Geography. These models imply that convergence can be an exclusive property of a selected set of economies, due to the operation of spatial dynamic externalities, spatial agglomerations and gaps in the levels of technology across regions. Such an approach implies the possibility of convergence amongst sets of economies with similar structural characteristics, i.e. as 'club convergence' and is the focus of the next chapter.

---

[31] A similar outcome is implied by the endogenous growth model of Tamura (1991) in which convergence in growth rates is evident among few individual countries (e.g. the highly industrialised countries) and divergence across groups of countries (e.g. between the developing and developed countries). Goodfriend and McDermott (1998) develop a similar model.

Chapter 4
Club Convergence

4.1 Introduction

Although the concept of 'club convergence' emerged from empirical evidence, its theoretical underpinnings can be found in neoclassical and endogenous growth models, outlined in Chaps. 2 and 3. Indeed, a prediction of several Endogenous Growth models, such as the 'Technological Diffusion-Gap' model, is that economies do not converge towards a common equilibrium. 'New Economic Geography' implies a polarisation of regions into different 'clusters', poor or 'peripheral' regions and rich or 'central-core' regions, with growing disparities and divergence among clusters. It is the purpose of this chapter to examine the theoretical framework for club convergence. Firstly, the notion of 'club convergence', as this has emerged from empirical studies, is introduced in Sect. 4.2. Section 4.3 outlines two theoretical approaches to multiple equilibria and club convergence proposed by Galor (1996) and Azariadis and Drazen (1990), which are, essentially, a reformulation of the neoclassical model. Section 4.4 describes the club convergence pattern within the framework of Endogenous Growth Theory, in which club convergence is attributed to the diffusion of technological innovations from leading economies. This process, however, appears to be exogenous and very little is said about how is determined. Diffusion of technology is not a simple and automatic process. Instead, it requires that lagging economies (countries or regions) should have the appropriate infrastructure or conditions to adopt or absorb the technological innovations. A simple model is developed in Sect. 4.5 in which club convergence is attributed to differences in the absorptive abilities of regions. Finally, Sect. 4.6 provides some conclusions.

4.2 'Club Convergence': An Empirical Fact

'Club convergence' refers to the possibility that absolute convergence may be restricted to a specific set of economies. Thus, a convergence club can be defined as a subset of economies for which convergence applies, while economies outside

S. Alexiadis, *Convergence Clubs and Spatial Externalities*,
Advances in Spatial Science, DOI 10.1007/978-3-642-31626-5_4,
© Springer-Verlag Berlin Heidelberg 2013

the club do not experience convergence vis-à-vis those in the club (Funke and Strulik 1999). Several empirical studies of national economies suggest that convergence is apparent only among a specific group of highly developed economies (e.g. Dowrick and Nguyen 1989; Dowrick and Gemmell 1991; Je-Su 2003; Savvides and Stegnos 2000; Johnson and Takeyama 2001; Canova 2004; Castellacci and Archibugi 2008). Some regional studies have also examined, and confirmed, this phenomenon (e.g. Chatterji and Dewhurst 1996; Kangasharju 1999; Baumont et al. 2003; Corrado et al. 2005).

Baumol (1986) introduced the concept of club convergence in order to describe a subset of national economies within the world economy, which demonstrate the property of convergence, reflected in a negative relationship between growth and initial level of per-capita income. Baumol (1986) also defines a convergence club as a 'very exclusive organisation' (p. 1079). Analysing 72 countries between 1950 and 1980, Baumol (1986) concludes that, in fact, 'there is more than one convergence club' (p. 1080) in the sense that income levels converged within the industrialised countries, the centrally planned economies and the middle-income market economies, but not within the group of low-income countries. Moreover, between these groups income levels appeared to diverge. As pointed out, however, by De Long (1988) there is an ex-post selection bias in this study. Subsequently, Baumol and Wolff (1988), utilising data from 72 countries provided by Maddison (1982), demonstrate that middle income countries (17 out of 72 countries included in the sample) have grown the fastest and the poorest countries have diverged from the others. Barro (1991) provides further support for this conclusion by arguing that over a 40 year period (1950–1988) convergence is restricted to OECD countries while it is almost absent between the OECD and the less developed countries. Consequently, the world economies can be classified into the following three sets or clubs:

> [...] the richer OECD countries may form one 'convergence club', the developing countries another and the underdeveloped yet another. (Martin and Sunley 1998, p. 203)

However, Canova (2004) suggests that even among the OECD countries convergence is not apparent. In other words, there is evidence of club convergence even within the economies of a convergence club identified by others. More specifically, Canova (2004) argues that the initially poor countries in the OECD diverge from the initially rich countries, and it is the latter which form the exclusive convergence club. Persistent inequalities between different clubs suggest different steady-states, or multiple equilibria. Durlauf (1994; 1996), and Durlauf et al. (2001) present empirical evidence to support the existence of multiple steady-states and polarisation of the world economies into distinct groups,[1] arguing that this is due to

---

[1] There is, however, a positive probability for an economy to move from one group to the other, i.e. the bimodal distribution is ergodic, allowing for 'economic miracles' (initially poor economies that grow rapidly, such as Hong Kong, Taiwan, South Korea, Singapore, although it the late 1990s a 'reversal of fortune' was notable) and 'economic disasters' (initially rich economies reaching low levels of income, such as Argentina and Venezuela).

heterogeneity in initial conditions. Only economies with similar initial conditions are likely to experience similar tendencies of convergence, to form a 'convergence club'. The same argument is found in Baumol and Wolff (1988) and in Martin and Sunley (1998) who claim that:

> [...] only countries that are similar in their structural characteristics and that have similar initial conditions will converge to one another. (p. 203)

Similarly, Islam (2003), in a survey of the literature on economic convergence, describes the process of club convergence as follows:

> Which of these different equilibrium an economy will reach, depends on its initial position or some other attribute. A group of countries may approach a particular equilibrium if they share the initial location or attribute corresponding to that equilibrium. This produces club-convergence. (p. 315)

Although the notion of club convergence as an empirical fact can be traced back to Baumol (1986), its theoretical development can be found in models that emphasise different characteristics or initial conditions. For example, some models demonstrate the potential for club convergence arising from different rates of human capital accumulation (e.g. Azariadis and Drazen 1990; Durlauf 1993), while others introduce capital market imperfections (Aghion and Bolton, 1996; Benabou 1994, 1996; Becker et al. 1990) and differences in capital utilisation (Dalgaard and Hansen 2005). Club convergence can also emerge using models that implement statistical techniques, such as Markov chain models with probability transitions to estimate the evolution of income distribution, as developed by Quah (1996a), who identifies three equilibria, i.e. complete equality of per-capita incomes, stratification and continually increasing inequality. Convergence clubs or coalitions are attributed to three reasons. First, the degree of interaction across economies, second the fact that different groups of economies exploit returns to scale due to specialisation and third, the creation of 'ideas', which determines the pattern of growth and is limited to a specific group of economies. Poor economies fail to catch-up with rich economies, leading to a polarised pattern at the extremes of the income distribution.[2]

Two different perspectives on club convergence within the neoclassical framework can be found in Azariadis and Drazen (1990) and Galor (1996). In the latter case club convergence is explained by a reformulation of the neoclassical model while Azariadis and Drazen (1990) offer a framework that allows for multiple equilibria and club convergence due to threshold externalities. Galor (1996) provides a general framework within the neoclassical model, which produces testable predictions for club convergence. Azariadis and Drazen (1990), on the hand, outline a general model that emphasises externalities in promoting club

---

[2] Quah (1996b, 1997) claims that implementing the conventional approaches (based on the neoclassical model) to convergence can mask this polarisation and the presence of convergence clubs. However, this is not necessarily true. As will be demonstrated in section 4.3, the neoclassical framework is flexible enough to accommodate club convergence as a distinct possibility.

convergence, a factor that is not included explicitly in Markov chain models. Therefore, the models by Galor (1996) and Azariadis and Drazen (1990) are discussed in the next section.

4.3 Club Convergence in the Neoclassical Model

In the conventional one-sector neoclassical model it is assumed that economic agents are homogeneous with respect to preferences, and regions are homogenous 'dimensionless points', characterised by identical production functions and perfect competition. However, a relaxation of these assumptions can lead to a prediction of club convergence:

> Once the neoclassical growth models are augmented so as to capture additional empirically significant elements such as human capital, income distribution, and fertility, along with capital market imperfections, externalities, non-convexities and imperfectly competitive market structures, club convergence emerges under broader plausible configurations. (Galor 1996, p. 1061)

In order to explain the prediction of club convergence, it is first necessary to review briefly the simple one-sector model of growth, presented in Chap. 1. The specific production function, assuming no technological progress, is characterised by constant returns to scale and diminishing marginal productivity of individual factors. Production in each region (i) is a function of the capital-labour ratio ($k_{i,t} \equiv K_{i,t}/L_{i,t}$) in each time period ($t$) and assuming constant returns to scale, production can be represented as follows:

$$Y_{i,t} \equiv L_{i,t} f(k_{i,t}) \tag{4.1}$$

The regional endowments of labour (L) and capital (K) at time $t + 1$ are given by:

$$L_{i,t+1} = (1 + n)L_{i,t} \tag{4.2}$$

$$K_{i,t+1} = (1 - \delta)K_{i,t} + S_{i,t} \tag{4.3}$$

where n and δ represent the rate of population growth and the rate of capital depreciation ($0 < \delta \leq 1$), which are assumed to be the same for all regions. Total savings $S_{i,t}$ are a constant fraction of output and this propensity to save (s) is the same across regions:

$$S_{i,t} = sY_{i,t} = sL_{i,t} f(k_{i,t}) \tag{4.4}$$

Combining Eqs. 4.2, 4.3 and 4.4, the evolution of the capital-labour ratio is described by:

$$k_{i,t+1} = \frac{(1 - \delta)k_{i,t} + sf(k_{i,t})}{(1 + n)} \equiv \phi(k_{i,t}) \tag{4.5}$$

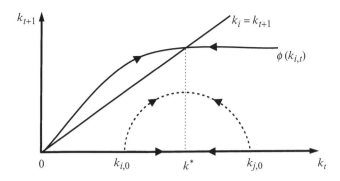

Fig. 4.1 Absolute convergence in the neoclassical model (Based on Galor 1996, p. 1058)

In steady-state equilibrium the capital-labour ratio $k^*(= k_{i,t} = k_{i,t+1})$ satisfies the following condition:

$$\frac{sf(k^*)}{k^*} = n + \delta \tag{4.6}$$

Consequently, if all regions have the same production function, and share the same characteristics (n, δ and s), all regions reach the same 'steady-state' capital-labour ratio. It follows that poor regions catch up with rich regions regardless of their initial capital-labour ratio, as shown in Chap. 1.

This outcome, depicted in Fig. 4.1, is known as the 'standard Solow diagram', where the 45 ° line represents the equilibrium condition:

The evolution of the capital-labour ratio for any region is depicted by $\phi(k_{i,t})$, and shows the movement towards equilibrium at k^*. Thus, a region with an initial capital-labour ratio of $k_{i,0}$ will exhibit positive growth towards the steady-state k^*, whilst a high initial ratio of $k_{j,0}$ leads to negative growth, but again convergence towards k^*. Galor (1996), however, shows that a change to the assumptions concerning savings behaviour can lead to the possibility of multiple steady-state equilibria and, hence, the emergence of convergence clubs. This approach is discussed next.

4.3.1   Multiple Equilibria and Club Convergence

Galor (1996) focuses on differences in the propensity to save and proceeds as follows. In each period per-capita output is distributed according to the marginal productivity of the factors of production:

$$f(k_{i,t}) = w(k_{i,t}) + r(k_{i,t})k_{i,t} \tag{4.7}$$

where $f(k_{i,t})$ is per-capita output, $w(k_{i,t})$ is the labour share of output and $r(k_{i,t})k_{i,t}$ is the capital share. Expressing the marginal product of capital as $r(k_{i,t}) \equiv f'(k_{i,t})$, the labour share is defined as follows:

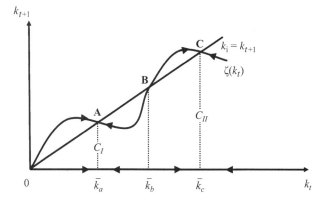

Fig. 4.2   Club convergence in the neoclassical model (Based on Galor 1996, p. 1059)

$$w(k_{i,t}) \equiv f(k_{i,t}) - f'(k_{i,t})k_{i,t} \tag{4.8}$$

The essence of the analysis is that, instead of a uniform propensity to save, Galor (1996) proposes different propensities to save according to the source of income, labour or capital, that is, there are different propensities to save out of wages and profits. If s^w and s^r are the corresponding propensities then the evolution of the capital-labour ratio is given by:

$$k_{t+1} = \frac{(1 - \delta)k_t + s^w f(k_t) + (s^r - s^w)f'(k_t)k_t}{1 + n} = \zeta(k_t) \tag{4.9}$$

If the capital-labour ratio converges to a steady-state, such that $\bar{k} = k_{i,t} = k_{i,t+1}$ then substitution of this condition into Eq. 4.9 gives an expression for the steady-state equilibrium:

$$s^w \left[\frac{f(\bar{k})}{\bar{k}} \right] + (s^r - s^w)f'(\bar{k}) = n + \delta \tag{4.10}$$

How is it then, possible for 'convergence clubs' to emerge? Galor (1996) demonstrates that the dynamic non-linear system, expressed in terms of Eq. 4.9, can be characterised by multiple locally stable equilibria, depending on the nature of the production function. Galor (1996) assumes a constant elasticity of substitution (CES) production function and this situation is depicted in Figure 4.2.

Here, the equilibrium condition is satisfied at three points, A, B and C; a phenomenon entirely due to the different propensities to save. However, B is not a stable equilibrium in that regions with an initial capital-labour ratio in the interval $[0, \bar{k}_b]$ converge to the low equilibrium $\bar{k}_a$, (point A) whereas those with an initial capital-labour ratio in the interval $[\bar{k}_b, \infty]$ converge to the higher equilibrium $\bar{k}_c$ (point C). Thus, any initial regional distribution of the capital-labour ratio gradually becomes polarised as two regional clusters (C_I and C_{II}) emerge over time. In the transitional phase, there exists an inverse relationship between the growth rate and initial level of output per-worker within these clusters.

This polarisation (at the extremes of the income distribution) of regions into two 'convergence clubs' occurs despite the fact that regions exhibit the same rates of depreciation and population growth. The assumption of different propensities to save out of wages and profits is sufficient to produce more than one convergence point. This is because regions, which differ in terms of the distribution of wages and profits at any point in time, will have different average propensities to save out of total income, even though they have the same individual propensities to save out of wages and profits.

4.3.2 Club Convergence: Permanent or Transitory?

The conclusion of the model, outlined in Sect. 4.3.1, is that economies which are similar in their structural characteristics as well as initial per-capita output, but differ in their initial distribution of income, will converge towards different 'steady-states'. The convergence clubs, which emerge from the processes outlined above, are presumed to be permanent rather than transitory. Nevertheless, there is a question as to whether, in the very long-run, it might be possible for absolute convergence to emerge. In fact, this is the case when technological change is included in the model. It is possible to demonstrate that improvements in technology, not associated with labour, and the diffusion of such technology have the potential to restore a unique equilibrium. This possibility is depicted in Fig. 4.3.

If the production function embodied within $\zeta(k_t)$ is characterised by a technological shift parameter, λ, then as Fig. 4.3 indicates, improvements in technology (from λ_1 to λ_2) result in an upward shift of the curve $\zeta(k_t)$. A significant change in technology can lead to a unique equilibrium, with a capital-labour ratio $\bar{k}_\lambda$, as shown in Fig. 4.3. Thus, the system is characterised by club convergence and polarisation only in the 'medium term', whereas in the very long-run the final outcome will be absolute convergence, provided that all regions are able to adopt the improvements in technology to the same degree.

The above model is not unique in the sense that other models in the neoclassical tradition may also produce multiple equilibria by assuming differences in a variety of factors, for example, in the savings ratio, economic structure or levels of education (Tondl 1999). Thus, Johnson (1966), following Nelson (1960), assumes that the propensity to save differs at different levels of capital and output per-worker, whilst other approaches demonstrate the potential for club convergence due to different rates of human capital accumulation. Galor and Zeira (1993), Galor and Tsiddon (1991, 1997) and Desdoigts (1999), for example, present models where initial wealth differs between individuals and conclude that economies with an unequal wealth distribution will accumulate less human capital compared to those with a more equal distribution and, hence, will experience lower growth in the presence of increasing social returns to scale from human capital. Hence, countries

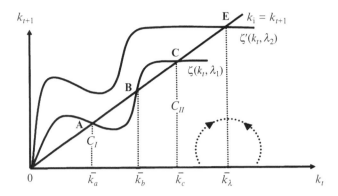

Fig. 4.3 Club convergence in the long-run (Based on Galor 1996, p. 1068)

with identical structural characteristics but different initial levels of human capital may cluster around different steady-state equilibria.

Human capital accumulation also features in the model of Azariadis and Drazen (1990). Here different returns to human capital are associated with substantial threshold externalities, which in turn result in multiple equilibria such that economies with high (low) rates of human capital reach a high (low) equilibrium. The next section outlines this approach.

4.3.3   Threshold Externalities and Multiple Equilibria

As with most contributors in the convergence debate, Azariadis and Drazen (1990) start their analysis from empirical observations about national economies.

> Some countries manage to sustain high growth rates over long periods of time; others advance at acceptable if not spectacular rates; while still others seem to stagnate in low growth "traps", exhibiting persistently low rates of growth or relative low levels of economic development, or both. (Azariadis and Drazen 1990, p. 501)

In seeking an explanation for this, Azariadis and Drazen (1990) augment the standard neoclassical model of economic growth with technological externalities that include a 'threshold property', to produce multiple, locally stable balanced growth paths in equilibrium. In broad terms, the explanation rests on physical capital and/or the stock of 'knowledge' surpassing certain critical or threshold values, at which points aggregate production possibilities expand rapidly.

Azariadis and Drazen (1990) build the structure of their model on Diamond (1965) and Romer (1986), two models that allow for multiple equilibria to emerge. Azariadis and Drazen (1990) employ the following production function:

$$Y_t = A_t F(k_{i,t}) \tag{4.11}$$

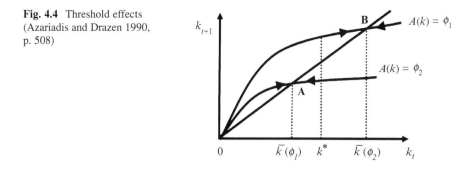

Fig. 4.4 Threshold effects (Azariadis and Drazen 1990, p. 508)

where A_t is a scale factor. Factors of production are separated into private and social, as proposed by Romer (1986), where the former are those inputs controlled by individual producers. The external effect, A_t, means that individual firms are operating under conditions of constant returns to scale but the economy as a whole (or a sector of the economy) operates at increasing returns. Azariadis and Drazen (1990) further assume that the scale factor is a function of the capital-labour ratio:

$$A_t = A(k_i) = \phi, \quad \forall k_t \tag{4.12}$$

They prove that it is possible to identify two non-trivial stable steady-states if the concept of a threshold value of k^* is introduced. Figure 4.4 illustrates this probability showing a bifurcation in the growth of k, which is dependent on the initial capital-labour ratio. These bifurcations or 'threshold effects', show radical differences in the dynamic behaviour of economies arising from variations in social returns to scale, as measured by the scale factor A_t.

Economies with an initial capital-labour ratio below the critical value k^* will converge monotonically to the low steady-state equilibrium $\bar{k}(\phi_1)$. On the other hand, economies initially above the critical value converge towards the higher steady-state equilibrium $\bar{k}(\phi_2)$. By definition, almost, low capital accumulation is likely to lead to a value for k_t below k^*, whereas the higher is k_t, the greater the external effect, captured by the scale factor A_t, as implied by Eq. 4.12. Azariadis and Drazen (1990) argue that small differences in k_t can lead to quite different growth paths:

> Externalities in the technology of human capital accumulation will then imply bifurcations that yield quite different development paths out of small differences in initial conditions. (p. 513)

The emphasis is thus on a combination of different initial conditions and external effects, which produce these different paths. Essentially, Azariadis and Drazen (1990) reformulate the neoclassical model in such a way as to produce multiple equilibria, by introducing discontinuities in technology captured by the scale factor. By assuming that technology depends on the capital-labour ratio, this model includes an endogenous mechanism to the growth paths. The next section, however, provides an explanation for the emergence of convergence clubs, which is clearly within the framework of Endogenous Growth Theory and which emphasises the role of technology gaps and technology diffusion.

4.4   Club Convergence: Technology Diffusion and the Technological Gap

Bernard and Jones (1996a) claim that a single equilibrium is the exception rather than the rule as a consequence of technological differences.[3] Furthermore, they argue that empirical studies on convergence have over-emphasised the role of capital accumulation in generating convergence at the expense of the diffusion of technology:

> To the extent that the adoption and accumulation of technologies is important for convergence, the empirical convergence literature is misguided. (Bernard and Jones 1996a, p. 1037)

They conclude that

> [...] future work on convergence should focus much more carefully on technology. (p. 1043)

On similar lines, Fagerberg and Verspagen (1996) argue that any theory aims to throw light on the convergence-divergence phenomena has to take account for factors related to technology diffusion. This section, therefore, outlines some key models that emphasise the role of technology gaps and technological choices through adoption and diffusion in club convergence.

In examining convergence, Baumol (1986) acknowledges the importance of the diffusion of innovations from leading to lagging economies (or 'innovation-sharing').

> For the laggards have to learn from the leaders, and that is why the process makes for convergence. (p. 1078)

Furthermore, given that an important channel for the spread of technology is via international trade, another prediction is that the higher the degree of trade liberalisation the faster the process of technology diffusion will be.

However, Baumol (1986) also recognises that differences in technology may lead to the more limited case of club convergence. Such technology differences can occur due to circumstances in some economies during the early stages of their development, generating productivity advantages. Cetorelli (2002) similarly argues

---

[3] Using a Cobb-Douglas technology framework, Bernard and Jones (1996a), demonstrate that the presence of substantial technological gaps across the OECD economies. They argue that this implies limited convergence possibilities. They aptly summarise this point by suggesting that '[T]his leads to a world in which similar steady-states outcomes are the exception rather than the rule.' (p.1040). In other words, they suggest a pattern of club convergence.

that club convergence is generated as the result of history dependence, since technology creation is based, to a certain extent, on historical factors. Nevertheless, the idea that differences or 'gaps' in technology account for disparities across economies pre-dates this. The argument has been presented in economic historians such as Gerschenkron (1962) and Gomulka (1971, 1990), for example, where the 'dual' role of technology is highlighted. In particular, technology is recognised as a factor promoting convergence through the diffusion of innovations but it is also acknowledged that, if technological advantages are maintained or even magnified, differences in economic performance will not be eliminated.[4]

The essence of the 'technology gap' model can be summarised as the 'advantages of relative backwardness', proposed initially by Gerschenkron (1962)[5] and Gomulka (1971; 1986). While advanced economies grow by means of innovative activity, lagging economies rely on the imitation and adoption of technologies from the leading economies. Imitators do not incur research and development costs. The rate of technology transfer from advanced to backward economies is a fundamental force driving growth in the latter and, ceteris paribus, the faster the rate of innovation in advanced economies, the higher the potential for growth via imitation for lagging economies. The rationale for the catching-up phenomenon has been explained, more fully, by Abramovitz (1986)[6]:

> When a leader discards old stock and replaces it, the accompanying productivity increase is governed and limited by the advance of knowledge between the time when the old capital was installed and the time it is replaced. Those who are behind however have the potential to make a larger leap. New capital can embody the frontier of knowledge, but the capital it replaces was technologically superannuated. So the larger the technological and therefore the productivity gap between the leader and follower, the stronger the follower's potential for growth in productivity; and other things being equal, the faster the follower's growth rate to be. Followers tend to catch up faster if they are initially more backward. (pp. 386–387)

The argument, therefore, is that the size of the technological gap is a primary determinant of an economy's rate of technological progress and hence growth. Backward economies can converge with the more advanced economies, provided that they are able to imitate or adopt innovations. Furthermore, technology transfer may be relatively cheap for lagging economies compared to leading economies that are already employing 'state of the art' technology, and which must devote resources to innovation activities in order to progress further. However, such

---

[4] See also Ames and Rosenberg (1963), Nelson and Winter (1974), Alesina and Rodrik (1994), Walters (1995), Kenny and Williams (2001), Persson and Tabellini (1994). Nelson and Winter (1982) also express a similar view. Their approach is an application of the theory of bounded rationality and decision-making under conditions of uncertainty, formulated by Simon (1972), to industrial innovation.

[5] Although Gerschenkron (1962) is acknowledged as the initiator of this view, nevertheless, the basis of the argument is based on Veblen (1915). See also Fagerberg (1994).

[6] In this light convergence is a manifestation of a 'technological' catch-up (Capolupo 1998).

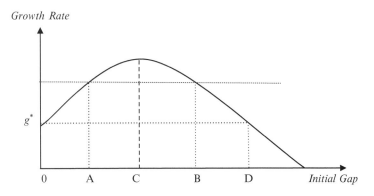

Fig. 4.5 Club convergence and technology diffusion (Chatterji 1992, p. 63)

low technology economies must possess the necessary social and political infrastructures to adopt technology.

One of the first attempts to formalise the role of the technology gap and technology diffusion in club convergence is undertaken by Chatterji (1992). Here, the growth of technology is approximated by the growth of real income per-capita so that the 'technology gap' between two economies is represented by the difference in per capita incomes. The contribution of diffusion to a pattern of club convergence is depicted in Fig. 4.5, which shows a relationship between growth in per-capita income over a particular time interval and the size of the gap with the leading economy, i.e. an economy with the highest per-capita income, at the start of the time period. This relationship is assumed to be non-linear and takes an inverted U-shape, as shown in Fig. 4.5. Chatterji (1992) rationalises this particular relationship by stating that:

> [...] countries with a very small gap are under little pressure to imitate the leader whilst countries with a large gap are under high pressure to mimic but lack the ability to do so.
> (p. 62)

Due to the diffusion of technology some economies will converge to the leader and in the long run will grow at the same rate (g^*) as the leader, whose growth rate is assumed to be exogenously determined. Chatterji (1992), however, argues that over the short run, or during the 'adjustment phase', there is no inverse relationship between growth and initial level of per-capita. Consider two economies that differ substantially in terms of initial per capita income, denoted by points A and B. These two economies, in the short run, exhibit the same rate of growth and the negative relation between initial per capita income and growth rate is apparent only for economies whose initial gap is less than C. According to Chatterji's argument above, the economy at A is 'under little pressure to imitate the leader' whereas the economy at point B 'lacks the ability to do so', but both exhibit the same rate of growth. For economies with a gap less that C, the property of absolute β-convergence exists, as a higher gap (i.e. lower initial per capita income) is associated with a higher rate of growth. However, all economies with a positive gap within the range 0 to D will be growing faster than the leading economy, and according to Chatterji (1992), constitute a convergence club. Economies with a gap greater than D are excluded from the convergence club; their growth is lower than that of the leading economy, and hence they never catch-up. Point C, where the function reaches a maximum, represents a 'threshold' technology below which the difficulties of adopting technology have negative impacts on growth. Although economies in the range C to D converge with the leader, the rate of growth is inversely related to the size of the gap.

This model, therefore, predicts the development of a convergence club and three kinds of economies are included in this convergence club. The first kind consists of those with a relatively small technological distance from the leading economy and the second are economies that exhibit a substantial gap but posses some capacity to adopt technology and grow accordingly. Finally, the third category includes economies with 'middle-sized' gaps possessing a suitable level of infrastructure, an educated labour force and an R&D sector all of which provide a capacity to benefit substantially from technology transfer (Chatterji 1992). Excluded from the convergence club are economies at some distance, technologically, from the leading economy and lacking the appropriate infrastructure.[7] Chatterji (1992) uses a descriptive approach to explain the development of convergence clubs. A model which examines the impact of technology gaps and diffusion in a more formal way is developed by Verspagen (1991 and 1992). This model, which also shows that threshold externalities can lead to different growth paths, is discussed next.

Verspagen (1991 and 1992), following Gomulka (1971, 1986) hypothesises a non-linear relationship between labour productivity growth and the size of the technological gap with the leading economy, which allows for both catching up and falling behind. A basic equation of this model is the following:

$$G = \ln\left(\frac{y_L}{y_i}\right) \tag{4.13}$$

where y_L and y_i are the levels of output per-worker in the leading and lagging economies, respectively, and G is interpreted as the technology gap. The growth rate of labour productivity in the leading economy is assumed to be exogenous, and based on the assumption that most research activities and innovations are conducted by the leading economy. It follows, then, that productivity growth in the followers derives from the diffusion of technology from the leading economy.[8] The growth rate of the technology gap is assumed to depend upon two factors, the leader's

---

[7] Gerschenkron (1962) also puts emphasis on the importance of ideologies. In backward nations there will be powerful parts of society that resist any kinds of changes (technological or institutional). See also Inkster (2002). A parallel set of arguments can be applied in a regional context, as well. Backward regions, especially those with an agricultural tradition, adopt technological innovations very slowly or even reject them. Rodríguez-Pose (1999b) argues along similar lines.

[8] It is not entirely clear if autonomous innovation occurs only in the leading economy. Nevertheless, even though some innovation may take place elsewhere, the presumption is that following economies rely principally on diffusion and imitation.

differential advantage in terms of autonomous innovation, $\bar{c}_i$, and the diffusion, or spillover effects, from the leader to the follower, SE_i. Thus:

$$\frac{dG_i}{dt} = \bar{c}_i - SE_i \tag{4.14}$$

Spillover effects, experienced by a following economy, are assumed to be a non-linear function of the technological gap, as follows:

$$SE_i = aG_i e^{-\frac{G_i}{v_i}} \tag{4.15}$$

where $0 < a \leq 1$ and $0 < v_i < 1$.

The rate of change in the gap is given as follows:

$$\frac{dG_i}{dt} = \bar{c} - aG_i e^{-\frac{G_i}{v_i}} \tag{4.16}$$

Spillovers are proportional to the technological gap, G_i and to the 'learning capability', $e^{-\frac{G_i}{v_i}}$, which is also dependent on the size of the gap. Of particular importance is the parameter v_i, which represents the degree to which an economy is able to adopt the innovations created by the leading economy. If an economy has a relatively high value of v_i, ceteris paribus, this indicates a high capacity for technology absorption through imitation. Thus, the learning capability is inversely related to the size of the gap (G_i) and positively related to the absorption parameter v_i. In reality, it is likely that a high value for G_i would be associated with a low value for v_i, i.e. a severely lagging economy would have a limited capacity for technology adoption.[9]

Furthermore, the process of convergence is affected also by the value of $\bar{c}_i$, which represents the differential advantage in terms of autonomous innovation, the higher its value, ceteris paribus, the slower any convergence process will be, since the distance between the leader and the follower is larger. Overall, the extent of catching up depends on the value of SE_i relative to $\bar{c}_i$; if $\bar{c}_i > SE_i$ then the gap is increasing. By imposing different values for the parameters in Eq. 4.16, it is possible to separate economies into two distinct groups, one converging with the leader and one falling.

A similar but alternative approach to the analysis of technology gaps and the diffusion process is provided by de la Fuente (1997, 2000). This model is based on the usual assumption that technological progress depends on the extent of technology diffusion from the most advanced economy but income disparities are also attributed to differences in the levels of investment in physical capital and technology, i.e. there is indigenous innovation possible in any economy.[10] Although this model does not

---

[9] It is interesting to note that Targetti and Foti (1997) claim that equation (4.16) encapsulates the neoclassical process of convergence as a special case. To be more precise, assuming that technology is a free good, as the neoclassical model assumes, then autonomous productivity growth is equal for all economies, which implies that $\bar{c}_i = 0$ and diffusion is effectively instantaneous, leading thus to absolute convergence in the long-run.

[10] Pigliaru (2003) develops a similar model in which technology accumulation in a region depends not only on technology diffusion from the leading region but also on the proportion of regional output devoted to innovation.

test the hypothesis of regional club convergence directly, some modifications of the model can lead to a club convergence prediction, as developed in a subsequent section.

In order to describe the production process, de la Fuente (2000) uses an aggregate Cobb-Douglas production function for an economy, assumed to be Harrod-neutral for all capital-labour ratios and taking the following form:

$$Y = \Phi K^a (AL)^{1-a} \tag{4.17}$$

where K includes both physical and human capital. The term A is an index of labour augmenting technical progress and by defining the capital-labour ratio in efficiency units as $k = \frac{K}{AL}$ Eq. 4.17 can be written as follows:

$$Y = \Phi A L k^a \tag{4.18}$$

The term Φ is the factor which is used to generate a further impact of capital accumulation upon output, operating in a way similar to that implied by Azariadis and Drazen (1990), discussed in Sect. 4.3.3. Specifically,

$$\Phi = k^\beta \tag{4.19}$$

where β is a parameter. According to de la Fuente (2000), this captures the external effects on output in that capital accumulation generates positive spillover effects. Equation 4.19 is similar to that proposed by Romer (1986), which in turn is based on 'learning-by-doing' mechanism proposed initially by Arrow (1962).

Combining Eqs. 4.18 and 4.19 leads to output per worker expressed as follows:

$$y = A k^\lambda \tag{4.20}$$

where $y = \frac{Y}{L}$ and the parameter $\lambda = a + \beta$ measures the degree of returns to scale to broad capital.

If s, n and δ are the share of savings in total output, the growth rate of labour and the rate of depreciation, respectively, then, as shown in Chap. 2, the capital-labour ratio (k) grows in accordance with the following relation:[11]

$$g_k = s k^{\lambda-1} - (n + g_A + \delta) \tag{4.21}$$

where g_A denotes the growth rate of technology.

In equilibrium, the growth rate of the capital-labour ratio is zero, so setting $g_k = 0$ gives a steady-state value of k as follows:

$$k^* = \left(\frac{s}{n + g_A + \delta}\right)^{\frac{1}{1-\lambda}} \tag{4.22}$$

---

[11] Output per-worker grows as follows: $g_y = (1 - \lambda)g_A + \lambda s k^{\lambda-1} - \lambda(n + \delta)$.

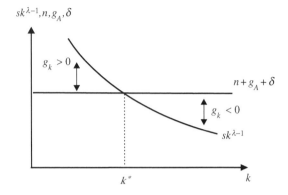

Fig. 4.6 Dynamics of capital accumulation when $\lambda < 1$ (de la Fuente 2000, p. 29)

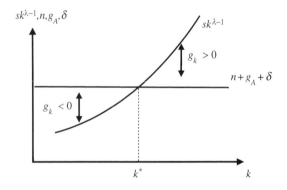

Fig. 4.7 Dynamics of capital accumulation when $\lambda > 1$ (de la Fuente 2000, p. 29)

The distinguishing feature of this model, thus far, is the parameter λ, which consists of the direct contribution of the capital stock to output (a) and the external effects of capital accumulation (β). In this respect, the model predicts, as in the standard neoclassical model, that if decreasing returns prevail ($\lambda < 1$) there will there be a process of convergence to the steady-state value for the capital-labour ratio, as shown in Fig. 4.6:

The situation is completely different if external effects, represented by β, are strong enough, so that $\lambda > 1$. In this case the system diverges from the equilibrium value k^* i.e. this is not a stable equilibrium. Returns to investment are now an increasing function of k and the higher (smaller) is k, the higher (smaller) is the growth rate of k, moving away from equilibrium, as shown on Fig. 4.7.

Thus, de la Fuente (2000) claims that the steady-state value of k in Eq. 4.22

[...] must be interpreted as a threshold for growth rather than as a long-run equilibrium. (p. 30)

In a multi-regional system, λ may be different across regions for a number of reasons. For example, the agglomeration of economic activities in relatively few regions may lead to greater positive externality effects (a higher λ). Thus, regions with high values of λ will follow a different growth path and, eventually, will diverge from regions with relatively low values of λ. Essentially, the development of different clusters of regions is attributed to different parameters values. Furthermore, if there are increasing returns to broad capital, i.e. $\lambda > 1$, then this alone is sufficient to generate divergence.

However, de la Fuente (2000) takes the model further by modelling technological progress in an economy. This is assumed to be an increasing function firstly of the proportion of output invested in R&D to produce 'technological capital' $(\theta)^{12}$ and secondly the opportunities for 'technological catch up', as measured by the gap between the existing level of technology in a region and that of a 'technological best-practice frontier', (b). Technological progress, therefore, is expressed as the sum of these two elements:

$$\dot{a}_i = g_A = \gamma\theta + \varepsilon b \quad \text{with } \gamma, \varepsilon > 0 \tag{4.23}$$

The parameter γ measures the productivity of innovation in augmenting technology while ε represents the rate of diffusion of technology across economies and, hence, reflects the opportunities for technological catch-up, similar to Verspagen (1991). The technological distance (b_i) is defined as the difference between a best-practice frontier (x), which is determined exogenously, and the prevailing level of technology in a region, represented by some index a_i. Thus:

$$b_i = a_i - x \tag{4.24}$$

Thus, in the cases of a leading region and a following region the technological distances are given by:

$$b_l = a_l - x \tag{4.25}$$

$$b_f = a_f - x \tag{4.26}$$

where the subscripts l and f denote the leader and the follower, respectively.

As illustrated in Fig. 4.8, the gap between the levels of technology in these two regions, assuming for the moment that no change occurs over time, can be expressed as follows:

$$b_{lf} = b_f - b_l \tag{4.27}$$

---

[12] De la Fuente (1997, p. 25) defines technological capital as 'the accumulated stock of useful technical knowledge' and argues that it is subject to the same constraint as physical capital, namely exhibiting diminishing returns. This variable represents indigenous innovation in an economy.

Fig. 4.8 Technological distance from the best-practice technology

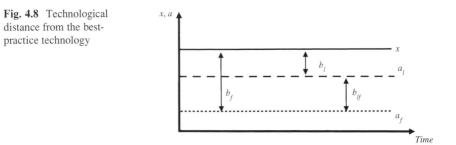

From this basis, de la Fuente (2000) examines the conditions under which convergence will occur. Assuming that each region devotes a different proportion of its output to R&D, Eq. 4.23 is used to show the growth of technology in the leading and following regions:

$$\dot{a}_l = \gamma \theta_l + \varepsilon b_l \tag{4.28}$$

$$\dot{a}_f = \gamma \theta_f + \varepsilon b_f \tag{4.29}$$

The growth rate for the technology gap between the two regions is therefore:

$$\dot{b}_{lf} = \dot{a}_l - \dot{a}_f = \gamma(\theta_f - \theta_f) + \varepsilon(b_l - b_f) \tag{4.30}$$

Given that $b_{lf} = b_f - b_l$ Eq. 4.30 can be written as follows:

$$\dot{b}_{lf} = \gamma \theta_{lf} - \varepsilon b_{lf} \tag{4.31}$$

where $\theta_{lf} = (\theta_l - \theta_f)$.

Assuming that $\theta_l > \theta_f$, convergence patterns are determined by the value of parameter ε, which represents the degree of technological diffusion between the leader and the follower. The absence of any technological diffusion ($\varepsilon = 0$), for example, implies that the rate of change in the gap ($\dot{b}_{lf}$) is positive and constant as shown in Fig. 4.9.

However, if $\varepsilon > 0$, then a degree of technological catch-up occurs between the leader and the follower and if this equals the rate of innovation differential exactly there will be no overall change in the gap, i.e. $\dot{b}_{lf} = 0$. Thus, the technological gap reaches a constant finite value b_{lf}^* where the condition $\dot{b}_{lf} = 0$ is satisfied, when

$$b_{lf}^* = \frac{\gamma \theta_{lf}}{\varepsilon} \tag{4.32}$$

As illustrated in Fig. 4.10, when the gap between leader and follower is below b_{lf}^*, the dynamics of the system cause the gap to grow towards its steady-state value, since the rate of innovation investment outweighs the effect of technology diffusion. Conversely, when the gap is greater than b_{lf}^*, there is movement towards equilibrium since $\dot{b}_{lf}$ is negative. This model, as represented by Eqs. 4.23 and 4.31, states that in

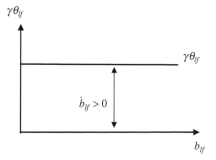

Fig. 4.9 Technological divergence (de la Fuente 2000, p. 31)

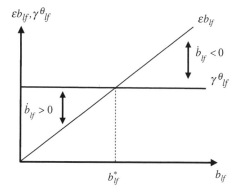

Fig. 4.10 Technological catch-up (de la Fuente 2000, p. 31)

the long-run the technology gap between the leader and the follower is directly proportional to the difference in the rates of investment in R&D, and inversely proportional to the speed of technological diffusion. In the absence of technological diffusion between the two economies ($\varepsilon = 0$), then the two economies will diverge. On the other hand, a catch-up process among the two economies will take place if there are decreasing returns to capital ($\lambda < 1$), and, technology diffusion ($\varepsilon > 0$) is taking place between the leader and the follower. According to De la Fuente (2000):

> [...] both convergence mechanisms tend to mitigate the level of international inequality induced by cross-country differences in fundamentals, but not eliminate it. (p. 31)

This is because an equilibrium differential remains which is determined by the differential in innovation and R&D. For the purposes of the present study, three key features of de la Fuente's (2000) model are of particular importance. First, this model places particular emphasis upon indigenous innovation, as this is represented by R&D investment. Second, apart from indigenous innovation, this model emphasises technology diffusion and its impact on gaps in technology across economies. Third, a mechanism is presented that can lead to divergence, which in this model relies on the external effects from broad capital accumulation.

In summary, de la Fuente (2000) implies the co-existence of both catching-up and falling behind mechanisms, in a way similar to that implied in the model by Verspagen (1991). The next section extends de la Fuente's model (2000) a step further by focusing in particular on the absorptive parameter that determines the pattern of convergence.

4.5   A Simple Model of Club Convergence

As discussed above, technological progress in de la Fuente's model is attributed to two factors, namely the intentional creation of technology through innovation and the diffusion of technology. The actual impact of diffusion depends upon the size of the technological gap and the value of the parameter ε, which is referred to as the speed of diffusion. An implicit assumption of this model is that all economies are able to absorb technology to the same degree, so that the higher the technological gap the higher the effect on growth, ceteris paribus. However, it may be argued that large gaps do not necessarily promote convergence in this way. It is quite possible that a significant technological gap is associated with unfavourable conditions for the adoption of new technology. Kristensen (1974) points out that technological spillovers are not likely to be effective if the capability of the receiving economy is too low:

> The most rapid economic growth should be expected to take place in countries that have reached a stage at which they can begin to apply a great deal more of the existing knowledge (p. 24)

On similar lines, Abramovitz (1986) recognises this possibility by arguing as follows:

> Countries that are technologically backward have a potentiality for generating growth more rapid than that of more advanced countries, provided their social capabilities are sufficiently developed to permit successful exploitation of technologies already employed by the technological leaders (p. 225)

In other words, if 'social capabilities' or infrastructure conditions are not 'sufficiently developed' then it cannot be presumed that there is an 'advantage of backwardness' associated with a high technological gap. The absorptive ability of a regional economy is therefore of paramount importance to the convergence process.

In terms of existing literature, Baland and Francois (1996), Keller (1996), Parente and Prescott (1994, 1999), Teixeira and Fortuna (2010) consider the implications of technology absorption for economic growth in national economies, and express the absorptive ability in terms of human capital. Griffith et al. (2003) argue that R&D affects both innovation and the assimilation of others' discoveries, i.e. the 'absorptive capacity'. At the firm level, Saito and Gopinath (2011) approximate the absorptive capacity in terms of employment of skilled workers. However, these models do not consider the implications for convergence, at least in an explicit way. Four regional models emphasise the absorptive ability of regions in promoting economic growth, with each highlighting different factors. Acs et al. (1994) put emphasis on the average size or age of local firms, Dosi (1988) considers the dominant production structure and the existence of networks, Henderson (2003b) uses available human capital in a location while in Drifflied (2006) the spillover effects from foreign direct investment are the focus. In these models, however, no implications for regional convergence are directly considered. A link between the absorption of technology and economic convergence is considered explicitly in a further four models. In particular, Barro and Sala-i-Martin (1997), Detragiache (1998), and Howitt and Mayer-Foulkes (2005) examine this relationship for national economies while Peri and Urban (2006) assess regional convergence in the light of spillovers from foreign direct investment, which are used to approximate regional adoption of technology.

Of particular importance for the purposes of the present study is a model by Howitt and Mayer-Foulkes (2005), based on Schumpeter (1934). Here, club convergence is recognised as a distinct possibility due to the implementation of advanced technology from leading regions. Following Nelson and Phelps (1966), Phelps (1966) and Nelson (1956; 1960 and 1981), Howitt and Mayer-Foulkes (2005) approximate the ability of an economy to absorb technology in terms of levels of human capital and the endogenous rate of innovation. An important issue is whether 'lagging' economies are able to develop a sufficiently modern R&D sector, described as a 'window of opportunity'. Countries are separated into three groups. The 'highest' group includes countries with an advanced R&D sector, an 'intermediate' group, consists of those in the initial stages of establishing a modern R&D sector and the 'lowest' group contains the technologically lagging countries. In this model a convergence club emerges when 'intermediate' countries converge with the countries in the 'highest' group. The remainder of this section continues to focus upon the diffusion process and the role of infrastructure in facilitating or impeding such diffusion by developing a simple model of regional club convergence.[13] Particular emphasis is placed upon the approach in de la Fuente (2000) rather than Howitt and Mayer-Foulkes (2005) because the former is more flexible and suitable for empirical application. As will be shown, the model in this section yields two 'outcomes' under certain conditions; a 'high' and a 'low' outcome. Whether economies converge towards a high or a low outcome depends on the degree to which infrastructure conditions are appropriate for the adoption of the latest technological improvements. The key feature in this model is that the rate of diffusion of technology (ε) is assumed to be a non-linear function of the technological gap. Thus,

$$\varepsilon_i = \frac{\rho}{b_{lf,i}^{\pi}} \qquad (4.33)$$

---

[13] See also Alexiadis (2010b,c; 2011).

where $\rho, \pi > 0$ are parameters.

The intuition behind Eq. 4.33 is that the rate of diffusion is not constant but varies across regions, according to the size of the gap. Thus, for a given value of ρ, a high technological gap implies a low capacity to absorb technology. The parameter ρ can be interpreted as a constant underlying rate of diffusion, which would apply to all economies if there were no infrastructure/resource constraints upon technological adoption. However, the existence of such constraints causes the actual rate to diverge from ρ. In other words, the higher the technological gap, the slower the rate of technological diffusion (ε). Of critical importance is the parameter π, which determines the extent to which the existing gap, and implicitly therefore the existing infrastructure, impacts on the rate of diffusion. This parameter can be viewed as a measure of the appropriateness or suitability of regional infrastructure to adopt technology.[14] Thus, the rate of technology diffusion is endogenously determined. As $b_{lf,i} \to \infty$, $\varepsilon_i \to 0$, i.e. for a regional economy with a high initial technological gap, the rate of diffusion is low, severely limited by a lack of appropriate infrastructure conditions. Conversely, as $b_{lf,i} \to 0$ then $\varepsilon_i \to \infty$ to reflect a high absorptive ability while instantaneous absorption occurs when $\varepsilon_i = \infty$. The implications of modelling the rate of diffusion in this way can be seen by substituting Eq. 4.33, into de la Fuente's framework (Eq. 4.28) to yield an expression for the rate of change in the technological gap as follows:

$$\dot{b}_{lf} = \gamma \theta_{lf} - \rho b_{lf}^{(1-\pi)} \tag{4.34}$$

In equilibrium $\dot{b}_{lf} = 0$ so that:

$$\gamma \theta_{lf} = \rho b_{lf}^{(1-\pi)} \tag{4.35}$$

which gives an equilibrium value for the technological gap:[15]

$$b_{lf}^* = \left(\frac{\gamma}{\rho} \theta_{lf}\right)^{\frac{1}{1-\pi}} \tag{4.36}$$

It is interesting to consider, however, the implications for an economy when its gap with the leading economy is not at this equilibrium level. The outcome turns upon the value of the parameter π. If $\pi = 0$, then according to Eq. 4.33 $\varepsilon_i = \rho$ and the diffusion of technology occurs at a constant autonomous rate equal to ρ, as in de la

---

[14] Generally, appropriateness or suitability of regional infrastructure includes factors such as human capital, a suitable industry mix, advanced financial arrangements, a good investment climate, etc. More specifically, these conditions can also be approximated in terms of sectors that implement advanced technology, such as information and data processing, scientific and electrical equipment production, pharmaceutical and chemical production, etc.

[15] Note that if $\left(\frac{\gamma}{\rho} \theta_{lf}\right) > 1$ and $\pi = 1$, then $b_{lf}^* \to \infty$ while if $\left(\frac{\gamma}{\rho} \theta_{lf}\right) < 1$ and $\pi = 1$, then $b_{lf}^* \to 0$.

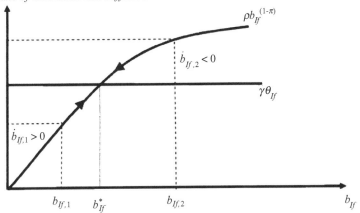

Fig. 4.11 Convergence pattern implied by $\pi < 1$

Fuente (2000), while if $\pi = 1$ the size of the technological gap changes in accordance with the rate is unrelated in the process of technological diffusion depends on the productivity of innovation and the constant rate of diffusion (if given $\pi = 1$, then $\dot{b}_{lf} = \gamma\theta_{lf} - \rho$). Two distinct patterns of convergence arise, however, when $\pi < 1$ and when $\pi > 1$.

Figure 4.11 portrays the pattern of convergence implied by $\pi < 1$.

This implies a pattern of convergence similar to that proposed by de la Fuente (2000), but now convergence is non-linear (as opposed to a linear process when $\pi = 0$). When the gap between leader and follower is below b_{lf}^*, the dynamics of the system cause the gap to grow towards its steady-state value, since the rate of innovation investment outweighs the effect of technology diffusion and, hence, $\dot{b}_{lf_i} > 0 \; \forall i \in [0 \; b_{lf}^*]$. Conversely, when the gap is greater than b_{lf}^*, there is movement towards equilibrium since $\dot{b}_{lf}$ is negative, i.e. $\dot{b}_{lf_i} < 0 \; \forall i \in [b_{lf}^* \; \infty]$. Assuming that the leading region maintains its leading position over a given time period, then economies with a large technology gap, i.e. above b_{lf}^*, converge towards equilibrium but at slower rates compared to those economies where the gap is below b_{lf}^*. Thus, when $\pi < 1$ convergence towards a single equilibrium is possible but regions with unfavourable infrastructure conditions reflected in a large technological gap move towards equilibrium at a slower pace. However, if $\pi > 1$, then convergence towards a unique equilibrium, for all but the leading region, is no longer the case, and b_{lf}^* represents a threshold value now.

As Fig. 4.12 shows, economies on either side of the threshold b_{lf}^* move in different directions. This pattern of convergence and divergence can be illustrated using a simple example. Consider an economy divided into three regions, one 'leader' and two followers. Assuming that the leading region is at the technological frontier ($b_l = a_l - x = 0$) so that steady-state equilibrium is, therefore,

Rate of Innovation and Diffusion

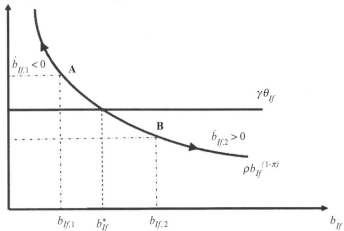

Fig. 4.12 Club convergence

approximated by the leading region, then convergence with the leading region requires that the gap at a terminal time (T) should be zero, i.e. $b_{lf,T} = 0$. However, as Fig. 4.12 indicates, a zero gap with the leader is not feasible, since by definition the curve $\rho b_{lf}^{(1-\pi)}$ is asymptotic to the axis of the graph. Hence, a more realistic condition would be that the technological gap tends towards zero over a given time period, i.e. $b_{lf,T-0} \rightarrow 0$. For simplicity assume that regions 1 and 2 devote the same proportion of output to R&D, i.e. $\theta_1 = \theta_2$, so that $\theta_{lf,1} = \theta_{lf,2}$ and that $\gamma_1 = \gamma_2$. It is also assumed that ρ is the same for both regions.[16] If, however, the initial technological gaps differ between these regions[17] ($b_{lf,1} < b_{lf}^* < b_{lf,2}$), then region 1 is able to close the technological gap with the leader at a faster rate than region 2, and the gap approaches zero asymptotically. Despite a lower rate of innovation compared to the leader, this region is able to adopt technology from the leading region and it is this latter effect which dominates. However, region 2, with a high gap and hence poor infrastructure conditions exhibits too slow a rate of technology absorption and, as a result, the gap with the leader increases over time. Convergence, therefore, is a

---

[16] Different values of ρ would result in shifting the curve $\rho b_{lf}^{(1-\pi)}$.

[17] Assume, for example, that output in each region is produced by two sectors; a technologically advanced and a 'traditional' sector: $Y_i = Y_A + Y_T$. The technological gap can be approximated in terms of a decreasing function of the labour employed in the technologically advanced sector: $b_i = f(l_{A,i})$ with $f' < 0$. Assume further that productivity and wages are higher in the advanced sector: $w_A - w_T > 0$. This framework implies that $l_{A,i} = h(r_i)$, where $r_i = w_{A,i1}/w_{T,i2}$ with $h' > 0$ and $b_i = f \cdot h(r_i)$, with $f' \cdot h' < 0$. The condition $w_A - w_T > 0$ induces labour to move from the 'traditional' to the advanced sector. If $r_1 - r_2 > 0$, then the advanced sector in region 1 attracts labour from the 'traditional' sector in that region and labour from both sectors in region 2, leading to $b_1 - b_2 < 0$.

property apparent only for region 1 and the leading region, which constitute an exclusive convergence club. In terms of Fig. 4.12, the convergence club includes any region with a technological gap in the range $(0, b_{lf}^*]$ while regions with gaps in the range $[b_{lf}^*, \infty)$ diverge from the leader and the remaining regions. In other words, the technological advantages of particular regions would accumulate and militate against convergence for all. In this light, b_{lf}^* is not an 'equilibrium' level for the technology gap, but rather a 'threshold' level, which distinguishes between converging and non-converging regions. It is possible to incorporate the impact of technological spillovers in the framework developed by Cameron et al. (2005). The rate of growth in a region-follower is generated by the size of the technological gap. Thus,

$$\Delta \log(A_{F,t}) = \upsilon_F - \alpha \log \left(\frac{A_{F,t-1}}{\varsigma A_{L,t-1}} \right) \tag{4.37}$$

In Eq. 4.37 υ_F is the autonomous rate of technological growth, ς denotes the proportion of technologies that can be adopted by a region-follower while the term $\alpha \log \left(\frac{A_{F,t-1}}{\varsigma A_{L,t-1}} \right)$ can be interpreted as a measure of technological spillovers. The leading region is assumed to grow autonomously:

$$\Delta \log(A_{L,t}) = \upsilon_L \tag{4.38}$$

Given that $\Delta X = X_t - X_{t-1}$, then the relation in Eq. 4.37 can be written in terms of the following first-order differential equation:

$$\log G_t = (\upsilon_F - \upsilon_L) - \alpha \log \varsigma + (1 - \alpha) \log G_{t-1} \tag{4.39}$$

where $G = \left(\frac{A_F}{A_L} \right)$

In the steady-state equilibrium all regions grow at the same rate, namely at the rate of the leading region, and $G_t = G_{t-1} = G^*$. Hence,

$$\log G^* = \left(\frac{\upsilon_F - \upsilon_L}{\varsigma} \right) + \log \alpha \tag{4.40}$$

A high initial technological gap implies that conditions are not favourable for the adoption of technology, which can be reflected in relatively low values of the parameters α and ς. Assuming that ς is a decreasing function of *geographical distance* with the leader, $\varsigma = f(d_L)$ with $f' < 0$, then spillovers are stronger in a region located closely to the leader. In the example with the two regions, and given that conditions are more favourable in region 1, then $\alpha_1 - \alpha_2 > 0$ and $\varsigma_1 - \varsigma_2 > 0$, implying that region 1 converges with the leader while region 2 is falling behind. Following Bode et al. (2012), it is possible to incorporate these considerations by modifying the term A in Eq. 4.11. Thus,

Fig. 4.13 Club convergence
when $\pi > 1$ and $\theta_{lf,1} \neq \theta_{lf,2}$

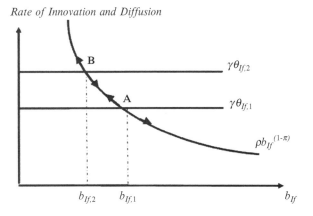

$$A_{i,t} = A_{i,0} \left(\prod_{j=1}^{n} \Theta_{j,t}^{\delta_{\Theta} w_{\Theta_{ij}}} \right) \left(\prod_{j=1}^{n} E_{j,t}^{\delta_{E} w_{E_{ij}}} \right) \tag{4.41}$$

Equation 4.41 blends elements of technology innovation and adoption, measured by $\Theta_{j,t}$ and $E_{j,t}$, respectively, in order to capture the potential in generating technological externalities in a region. Such an approach is explicitly spatial given that the output elasticities of the potentials of externalities (δ_{Θ} and δ_{E}) are adjusted by spatial weights which depend on the distance between two regions ($w_{\Theta_{ij}}$ and $w_{E_{ij}}$).

Nevertheless, the important point to grasp is that the modification of de la Fuente's model imposes a non-linear process of technological diffusion (i.e. $\pi > 1$) that depends on infrastructure conditions as embodied in the size of the gap at a point in time. To be more precise, if the adoption of technology is related in a particular way to the size of the initial technological gap and associated infrastructure conditions, then two groups of regions can emerge; one which is a convergence club while a second group that does not exhibit an 'equilibrium'. Whether a region belongs to the convergence club depends on its capacity to adopt technology, and this capacity declines the higher the initial technology gap. The assumption in the preceding example with two following, or lagging, regions is that both exhibit the same characteristics, such as the propensity to innovate.

A more complicated picture arises if this assumption is relaxed, allowing the creation of technology to differ between the lagging regions, for example.

Figure 4.13 shows a situation where region 1 has a higher rate of technology creation, compared to region 2, which is reflected in a lower differential in technology creation with the leader, i.e. $\theta_{lf,1} < \theta_{lf,2}$. Point B represents the critical threshold for region 2, showing that a large difference in innovation rates requires a high rate of technology absorption in order to prevent the region moving further away from the leading region in terms of overall technology growth. On the other hand, point A is the threshold for region 1, which has a lower innovation differential compared to the leader. As a result, the rate of technology absorption that is required to prevent region 1 from following a divergent path, is lower compared to that of region 2. A diverging path for region 1 corresponds to movements to the right of point A. Hence, by imposing different abilities to create and absorb technology, two thresholds exist, one that corresponds to $b_{lf,1}$, with low θ_{lf} and another to b_1, with high θ_{lf}. Broadly speaking, this model suggests that only economies with low technology gaps, relative to leading economies, are likely to converge towards a steady-state equilibrium growth path, as represented by the growth rate of the leading economy. Economies with relatively large technology gaps may fall progressively behind. Club convergence can emerge dependent on value of the absorptive parameter π. In particular, two distinct cases can be identified. If $\pi < 1$, then this model predicts a constant equilibrium gap, with different equilibrium positions possible depending upon whether economies share the same characteristics or not. The pattern of convergence implied by $\pi > 1$ is the most interesting. In this case, a convergence club emerges, even when all economies share the same characteristics, or parameters, apart from their initial position with regard to the size of the technological gap. It is the size of this initial gap that distinguishes whether an economy follows a convergent or divergent path. Further, if economies also differ with respect to their structural characteristics (i.e. in terms of θ_{lf} or the values of parameters ρ and γ), then the membership of the convergence club is more 'complex' to establish but fundamentally there is still one convergence club. This club is most likely to include economies with structural characteristics similar to the leader. The simple model, discussed in this section, clearly indicates that convergence towards leading economies is feasible only for economies with sufficient absorptive capacity, which is assumed to be a function of infrastructure conditions in an economy.

4.6 Conclusions

The concept of club convergence has emerged to some extent from empirical observation of economic development patterns. However, the theoretical underpinnings of this concept can be linked to both standard neoclassical and endogenous growth theory, as this chapter has demonstrated.

The theoretical discussion has demonstrated that convergence may be restricted to a selected subset of economies. Only economies, which are similar in their initial income conditions and/or their structural characteristics, may exhibit a tendency to converge, constituting a 'convergence club'. On that respect, Galor (1996) provides a theoretical model that predicts a situation that can be described as club convergence. However, this situation is transitory and, in the long-run, overall convergence will prevail if technology diffusion occurs across regions. Club convergence can also emerge in the context of two other models. Azariadis and Drazen (1990) develop a model in which club convergence is attributed to externalities, which 'lock-in' regions into different growth paths. Moreover, the 'technological gap' model raises issues about technology diffusion in shaping a pattern of club convergence.

Finally, a simple model is developed in this chapter, which shows the conditions that lead some economies to converge towards a leading economy, this has focused on differences in the ability of regions to adopt technology as a primary force in convergence. In a regional context, however, there are several other factors that operate to promote convergence or divergence, such as externalities from spatial agglomeration, regional specialisation, and diversity of economic activities. It is a possible theory; one cannot adopt it without more exact knowledge of their performance in a specific empirical framework. Therefore, the impact of these factors on regional growth and convergence will be discussed and tested empirically in the context of the regions of the EU-27 in a subsequent chapter. Prior to this, however, the next chapter reviews the most commonly used empirical measures of convergence and club convergence.

Chapter 5
Empirical Measures of Regional Convergence

5.1 Introduction

The theoretical analysis of convergence presented thus far has examined the circumstances in which an economy converges towards an equilibrium level of output per-worker or a steady-state rate of growth. The possibility that groups of economies are likely to converge towards the same steady-state (absolute convergence) or towards different steady-states (conditional convergence) has also been examined. In discussing club convergence, the possibility of convergence towards a leading economy has also been addressed. In reality economies are not in equilibrium and are subject to all manner of shocks at different points in time. Therefore, an important question arises: 'how is possible to test for convergence, when the steady-state is never achieved?' The approach, in practice, is to direct empirical measures of convergence towards the process of convergence, rather than the equilibrium outcome.

The fundamental issue behind the convergence debate is the extent to which there is increasing or decreasing inequality among economies. 'Inequality' is typically measured by reference to the distribution of per-capita income or output across countries or regions. In a very broad sense, therefore, one would expect changes in the distribution of income across economies to be a focus for attempts to measure convergence. For example, Baumol (1986) addresses questions of long-run growth and welfare among economies, and following the ideas of Abramovitz (1986), suggests that convergence occurs when poor economies grow faster than rich economies, such that the poor economies catch up in terms of the level of per-capita income through time. Alternatively, Barro and Sala-i-Martin (1992a, 1995) consider a different definition of convergence, which is a decline in income inequalities over time. Overall, the issue of convergence can be addressed in terms of per-capita income, output per-capita or output per-worker. In this chapter, however, for the sake of consistency in any general discussion, output per-worker is used, given that this is a primary concern of the theoretical model underlying the issue of convergence. There are many acceptable approaches to testing for regional convergence, ranging from simple statistical measures, such as the standard

S. Alexiadis, *Convergence Clubs and Spatial Externalities*,
Advances in Spatial Science, DOI 10.1007/978-3-642-31626-5_5,
© Springer-Verlag Berlin Heidelberg 2013

deviation to cross-section regressions (e.g. Baumol 1986; Barro and Sala-i-Martin 1992a), time series analysis (e.g. Bernard and Durlauf 1995; Carlino and Mills 1993; Kane 2001; Nahar and Inder 2002) and transitional dynamics (e.g. Maurseth 2001; Hobijin and Frances 2001; Bishop and Gripaios 2005, 2006). It is the purpose of this chapter to outline the main approaches that are subsequently used in the empirical analysis of this thesis so as to provide a background context for the empirical work of Chaps. 6 and 7.

The most common measures of convergence, namely σ and β convergence, are analysed in Sects. 5.2 and 5.3 respectively, while Sect. 5.4 outlines the approach to measuring conditional convergence. Of particular relevance to regional convergence are the effects of spatial interaction and these are also discussed in this section. Section 5.5 is devoted to empirical tests of club convergence and examines in particular two methodologies found in Baumol and Wolff (1988) and Chatterji (1992), and their application in empirical studies. All of the measures above employ cross-section data and criticisms of this cross-sectional approach are therefore discussed in Sect. 5.6, followed by an alternative test based on the concept of stochastic convergence using time-series data. A more extended test for stochastic convergence, which distinguishes between groups of economies that follow different trends, i.e. a time-series test for convergence clubs, is also outlined in this section. Finally, Sect. 5.7 concludes.

5.2 Measurement of σ-Convergence and Empirical Applications

The concept of σ-convergence is measured by reference to the cross-sectional dispersion in per-capita income through time. It is argued, for example, that a set of regional economies exhibits σ-convergence if the dispersion of income per-capita displays a declining trend. Although several descriptive measures have been put forward to measure the trends in reducing regional inequalities (Lichtenberg 1994; Esteban 2000; Canaleta et al. 2004; Kang and Lee 2005; Salardi 2009), the notion of σ-convergence is typically measured by calculating either the coefficient of variation or the standard deviation of per-capita income or output[1] (Cowell 1995; Fan and Casetti 1994; Formby et al. 1999; Rietveld 1991; Breunig 2001). Barro and Sala-i-Martin (1992a) introduced the term σ-convergence to describe one of the earliest approaches used to assess the extent of regional convergence (e.g. Easterlin 1958; Hanna 1959; Roberts 1979). Table 5.1 illustrates indicative main findings of

---

[1] Standard deviation ($\sigma_{i,t}$) is measured as $\sigma_{i,t} = \sqrt{\frac{1}{n} \sum_{i=1}^{n} \left[\log\left(\frac{y_i}{y^*}\right) \right]^2}$, where $\log y^* \equiv \frac{1}{n} \sum_{i=1}^{n} \log y_i$

(Dalgaard and Vastrup 2001). σ-convergence is signified when $\sigma_{i,T} < \sigma_{i,0}$ or more generally, when $\sigma_{i,t} \to 0$, as $t \to T$, where T is a terminal time. The coefficient of variation ($c_{i,t}$) is defined as the ratio of the standard deviation to the mean (μ):$c_{i,t} = \frac{\sigma_{i,t}}{\mu_{i,t}}$

Table 5.1   Coefficient of variation for the regions of UK and US

Coefficient of variation in per-capita personal income, US 1880–1950			
1880	1900	1919–1920	1949–1951
57.9	42.5	30.4	23.4
Coefficient of variation in per-capita regional income, UK 1949–1965			
1949–1950	1959–1960	1964–1965	
15.7	16.6	14.9	

Source: Easterlin (1958), Richardson (1973b)

Table 5.2   Empirical studies on σ-convergence using the coefficient of variation

Study	Time period	Main findings
Dunford (1993)	1960–85	convergence in 1970s, divergence in 1980s
Button and Pentecost (1995)	1977–90	convergence in 1970s, divergence in 1980s
Dunford and Smith (2000)	1980–96	divergence in 1980s and 1990s

two early studies for the regions of two leading economies, namely the USA by (Easterlin 1958) and the UK (Richardson 1973b).

During the interval 1880–1950 there was a convergence trend across the nine main regions of the USA (New England, Mid-Atlantic, excluding New York State, East-North Central, West-North Central, South Atlantic, East-South Central, West-South Central, Pacific and New York), as indicated by a progressive decline in the coefficient of variation. In the case of the ten UK regions, the coefficient of variation indicates a convergence trend only after 1960, although this is hardly confirmed given the short time period. Another important empirical application is that by Williamson (1965), in which the coefficient of variation is measured for regions within a wide range of countries. His analysis reveals a uniform pattern of widening regional disparities, referring to regions within countries, as countries reach higher levels of economic development,[2] until a peak is reached, at which point, the disparities start to diminish.[3] More recent studies of regions of individual countries or group of countries like the EU, using the coefficient of variation, reveal a mixed picture. For example, Dewhurst (1998) examining σ-convergence in UK regions using household income for the period 1984–1993, suggests that σ-convergence occurs during booms but not during slumps. Table 5.2 provides the

---

[2] According to the 'Williamson's Law', regional disparities are expected to stronger during the early phases of an integration process and they slowdown or even reverse as this process evolves (Camagni and Capello 2010).

[3] Fisch (1984), also, supports, and extends Williamson's argument, as by considering regional inequalities in terms of personal incomes across the US states in comparison to the national average.

main findings of some indicative empirical studies on σ-convergence, with respect to the regions of EU.

According to Dunford (1993, 1996) income differences among EU regions were in decline up to the mid-seventies. This phase of convergence was followed by a phase of divergence, which lasted up to the mid-eighties and as a result, regional differences reached the level of 1970 once again. Since the mid-eighties, regional differences have been stable, although there is some evidence that they may have increased at the beginning of the 1990s.[4] The decomposition of European regional inequalities into a cross-country and a within-country component shows the former declining, whereas the latter has risen significantly over the 1980s and the 1990s (Dunford and Smith 2000). Button and Pentecost (1995) also identify a trend towards regional convergence across the EU-9 over the period 1977–1990, using the coefficient of variation to measure σ-convergence. Other studies have used the standard deviation. Gripaios et al. (2000), for example, examine the tendencies of convergence across the UK counties using the standard deviation of GDP per capita. According to their results, the evolution of the standard deviation has not remained constant over the 1977–1995 period. In particular, there is an increase in standard deviation, i.e. divergence over the period 1977–1993 while a fall in the standard deviation is apparent after 1995, i.e. tendencies towards convergence.[5] The standard deviation and the coefficient of variation are usually used interchangeably in the empirical literature since, essentially, they are equivalent and lead to similar conclusions. However, if the actual size of deviation is of importance, then the standard deviation provides a clearer view, compared to the coefficient of variation, which is normalised by the mean of the observational units included in a data set. Nevertheless, it is important to note that both measures provide a crucial view on the issue of σ-convergence. Although simple and highly practical, the σ-convergence measure is very sensitive to the impact of random shocks and disturbances, which might occur within a time period and increase dispersion in the short run. Moreover, the standard deviation and the coefficient of variation are ultimately only descriptive statistics, which do not provide any information about the underlying mechanisms behind regional convergence or divergence. An alternative measure, which embodies the essence of the neoclassical convergence process, estimates whether, and at what rate, poor regions are catching up to rich regions; a process known as β-convergence.

---

[4] Tondl (1999) attributes this pattern to the fact that throughout the 1980s several less prosperous members have jointed the EU.

[5] Examining σ-convergence in terms of output per-capita across the EC regions over 1980–1989, Neven and Gouyette (1995) reach similar conclusions and argue that the 'northern' regions are more homogenous in term of per-capita output than the regions located in the 'south' of Europe. Fagerberg and Verspagen (1996) aptly note that over the period 1980–1990 the gap in per capita GDP between the richest and poorest EU region is roughly the same order as the difference between Germany and a developing country, such as Costa Rica or South Africa.

5.3 Absolute β-Convergence

The term 'β-convergence' is introduced by Barro and Sala-i-Martin (1992a) and it is now used generally to describe the situation of a 'poor' economy exhibiting a tendency to grow faster than a 'rich' economy; 'monotone' convergence, as defined by Boldrin and Rustichini (1994). There are many empirical studies based on the measurement of β-convergence (e.g. Ferreira 2000; Goddard and Wilson 2001; Cunado et al. 2003; Kangasharju 1998; Mulder and de Groot 2007). Absolute β-convergence is identified as an inverse relationship between the growth rate during a given time period and the initial level of per-capita income (e.g. Baumol 1986, 1988; Barro 1991) leading eventually to the equalisation of per capita output across economies. This absolute β-convergence reflects the neoclassical argument that poor economies (nations or regions) with a higher marginal product of capital, will attract capital inflows and hence will grow faster than rich economies, where the marginal product of capital is lower. As discussed in Chap. 2, this difference in growth rates allows poor economies to 'catch up' to rich economies. This framework not only provides another practical approach to the measurement of convergence but also an expression for the speed at which convergence takes place. The process of catching up through transitional dynamics has been analysed more fully in Chap. 2 so that, in this section, the focus is primarily upon the empirical measurement of β-convergence.

5.3.1 The Measurement of β-Convergence

Although the early 'seeds' of the convergence issue can be found in Kuznets (1955, 1964), Rostow (1960), Gerschenkron (1962) and Gomulka (1971), all of which recognise how backward countries tend to grow faster than rich countries, the first statistical test of the hypothesis that poor economies will catch up with rich economies is found in Baumol (1986), generally regarded as a major contribution to the convergence debate.[6] In this paper Baumol (1986) examines the hypothesis of β-convergence, by means of the regression equation, which as shown in the Appendix I, can be obtained from the standard neoclassical model:

$$g_i = a + by_{i,0} + \varepsilon_i \tag{5.1}$$

---

[6] An interest in convergence can also be found to the writings of 'classical' economists, such as Ricardo, Marx and Malthus. In particular, for Ricardo the process of growth leads to convergence due to decreasing returns in agriculture and no institutional or technological change. Conversely, Marx and Malthus argue that growth exaggerates an already established unevenness leading to divergence. A more detailed discussion can be found in Boyer (1997).

where $y_{i,0}$ is the natural logarithm of output per-worker at some initial time for the ith economy, a is the constant term,[7] b is the convergence coefficient and ε_i is the random error term.[8] If the growth of output per-worker $(Y_{i,T})$ is represented as $Y_{i,T} = e^{g_i} Y_{i,0}$, then taking logarithms and solving for g_i, the growth rate over a period of time (g_i) is represented by $g_i = y_{i,T} - y_{i,0}$, where T is the terminal time.

The parameter b reflects the partial correlation between the growth rate and the initial level of output per-worker and its sign indicates whether economies, on average, are converging or not. The condition for convergence requires that the first derivative of Eq. 5.1 is negative. Thus:

$$\frac{\partial g_i}{\partial y_{i,0}} \equiv f'_{g_i, y_{i,0}} = b < 0 \qquad (5.2)$$

Romer (1996) describes perfect convergence as occurring when $b = -1$ while at the other extreme, a value of zero indicates that the economies included in the data set may even exhibit divergence. Alternatively, $b = 0$ implies $g_i = a$, which can be considered as an indication of an autonomous growth rate that maintains income differences across economies.

A distinction is made in the literature between the convergence coefficient b and the speed of convergence β. Following Barro and Sala-i-Martin (1992a) the convergence coefficient b may be expressed as follows:

$$b = -(1 - e^{-\beta T}) \qquad (5.3)$$

where T is the number of years included in the period of analysis. The term for $\beta = -\frac{\ln(b+1)}{T}$ indicates the speed at which economies approach the steady-state value of output per-worker over the given time period, i.e. the average rate of convergence.[9] If $b < 0$ then the parameter β will be positive and it follows that a higher β corresponds to more rapid convergence.[10]

In this context, Chatterji (1992, p.59) separates convergence into two categories: weak and strong convergence. In particular, Chatterji (1992) considers the following test for convergence: $\ln(Y_T/Y_0) = a + b_1 \ln Y_0$ and argues that weak convergence is associated with a value of b_1 less than zero while strong convergence exists in the case

---

[7] Barro and Sala-i-Martin (1995) claim that this term essentially represents the steady-state growth rate.

[8] The error term is assumed have zero mean and constant variance (uncorrelated with the initial level of output per-worker).

[9] The time at which output per-worker $(y_{i,t})$ is halfway between the value during the initial year and the 'steady-state' (y^*) satisfies the condition $e^{-\beta t} = \frac{1}{2}$. As T gets larger, the effect of the initial level of output per worker tends to decline.

[10] The convergence coefficient is bounded to the sign of β, implied by $\log(y_{i,t}) = (1 - e^{-\beta t}) \log(y^*) + e^{-\beta t} \log(y_{i,0})$.

where $-2 < b_1 < 0$.[11] Chatterji (1992) argues that the condition $b_1 < 0$ does not guarantee that economies will reach a steady-state where per-capita incomes are equalised, or that such a steady-state equilibrium exists. Alternatively, strong convergence is defined:

> [...] as requiring two conditions: first, the existence of a steady-state in which per capita real income is equalised; and secondly the presence of dynamic forces which in the long-run drive the world economy to this steady-state. (Chatterji 1992, p. 59)

In applying the test for β-convergence, Baumol (1986), exploits data provided by Maddison (1982), for 16 industrialised countries (United Kingdom, Australia, Netherlands, Belgium, Switzerland, Italy, Denmark, United States, France, Canada, Austria, Germany, Norway, Sweden, Finland, and Japan) over the period from 1870 to 1979. The estimate of b is very close to -1 indicating almost perfect convergence.

However, De Long (1988) regards these results as largely spurious, and identifies two major problems with respect to the data used; sample selection bias and measurement error. The argument for selection bias is that countries with long data series are generally those which are now the most industrialised. De Long (1988) points out that if more countries are included, particularly those that were at least as well off in 1870 but then fall behind, this then produces a lower rate of convergence. De Long (1988) adds seven new countries (New Zealand, East Germany, Ireland, Portugal, Spain, Argentina and Chile) in Baumol's sample and estimates a lower value for b (-0.566). Dowrick and Nguyen (1989) also point out that ex-ante and ex-post selection biases are present. The former occurs when economies with remarkable or exceptional growth rates are included. Such 'growth miracle' economies[12] may bias the results towards acceptance of the convergence hypothesis. Ex-post selection bias derives from the inclusion of economies that, ex-post, had higher rates of growth, whilst those that experienced high rates of growth at the beginning of the period but not at the end are excluded. In this case also there is a selection bias in favour of accepting the hypothesis of convergence. The second problem identified by De Long is measurement error. Estimates of output per-worker in 1870 are imprecise and it might be argued that such imprecision generates a bias towards accepting the convergence hypothesis. If income for 1870 is overstated, then growth over the period 1870–1979 is likely to be understated by an equal amount, and when 1870 income is understated, the reverse occurs. Thus, measured growth will tend to be lower in countries with higher measured initial income even if there is no relation between actual (i.e. true) growth and actual initial income.

---

[11] Reconciling b_1 with the expression in Eq. 5.3 involves substitution of the absolute value of b_1 into the expression for the rate of convergence (β).

[12] A notable example of a 'growth miracle' consists of the Japanese economy during the post-war era and some South East Asian economies during the 1980s and early 1990s.

The studies discussed so far are all concerned with the performance of national economies, which gives rise to the problem of sample selection when there is no clear rationale for including or excluding particular countries. However, when Baumol's technique for identifying β-convergence is applied to the regional context, the sample selection problem is far less acute.

5.3.2   Absolute β-convergence at the Regional Level

Empirical literature on regional convergence is extensive. The vast majority are concentrated on the USA (e.g. Austin and Schmidt 1998; Crikfield and Panggabean 1995; Drennan and Lobo 1999; Partridge 2005), but there are also many studies of the EU regions (e.g. Paci 1997; Ezcurra and Rapun 2006; Petracos and Artelaris 2009) in addition to 'within country' studies (e.g. Italy: Mauro 2004; Mauro and Podrecca 1994; Ireland: Birnie and Hitchens 1998; O'Leary 1997, 2001; South Korea: Dollar 1991; Germany: Keller 2000; Australia: Cashin and Strappazzon 1998; Canada: Coulombe 2000; Spain: Cuadrado-Roura et al. 1999; de la Fuente 2002; Marchante and Ortega 2006; Mexico: Chiquiar 2005).

Table 5.3 reports the estimated values for the speed of convergence (β) using Eq. 5.1 taken from a panel of indicative empirical studies. A value for the β coefficient which is positive but less than one is an indication of absolute regional convergence.[13] The results in Table 5.3, therefore, do appear to support the convergence predictions of the neoclassical model.

For example, in the much cited studies by Barro and Sala-i-Martin (1991, 1992b), Sala-i-Martin (1994, 1996a, b) the speed of convergence is estimated using data for per-capita GDP across the regions of the United States, Canada, Japan, Germany, UK, France, Italy and Spain. Thus, on the basis of these results Sala-i-Martin (1996a) concludes that for both regional and national economies:

> [...] the estimated speeds of convergence are so surprisingly similar across data sets, that we can use a mnemonic rule: *economies converge at a speed of about two percent per year.* (p. 1326) [Emphasis in the original]

Empirical studies undertaken by other authors for the same data set, but for different time periods, reveal similar results (for example, Coulombe and Lee 1995 and Mila and Marimon 1999).

Other studies have revealed slower rates of convergence. Using per-capita GDP of the Greek NUTS-2 regions over the period 1971–1996, Siriopoulos and Asteriou (1998) report an extremely slow rate of absolute convergence (0.1 %). On the other hand, at the prefecture level (NUTS-3) Benos and Karagiannis (2008) estimate that the NUTS-3 regions of Greece converge at an average rate equal to 3.5% per year. A slow rate of regional convergence (0.3%) is also estimated by Abler and Das

---

[13] Arbia et al. (2008) note the absolute convergence model can be thought as an approximation of the original Solow-Swan model.

Table 5.3 Estimates of the speed of convergence: regional applications

Country	Time period	Estimated value of β	Study
USA	1880–1990	0.017	Sala-i-Martin (1996a)
EU[a]	1950–1990	0.015	Sala-i-Martin (1996a)
EU[a]	1950–1960	0.016	Armstrong (1995a)
EU[b]	1950–1990	0.019	Barro and Sala-i-Martin (1991)
EU[b]	1975–1992	0.009	Armstrong (1995a)
EU[b]	1975–1985	0.010	Button and Pentecost (1999)
EU[c]	1975–1998	0.007	Martin (2001)
EU[b]	1975–2000	0.009	Le Gallo and Dall' erba (2008)
UK	1950–1990	0.030	Sala-i-Martin (1996a)
France	1950–1990	0.016	Sala-i-Martin (1996a)
Italy	1950–1990	0.010	Sala-i-Martin (1996a)
Japan	1930–1987	0.034	Barro and Sala-i-Martin (1992a)
Japan	1955–1990	0.019	Sala-i-Martin (1996a)
Canada	1961–1991	0.024	Coulombe and Lee (1995)
Sweden	1911–1993	0.023	Persson (1997)
Germany	1970–1994	0.006	Funke and Strulik (1999)
Austria	1961–1986	0.010	Hofer and Wörgötter (1997)
Australasia	1861–1991	0.029	Cashin (1995)
Finland	1934–1993	0.020	Kangasharju (1999)
Greece[b]	1971–1996	0.001	Siriopoulos and Asteriou (1998)
Greece[d]	1971–2003	0.035	Benos and Karagiannis (2008)
Spain	1981–1991	0.024	Mila and Marimon (1999)
India	1961–1991	0.003	Abler and Das (1998)
Mexico	1970–1980	0.006	Mallick and Carayannis (1994)

NUTS Nomenclature des Unités Territorial les Statistiques
Notes: [a]NUTS-1 Level [b]NUTS-2 Level [c]EU-16 (Regions of 15 European countries plus Norway), [d]NUTS-3 Level

(1998) for India. Funke and Strulik (1999) note that the gap of per-capita GDP across German regions has narrowed, but only at 0.6% per year while Hofer and Wörgötter (1997) estimate a rate of convergence for 84 districts in Austria of about 1%. These results contrast with a higher rate of convergence of 3% estimated by Cashin (1995) for the Australian colonies and 2.3% by Persson (1997) for Sweden.[14] Results are also sensitive to the convergence variable employed. The studies noted above have all been carried out using per-capita GDP which measures

---

[14] It is worthy of note that Persson (1997) identifies a weakness of most empirical studies concerning regional convergence in that data on regional per-capita income or output are often of poor quality and not adjusted for differences in the cost of living across regions; a technique which would permit comparisons of 'real' living standards across observational units. When such an adjustment is made, Persson (1997) finds stronger and more robust evidence on regional convergence across Swedish counties. The estimated convergence coefficient indicates a rate of 4% per year, which is almost double that obtained using unadjusted data (2.3%). This conclusion does tend to suggest that such 'real' comparisons are important.

the standard of living.[15] However, some studies investigate convergence in terms of productivity. Estimation of Eq. 5.1 using this variable has tended to produce, not surprisingly, different rates of convergence. In particular, for 90 regions of the EU, Sala-i-Martin (1996a) derives a convergence rate of 1.5% per year during the period 1950–1990, which is very close to the estimate of 1.6% in Armstrong (1995). Furthermore, in a report for the European Commission, Armstrong (1995b) analyses the pattern of convergence for both the NUTS-1 and NUTS-2 regions and suggests a varying pattern of regional convergence over time. In particular, between 1950 and 1960 EU regions converged at a rate of 1.2% but this increased during the 1970s to 2.5%. However, the pace of convergence slowed down again in the period 1975–1993, following the various phases of EU enlargement, to an average of 0.6% per year. Other studies, however, revealed a faster rate of convergence, close to Barro and Sala-i-Martin's 'stylised fact' of 2% per annum. Using data for the regions of the EU-12 countries, Tondl (1999) reports an average rate of convergence about 2% for the period 1950–1960 and a faster rate for the subsequent decade (about 3%).

In summary, it is evident that the empirical literature on regional convergence has made significant use of the concepts of σ and β-convergence. As Carree et al. (2000) aptly note:

> [. . .] a first choice a researcher is confronted with is whether to consider σ or β-convergence (p. 338)

However, σ and β-convergence are conceptually different. Sala-i-Martin (1996a) argues that σ-convergence examines how the distribution of income evolves over time while β-convergence considers the mobility of income within the same distribution, by seeking to establish whether poor economies grow faster.

Critics of β-convergence, such as Friedman (1992) and Cheshire and Magrini (2000), argue that β-convergence is a weak criterion due to the fact that it is a 'regression towards the mean' and that an unbiased index for convergence would be the shrinking over time of the variance of per-capita income.[16] Thus, Friedman (1992) claims that an unbiased estimate of β-convergence can be obtained by using the trend in the coefficient of variation. As a response to these criticisms, Barro and Sala-i-Martin (1995) argue that σ-convergence is a sufficient but not necessary condition for β-convergence, in the sense that σ-convergence may be constant over a period of time while the rankings of individual economies change, implying

---

[15] Other studies use the level of regional income (e.g. Doyle and O'Leary 1999; Cheshire and Magrini 2000, regional wages (Mora et al. 2005), regional welfare inequalities (e.g. Álvarez-Garcia et al. 2004; Ezcurra et al. 2005) or specific aspects of regional economies, such as manufacturing (e.g. Pascual and Westermann 2002; Gugler and Pfaffermayr 2004), regional agriculture productivity (e.g. Alexiadis and Alexandrakis 2008) and the wages in the agricultural sector (Tavernier and Temel 1997). Bassino (2006) examines σ and β convergence in terms of the height and health stature of the population across the prefectures of Japan.

[16] See also Quah (1993), Bliss (1999, 2000), Cannon and Duck (2000).

β-convergence.[17] Boyle and McCarthy (1997, 1999) propose a methodology to test for β-convergence that overcomes these difficulties. This methodology implements a Kendall's measure of rank concordance in conjunction with a measure of σ-convergence and is known as γ-convergence. Gripaios et al. (2000) and Bishop and Gripaios (2004) apply this measure of convergence across the counties of Great Britain between 1977 and 1995 and conclude that there is a notable north–south divide with the existence of γ-convergence in the northern counties over the 1990s.

It is clear, however, that σ and β convergence measures have their limitations; tests for σ-convergence rely on simple descriptive statistics, whilst the absolute β-convergence test, described thus far, omits a number of important factors, as will be seen in the following section.

5.4 Conditional and Spatial Convergence

Absolute convergence occurs when all economies converge to the same steady-state. Suppose, however, that different economies (or groups of economies) converge towards different steady-states. As discussed in Chap. 1 this outcome is described as conditional convergence. If different economies have different technological and behavioural parameters (such as different propensities to save or rates of population growth), then convergence is conditional on these parameters, giving rise to different steady states.

5.4.1 Empirical Tests for Conditional Convergence

The empirical test for conditional convergence derives from the key work of Mankiw et al. (1992), who test the neoclassical model in its standard and augmented version. As noted in Sect. 2.3.2 of Chap. 2, the 'augmented Solow' model implies that differences in the proportion of output invested in physical and human capital accumulation, lead to different levels of output per worker on the balanced growth path, which persist through time. This leads Mankiw et al. (1992) to provide a formal test of conditional convergence by introducing differences in human capital.

However, the most frequently used test for conditional convergence has been put forward by Barro and Sala-i-Martin (1992a), which is based upon the argument that different regional characteristics will lead to different steady-states. Thus, a range of regional structural characteristics are incorporated into the framework of Eq. 5.1, as follows:

---

[17] For a more detailed analysis of the relation between β and σ-convergence, see Furceri (2005).

$$g_i = a + b_1 y_{i,0} + b_2 \mathbf{X_i} + \varepsilon_i \tag{5.4}$$

where $\mathbf{X_i}$ represents a vector of variables to control for differences across regions.

Absolute (unconditional) convergence is signalised by $b_1 < 0$ and $b_2 = 0$ while conditional convergence depends upon $b_1 < 0$ and $b_2 \neq 0$.[18] Having selected appropriate variables to represent the institutional, structural, preference and environmental variables that characterise the steady-state value of per-capita income it remains the case that convergence is said to be occurring when higher initial levels of per-capita income are associated with lower rates of growth, over a given time period.[19]

Obviously, the particular variables that are included in vector $\mathbf{X_i}$ are of critical significance. In the empirical literature on regional conditional convergence (e.g. Gouyette and Perelman 1997; Boltho et al. 1999; Dobson and Ramlogan 2002) the variables used most frequently to distinguish regional characteristics include investment ratios, population growth and measures of human capital. Thus, several empirical studies approximate human capital in terms of school enrolment rates, number of students with high school or university degrees, etc. (e.g. Albelo 1999; Barro 1997; Barro and Lee 1993; Benhabib and Spiegel 1994; de la Fuente and Vives 1995). Other studies use institutional innovations, such as the creation of custom unions, fiscal and monetary characteristics, such as the public sector's share of GDP or tax policy (Yamarik 2000), macroeconomic characteristics, (e.g. monetary shocks, variability of inflation, the sectoral composition of regional GDP[20]), or variables related to regional and development policies in the EU,[21] such as the European Structural Funds (Rodríguez-Pose and Fratesi 2004).

---

[18] Sala-i-Martin (1996a) claims that the conditional convergence and the absolute convergence hypotheses coincide, only if economies have the same steady-state. Furthermore, he claims that if the study of convergence is restricted to selected sets of economies, then the hypothesis of similar steady-states is apparent.

[19] Martin and Sunley (1998) propose an alternative way to test for conditional convergence. According to their method, the analysis of convergence is restricted to sets of economies for which the assumption of similar structural characteristics or 'fundamentals' is not unrealistic. Thus, similar economies (countries or regions) should exhibit absolute β-convergence.

[20] Button and Pentecost (1995), for example, use the share of agriculture in order to capture two factors. First, the differences in the composition and the structure of economic activities across the EU regions and second the impact of transfer payment through the CAP.

[21] Development policies have become after the CAP the second largest policy area in the EU. In budgetary terms, development policies have grown from a mere 10% of the European Community's budget and 0.09% of the EU-15 in 1980 to more than one-third of the budget and about 0.37% of the EU GDP, on average, in the period 1988–2001.

5.4.2   *Spatial Dependence and Regional Convergence*

It has been argued, particularly in the case of regional economies, that spatial characteristics are significant in determining patterns of economic development and hence in contributing to any convergence mechanisms. The location of a region within a system of regional economies is a unique characteristic, and in the same way as other structural characteristics, has the potential to impact on growth and development. Martin and Sunley (1998) claim that in the majority of empirical studies regions are treated as 'isolated islands' with no explicit recognition of interaction between economies. Such treatment tends to overlook the fact that regions are not dimensionless points but vital functional parts of an inter-dependent system of regional economies. Several authors (e.g. Quah 1993a; 1996a; 1996b) have claimed that models of regional convergence only relate a region's growth to its own history, and not to the interregional system of which it is a part. As Martin and Sunley (1998) argue:

> [...] the growth trend of a region may actually depended crucially (either positively or negatively) on the growth *trajectories* of others. (p. 207) [Emphasis added]

This economic inter-dependence is partly a function of spatial inter-dependence. As discussed in previous chapters, the processes underlying regional convergence depend upon the relative extent of mechanisms such as factor mobility, price flexibility and knowledge or technology spillovers. Where such mechanisms exist, they are likely to be enhanced, rather than reduced, by spatial proximity. Although the impact of spatial factors on the process of regional economic development in general has long been recognised,[22] Rey and Montouri (1999) point out that this has often been ignored in the literature on regional convergence. According to Rey and Montouri (1999) a 'conventional' model of convergence, when applied in a regional context, is misspecified if it does not take any account of geographical factors, because the presence of spatial autocorrelation is more intense at the regional level. Lopez-Bazo et al. (2004) aptly note that

> Economies interact with each other and, in the case of regional economies, linkages are assumed to be stronger than across heterogeneous countries. (p. 43)

Indeed, regions are more open compared to national economies, and it might reasonably be expected that economic interactions, such as trading relations, labour movements or technology spillovers, will be stronger with neighbouring regions. More recently, however, there have been a number of studies examining the process of regional convergence from a spatial econometric perspective in various regional contexts, for example the regions of Europe (e.g. Fingleton 2001; Carrington 2003;

---

[22] Early studies on spatial econometrics include Douglas-Carrol (1955), Fisher (1971), Hordijk (1974), Paelnick (1978), Steinnes (1980), Bennett and Hordijk (1986). For a more updated analysis of spatial econometrics see Kelejian and Prucha (2002), Dubin (2003), Saaverda (2003) and Arbia (2006).

Basile 2008) or the regions of individual countries, (e.g. USA: Dobkins and Ioannidis 2001; Lall and Yilmaz 2001; UK: Roberts 2004; Turkey: Gezici and Hewings 2004; Spain: Villaverde 2005).[23] Spatial dependence can be incorporated into convergence analysis, through three econometric models (Rey and Montouri 1999), namely the spatial error, the spatial lag and the spatial cross-regressive models. Building upon the β-convergence model of Eq. 5.1, the first of these, the spatial error model, assumes that any effects from spatial interaction are captured in the error term. Thus the usual assumption of independent error terms is abandoned, which is not implausible given the fact that regions, as previously noted, are typically very open economies exhibiting a high degree of interaction with their neighbours. Following Rey and Montouri (1999), therefore, the error term incorporating spatial dependence is shown as follows:

$$\varepsilon_t = \zeta \mathbf{W}\varepsilon_t + u_t = (\mathbf{I} - \zeta \mathbf{W})^{-1} u_t \tag{5.5}$$

where $\mathbf{W}$ is a spatial weights matrix and u_t is the new, spatially correlated, error term.[24]

In Eq. 5.5 ζ is a scalar spatial error coefficient to be estimated. If $\zeta = 0$, then there is no spatial correlation in the error terms and the model reduces to the usual model of absolute convergence. A pattern of spatial dependence is detected if $\zeta \neq 0$.

The spatial links between regions are generated by means of a spatial-weights matrix $\mathbf{W}$, the elements of which (w) may be devised in various ways. For example, a common practice is to allow these weights to take the value of 1 if a region is contiguous to another and 0 otherwise (a binary connectivity matrix). Alternatively, the spatial weights may be continuous variables, constructed so as to produce declining weights as distance between regions increases, as follows:

$$w_{ij} = \frac{1/d_{ij}}{\sum_j 1/d_{ij}} \tag{5.6}$$

Here, d_{ij} denotes the distance between two regions i and j. The denominator is the sum of the (inverse) distances from all regions surrounding region i, within a selected boundary. Equation 5.6 implies that interaction effects decay as the distance from one area to another increases (weights decline as distance increases).

It is therefore possible to introduce spatial interaction into the conventional test for absolute convergence by substituting the error term of Eq. 5.5, into Eq. 5.1. Thus,

---

[23] The studies by Bernat (1996), Novell and Viladecans-Marsal (1999), Beardsell and Henderson (1999) are also relevant, although they refer to a context other than regional convergence. For a more detailed review on the empirics of spatial growth and convergence, see Fingleton (2000), Rey and Janikas (2005), Abreu et al. (2005).

[24] $u \sim N(0, \sigma^2 I)$. For a more detailed analysis of the econometric treatment of spatial error terms see Anselin and Moreno (2003).

$$\mathbf{g_i} = a + b\mathbf{y_{i,0}} + (\mathbf{I} - \zeta\mathbf{W})^{-1}u_t \tag{5.7}$$

where $\mathbf{W}$ is the $n \times n$ matrix of distance weights.

The interpretation of this model is that regions constitute a linked network such that the effects of a random shock on the growth rate of any one region will disperse beyond that region's boundaries, impacting upon growth in surrounding regions and, beyond. Such spillover effects will ripple throughout the national economy, their size and distribution determined by the elements of the spatial transformation matrix $(\mathbf{I} - \zeta\mathbf{W})^{-1}$. In this light, therefore, a region is not an independent unit (or 'isolated island') but is a member of an interconnected system of regions. Nevertheless, the test for convergence remains the same, that is, a negative relationship between growth and starting levels of output per-worker ($b < 0$), implies that converging regions are moving towards the same steady state. An alternative approach to spatial interaction, according to Rey and Montouri (1999), is to introduce the spatial weights matrix directly, either via regional growth rates or starting levels of output per-worker. Adopting the former strategy leads to the spatial lag model shown below:

$$\mathbf{g_i} = a + b\mathbf{y_{i,0}} + \rho(\mathbf{Wg_i}) + \varepsilon_i \text{ with } \varepsilon_i \sim N(0, \sigma^2) \tag{5.8}$$

where ρ is a scalar autoregressive parameter to be estimated. Thus, a region's growth depends not only upon its initial level of output per-worker as before, but is also directly linked to growth in surrounding regions, with the relative extent of these linkages determined by the spatial weights matrix. Consequently, the significance of any spillover effects arising from spatial interaction is encapsulated in the parameter ρ.

Rey and Montouri (1999) present two interpretations of Eq. 5.8. The filtering perspective focuses on the convergence pattern, i.e. the relationship between growth and initial output per-worker, after the spatial effect has been incorporated. Formally, this can be expressed in terms of the following equation:

$$(\mathbf{I} - \rho\mathbf{W})\mathbf{g_i} = a + b\mathbf{y_{i,0}} + \varepsilon_i \tag{5.9}$$

The second interpretation focuses on the expected value of the growth rate, which may be expressed as follows:

$$E(\mathbf{g_i}) = E(\mathbf{I} - \rho\mathbf{W})^{-1}(a + b\mathbf{y_{i,0}}) + E[(\mathbf{I} - \rho\mathbf{W})^{-1}u_i] \tag{5.10}$$

According to Eq. 5.10, the expected value of the growth rate in a region is related to both its initial level of output per-worker and to the initial output per worker of the surrounding regions via the spatial weights matrix. Also, as in the spatial error model, using $\varepsilon_i = (\mathbf{I} - \zeta\mathbf{W})^{-1}u_i$, although the expected value of the error term is zero, any non-zero shock to a given region will, nevertheless, have impacts on surrounding regions through the data generating process (Rey and Montouri 1999).

Nevertheless, it is important to note that the estimated coefficients in the spatial lag model include only the direct marginal effect of an increase in the explanatory variables, excluding all indirect induced effects.[25] The coefficients obtained by Ordinary Least Squares (OLS) represent the total marginal effect. Consequently, it is incorrect to compare the coefficients of a spatial lag model with the coefficients from spatial error estimates or from an OLS (Arbia et al. 2008).

Finally, the spatial cross-regressive model shows a region's growth as dependent upon its initial output per-worker, and output per-worker of other regions in the system:

$$\mathbf{g_i} = a + b\mathbf{y_{i,0}} + c(\mathbf{Wy_{i,0}}) + \varepsilon_i \qquad (5.11)$$

Thus, the effects of any spatial interaction flow purely from the spatial pattern associated with the initial conditions in output per-worker. An interesting issue that emerges from the discussion of the three spatial econometric models regards the sign of the spatial coefficients. Although in the empirical literature this is not a specific concern, nevertheless both 'positive' and 'negative' spillover effects are possible. More specifically, if growth in one region is enhanced by proximity to another successful region then a positive sign is expected for the coefficients ζ, ρ and c in Eqs. 5.7, 5.8 and 5.11, respectively. On the other hand, a negative sign may be considered as an indication that successful regions may be growing at the expense of the surrounding regions. However, this is ultimately an empirical issue, dependent upon particular circumstances. The three spatial econometric models represent an approach to testing for β-convergence,[26] that is conditional upon the spatial distribution of regions and this will be examined more fully in Chaps. 6 and 7 in the context of the European NUTS-2 regions.

5.5 Club Convergence: Empirical Tests

Notwithstanding the substantial differences, Fischer and Stirböck (2006) claim that it is not easy to distinguish empirically club from conditional convergence. Consequently, in the relevant literature several different empirical approaches have been suggested. As Chap. 4 explains, one possibility involves identification of multiple

---

[25] The spatial lag model can be written equivalently as $\mathbf{g_i} = (\mathbf{I} - \rho\mathbf{W})^{-1}(b\mathbf{X}_i + \varepsilon_i)$, where $\mathbf{X}_i$ is an $(n \times 2)$ vector containing the constant term and the observations of the initial per-capita income. Given that $(\mathbf{I} - \rho\mathbf{W})^{-1} = \mathbf{I} + \rho W + \rho^2 W^2 + \rho^3 W^3 + \ldots$, then the growth rate in a region is affected by a marginal change in the explanatory variable in this region and by marginal changes in the explanatory variables in the remaining regions.

[26] There is also an alternative approach using Bayesian methods (e.g. Ertur et al. 2007; Arbia et al. 2008). This method tackles with problems due to heteroscedasticity and outliers from 'enclave effects', i.e. where a particular observation exhibits divergent behaviour from nearby observations.

equilibria, which can emerge using models that implement statistical techniques, such as Markov chain models, to estimate the evolution of income distribution, developed by Quah (1993a; 1996a; b; c; 1997). Markov chain models estimate the movement of income distributions over time, allowing an analysis of changes in the intra-distribution dynamics and the shape of the distribution. However, this approach is sensitive to the choice of the intervals by which income is classified, which may bias the Markov properties.[27]

Nevertheless, this approach constitutes a useful descriptive tool and has been used extensively in recent empirical studies. For example, Fingleton (1997), Fischer and Stumpner (2008) and Webber (2002) use this approach to test for clustering across the EU regions in terms of per-capita incomes and labour rewards, respectively. More detailed studies have been undertaken for individual countries, e.g. US (Yamamoto 2008), Finland (Pekkala 2000), Greece (Tsionas 2002), Spain (Salinas-Jiménez 2003; Tortosa-Ausina et al. 2005), Russia (Carluer 2005), Brazil (Andrade et al. 2004), Japan (Kakamu and Fukushige 2006) and UK (Bishop and Gripaios 2006).

However, as previously stated Baumol (1986) introduced the concept of club convergence in order to describe an empirical fact, which was the existence of only a subset of national economies within the world economy which exhibited β-convergence. Nevertheless, in the relevant literature, two formal empirical tests for club convergence have since been put forward. The first derives from the work of Baumol and Wolff (1988) while the second from Chatterji (1992). These tests are examined in the following sections.

5.5.1   Club Convergence tests: Baumol and Wolff (1988)

Baumol and Wolff (1988) reformulate the test for absolute convergence using the following model:

$$g_i = a + b_1 y_{i,0} + b_2 y_{i,0}^2 \qquad (5.12)$$

This quadratic function allows for non-linearities and is illustrated in Fig. 5.1. It is drawn on the assumption that b_1 is positive and b_2 negative, which are the conditions required for the existence of a convergence club.

---

[27] One way to avoid this problem is by estimating a stochastic kernel, which can be regarded as a continuous version of the transition probability matrix. Nevertheless, Neven and Gouyette (1995) show that using the measures of σ-convergence (e.g. coefficient of variation), β-convergence and Markov-chain (movements-matrix) produce consistent results.

Fig. 5.1 A convergence club

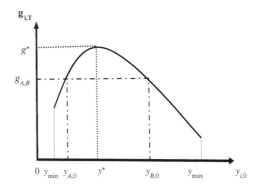

Growth reaches a maximum when

$$\frac{\partial g_i}{\partial (y_{i,0})} = b_1 + 2b_2(y_{i,0}) = 0 \tag{5.13}$$

Solving Eq. 5.13 for $y_{i,0}$ yields

$$y^* = \frac{-b_1}{2b_2} \tag{5.14}$$

where y^* is the level of output per-worker that corresponds to maximum growth.

It is this turning point which is used to identify members of the convergence club. For economies with an initial level of output per-worker in excess of the threshold y^*, growth is inversely related to the initial level of output per-worker. It may therefore be argued that these economies constitute a 'convergence club' by exhibiting β-convergence. The opposite holds for economies where output per-worker lies below y^*. In this case, growth is positively related to initial output per-worker (provided that $b_1 > 0$ of course). It follows, therefore, that the initial conditions, as expressed in terms of output per-worker, of the member-economies in the 'convergence club' are likely to be similar (Feve and lePen 2000). In other words, a convergence club is unlikely to consist of economies with markedly different levels of output per-worker levels; all must lie within a range that is equal to, or above, the threshold value y^*.

The following example is illustrative. Consider two regions, A and B, each exhibiting identical growth rates $(g_{A,T} = g_{B,T})$ with $y_{A,0} - y^* < 0$ and $y_{B,0} - y^* > 0$, implying that $y_{A,0} - y_{B,0} < 0$. If regions A and B continue to grow at the same rate, i.e. if $(g_{A,T} - g_{B,T})_{\tau} = 0$, then $(y_A - y_B)_{\tau} < 0$ as $\tau \to \infty$. Region A, therefore, is unable to close the gap with region B. Convergence between these two regions is feasible only if $(g_{A,T} - g_{B,T})_{\tau} > 0$, as $\tau \to \infty$. In this context it is reasonable to assume that the rates of convergence will differ between the regions included in a convergence-club and the regions excluded from the club, i.e. $\beta_c - \beta_{nc} \neq 0$. Given that $f'_{g_{i,T}y_{i,0}} < 0$ implies β-convergence, then the regions in the club will exhibit a rate of convergence faster compare to the regions excluded from the club, i.e. $\beta_c - \beta_{nc} > 0$; a condition in accordance with the view on club convergence put forward by Fischer and Stirböck (2006).

A relatively high (low) level of initial labour productivity, defined as $y^* - y_{i,0} < 0$ ($y^* - y_{i,0} > 0$), ensures β-convergence (divergence). Once this knowledge is introduced, it comes as no surprise that the initial conditions, as expressed in terms of labour productivity, determine the composition of the convergence-club. Stated in alternative terms, a convergence-club is unlikely to consist of regions with markedly different levels of labour productivity; all must lie within a range that is equal to, or above, the *threshold* value y^*, i.e. $y_{i,0} - y^* \geq 0$. A pattern of club-convergence can be attributed not only to conditions related to the initial level of labour productivity, that is to say initial economic conditions, but also to certain structural characteristics. These characteristics can be conceived as '*threshold conditions*' that determine the composition of a convergence-club.

5.5.2   Club Convergence Tests: Chatterji (1992)

The above approach to club convergence is based on the now familiar definition of β-convergence. There is a particular problem associated with this definition, however. As Chatterji (1992) notes, there is no guarantee that the variance of per-capita income will be lower at the end of the period than at the beginning. Inequality is not necessarily reduced and the absolute gap between two economies can be higher at the end of the period than at the beginning, despite the existence of the negative relation between growth and initial level of per-capita income. Chatterji (1992) addresses these difficulties in the analysis of convergence by focusing not upon levels of output per-worker, but upon differences in levels, or gaps, with respect to a leading economy. A process of convergence, therefore, implies that such differences diminish over time. Implicit in this argument is that the 'steady-state' (convergence point) is approximated by the output per-worker of the leading economy.

Building on the general framework introduced by Baumol (1986) as the basis for their analysis, Chatterji and Dewhurst (1996) employ the technology gap concept from the diffusion model of Chatterji (1992). Thus, Eq. 5.1 is retained but the emphasis is placed upon the gaps in output per-worker between a leading region and all other regions. Thus,

$$y_{L,T} - y_{L,0} = \alpha + b y_{L,0} \qquad (5.15)$$

where the subscript L refers to the leading region.

For the remaining regions:

$$y_{i,T} - y_{i,0} = \alpha + b y_{i,0} \qquad (5.16)$$

Subtracting Eq. 5.16 from Eq. 5.15 yields:

$$(y_{L,T} - y_{L,0}) - (y_{i,T} - y_{i,0}) = b(y_{L,0} - y_{i,0}) \tag{5.17}$$

Equation Eq. 5.17 is rearranged as follows:

$$(y_{L,T} - y_{i,T}) = (1 + b)(y_{L,0} - y_{i,0}) \tag{5.18}$$

Equation Eq. 5.18 can be written equivalently as follows:

$$G_{i,T} = \gamma G_{i,0} \tag{5.19}$$

where $\gamma = (1 + b)$ and G_i represents the gap in output per-worker between any region and the leading region.

Weak and strong convergence are also relevant in this context (Chatterji and Dewhurst 1996). Strong convergence requires that $-2 < b < 0$, i.e. $-1 < \gamma < 1$, and for the existence of weak convergence $\gamma < 1$, i.e. $b < 0$.

Very simply, the terminal gap is proportional to the size of the initial gap, and convergence is defined in general as a narrowing of the gap between any region and the leading region over the given time period. The presumption is that the same region remains the leading region at the initial and terminal times.

By including further powers of the initial gap $G_{i,0}$ as follows:

$$G_{i,T} = \sum_{k=1}^{K} \gamma_k (G_{i,0})^k \tag{5.20}$$

more than one convergence club can be identified. For example, the following non-linear specification of convergence clubs, is used by Armstrong (1995a) and Kangasharju (1999):

$$G_{i,T} = A_1(G_{i,0}) + A_2(G_{i,0})^2 + A_3(G_{i,0})^3 \tag{5.21}$$

This implies the existence of three equilibria where the initial gap is equal to the terminal gap, i.e. $G_i^e = G_{i,0} = G_{i,T}$. These points of equilibrium are the means by which regions are separated into groups, and the number and membership of convergence clubs identified.

In Fig. 5.2 below, the 45° line represents the equilibrium condition, and function Eq. 5.21 is represented by $0\ °C$ on the assumption that $A_1 < 1$ (Kangasharju 1999, p. 210).

Convergence clubs are determined using the principle that points above the 45° line indicate an initial gap lower than the terminal gap, clearly a case of divergence from the leading region during the time interval $[0, T]$. By similar reasoning, points below the 45° line are an indication of convergence. Therefore, those regional economies positioned in the range 0 to G_2^0 are converging towards the leading economy.

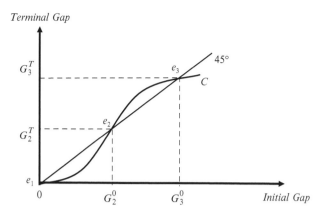

Fig. 5.2 Convergence clubs under the condition of $A_1 < 1$

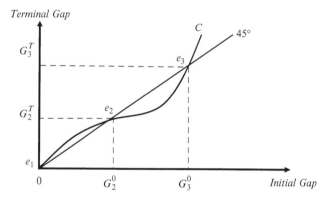

Fig. 5.3 Convergence clubs under the condition of $A_1 > 1$

On the other hand, the range from G_2^0 to G_3^0 contains economies which are diverging from the leader, but converging towards the point e_3. The very poorest economies with the highest initial gaps ($> G_3^0$) are improving their position but only towards the equilibrium point e_3 . Thus, there are two convergence clubs distinguished by the threshold gap of G_2^0 at the start of the time period. The first consists of richer economies that are converging towards the leading economy, with remaining economies converging towards a different 'lower' equilibrium.

A different scenario is shown in Fig. 5.3, which assumes the coefficient A_1 to be greater than one, i.e. a situation in which $b > 0$ (Kangasharju 1999, p.210).

Regions in the range $(0, G_2^0]$ now diverge from the leader, converging towards e_2 irrespective of a relatively low initial gap. Although regions in the range $[G_2^0, G_3^0]$ can be said to be catching up with the leader, this occurs only up to the equilibrium point e_2. Finally, all regions with initial gaps greater than G_3^0 are not only falling behind the leading region, but also all other regions. In this case, therefore, there is only one convergence club that includes all regions with an initial gap less than G_3^0. However, convergence is towards a level of output per-worker that is lower than that achieved by the leading economy, which retains its leading position. The only regions that could be said to demonstrate any form of catching-up are those in the range $[G_2^0, G_3^0]$ given that their gap is actually reduced over the time period. In this way, estimation of Eq. 5.21 permits the identification of sub-sets of economies for which convergence is apparent (i.e. convergence clubs). Essentially, this methodology relies on the existence of multiple equilibria, as discussed in Chap. 4.

Nevertheless, in this context an interesting question arises: are these two specifications of club convergence able to reflect the reality of circumstances? It is possible to approach this issue by examining the studies that test empirically Baumol and Wolff's (1988) and Chatterji's (1992) specification of convergence clubs.

5.5.3 Club Convergence: Empirical Evidence

The hypothesis of convergence clubs has been tested empirically for both world economies and for regions of individual countries. Chatterji (1992), for example, estimates Eq. 5.21 for a set of national economies over the period 1960–1985 using data provided by Heston and Summers (1984; 1988). The set of countries used in the empirical application excludes countries with populations of less than one million and also the oil producing countries, while the USA is taken to be the leading economy at both the initial and terminal times.

The outcome is similar to that shown in Fig. 5.2, suggesting the existence of two distinct clubs, one 'poor' and one 'rich'.[28] The approach by Chatterji (1992) has also been the subject of three major studies, as shown in Table 5.4.

Using Eq. 5.21, Armstrong (1995a) reports a pattern of divergence between the 'leading-region' (Ile de France) and the remaining regions of the EU, which are converging towards a lower equilibrium level, estimated to be 84% of the income level of the leading region in the period 1950–70 and only 66% in the subsequent period 1970–90. Chatterji and Dewhurst (1996), using Eq. 5.20 for different values of K, came to a similar conclusion for UK regions between 1977 and 1991. Greater London maintained a substantial per-capita income lead over the period 1977–1991, with the remaining counties of the UK converging towards a substantially lower equilibrium level. Finally, estimating Eq. 5.21 with data on incomes

---

[28] It is interesting to note that these conclusions are already familiar to development economists. Indeed, according to Nelson (1960) and Leibenstein (1957) some poor economies are 'stuck' in a 'low level equilibrium' (the poor 'club') or 'poverty trap' and a 'big push' is required in order to achieve high levels of per-capita income. Moreover, Nelson (1956) argues that even if production techniques are not improved and even in the absence of a massive investment, the 'trap' may still be escaped if the socio-political environment is favourable. A similar argument can be found in Folloni (2009).

Table 5.4 Convergence clubs: major regional studies

	Number of regions	Leading region	Time period	Clubs
Armstrong (1995a)	85 EU regions	Ile-de-France	1950–1970 1970–1990	Leading region & remaining regions
Chatterji and Dewhurst (1996)	61 UK counties	Greater London	1977–1991	Leading region & remaining regions
Kangasharju (1999)	88 Finish regions	Helsinki	1934–1990	One single club

accruing from personal, industrial and property activities, Kangasharju (1999) concludes that all Finnish regions constitute a single convergence club with the process of catching up increasing in proportion to size of the initial gap. In the case of Finnish regions, there is no evidence of multiple equilibria, and hence to a 'superior' or 'inferior' club. Kangasharju (1999) attributes this uniform pattern of regional convergence to the fast diffusion of technology and innovation across Finland.

The three regional empirical studies reviewed above are attempts to establish the existence of convergence clubs using the methodology of Chatterji (1992), which is based upon the concept of 'technology-income' gap. However, as the results show the technique has succeeded in separating the leading region from all other regions in two instances, but has not identified any further convergence clubs. Chatterji's (1992) technique is 'capable' of identifying several convergence clubs; the fact that it does not do so in the empirical studies may be attributable to the technique, but may also reflect the reality of circumstances. On the other hand, the methodology of Baumol and Wolff has not been tested empirically, as a means of detecting a regional convergence club.[29]

5.5.4 Cross-Section Analysis: Implications for Convergence

The tests for β-convergence and for convergence clubs outlined thus far are essentially cross-sectional techniques, in that the performance of a number of regional or national economies over a particular time period is examined, and only data at the start and end of the time period are required.[30]

A number of issues are associated with the implementation of this cross-section approach. A possible source of bias, particularly relevant at the international level,

---

[29] The study by Leonida et al. (2003) employs the quadratic specification in the context of Italian regions, but does not addresses the issue of a convergence club directly.

[30] Several studies (e.g. Soukiazis and Castro 2005; Badinger et al. 2004; Evans and Karras 1996a; Lee et al. 1998) implement panel data, which allow for time-varying and country-specific steady states.

concerns the selection of economies for analysis, as already discussed in Sect. 5.2, which may bias the results towards acceptance of the β-convergence hypothesis. It may be argued that this form of selection bias is virtually non-existent in empirical studies of regional convergence since, normally, such studies use data for all regions within a country and sample selection is not an issue. Nevertheless, there are circumstances in which a similar problem of selection bias might be identified at the regional level, for example, when testing for convergence between regions from a selected set of countries. Of particular significance is the potential sensitivity of the cross-section analysis to the choice of time period. In other words, choosing different initial and terminal years could lead to different conclusions. Furthermore, data relating to the interim period are not utilised, thus excluding a considerable amount of potentially useful information, as pointed out by several authors (e.g. Bernard and Durlauf 1995; Quah 1993a; 1996a; Levine and Renelt 1992; Mankiw 1995). Such information has the potential to reveal further interesting aspects of patterns of convergence or even to change the conclusions derived from the cross-section approach, as discussed so far. As den Haan (1995) notes:

> [...] if income is influenced by *more than one factor*, then we cannot expect a given cross-section of income levels to converge in the same manner at every point in time and for every set of countries, even if each country's income level is generated by the same economic model. (p. 65) [Emphasis added]

Because cross-section tests of convergence utilise only two end-observation points, and take no account of any trends in observational variables through time, possible tendencies to convergence or divergence within the time period are not revealed. In other words, whilst economies may converge in the long-run at an 'average rate' in the short-run different economies may converge at different rates, due to different individual circumstances. Cross-section tests are not able to detect these trends. A permanent 'shock' to a national economy occurring at a particular point within the time period will have differential impacts upon regional economies, in terms of magnitude and timing, but such trends will not be apparent in the analysis.

In summary, the previous section has outlined a number of cross-section techniques that can be employed to test for convergence, whether this is in the form of absolute, conditional or club convergence. These techniques are typically rooted in the neoclassical theory of growth and convergence. Although their effectiveness in testing this model may be questioned, nevertheless, there is an underlying theoretical basis.

5.6 Time-Series or Stochastic Convergence Tests

Some of the problems that arise when testing for convergence using cross sectional data can be overcome by an alternative approach, based on the concept of stochastic convergence using time-series data. Advocates of this approach (e.g. Bernard and

Jones 1996a; b; c; Bernard and Durlauf 1995) claim that convergence is, by definition, a dynamic concept that cannot be captured by cross-sectional studies. This section therefore provides a definition of stochastic convergence and discusses the main statistical tests associated with this approach. However, it should be noted that stochastic convergence lacks an explicit theoretical background.

Empirical tests of stochastic convergence have been applied across the OECD countries, (e.g. Oxley and Greasley 1995, 1999; Greasley and Oxley 1997; Ben-David 1993, 1996, 1998; Evans and Karras 1993; Miller 1996; Ben-David and Papell 2000; Linden 2002; Datta 2003; Bentzen 2005), the EU and groups of individual countries (e.g. Hossain and Chung 1999; Tsionas 2000a). There has been an interest in testing for stochastic convergence across the regions of individual countries. Such regional studies[31] concentrate to a large extent on the US (e.g. Carlino and de Fina 1995; Bernard and Jones 1996b; Carlino and Mills 1993, 1996, 1996a; Loewy and Papell 1996; Evans 1997; Evans and Karras 1996a; Strauss 2000; Johnson 2000; Tsionas 2000b, 2001; Drennan et al. 2004). Empirical studies for stochastic convergence have also been conducted for the regions of the UK (McGuinness and Sheehan 1998), Austria (Hofer and Wörgötter 1997), Italy (Proietti 2005), Greece (Alexiadis and Tomkins 2004) and the EU (Hobijn and Frances 2000). Underpinning all these studies is a dynamic concept of convergence. The associated convergence tests are based on whether the dispersion in output per-worker between two (or more) regions has narrowed during a time period, and all observations from that time period are used (Durlauf and Quah 1999). Thus, convergence is identified, not as a property of the relationship between initial output per-worker and growth over a fixed sample period, but instead is defined by the relationship between long-run forecasts of the time-series in output per-worker. It follows, then, that this approach takes into account all the relevant information available throughout the given time period, although it might be argued that the issue of choice of time period remains. By definition, the impacts of random shocks to national and regional economies are taken into account, in predicting long-run trends. More specifically, following Bernard and Durlauf (1995), stochastic convergence between two economies i and j occurs if the long-run forecasts of output per worker for both economies (countries or regions) are equal. The convergence property can be defined in formal terms as follows (Bernard and Durlauf 1995, p. 99):

$$\lim_{k \to \infty} E(y_{i,t+k} - y_{j,t+k}|I_t) = 0 \qquad (5.22)$$

where E is the mathematical expectation, y_i is the logarithm of real output per worker in economy i, and I_t describes the information set available at time t.

---

[31] There have also been studies using time-series data on regional employment or unemployment. See for example Baddeley et al. (1998), Fagerberg et al. (1996), Martin and Tyler (2000), Muscatelli and Tirelli (2001), Gray (2004). In this context, the Error-Correction-Model (ECM) is a useful econometric tool. See for example Martin (1997), Gray (2005), Alexiadis and Eleftheriou (2010), among others.

The above definition can be extended to n regions as follows. Economies $i = 1, \ldots, n$ converge if the long run forecasts of output per-worker for all regions are equal. Thus,

$$\lim_{k \to \infty} E(y_{1,t+k} - y_{i,t+k} | I_t) = 0 \, \forall i \neq 1 \tag{5.23}$$

Equation 5.23 represents the conditions required for absolute convergence to exist between all the regions included in the test. However, a critical issue is the determination of specific econometric tests for stochastic convergence. One of the most widely used such tests is the Augmented Dickey Fuller (hereafter ADF) test, which takes the following form:

$$\Delta(y_{i,t} - y_{j,t}) = \mu + \alpha(y_{i,t-1} - y_{j,t-1}) + \beta t + \sum_{k=1}^{n} \delta_k \Delta(y_{i,t-k} - y_{j,t-k}) + \varepsilon_t \tag{5.24}$$

where μ is the constant term, t denotes the time trend and ε_t is the error term of the regression.

Of critical importance is the coefficient on the difference between the two output per-worker series, $\alpha = (\rho - 1)$, where ρ is the unit root. If this difference contains a unit root (i.e. if $\rho = 1$, which implies that $\alpha = 0$), then output per-worker in the two economies will not converge while the absence of a unit root ($\alpha < 0$) is an indication of convergence between the two economies.[32] It might be argued that stochastic convergence in the long run implies two properties; firstly that the disparity in output per-worker between the two economies is disappearing and secondly that movement towards long run equilibrium is occurring. However, the unit root test detects 'catching-up' convergence only, i.e. the first of the two properties. In order to assess for convergence towards long-run equilibrium also, then it must be the case that the coefficient on the time trend is equal to zero ($\beta = 0$). Thus, long run convergence between two economies is occurring if $\alpha < 0$ and $\beta = 0$ (Oxley and Greasley 1995). The test for stochastic convergence described thus far essentially examines the convergence possibilities between 'pairs' of economies only, with the presumption of convergence towards the same steady-state. Using simple ADF tests, it is therefore difficult to identify whether particular groups of economies follow a common convergence path, as will be seen in Chap. 7. Nevertheless, a recently developed technique by Nahar and Inder (2002) allows such groups to be detected, using time-series data. Therefore, the remainder of this section articulates the methodology proposed by Nahar and Inder (2002). In a critical appraisal of stochastic convergence Nahar and Inder (2002) point out that the test of stochastic convergence proposed by Bernard and Durlauf (1995) suffers

---

[32] The approach to cointegration and the unit root hypothesis has been developed by Dickey and Fuller (1979, 1981), Engle and Granger (1987). For a more detailed review of the associated econometric test see Lee and Mosi (1996), Pesaran and Smith (1995), Lopez (1997).

from a number of weaknesses. Firstly, there is the possibility of an incorrect conclusion, as follows. The definition of convergence encapsulated in Eqs. 5.22 and 5.23, rests on the long-run forecasts of output per-worker differences tending to zero as the forecasting horizon approaches infinity. Thus, convergence is detected if the difference $y_i - y_j$ is a mean zero stationary process. However, it is also possible, that certain non-stationary processes can be convergent even though the unit root hypothesis ($\alpha = 0$) is accepted. The underlying process is convergent, but the ADF test suggests otherwise.[33] A second, and more general comment, is that an ADF test is able to identify convergence only between pairs of economies, as noted above. It can therefore be difficult to identify groups of economies that follow a common convergence pattern towards the same steady-state, and as a consequence the ability of ADF test to detect convergence clubs is limited. In addition to the question of how to identify those economies which belong to a club, there is the further question of what is the steady-state equilibrium towards which club members are progressing in the long-run. In recognition of this second issue, Nahar and Inder (2002) propose a test for stochastic convergence that explicitly acknowledges a steady-state level of output per-worker and convergence is assessed with reference to this long-run equilibrium point. In doing so, it also becomes possible to identify members of a convergence club. In an empirical setting, two proxies are suggested to represent the steady-state. The first is average output per-worker of all economies included in the set and the second is the output per-worker of the leading economy. Convergence is now defined as either declining deviations from average output per-worker or as declining differences in output per-worker compared to the leader. In both cases, the underlying concept of convergence that is being tested is that of absolute convergence. Using average output per-worker as the steady-state proxy, absolute convergence is said to occur when the distance of an economy's output per-worker from the average approaches zero over time. Nahar and Inder (2002), employ the following econometric test:

$$\phi_{i,t} = \theta_0 + \theta_1 t + \theta_2 t^2 + \ldots + \theta_{k-1} t^{k-1} + \theta_k t^k + u_{i,t} \qquad (5.25)$$

where $\phi_{i,t}$ is the ith economy's squared deviation from the average and θ_i's are parameters. The condition for convergence requires that the squared deviations decline through time, that is to say, the average slope of the function Eq. 5.25 is negative, i.e. $\frac{1}{T} \sum_{t=1}^{T} \frac{\partial \phi_{i,t}}{\partial t} < 0$ and given by:

$$\frac{1}{T} \sum_{t=1}^{T} \frac{\partial \phi_{i,t}}{\partial t} = \theta_1 + \theta_2 r_2 + \ldots + \theta_{k-1} r_{k-1} + \theta_k r_k = \boldsymbol{\theta} \mathbf{r}' \qquad (5.26)$$

---

[33] Nahar and Inder (2002) use the following example. Suppose that the difference in income between two economies, $y_{i,t} - y_{j,t}$, is a non-stationary process and is represented by $y_{i,t} - y_{j,t} = \frac{\theta}{t} + u_t$ in which $E(u_t) = 0$ and u_i is a stationary process. As $t \to \infty$, then $\frac{\theta}{t} \to 0$ and $y_{i,t} - y_{j,t}$ is also converging since $\lim_{k \to \infty} E(y_{i,t+k} - y_{j,t+k}|I_t) = 0$.

where $r_2 = \frac{2}{T} \sum_{t=1}^{T} t, \ldots, \quad r_{k-1} = \frac{(k-1)}{T} \sum_{t=1}^{T} t^{k-2}, \quad r_k = \frac{k}{T} \sum_{t=1}^{T} t^{k-1} \mathbf{r}' = \begin{bmatrix} 0 & 1 & r_2 & \cdots \end{bmatrix}$
$r_{k-1} r_k]$ and $\boldsymbol{\theta} = \begin{bmatrix} \theta_0 & \theta_1 & \cdots & \theta_{k-1} & \theta_k \end{bmatrix}$.

Application of this test involves three steps. First, Eq. 5.26 is estimated using ordinary least squares (hereafter OLS) and, secondly the average slope (i.e. the $\boldsymbol{\theta} \mathbf{r}'$ vector) is estimated for each economy. Finally, the null hypothesis of non-convergence, i.e. $H_0 : \boldsymbol{\theta} \mathbf{r}' \geqslant 0$, is tested against the alternative $H_a : \boldsymbol{\theta} \mathbf{r}' < 0$.

When the steady-state is approximated by the output per-worker of the leading economy a similar approach is employed. The model to be estimated is expressed as follows:

$$(y_{i,t} - y_{L,t}) = \theta_0 + \theta_1 t + \theta_2 t^2 + \ldots + \theta_{k-1} t^{k-1} + \theta_k t^k + u_t \qquad (5.27)$$

where $y_{i,t} - y_{L,t}$, is the gap between an economy's output per-worker ($y_{i,t}$) and the leading economy ($y_{L,t}$). Convergence is therefore said to occur when the gap from the leader approaches zero through time, implying that the rate of change in the 'gap' variable with respect to time is positive. As in the previous case, the non-convergence hypothesis $H_0 : \boldsymbol{\theta} \mathbf{r}' \leqslant 0$ is tested against the alternative $H_a : \boldsymbol{\theta} \mathbf{r}' > 0$.

The proposed technique by Nahar and Inder (2002) has a major advantage over the simple bivariate ADF tests. A problem with these tests is their limited ability to distinguish groups of economies which are converging with each other because the tests are restricted to pair-wise comparisons. The advantage of a test based on deviations from a steady-state is that it identifies those economies that are converging towards a common steady-state from those which are not, thereby recognising also the concept of club-convergence.

5.7 Conclusions

This chapter has outlined various approaches that have been employed to test whether convergence is occurring, which may be applied to national economies or to regional economies. There are various ways in which these tests may be characterised, for example in terms of the nature of data requirements (cross-sectional or time series) or whether they are testing for absolute or conditional convergence. One important way in which the tests may be categorised is whether they represent an attempt at explaining the mechanisms behind convergence in the sense of being derived from an underlying model. Some approaches simply test for the presence or absence of convergence (e.g. σ-convergence or stochastic convergence). On the other hand, other approaches have a theoretical basis (e.g. absolute β-convergence, conditional convergence or spatial dependence models). However, the explanation provided by these tests can be limited, depending on the data employed. An issue also explored in this chapter is the question of whether all economies in a set demonstrate convergence properties or whether only subsets do, to form convergence clubs. The question of spatial clustering of regional economies has also been raised. There may be many explanations of why convergence clubs emerge, as shown in Chap. 4, but there are fewer ways of actually detecting these clubs. In particular, two alternative cross section tests for convergence clubs have been discussed in this chapter, as well as an alternative time series approach, which identifies groups that, in the long run, converge towards steady-state equilibrium, approximated either by average output per-worker or output per-worker in a leading economy. This chapter has also provided a brief review of the studies that examine empirically the hypothesis of regional convergence across Europe. Although there are few exemptions, (e.g. Ertur and Koch 2005; Fischer and Stirböck 2006), the existing empirical literature is concentrated in the regions of the EU-15. The remainder of this study, therefore, focuses on applying the various approaches discussed in this chapter in the context of the NUTS-2 regions of an enlarged Europe (EU-27).

Chapter 6
EU-27 Regions: Absolute or Club Convergence?

6.1 Introduction

Regional growth may be convergent or divergent, as discussed in Chaps. 2 and 3. Convergence may also be an exclusive property of a specific set of regional economies, which are likely to share similar characteristics. It is the purpose of this chapter to provide an assessment of whether or not absolute convergence is apparent across the regions of the EU-27, and whether this applies only to a selected club.

The remainder of this chapter is structured in the following way. The results of applying the most frequently used empirical tests for σ and β convergence to the NUTS-2 regions of the EU-27 are reported in Sect. 6.2. Estimation of a simple model of absolute convergence indicates that regional convergence in terms of regional productivity is apparent in Europe, but occurs at a relatively slow rate. The alternative notion of convergence, the club convergence hypothesis, is examined next by two cross-section tests for club convergence, specified by Baumol and Wolff (1988) and Chatterji (1992). Finally, Sect. 6.4 summarises the main conclusions.

6.2 Data Employed

Previous chapters have presented the theoretical and empirical context for an examination of regional convergence. It is apparent that there are several different perspectives on the underlying causes of regional growth trends, be they convergent or divergent, and several different ways of defining and measuring convergence. Before attempting to assess the extent of convergence across the regions of the EU, it is the purpose of this section to provide a brief overview of the context in which the empirical analysis will be conducted.

The limits of regions are usually defined by natural borders (such as rivers, mountains and coastlines), historical reasons and/or administrative boundaries, some of which may coincide. Nevertheless, the regional classification system that

S. Alexiadis, *Convergence Clubs and Spatial Externalities*,
Advances in Spatial Science, DOI 10.1007/978-3-642-31626-5_6,
© Springer-Verlag Berlin Heidelberg 2013

the European Statistical Office (EUROSTAT) follows is based mainly on the institutional divisions in the 27 Member States. Each EU country has a different way of dividing its territory into administrative units. For the purposes of managing programmes and comparing statistics, the EU devised the NUTS system – dividing each country into statistical units (NUTS regions). Thus, the EU is divided into three levels of Nomenclature of Territorial Units of Statistics (NUTS), namely NUTS-1, NUTS-2 and NUTS-3 regions.[1] The territorial units used in this study refer to 268 NUTS-2 regions.[2] The EU uses NUTS-2 regions as 'targets' for convergence, defined as the 'geographical level at which the persistence or disappearance of unacceptable inequalities should be measured' (Boldrin and Canova 2001, p. 212).

Despite considerable objections to the use of NUTS-2 regions as the appropriate spatial level for the assessment of convergence,[3] they are nevertheless sufficiently small to be able to capture sub-national variations (Fischer and Stirböck 2006). Given that the primary focus of the present study is the trends in regional economic disparities, the most important issue from a data perspective is how regional economic performance is to be measured. The issue of regional economic convergence is broadly concerned with reductions of regional disparities in welfare through time. The concept of welfare, however, is wide and potentially vague, leading to a number of interpretations. For example, welfare could be addressed in terms of personal disposable income, employment opportunities, environmental conditions and so forth. In most empirical studies of regional convergence the level of welfare is approximated either by the measure of income per-capita or output per-worker, since such data is widely available (both are also used in theoretical analysis). Given that these measures represent quite different aspects of regional performance, it is important to be clear about which particular measure is being used and why. For example, output or income per-capita is a measure of standard of living in economic terms while output per-worker measures productivity and is a measure of competitiveness. Nevertheless, the choice of measure typically depends on the purpose for which it is to be used and to a considerable extent on data availability.

---

[1] Essentially, the NUTS system is a hierarchical classification established by EUROSTAT to provide comparable regional breakdowns of the EU Member States. The first version of the NUTS system was set up in the early 1970s. A legal basis was obtained in 2003 (Regulation of the European Parliament and Council 1059/2003). NUTS-1 corresponds to Government Office Regions in England; NUTS-2 to English Counties.

[2] A list of the NUTS-2 regions used in this study is provided in Appendix IV.

[3] Boldrin and Canova (2001), for instance, put forward three objections. First, the large size of the NUTS-2 regions, second commuting in several NUTS-2 regions, e.g. the metropolitan area (an agglomeration zone constituting of several urban centres or a very large city) of Hamburg, which is defined as NUTS-2 region, and yet half of the population of this area lives in the nearby regions of Schleswig-Holstein and Lower Saxony; a similar situation emerges for Ile de France, the Bassin Parisien and Madrid and Castillas and Flevoland in the Netherlands, and third factor endowments and population density are very heterogeneous across the NUTS-2 regions of the EU. Furthermore, GDP is abnormally inflated in most capital cities of Europe due to a large concentration of state governments and headquarters of large national companies. As a result, GDP is attributed to headquarters or central government offices, even when production is taking place elsewhere.

Regionally disaggregated data, available from EUROSTAT, refer to gross value added. Therefore, gross value added per-worker is used to assess the existence and extent of convergence: $y_{i,t} = \ln\left(\frac{GVA_{i,t}}{L_{i,t}}\right)$, where GVA is total gross value added, expressed in Euros,[4] and L is total employment, defined as the economically active labour force less unemployment[5] in each NUTS-2 region i during a given time period, t, usually a fiscal year. GVA per-worker is chosen because it is a measure of regional productivity and in general this is a major component of differences in the economic performance of regions and a direct outcome of variation in factors that determine regional 'competitiveness' (Martin 2001; LeSage and Fischer 2009).

Due to lack of reliable data for the regions in the Central and Eastern Europe, the time period for the analysis extends from 1995 to 2006. This might be considered as rather short but Islam (1995), and Durlauf and Quah (1999), point out that convergence-regressions are valid for shorter time periods, since they are based on an approximation around the steady-state and are supposed to capture the dynamics toward the steady-state. The period 1995–2006 seems to be adequate for two reasons. First, this period includes the transition to the Euro and the enlargement towards Central and Eastern Europe countries. A change from a centrally planned process of industrialisation to a market economy took place in the regions of Central and Eastern Europe countries and economic recovery is taking place during this particular period. Second, regional data for GVA are comparable between the EU-15 and the Central and Eastern European regions after the mid 1990s (European Commission 1999).

6.3 Empirical Tests of Regional Convergence

This section applies the most frequently used cross-section techniques for testing regional convergence, as discussed in Chap. 5. At this point, the analysis will examine whether the evidence points to convergence, on average, across all regions; following sections examine whether convergence exists only within a subset of regions. The simplest approach to testing for convergence is to examine

---

[4] GVA is the net outcome of output at basic prices less intermediate consumption valued at consumers' prices. The estimates are in accordance with the European System of Accounts 1995. It is possible to use Gross Regional Product at market prices or to measure GVA in purchasing power standards (PPS). However, at the regional level this raises several problems (Ertur et al. 2007). To be more precise, the conversion should be made using regional PPS. However, since such data are not available, the adjustments are made using national price levels. Moreover, the relative figures of regional GVA can change not only due to differences in the rate of GVA growth in real terms but also due to changes in the relative price level. Changes due to reductions in the relative price level might have a different implication than one resulting from a relative growth in real GVA.

[5] Using total labour force may be misleading if the primary concern of the study is regional productivity. To be more specific, inclusion of unemployed labour force would distort the productivity measure when unemployment levels vary significantly across regions.

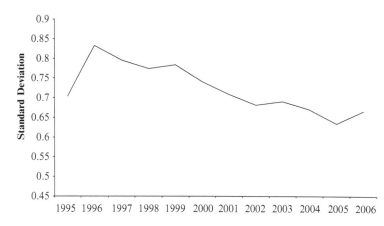

Fig. 6.1 GVA per-worker: standard deviation, EU-27 NUTS-2 regions

changes in standard deviation for regional GVA per-worker over the period 1995–2006. This test of convergence, when carried out for the 267 NUTS-2 regions, produces the outcome shown in Fig. 6.1.

It should be visible in Fig. 6.1 that over the examined period the long-run trend in the coefficient of variation suggests σ-convergence, although at both the beginning and the end of the period some slight increases are observed. A similar conclusion can be reached using the coefficient of variation (Fig. 6.2).

The conclusion to be drawn, therefore, on the basis of the σ-convergence test alone is that the NUTS-2 regions of EU27 have moved closer together as a group in that the dispersion of GVA per-worker at the end of the period is narrower than at the beginning.[6] As pointed out in Chap. 5, both the coefficient of variation and standard deviation are only simple descriptive tools and are not based on a model of regional convergence or divergence. There is no underlying explanation of a catching up process implicit in these measures. The examination of individual movements within the distribution, however, can provide considerable information about regional inequalities[7] and the mechanisms operating in the process of regional convergence. Some preliminary information can be obtained by

---

[6] Using the coefficient of variation for GDP per-head over the period 1995–2005 Michelis and Monfort (2008) reach similar conclusions.

[7] It is argued that within the EU income disparities have diminished between Member-States but increased between regions. Indeed, the richest regions are eight times richer than the poorest regions. Socio-economic inequalities within regions and countries constitute about 80 % of overall inequalities (Kanbur and Venables 2007) and for the majority of the Member-States were higher in 2007 than in 1980. For a more detailed description of regional inequalities and income polarization in the EU see Paci (1997), Magrini (1999), Puga (1999), Maza and Villaverde (2004), Martin (2005), Ezcurra (2009), Shucksmith et al. (2009) Bracalente and Perugini (2010), among others.

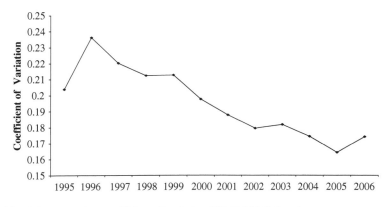

Fig. 6.2 GVA per-worker: coefficient of variation, EU-27 NUTS-2 regions

constructing a 'movements-matrix'.[8] Table 6.1 considers five categories of labour
productivity and reports the number of regions in each category at the beginning
(1995) and end (2006) of the observed period.

These categories were chosen to account for important benchmarks in the
context of European cohesion policy. In particular, the level of 75 % of the EU
average GDP per capita (measured in purchasing power parities and calculated on
the basis of Community figures for the last 3 years available) is a key criterion for
being eligible to support from the Structural Funds (Council Regulation 1260/99,
article 3).[9] For each category, Table 6.1 displays the percentage of regions which by
2006 either remained in the same category (this corresponds to the diagonal of the
matrix) or moved to another category.

---

[8] This is an exercise that a number of authors, including, Fingleton (1997), Quah (1996a), Puga
(2002) have undertaken. Neven and Gouyette (1995), however, argue that this approach is mostly a
descriptive analysis.

[9] These regions are characterised as Objective-1 regions. In 2003, 84 regions were below the 75 %
threshold with total population about 154 million inhabitants. The Objective-1 regions cover the
entire area of the 10 Member States that joined the EU in 2004 (with the exception of Bratislava,
Prague and Cyprus). A second criterion applies to the definition of Objective-1 regions: a low
population density (less than eight inhabitants per square kilometre). This criterion covers a
number of region in northern Finland and Sweden, the French overseas departments, the Canary
Islands, the Azores and Madeira. The European Commission (1996) observes that 'regions with
more than 500 inhabitants per square kilometre account only for 4 % of the land area of the Union
but for more than half the population. This implies that between two-thirds and three quarters of
the EU's total wealth creation occurs in urban areas' (p. 12). Regions under economic and social
restructure are classified as Objective-2 regions. In this case the following criteria are applied:
changes in key sectors due to declining employment in industrial and services sectors, economic
and social crisis in urban areas, decline of traditional activities and depopulation of rural areas.
Regions in which efforts are made to reduce unemployment are characterised as Objective-3
regions. The disadvantages areas of the EU, Objective-1 and 2 regions correspond to almost half of
the EU-25's total population (about 225 million inhabitants).

Table 6.1 'Movements- Matrix': EU-27 NUTS-2 regions, 1995–2006

	n [1995]	Labour productivity, 2006	[0–0.5)	[0.5–0.75)	[0.75–1)	[1–1.3)	[1.3–	n [2006]
Labour Productivity, 1995	7	[0–0.5)	**0.02**	0.00	0.00	0.00	0.00	6
	42	[0.5–0.75)	0.00	**0.10**	0.05	0.00	0.00	29
	35	[0.75–1)	0.00	0.00	**0.12**	0.01	0.00	53
	184	[1–1.3)	0.00	0.00	0.03	**0.66**	0.00	179
	0	[1.3–	0.00	0.00	0.00	0.00	**0.00**	1

The relative persistence in the distribution is indicated by the elements in the diagonal. About 66 % of the regions with labour productivity above the EU average in 1995 remained in the same range in 2006. Only 12 % of the regions with labour productivity less that 75 % of the EU average in 1995 retained their relative position throughout the examined period. Few upward movements can be detected. For example, 5 % of the regions in the range between 50 % and 75 % experienced a relative productivity rise in the range between 75 % and 100 % of the EU-27 average. On the other hand, 3 % of regions with relatively high levels of labour productivity in 1995 (in the range between 1 and 1.3 times the EU-27 average) exhibited a downward movement (in the range between 75 % and 100 % of the EU-27 average). Overall, Table 6.1 suggests that a process of regional convergence is at work among the EU-27 regions, although at a slow pace. As pointed out in Chap. 5, the notion of β-convergence is able to provide an indication of a catch-up process together with the rate at which this process takes place. This aspect of convergence is examined next. As explained in Chap. 5, one indicator of convergence is the presence of an inverse relationship between growth and initial level of per-capita income/output (Baumol 1986). Such β-convergence embodies the essence of the neoclassical argument that poor regions grow faster than rich regions and produces estimates of the rate at which poor regions are catching up with rich regions, should convergence be detected.

The potential or otherwise for such β-convergence is indicated in Fig. 6.3, which shows a scatterplot of the average annual growth rate against the initial level of GVA per-worker.[10]

At first sight, it could be argued that there are some tendencies for absolute convergence. A closer examination of Fig. 6.3, however, suggests that the convergence property is restricted to a group of regions exceeding a certain level of initial labour productivity in 1995 (about 3 in natural logarithms).[11] Bearing this in mind, one cannot be sure that the European regions exhibit fast convergence tendencies. Regions above an approximate threshold of 3 for initial GVA per-worker could be described as exhibiting β-convergence. On average this group has experienced a

---

[10] This scatterplot is known as the 'convergence picture' (Romer 1987b).

[11] Labour productivity is expressed in logarithmic terms given that the empirical literature has concentrated mainly on logarithms instead of levels.

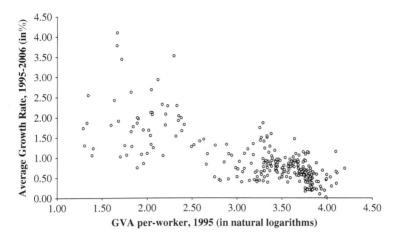

Fig. 6.3 Absolute convergence, EU-27 NUTS-2 regions

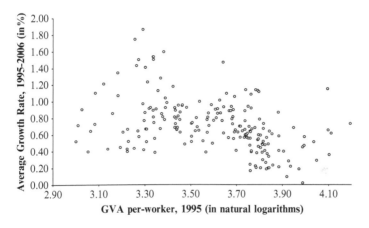

Fig. 6.4 β-convergence: regions with labour productivity above 3 in 1995

rate of growth over the period of 0.71 % per annum while the regions with initial GVA per-worker below the threshold have grown at a rate of 1.68 %. The presence of β-convergence in this group is ambiguous, as shown in Fig. 6.6. The latter group corresponds to almost one quarter of the total NUTS-2 regions of the EU27 while its composition refers mainly to regions from the New Member-States with fewer regions from the EU-15.

Figure 6.4 also indicates that there is a group of low-productivity regions exhibiting low rate of growth. This group is displayed in Fig. 6.5 and includes nine regions (PT11, PT20, PT30, GR11, GR21, PL61, PL62, MT00 and UKK3). In 1995, the average GVA per-worker in this group was less than 3 (in natural logarithms) while they exhibited average rates of growth of 0.66 % per annum,

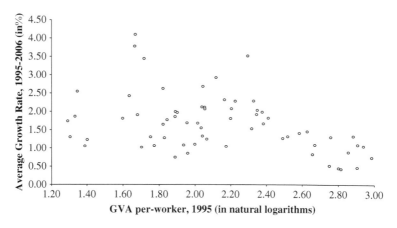

Fig. 6.5 β-convergence: regions with labour productivity below 3 in 1995

which is less that the average for all the NUTS-2 regions (0.94 % per annum). These regions seem to have fallen into a 'low-level trap' with low GVA per-worker and low rates of growth.

The presence (or absence) of absolute β-convergence, however, cannot be confirmed by visual inspection alone. As shown in Chap. 5, a more formal test for absolute β-convergence involves estimating the following equation:

$$g_i = a + by_{i,0} \tag{6.1}$$

The results, presented in Table 6.2, show the convergence coefficient (b) to be

negative and significant at the 95 %, implying a positive value for the rate of convergence (β), although in a relatively small range, estimated to be 0.65 % per annum.

This cross-section test provides some, albeit, very limited evidence that the NUTS2 regions of EU-27 are in the process of absolute β-convergence with low productivity regions growing, on average, faster than high productivity areas. But given the extremely slow convergence rate estimated,[12] it would take a very long time for all regions to reach a common level of productivity, as predicted by the absolute convergence model.[13] The model of absolute convergence has a poor

---

[12] This slow process of regional convergence can, possibly, be explained by the low degree of labour mobility that characterises the European regions, due to linguistic and cultural barriers. As Boldrin and Canova (2001, p. 243) state 'while capital is moving around Europe, labour is definitely not'. Obstfeld and Peri (1998) report that labour mobility in Germany, Italy and the UK over the period 1970–1995 was only about one-third of the US level.

[13] Recall that the notion of absolute convergence derives from the standard neoclassical model, which treats all economies (countries or regions) as similar. If this was true, then the economies will display absolute β-convergence as well as σ-convergence (Sala-i-Martin 1996a). While there is evidence for σ-convergence, the slow process of β-convergence implies that structural characteristics and overall conditions differ markedly across the EU-27.

Table 6.2 Absolute β-convergence and the speed of convergence, 1995–2006

OLS, estimated equation: $g_i = a + by_{i,0}$, sample: 268 EU-27 NUTS-2 regions				
a	b	R^2	[ser]	Implied β
0.5714**	−0.0747**	0.12492	[0.1397]	0.0065**
Ramsey reset test [p-value]: 9.0436 [0.000]				
LIK 147.552		AIC -291.104	SBC -283.929	

Notes: **Indicates statistical significance at 95 % level of confidence. [ser] denotes the standard error of the regression. AIC, SBC and LIK denote the *Akaike*, the *Schwartz-Bayesian* information criteria and Log-likelihood, respectively.

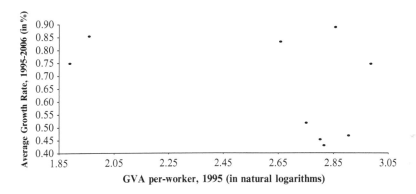

Fig. 6.6 Regions in a 'low-level trap'

explanatory power, as indicated by the value of R^2. Moreover, the probability associated with the Ramsey RESET test indicates that the null hypothesis (i.e. that the model specification is adequate) cannot be accepted at the usual levels of significance. Therefore, an alternative model may be more appropriate. As argued in Chap. 4, absolute convergence may be restricted to a sub-set of regional economies, known as a 'convergence club'. This possibility, implicit in the data of Figs. 6.3, 6.4 and 6.6, is now examined in the next section.

6.4 Club Convergence: Preliminary Evidence

A number of cross-section approaches have been developed to examine the presence of convergence clubs. For example, Baumol and Wolff (1988) use a quadratic version of Eq. 6.1, which can detect one club, while Chatterji (1992) implements a method based on the gaps or deviations from per-capita GDP of a leading economy.

Therefore, the aim of this section is to consider the hypothesis of club convergence using cross-section techniques. Following the discussion in Chap. 5, the hypothesis of club convergence may be tested, according to Baumol and Wolff (1988), by estimating the following regression equation:

$$g_i = a + b_1 y_{i,0} + b_2 y_{i,0}^2 \tag{6.2}$$

Table 6.3 Convergence clubs: Baumol and Wolff's specification, 1995–2006

2SLS, estimated equation: $g_i = a + b_1 y_{i,0} + b_2 y_{i,0}^2$ sample: 268 EU-27 NUTS-2 regions					
a	b_1	b_2	R^2	[ser]	Implied y^*
0.0567	0.3233**	−0.0704**	0.17261	[0.1361]	2.2926**
Ramsey Reset Test: 0.4344 [0.6480]			F-Statistic: $F_{(2,265)}$ 27.5374 [0.000]		
LIK	155.034	AIC	−304.068	SBC	−293.306

Notes: **Indicates statistical significance at 95 % level of confidence [ser] and [p-value] denote the standard error of the regression and the probability associated with each test, respectively. AIC, SBC and LIK denote the *Akaike*, the *Schwartz-Bayesian* information criteria and Log-likelihood, respectively

with the expectation of $b_1 > 0$ and $b_2 < 0$. The threshold value of initial GVA per-worker (y^*) that distinguishes which regions are included in the club is calculated as follows:

$$y^* = \frac{-b_1}{2b_2} \tag{6.3}$$

It should be noted, however, that introducing the initial level of productivity, raised to the square, as an additional explanatory variable result to high multicollinearity. In an attempt to overcome this problem, Eq. 6.2 is estimated using the method of 'Two-Stages Least Squares' (2SLS).

In this case, there is some limited improvement in the overall fit of the model, compared with the absolute convergence model in Table 6.2. Nevertheless, the probability associated with the F-statistic[14] for overall significance of the regression rejects the null hypothesis of zero coefficients. The p-value of the Ramsey-RESET test suggests that the null hypothesis is accepted, indicating that the club convergence model is well specified. Indeed, successive enlargements of the EU have brought countries with several less productive regions and convergence towards a single steady-state might not be the case.

The outcome is also consistent with the presence of a convergence club, in that the estimated coefficients are as expected. As can be seen from Table 6.3, the coefficient b_1 is positive while the coefficient b_2 is negative. In order to identify convergence club members the threshold value of initial GVA per-worker (y^*) is determined using Eq. 6.3, which is statistically significant at 95 % level of confidence.

---

[14] This is computed as $F = \frac{ESS/k-1}{RSS/n-k}$, where ESS is the explained sum of squares, RSS is the residuals sums of squares (the total sum of squares is $TSS = ESS + RSS$), k is the number of parameters including the constant and n is the number of observations. The null hypothesis associated with this test is that all the regression coefficients are equal to zero. A low probability value implies that at least some of the regression parameters are nonzero and that the regression equation does have some validity in fitting the data (i.e., the independent variables are not purely random with respect to the dependent variable).

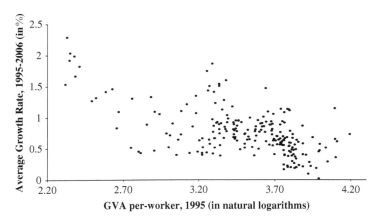

Fig. 6.7 β-convergence amongst the convergence club

Table 6.4 β-convergence in the converging and diverging club

OLS, estimated equation: $g_i = a + by_{i,0}$, sample: 226 NUTS-2 regions		
a	b	Implied β
0.7444**	−0.1238**	1.102**
OLS, Estimated equation: $g_i = a + by_{i,0}$, Sample: 42 NUTS-2 regions		
a	b	Implied β
−0.0871**	0.2766**	−2.035**

Notes: ** Indicates statistical significance at 95 % level of confidence while * indicates signifi-cance at 90 % level.

At this point the conclusion that the simple model of club convergence provides a better explanation of the data than the simple absolute convergence model is tentative. The overall fit remains poor, and the power to discriminate between those regions which exhibit β-convergence, and those which do not, must be therefore be viewed with caution.

According to Baumol and Wolff's (1988) specification of convergence club, the property of β-convergence is apparent for the regions with an initial level of GVA per-worker in excess of the estimated threshold value of initial labour productivity. Figure 6.7 and Table 6.4 provide support to this argument.

The regions included in the converge club grow at an average rate 1.1 % per annum. An opposite picture is revealed for the regions excluded from the conver-gence club (Fig. 6.8), which exhibit *diverging* tendencies, at a rate about 2 % per annum, on average.

While the diverging areas clearly exhibit an average rate of growth faster than the regions included in the convergence club (Table 6.5), nevertheless there seems to be an intra variation within the diverging group. There is a group of 12 regions that their growth rates and the initial levels of labour productivity are both below the average of the regions in the diverging group. These regions locked in a 'low

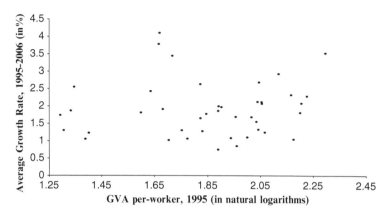

Fig. 6.8 Diverging regions

Table 6.5 Average growth rates in the converging and diverging club

Average growth of all regions	Average growth in the convergence club	Average growth in non-members of the convergence club
0.94 %	0.76 %	1.9 %

level equilibrium trap' and exhibit an average growth rate less than the diverging and the convergence club (about 0.4 % per annum).

The location pattern of the regional groupings identified in this section is given in Fig. 6.9. The convergence club includes, almost exclusively, regions from the 'advanced' members-states of the EU-15.

Such an outcome is consistent with the view put forward by Dunford and Smith (2000) on a '*development divide*' between the EU-15 and the East Central Europe. Indeed, according to the threshold value of the initial level of labour productivity very few regions form the new member-states are included in the converging group. Most of these regions are located in Czech Republic; a relatively advanced economy of the East-Central Europe in which two regions (Prague and Bratislava) with GDP per capita above 75 % of the EU average, are located.

Conversely, the diverging regions are found mainly in relatively backward Eastern European countries (e.g. Slovakia, Latvia, Hungary and Poland) while the majority of regions, identified as 'locked in a low level equilibrium trap' are found in Romania and Bulgaria. These countries are characterised by substantial internal disparities between urban areas or regions bordering the EU-15, which have benefited from the expansion of the service sector and the remaining regions.

Clearly, the existing economic disparities between the regions of the EU-15 and the regions in the East Central Europe is a factor that constraints any possibilities for overall convergence across the EU-27. Indeed, as Moucque (2000) notes, even if the countries of East-Central Europe maintain a 2 % growth differential with the remaining countries of the EU, it will take about half a century before most of them approach the EU average.

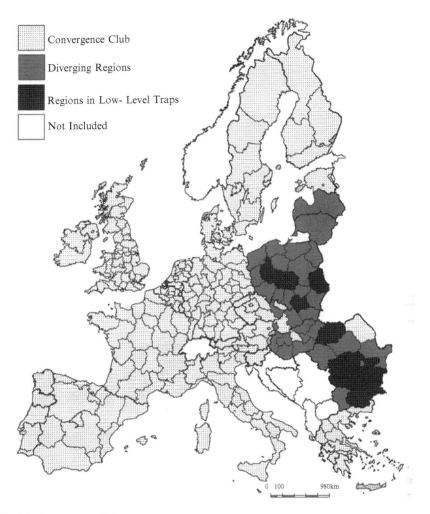

Fig. 6.9 Convergence club

Chatterji (1992) recommends an alternative approach to testing the convergence club hypothesis, which defines convergence in terms of the narrowing of gaps between the leading region and other regions. As shown in Chap. 5, Chatterji's specification takes the following form:

$$G_{i,T} = A_1(G_{i,0}) + A_2(G_{i,0})^2 + A_3(G_{i,0})^3 \qquad (6.4)$$

or more generally

$$G_{i,T} = \sum_{k=1}^{n} A_k(G_{i,0})^k \qquad (6.5)$$

Table 6.6 Convergence clubs: Chatterji's specification

Non-Linear OLS, estimated equation: $G_{i,T} = A_1 (G_{i,0}) + A_2 (G_{i,0})^2 + A_3 (G_{i,0})^3$				
Sample: 268 NUTS-2 regions				
A_1	A_2	A_3	$G_{2,0}$	$G_{3,0}$
1.3211**	−0.3885**	0.1013**	1.205**	2.629**

Notes: An asterisk (*) indicates *statistical* significance at 95 % level of confidence.

where $G_{i,0}$ and $G_{i,T}$ denote the initial and terminal gap of region i with the leading region (L), respectively.

In choosing the leading region, several possibilities were considered.[15] Nevertheless, the region of Luxemburg (LU) was chosen since this is the region with the highest level of labour productivity in the initial year of the analysis.

Following the discussion in Chap. 5, Sect. 5.5.2, the leading region represents one equilibrium point since $G_{L,0} = 0$ by definition, while the equilibrium points that determine the club(s) depend on the values of $G_{2,0}$ and $G_{3,0}$, which can be calculated as follows:

$$G_{2,0} = \frac{-A_2 - \sqrt{(A_2)^2 - 4A_3(A_1 - 1)}}{2A_3} \text{ and}$$

$$G_{3,0} = \frac{-A_2 + \sqrt{(A_2)^2 - 4A_3(A_1 - 1)}}{2A_3}$$

$$(6.6)$$

The results of applying this methodology to NUTS-2 regions of the EU-27 are shown in Table 6.6. The values of the equilibrium points $G_{2,0}$ and $G_{3,0}$, are also shown.

The fact that $A_1 > 1$ implies that regions with an initial gap less than $G_{2,0}$, actually diverge from the leading region. It should be noted, however, that there is a group of four regions that their terminal level of labour productivity exceeds that of the leading region; these are Brussels (BE10), Ile de France (FR10), where the capital cities of Belgium and France are located, Hamburg (DE60) with the main port of Germany and Groningen (NL11), the centre of the Dutch gas industry.[16]

---

[15] As a matter of fact, Chatterji's specification was tested using these four regions as leaders. In any case, the results clearly indicate that the NUTS-2 regions of the EU-27 diverge from the leading regions. Nevertheless, using LU as the leading region produces more robust results from econometric point of view, compare to the four other regions, and therefore was chosen.

[16] Neven and Gouyette (1995) exclude the region of Groningen from their empirical analysis. They argue that output recorded in that region is somewhat of artificial nature, which includes all production of gas from the North Sea in the Netherlands. This region was the most affluent in the EC in the early 1980s, but declined markedly relatively to others as energy prices fell throughout the second part of the 1980s. The authors argue that the inclusion of Groningen in the sample would bias the estimates in favour of finding convergence. On similar lines, Maurseth (2001) takes account of the fact that Groningen was hard hit by the 'Dutch disease' in the 1980s and excludes this particular region from the empirical analysis.

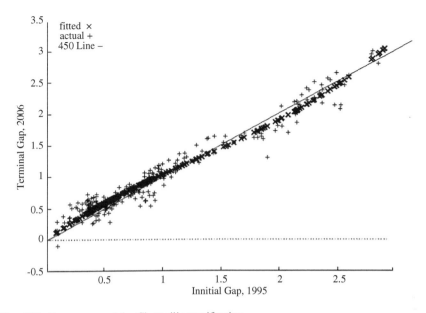

Fig. 6.10   Convergence clubs, Chatterji's specification

Based on the estimations results, it might be argued that this group together with Luxembourg constitute a single leading club.[17] On the other hand, regions with gaps in the range [1.2, 2.6] during the initial time of the analysis (1995), although they were able to reduce their gaps at the end of the period (2006), nonetheless, they converge to a lower equilibrium. Divergence from the leading region is also detected for the regions with an initial gap in excess of $G_{3,0}$. These regions can be conceived as regions in 'low-level' traps. Figure 6.10 shows the two equilibrium gaps, obtained by Eq. 6.4.

As shown in Fig. 6.10, the fitted curve 'cuts' the 45° line at 2.08, which corresponds to $G_{2,0}$, i.e. the common gap towards which all the NUTS-2 regions converge. Thus, it may be concluded that over a 12 year period, two distinct groups emerge from Chatterji's specification. The first includes the leading region of Luxemburg and the second the remaining regions. Thus, convergence with the leading region is not suggested by Chatterji's model. In this light, it might be argued that the group of leading regions are exceptional cases and not representative of the majority of European regions.

---

[17] The presence of 'outlying' or 'leading' regions might influence the process of overall regional convergence (Button and Pentecost 1995).

6.5 Spatial Interaction in EU-27: Preliminary Evidence

The empirical tests reported in this chapter have shown that across the NUTS-2 level of territorial division of EU-27 the process of absolute convergence is extremely slow. For example, the standard cross-section econometric test for absolute convergence indicates that over the period 1995–2006 the 268 NUTS-2 regions converge at an average rate of 0.66 %, per annum. Further empirical tests show convergence to be restricted to a group of regions suggesting a pattern of club convergence. A preliminary inspection of the composition of the convergence club shows that its members are located almost exclusively in the EU-15. The subsequent empirical analysis provides a preliminary examination of spatial interaction across the European regions.

As a first step, the extent of spatial interaction across the NUTS-2 regions is assessed by means of simple descriptive statistics. Several statistics have been put forward to describe interaction across space and one measure of spatial dependence that is used extensively in empirical studies is the Moran's I statistic, calculated as follows:

$$I_t = \frac{n}{s} \frac{\sum_i \sum_j w_{ij}(x_i - \mu)(x_j - \mu)}{\sum_i (x_i - \mu)^2} \quad i \neq j \qquad (6.7)$$

where n is the number of observations for a variable x and w_{ij} represents the spatial weight for each pair of regions i and j. The term μ denotes the mean of the data set for the variable x while s is a scaling constant, calculated as the sum of all spatial weights.

In this task a principal issue is the construction of the spatial weights. A common practice is to allow these weights to take the value of 1 if a region is contiguous to another and 0 otherwise. In this case spatial interaction is presumed to occur only between regions that share a common border. Alternatively, the spatial weights may be continuous variables, constructed so as to produce declining weights as distance between regions increases. Thus,

$$w_{ij} = \frac{1/d_{ij}}{\sum_j 1/d_{ij}} \qquad (6.8)$$

Here, d_{ij} denotes the distance between two regions i and j, typically represented by the distance between the regions' main cities where the majority of economic activities are located (the centroid of a region). The denominator is the sum of the (inverse) distances from all regions surrounding region i, within a selected boundary. Equation 6.8 implies that interactions between regions, such as spillover effects, decay as the distance from one area to another increases (hence weights decline as distance increases) and that such effects are dominated by the leading area.[18]

In constructing the spatial weights matrix to examine spatial dependence amongst NUTS-2 regions a similar approach is adopted, where the weights are calculated using distances between the main cities of regions, given that economic activities are typically concentrated in the main city of each region. The numerator, thus, consists of the distance of the nearest main city in a region from the main city of the contiguous region with a higher GVA per-worker.[19] This choice is based on the assumption that spillover effects are dominated by a leading area, and that such effects from a location with high GVA per-worker are greater in the nearby locations. Moreover, Eq. 6.8 allows accounting for the existence of island regions in the data set. To be more precise, in a simple contiguity matrix the weights for island-regions would be zero. That would change the sample size and the interpretation of the results. A spatial matrix based on the geographical distance provides a better approach to the issue of spatial dependence.

Depending upon the spatial weights matrix, if $I_t > 0$ then this is indicative of high spatial autocorrelation, suggesting positive perfect spatial dependence. On the other hand, if $I_t < 0$, then this implies perfect negative spatial autocorrelation while if $I_t = 0$, then this indicates the absence of spatial dependence, that is no significant spatial links among the observational units.

In 1995 and in 2006, the Moran's I statistic values are both positive indicating some degree of spatial interaction across the NUTS-2 regions of the EU-27. Moreover, the correlation between the coefficient of variation and Moran's I statistic is -0.78, indicating that changes in the degree of spatial dependence follow a dissimilar trend to that of changes in regional distribution of productivity. Figure 6.11 displays the evolution of the coefficient of variation and Moran's I statistic for the 1970–2000 period.

According to Rey and Montouri (1999), the general expectation is that σ-convergence, as measured by a decline in the coefficient of variation, is associated with an increase in Moran's I statistic. This condition characterizes the period 1995–2000. On the other hand, during the period 1996–2006 there is a declining

---

[18] Equation (6.1.1) is used extensively in the empirical literature on spatial econometrics (e.g. Richardson 1974; Cliff and Ord 1981; Attfield et al. 2000; Ravallion and Jalan 1996; Fingleton 2000; Frizado et al. 2009). Nevertheless, the spatial matrix can be constructed also using the inverse distances to the square as denominator. Results using this kind of spatial matrix were very similar.

[19] Choosing cities according to their level of GVA per-worker may cause problems of endogeneity in estimating spatial econometric models. However, such a criterion is used extensively in the relevant empirical literature. Nevertheless, one way to overcome this endogeneity problem is to choose the most populated cities. Such a choice does not serve any purpose since cities with high GVA per-worker are normally associated with high population and most economic activities are concentrated here also.

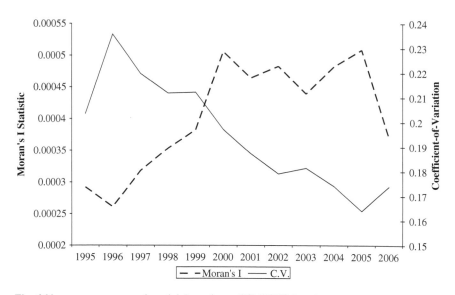

Fig. 6.11 σ-convergence and spatial dependence, 268 NUTS-2 regions

tendency for the dispersion of regional productivity across the NUTS-2 regions of Europe,[20] the evolution of the Moran's I statistic follows an opposite tendency.

Spatial interaction can also be depicted in a different manner by Moran's scatterplot, which plots a region's GVA per-worker against its spatial-lag (Anselin 1988). According to Rey and Montouri (1999) a region's spatial-lag is the weighted average of GVA per-worker of its surrounding regions. On the vertical axis in Moran's scatterplot the spatial-lag of regional GVA per-worker is measured while the horizontal axis measures regional GVA per-worker. Thus, each Moran's scatterplot contains four quadrants that identify four different kinds of spatial interaction between regions (Fig. 6.12). Quadrant I includes regions with high (above average) GVA per-worker that are surrounded also by high GVA per-worker, while quadrant III refers to those regions with low GVA per-worker which are surrounded also by low GVA per-worker. These two quadrants indicate positive spatial association, or correlation. On the other hand, quadrant II represents regions with low GVA per-worker, which are surrounded by regions with high GVA per-worker, while the reverse case is found in quadrant IV. Thus, quadrants II and IV exhibit negative spatial association.

Significant positive spatial association implies that regions would spatially cluster into two distinctive groups, i.e. rich and poor regions, in quadrants I and III. On the other hand, negative spatial association suggests regional grouping in quadrants II and IV, described by Rey and Montouri (1999) as 'doughnut' and

---

[20] The measures of σ-convergence are not reliable in the presence of spatial autocorrelation (Rey and Dev 2006). Nevertheless, these measures are used only indicative.

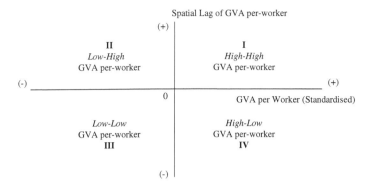

Fig. 6.12 Spatial autocorrelation in Moran's scatterplot

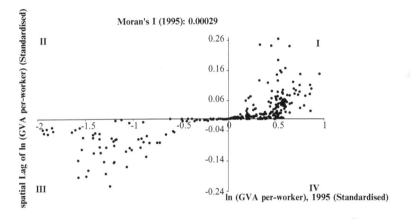

Fig. 6.13 Moran scatterplot, 1995, EU-27 NUTS-2 regions

'diamond in the rough'. It may be argued, therefore, that if observations scatter in both quadrants I and III, then a pattern of club convergence is a possibility, in the sense that rich and poor regions constitute two separate clubs. If, on the other hand, regions are scattered in quadrant IV, then this is compatible with a 'core and periphery' pattern, in the sense that high productivity regions (centre or core) are surrounded by low productivity regions (periphery) implying a pattern of regional divergence.

Figures 6.13 and 6.14 present the Moran's scatterplots[21] for the years 1995 and 2006, for the NUTS-2 regions of the EU-27.

---

[21] Baumont et al. (2003) put forward the argument that convergence clubs can be detected using a Moran's scatterplot. They support this argument using data for the EU regions. Similar results are reported by Maza and Villaverde (2004) and Mora (2004, 2005).

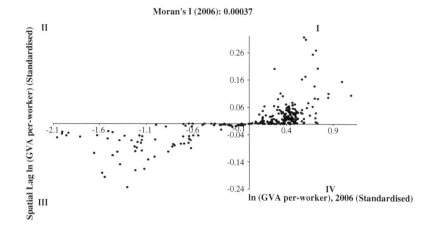

Fig. 6.14 Moran scatterplot, 2006, EU-27 NUTS-2 regions

Figures 6.13 and 6.14 clearly suggest a pattern of clustering in the first and the third quadrants of both figures such that high-productivity regions are likely to be neighbours of other high-productivity regions, and low-productivity prefectures are similarly grouped. This pattern is observed both at the beginning and at the end of the time period, suggesting that the data are not randomly distributed, but indicate a systematic spatial pattern, which is compatible with the club convergence hypothesis, where there are two spatially connected clubs, a poor and a rich club. Identifying spatial dependence across this set of observational units suggests that the conventional tests of regional convergence should be modified to include an explicit spatial dimension.

6.6   Conclusions

In this chapter an attempt has been made to test for convergence across the NUTS-2 regions of EU-27. Hurst et al. (2000) note that '[...] there are regions that have been very similar to start with, but nonetheless have developed at very different rates' (p. 16). Overall, the results reported in this chapter suggest that while there is no uniform pattern of growth across all the European regions, a group of regions appear to be following a convergence path. This conclusion provides support to the view held by Button and Pentecost (1999), that the EU is not a homogeneous economic space.

Examination of σ-convergence for the period 1995–2006 indicates that there is a tendency towards declining regional inequalities, suggesting that convergence is a possibility. On the other hand, formal tests for β-convergence provide scant support for this possibility. The NUTS-2 regions of the EU-27 converge at an extremely low rate, suggesting that club convergence may be a possibility. This view receives further support by the Moran scatterplot, which suggests a pattern of geographical clustering across the European regions.

Using Baumol and Wolff's (1988) specification, some evidence of club convergence is detected, in the sense that the property of an inverse relation between growth and initial level of GVA per-worker is apparent within a group of regions. Using an alternative methodology (Chatterji 1992), suggests a different pattern. Application of this model to the European regions shows that a group of 'leading' regions constitutes a single club while all remaining regions diverge from this group. In this light, a variation *within* the convergence club arises as a distinct possibility.

Several empirical studies focusing on tests of absolute and conditional convergence across the European regions conclude that a pattern of club convergence might be a probable outcome. Neven and Gouyette (1995, p. 60), for instance, note that '[...] our convergence equations may be misspecified. Differences in the steady-state values of output across regions may have not been accounted properly.'

In Chap. 4 a model is developed that attributes club convergence to differences in the steady-states due to dissimilarities in the degree of technology diffusion across regions. Therefore, the next chapter considers the possibility of club convergence more thoroughly by examining the relationship between patterns of regional growth, technology diffusion and the adoption of innovations across the regions of the EU-27 in a context of spatial interaction.

Chapter 7
'Club Convergence': Geography, Externalities and Technology

7.1 Introduction

The previous chapter has examined club convergence in the context of the EU-27 regions, thus providing an alternative perspective on the issue of regional convergence in an enlarged Europe. While previous studies on European regions claim that convergence is slow, the empirical tests reported on Chap. 6 establish that convergence is a property that characterises the regions of the 'old' member-states of the European Union together with a selected set of regions located in new member-states.

It is the purpose of this chapter, therefore, to extend the analysis of club convergence by taking account of spatial interaction between regions. In addition, the model which is tested is based extensively on the model of club convergence, developed in Chap. 4, which examines the role of technology creation and diffusion across regions. Furthermore, factors regarding spatial agglomerations are also introduced into this single club convergence model.

This chapter is divided into five sections. Section 7.2 provides a formal examination of spatial interaction, using spatial econometric models. In Sect. 7.3 an econometric model is presented which incorporates some factors that may lead regions to formulate convergence clubs, specifically technology creation and adoption, and localisation and diversification effects. Club convergence is examined in Sect. 7.4, using both a simple and a spatial specification. Section 7.5 tests empirically a model that attributes club convergence to the interaction of three factors, namely geography, agglomeration externalities and technology. Finally, Sect. 7.6 assesses the implication of the results for the debate concerning the pattern of regional convergence in an enlarged Europe.

S. Alexiadis, *Convergence Clubs and Spatial Externalities*,
Advances in Spatial Science, DOI 10.1007/978-3-642-31626-5_7,
© Springer-Verlag Berlin Heidelberg 2013

7.2   Spatial Interaction in the Process of Regional Convergence

Empirical tests in Chap. 6 have shown that across the NUTS-2 level of territorial division of EU-27 the process of absolute convergence is extremely slow. For example, the standard cross-section econometric test for absolute convergence indicates that over the period 1995–2006 the 268 NUTS-2 regions converge at an average rate of 0.66 %, per annum. Further empirical tests show convergence to be restricted to a group of regions suggesting a pattern of club convergence. A preliminary inspection of the composition of the convergence club shows that its members are located almost exclusively in the 'advanced' members of the European Union (EU-15). The subsequent empirical analysis provides an extensive examination of the impact of spatial dependence and interaction in the process of regional convergence across the European regions. The basic model of absolute convergence is represented as a negative relation between growth rate over a given time period and the initial level of GVA per-worker:

$$\mathbf{g_i} = a + b\mathbf{y_{i,0}} + \varepsilon_i \qquad (7.1)$$

where $\mathbf{g_i} = \ln \mathbf{y_{i,T}} - \ln \mathbf{y_{i,0}}$, $b = -(1 - e^{-\beta t})$ and $\beta = -\frac{\ln(b+1)}{T}$.

As discussed in Chap. 5, this model can be extended to incorporate spatial dependence in the form of the spatial-error, spatial-lag and spatial cross-regressive models as follows (Rey and Montouri 1999):

$$\mathbf{g_i} = a + b\mathbf{y_{i,0}} + (\mathbf{I} - \zeta\mathbf{W})^{-1} u_t \qquad (7.2)$$

$$\mathbf{g_i} = a + b\mathbf{y_{i,0}} + \rho(\mathbf{Wg_i}) + \varepsilon_i \qquad (7.3)$$

$$\mathbf{g_i} = a + b\mathbf{y_{i,0}} + c(\mathbf{Wy_{i,0}}) + \varepsilon_i \qquad (7.4)$$

Each spatial model implies a different interpretation of spatial dependence, as discussed in Chap. 5. The spatial-error model, i.e. Eq. 7.2 captures the impact of regional spillovers in convergence through the spatial transformation matrix $(\mathbf{I} - \zeta\mathbf{W})^{-1}$. Spatial interaction is captured by the term $\mathbf{Wg_i}$, in the spatial-lag model in Eq. 7.3. On the other hand, the spatial cross-regressive model, i.e. Eq. 7.4, provides a simple treatment of spatial interaction by assuming that any spatial effects are captured in initial level of GVA per-worker adjusted by geographical distance ($\mathbf{Wy_{i,0}}$). Nevertheless, in all three spatial models the condition for convergence requires a negative relationship between growth and starting levels of GVA per-worker, i.e. $b < 0$. At this stage, however, it is important to comment on the estimation methods for these spatial econometric models. Thus, estimation of the spatial error model is carried out by the maximum likelihood method (ML), based on the eigenvalues of the spatial weights matrix, as OLS may result in problems of bias. To be more specific, the presence of spatial interaction in the error term leads to the following non-spherical covariance matrix (Rey and Montouri 1999, p. 149):

Table 7.1   Absolute convergence: non-spatial specification, EU-27, 1995–2006

OLS, Estimated equation: $g_i = a + by_{i,0}$, Sample: 268 EU-27 NUTS-2 regions				
a	b	R^2	[ser]	Implied β
0.5714**	−0.0747**	0.12492	[0.1397]	0.0065**
LIK	147.552	AIC −291.104	SBC	−283.929
Test statistics for heteroscedasticity [p-value]				
White		16.2553 [0.000]		
Breusch-Pagan		21.2656 [0.000]		
Koenker		15.1542 [0.000]		
Test statistic for normality of the residuals [p-value]				
Chi-squared		14.6936 [0.000]		

Notes: ** indicates statistical significance at 95 % level of confidence. [ser] denotes the standard error of the regression. AIC, SBC and LIK denote the *Akaike*, the *Schwartz-Bayesian* information criteria and Log-likelihood, respectively.

$$E[\varepsilon_t \varepsilon_t'] = (\mathbf{I} - \zeta \mathbf{W})^{-1} \sigma^2 \mathbf{I}(\mathbf{I} - \zeta \mathbf{W})^{-1'} \tag{7.5}$$

The presence of non-spherical errors results in unbiased OLS estimators but biased estimations of a parameter's variance. Bernat (1996) notes that the presence of spatial autocorrelation invalidates the standard tests in OLS regressions in a way similar to heteroscedasticity.[1] Thus, all inferences based on that model are invalid. Hence, the recommended estimation method is through ML (Anselin and Bera 1998) or Two-Stages Least Squares (2SLS). Fingleton (2001).[2]

When applied to the spatial-lag model, OLS estimators are inconsistent due to the simultaneity introduced through the spatial dimension. Ignoring the term $\mathbf{W}g_i$ the estimation of the convergence coefficient would be biased due to an omitted variable. Thus, the recommended estimation method is once again ML (Anselin 1988; Anselin et al. 1996; Pace 1997) or 2SLS (Elhorst 2010). In contrast to the two previous models, the spatial cross-regressive model treats the spatial variable as exogenous and, hence, estimation is possible through the OLS method. Before proceeding with the estimation of the spatial models, the results of estimating the non-spatial model of absolute convergence are presented in Table 7.1. Although these are discussed in Chap. 6, it is appropriate at this stage to present the relevant results again, in order to facilitate comparison. Table 7.1 also shows some diagnostic tests for heteroscedasticity.

As shown in Table 7.1, there is a statistically significant inverse relationship between growth over the time period, and the level of GVA per-worker at the start of the period. Nevertheless, the rate of convergence of labour productivity is a slow one, estimated to be 0.65 % per annum.

---

[1] Heteroscedasticity occurs when the disturbance variance is not constant and arises due to measurement problems, inadequate specification or omitted variables.

[2] An alternative is to include a spatial moving average error, $\varepsilon = \lambda \mathbf{W} v + v$, with, $v \sim N(0, \sigma^2 \mathbf{I})$ or a spatial error component model, $\varepsilon = \mathbf{W} v + \psi$, with two independent error components, one associated with the 'region' (weighted average of neighbour's error), and one which is location-specific (Acosta 2010).

In a spatial context, a frequent problem is the presence of heteroscedasticity (non-constant variances). This is mainly due to problems related to data collection. These refer to the different dimensions or sizes of the various spatial units that compose the area under consideration, the unbalanced distribution of population/ economic activities within regions, variations in the degree of urbanisation, the presence of relatively large rural areas, and so forth. The three tests set out in Table 7.1 accept the alternative hypothesis of heteroscedasticity. This is, perhaps, not so surprising if one considers the heterogeneity of the regions in the EU.[3] Based on the aforementioned tests, the null hypothesis of homoscedasticity (or the assumption of constancy of the conditional variance) for the model of absolute convergence cannot be accepted, at the usual levels of significance.[4] Furthermore, the null hypothesis of normal distribution of the residuals is rejected, enhancing the argument that the process of regional convergence in Europe is affected by spatial dependence. A spatial specification of the absolute convergence model, therefore, seems to be more appropriate in the case of the EU-27 regions. According to Lopez-Bazo et al. (2004) and Fingleton (1999), a spatial dimension is necessary in order to avoid misspecification. Table 7.2 presents the results from the estimation of the three spatial models for the period 1995–2006.

When spatial interaction is included,[5] the rate of convergence ranges from 0.64 % to 0.71 % per annum. Bearing in mind, however, that the spatial lag model represents only the direct marginal effects of an increase in the initial level of labour productivity, any conclusions should be treated with caution. In all cases, the spatial coefficient is statistically significant and positive, showing that spatial interaction plays a positive role in the convergence process. The superiority of the spatial models is supported by both the criteria for model selection applied here, namely the *Akaike* (AIC) and the *Schwartz-Bayesian* (SBC) information criteria, calculated as $AIC = -2L + 2K$ and $SBC = -2L + K \ln(T)$, where L is the value of the log likelihood function, T is the number of observations and K stands for the number of parameters estimated, including the constant term.[6] Further support is also provided by the value of the Log-likelihood (LIK), which increases, as perhaps anticipated, with the introduction of spatial interaction. According to this criterion the best fitted model is the one that yields the greatest value of the LIK (Anselin 1988). It should be noted that compared to the simple model of convergence the calculated values of the LIK statistic confirm the superiority of the spatial models suggesting therefore, that the conventional model of regional convergence is

---

[3] For example, entire countries (e.g. Denmark, Cyprus, Latvia, Lithuania and Slovenia) are treated by EUROSTAT as NUTS2 regions.

[4] If the obtained p-value is less that 0.10, 0.05 and 0.01 then the H_O hypothesis is rejected and the alternative H_a is accepted at 10 %, 5 % and 1 % level of significance, respectively.

[5] The presence of spatial autocorrelation makes the R^2 an unreliable measure of the goodness of fit and so is not reported.

[6] As a rule of thumb, the best fitting model is the one that yields the smallest values for the AIC or the SBC criterion. The SBC has superior properties and is asymptotically consistent, whereas the AIC is biased towards selecting an overparameterized model (Enders 1995).

Table 7.2 Absolute convergence: spatial econometric models, 1995–2006

I. Spatial-Error model $\mathbf{g_i} = a + b\mathbf{y_{i,0}} + (\mathbf{I} - \zeta\mathbf{W})^{-1}u_t$ ML,

Sample: 268 NUTS-2 regions

a	b	ζ	Implied β
0.5985**	−0.0819*	0.7506**	0.0071**
AIC −534.5256	SBC −523.7526	LIK 270.2628	

II. Spatial-Lag model $\mathbf{g_i} = a + b\mathbf{y_{i,0}} + \rho(\mathbf{Wg_i}) + \varepsilon_i$ ML,

Sample: 268 NUTS-2 regions

a	b	ρ	Implied β
0.5482**	−0.0770	0.1148*	0.0068
AIC −534.2128	SBC-523.4452	LIK 270.1091	

III. Spatial cross-regressive model $\mathbf{g_i} = a + b\mathbf{y_{i,0}} + c(\mathbf{Wy_{i,0}}) + \varepsilon_i$ OLS, Sample: 268 NUTS-2 regions

a	b	c	Implied β
0.5743**	−0.0741**	0.5979**	0.0064**
AIC −323.9148	SBC −313.1418	LIK 164.9574	

Notes: ** indicates statistical significance at 95 % level of confidence while * indicates significance at 90 % level. AIC, SBC and LIK denote the *Akaike*, the *Schwartz-Bayesian* information criteria and Log-Likelihood, respectively.

misspecified, by omitting geographical factors. The calculated values of the LIK criterion confirm the superiority of the spatial-error model. Thus, the approach to regional convergence, which is conditional upon spatial interaction operating through the disturbance term, provides a better explanation of the pattern of regional convergence than the other two specifications investigated in this section.

Overall, the results of estimating the spatial models confirm the previous conclusion that the European regions have been converging at a very slow rate. Incorporation of spatial interaction has improved the econometric performance of the model to some limited degree, but has not radically changed the conclusions. It may be the case that absolute convergence towards a unique 'steady-state' is not the underlying position for the 268 NUTS-2 regions of Europe. In order to investigate this further, it is appropriate to consider the possibility of conditional convergence, which implies that economies (countries or regions) converge towards different 'steady-states'. As noted by De la Fuente (2000) even where convergence forces prevail, long-run income levels can vary across regions, reflecting underlying differences in structural factors. A critical question, however, is the selection of appropriate variables to represent structural differences. Sala-i-Martin (1996a) argues that:

> [...] economic theory should guide our search for such variables. Different growth models suggest different variables (p.1028).

As shown in Chap. 4, contemporary models of economic growth suggest that technology creation and diffusion play a critical part in regional growth. The next section, therefore, tests the hypothesis of conditional convergence using variables that approximate regional differences in terms of the degree of regional capacities to create or adopt technology together with spatial factors, such as regional specialisation or diversity.

7.3 Conditioning for Technology and Agglomeration Externalities

Chapter 3 has demonstrated how the accumulation and diffusion of knowledge and innovation has the potential to play a significant role in the operation of agglomeration externalities and how, more generally, the diffusion of technology can be a significant factor in the convergence process. This section, therefore, examines the hypothesis of conditional convergence by taking account of the differences between the European regions in terms of these characteristics. In the first instance, the focus is upon technological change. As argued in Chap. 4, the empirical literature on convergence has focused on the contribution of physical capital accumulation in economic convergence at the expense of technological factors. Apart from some notable exceptions (e.g. de la Fuente 1997, 2000; Pigliaru 2003; Paci and Pigliaru 1997) technology is assumed to be uniform across observational units (countries or regions). However, not all economies have access to technological innovations and, more importantly, do not have the appropriate conditions or abilities to adopt technological innovations.

As acknowledged by Abramovitz (1986), technological progress is driven not only by indigenous innovation but also by the process of absorption of new technologies. More specifically, the possibility of imitating, at low cost, technologies developed elsewhere should allow poor regions to grow faster than rich ones, ceteris paribus – the 'technological catch-up effect'. In this section, therefore, the impact of technology in the process of regional growth is considered from these two broad perspectives.

7.3.1 Convergence due to Creation and Adoption of Innovation

A simple model developed in Chap. 4, has shown that the inclusion of technological factors, namely the intentional creation and adoption of technology, implies that club (local) convergence is a more probable outcome than absolute convergence. Technology creation and adoption, together with externalities arising from spatial agglomerations, have been acknowledged to be of paramount importance in determining patterns of regional growth and, hence, convergence. The remainder of this section formulates a model of regional growth based on technology and agglomeration externalities in a way that is amenable to econometric assessment. Production in region i is assumed to be a function of three inputs, namely capital, labour and technology in conjunction with a set of factors related to spatial agglomerations, which are represented as a separate element (E_i) in the production function. Thus,

$$Y_i = K_i^{\alpha}(E_iA_iL_i)^{1-\alpha} \tag{7.6}$$

An additional assumption is that production functions are identical across regions. Of critical importance for the purposes of this study are two elements of Eq. 7.6, representing technology (A_i) and externalities from spatial agglomeration

(E_i).[7] Technology is represented by a multiplicative function, which takes the following form:

$$A_i = IC_i ADP_i \quad \text{with} \quad \frac{\partial A_i}{\partial IC_i} > 0 \quad \text{and} \quad \frac{\partial A_i}{\partial ADP_i} > 0 \qquad (7.7)$$

where IC_i and ADP_i represent intentional creation and adoption of technology, respectively.[8]

The intuition behind Eq. 7.7 is that creation of technology, which is assumed to occur exogenously, does not occur globally, so that all regions are not able to produce technological innovations to the same degree; a statement that is supported by several studies (e.g. Moulaer and Seria 2003; Breschi 2000; Gordon and McCann 2005; Varga and Schalk 2004). In this case, technology development in these regions depends to a greater extent on adoption of innovations from advanced regions, represented by ADP_i.[9] In the case of agglomeration externalities, these appear in two distinct forms, namely localisation and diversity effects, as shown in Chap. 3; a separation which provides a convenient way for incorporating the differential impacts of agglomeration externalities into an empirical test for regional convergence. Thus, agglomeration externalities are assumed to be a multiplicative function of localisation and diversity effects, as follows:

$$E_i = LOC_i DVR_i \qquad (7.8)$$

where LOC_i and DVR_i denote localisation and diversity effects, respectively.

In general terms, gains from specialisation in one or more closely interrelated industries, are more likely to have positive effects on the growth of output rather on the growth of overall knowledge and technology. Such localisation effects may affect only the particular industry in which a region is specialised and are unlikely to create an appropriate environment for technology creation or adoption of technology, more generally.[10] An implicit assumption in Eqs. 7.7 and 7.8 is that both technology and agglomeration externalities are exogenously determined, in a manner similar to that implied by conventional neoclassical models. The

---

[7] This production function is similar to Barro and Sala-i-Martin (1997) in which technology adoption/diffusion is approximated by the quantity of non-durable inputs (X_j), modelled as a separate element in a production function, i.e. $Y_i = A_i L_i^{1-\alpha} \sum_{j=1}^{N} (X_j)^{\alpha}$.

[8] Equations 7.6 and 7.7 are in accordance with the model by de la Fuente (2000) in which growth of technology is assumed to be an increasing function of the fraction of GDP invested in R&D (intentional creation of technology) and a technological gap.

[9] This point is aptly summarised by Rosenberg (1982) when he suggests that: 'It may be seriously argued that, historically, European receptivity to new technologies, and the capacity to assimilate them whatever their origin, has been as important as inventiveness itself' (p. 245).

[10] See for example Alderman and Fischer (1992), Simmie (2003) and Morgan (2004).

development of agglomeration externalities depends, to some extent, on the geographical position of a region, such as whether a region is located in the periphery or in a centralised area, an outcome, at least partly, of historical and political factors. The next step forward is to develop an expression for regional growth incorporating technology and agglomeration externalities in such a way that it may be empirically tested. Thus, introducing each element of Eqs. 7.7 and 7.8 in terms of a regression equation yields:[11]

$$g_{i,T} = c + b_1 \log \left(\frac{Y}{L}\right)_{i,0} + b_2 \log IC_{i,0} + b_3 \log ADP_{i,0} + b_4 \log LOC_{i,0} + b_5 \log DVR_{i,0}$$

$$(7.9)$$

where $g_{i,T} = \log \left(\frac{Y}{L}\right)_{i,t} - \log \left(\frac{Y}{L}\right)_{i,0}$ is the growth rate of output per worker over a given time period $T = t - 0$, c is the constant term and $b_1 = -(1 - e^{-\beta t})$.

In Eq. 7.9 the variables related to technology and externalities are expressed in initial values. There are two primary reasons for such an approach. The first is related to the fact that R&D effort and adoption of innovations, normally, have future or long-run effects on regional growth.[12] In other words, future growth is affected by current efforts to enhance technology. Therefore, including technology creation and adoption at the initial time captures these long-run effects of technology on regional growth over a specific time period. A similar argument can be raised for the variables reflecting agglomeration externalities. A second reason for using initial values is that it tests the hypothesis that initial conditions 'lock' regions into a high or low position, for example, how high or low levels of technology affect the pattern of regional growth and convergence.

From an econometric point of view, inclusion of technological variables measured at the initial time helps to avoid the problem of endogeneity. Moreover, Pigliaru (2003) claims that models which include measures of technology require data on total factor productivity. In the absence of such data, econometric estimation requires that the variables related to technology ought to be included in initial values.

Despite its simplicity, this model aims to highlight the importance of initial conditions regarding spatial technology and agglomeration externalities in the process of regional growth and convergence. However, Eq. 7.9 treats regions as 'closed' economies, apart from the recognition of a technological gap with the leading region. It is possible to overcome this, clearly unrealistic, assumption by introducing in Eq. 7.9 the effects of spatial interaction. Thus, in general terms:

$$\mathbf{g_{i,T}} = c + b_1 \mathbf{EC_{i,0}} + b_2 \mathbf{T_{i,0}} + b_3 \mathbf{A_{i,0}} + b_4 \mathbf{SI_i} \qquad (7.10)$$

In Eq. 7.10 $\mathbf{EC_{i,0}}$ denotes the initial economic conditions in a region (i.e. initial levels of regional productivity), $\mathbf{T_{i,0}}$ refers to the initial technological factors, $\mathbf{A_{i,0}}$

---

[11] For a more detailed analysis see Appendix II.

[12] As Funke and Niebuhr (2005) claim: '[...] current R&D should affect future GDP.' (p. 149).

represents initial position regarding agglomeration externalities and finally, SI_i denotes spatial interaction, as captured in spatial econometric models outlined in Chap. 5 and Sect. 7.3. Thus, Eq. 7.10 offers an alternative test for regional convergence that takes into consideration technological factors, agglomeration externalities and spatial interaction.

It should be noted that contemporary empirical literature on regional convergence is based on models that combine conditional variables with spatial terms (that is to say 'spatial conditional convergence' models) focused mainly on the EU regions (e.g. Maurseth 2001; Arbia and Paelinck 2003; Alexiadis and Korres 2009, 2010) with fewer studies referring to individual countries (e.g. Funke and Niebuhr 2005 for Germany; Alexiadis 2010a for Greece). Equation 7.10 is consistent with this literature and can be applied to the regional context of any individual country, provided that the required data are available. Finally, Eq. 7.10 is sufficiently flexible that it can be used as a test for club convergence by simply modifying vector $EC_{i,0}$ to include a quadratic version of the initial level of labour productivity. Subsequent sections, therefore, are devoted to an empirical application of Eq. 7.10 in the context of the 268 NUTS-2 regions of the EU-27. Econometric estimation of Eq. 7.10 requires data on the level of technology and an approximation of agglomeration externalities. Such data, however, are not always readily available. In practice it is often the case that empirical analysis is limited by the extent and quality of data that is available at the required level of disaggregation. Therefore, the choice of appropriate proxies becomes an important issue. The next section outlines the proxies employed in the empirical analysis.

7.3.2 Technology Creation and Adoption in EU-27

A key feature of the model discussed in Sect. 7.4.1 is that technical change, leading to regional productivity growth, originates either from within the region or from other regions. In the former case, such internally generated technical change would be the outcome of R&D activities, patent applications and subsequent investment expenditures. The contribution of the R&D sector, and its spatial distribution, to regional growth has long been recognised in regional economics.[13]

As shown in Chap. 3, models of endogenous growth argue that the relationship between R&D and economic growth is not a simple linear process, due to strong threshold effects and external economies associated with investment in R&D. More

---

[13] Richardson (1973b), for example notes: 'Innovations and technical progress do not spread evenly and rapidly over space but frequently cluster in a prosperous region; for instance, technical progress may be a function of the levels of R and D expenditures which are higher in high-income regions.'(p. 56) while Hirschman (1962) argues along similar lines. More recently, Mulas-Granados and Sanz (2008) report evidence of a strong relationship between the distribution or technology indicators and the distribution of regional income in Europe.

recent models attribute the returns from investment in R&D to a number of specific factors such as human capital in a region (Cheshire and Carbonaro 1995, 1996), or the spatial concentration of R&D centres (Audretsch and Feldman 1996a; Audretsch and Feldman 1996b; Verspagen 1991; 1992). Nevertheless, all these various formulations acknowledge the importance of R&D. The practical problem, however, is effective measurement of R&D. In empirical studies (e.g. Fagerberg et al. 1997; Fagerberg 1987; Piergiovanni and Santarelli 2001), patent applications and patent citations are often used to approximate innovative activity,[14] although an alternative approach outlined by Pigliaru (2003) provides a more appropriate measure in the context of the observed slow rate of convergence across regions. According to this approach, technological growth is related to the 'propensity to innovate'. Thus, the resources devoted to innovation in a region as a share of total regional resources represents the propensity to innovate.

Problems arise, however, in choosing appropriate ways to measure the resources utilised in the knowledge producing sector. In the relevant empirical studies (e.g. Paci and Usai 2000a; b), R&D expenditures or patent applications and citations are used. Soete (1981), however, makes a distinction between technology output measures and technology input measures. Data related to patents[15] fall into the first category while R&D expenditures or labour employed in R&D activities belong in the second category. It is argued by both Soete (1981) and Fagerberg (1988, 1996) that the former category is a better measure of the impact of innovative effort since the latter often reflects efforts related to both innovation and diffusion. Ideally, therefore, an output measure of innovation would be preferable for the present study, given the objective of distinguishing between innovation and the diffusion of innovation. Nevertheless, in this study the propensity to innovate is defined as the number of patents (R_i) available to the total population of a region (P_i) in that region:[16]

$$IC_{i,t} = \frac{R_{i,t}}{P_{i,t}} \tag{7.11}$$

This ratio has some limitations; for example, not all inventions are systematically patented, not all patents have the same intrinsic value and that only a small proportion of them lead to technological breakthroughs. Especially, at the regional level the place of residence of the inventor, which is used by the major producers of patent statistics for the distribution of patent applications, and the place where the invention took place (e.g. research institute) are not necessarily in the same region).

---

[14] In an empirical study for OECD economies Verspagen (1995) assumes that the initial level of per capita GDP takes into account the effect of knowledge spillovers.

[15] Marjit and Beladi (1998) make a distinction between product and process patents.

[16] EUROSTAT is the main source for the data used in the empirical analysis in this chapter.

Nevertheless, this proxy is able to provide a useful and readily available measure of resources allocated to innovative activities at the regional level.[17]

Turning to the ability of regions to adopt technology and innovations, this is even more difficult to measure. Camagni and Capello (2009), for example, offer a measurement of the absorptive capacity by a binary dummy variable that takes the value of 1 if a firm's R&D expenditure is above the mean, 0 otherwise. Nevertheless, this approximation is more appropriate at the firm's level. Peri and Urban (2006) approximate technology adoption in terms of spillovers from foreign direct investment while Bode (2004) develops a model that distinguishes between spillovers from abroad and local spillovers. While such approaches are interesting, it is difficult to apply them directly in the present context due to data limitations. However, other approaches put emphasis on the role of dynamic, advanced technological sectors in driving the technology diffusion process. Here, the relative extent of technology adoption capacity is therefore approximated by the share of a region's resources found in such sectors. In other words, this approach involves identifying technically dynamic sectors, which are perceived to be the most receptive to innovation and its utilisation.

One of the first attempts to include industrial structure that recognizes high technology in a model of conditional regional convergence is by Gripaios et al. (2000). These authors select four high technology industries, as defined by the OECD, namely aerospace, pharmaceutical, TV-radio and communication equipment and computer and office equipment. Gripaios et al. (2000) use the proportion of employment in high technology industries as an explanatory variable in a test for regional convergence across the UK counties. This variable is used, in conjunction with a series of employment variables (traditional manufacturing, utilities and financial/business services) to approximate industrial structure, to test for the differential impacts of various sectors in shaping patterns of regional growth. According to Gripaios et al. (2000):

> [...] different sectors will have different growth patterns arising from long-term changes in technology and demand (p. 1165)

Similarly, Plummer and Taylor (2001a, 2001b) also select five such industrial sectors: pharmaceutical and veterinary, aircraft manufacturing, photographic, professional and scientific equipment, data-processing services and, finally, research and scientific institutions.[18] In this study a region's level of adoption capacity is measured as the percentage of total employment in technologically dynamic sectors, which include manufacturing activities such as aerospace and services such as computer and related activities. More formally, at time t,

---

[17] Jaffe et al. (1993) argue that knowledge spillovers as evidenced in spatial patterns of patent citations are strongly localized.

[18] Andonelli (1990) and Alderman and Fisher (1992) use a similar approach in identifying sectors that are able to adopt technological innovations, although in a context other than of regional convergence.

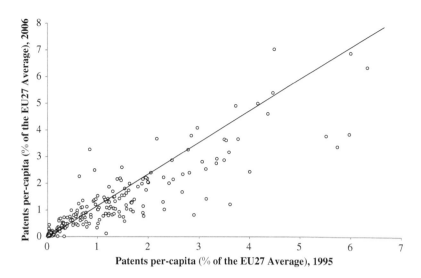

Fig. 7.1 Technology-creation, 268 NUTS-2 regions, 1995–2006

$$ADP_{i,t} = \frac{\sum_{\rho=1}^{k} \eta_{i,t}^{\rho}}{\sum_{j=1}^{m} L_{i,t}^{j}} \tag{7.12}$$

where $\eta_{i,t}^{\rho}$ refers to personnel employed in high-tech manufacturing and knowledge-intensive high-technology services ($\rho = 1, \ldots, k$), while $L_{i,t}^{j}$ is the employment in all the sectors ($j = 1, \ldots, m$) of a regional economy i.

As in the case of the propensity to innovate, the ability of a region to adopt technology, given by the ratio in Eq. 7.12, is measured for the initial years of the analysis (1995).

At this point it is important to provide some descriptive statistics on the two 'technological variables' (IC_i and the ADP_i). The analysis will be conducted in terms of a scatterplot that compares the initial and the terminal deviations from the EU-27 average (Figs. 7.1 and 7.2). The 45 ° line divides the regions into to categories. The first includes regions in which the variable in question was higher in the initial year compare to the terminal year while the opposite holds for the regions in the second category.

This simple descriptive approach reveals some interesting aspects of the regional distribution of technological activities in EU-27, in conjunction with the mobility of regions above or below the EU-27 average throughout a given time-period (1995–2006).

Figure 7.1 indicates a converging tendency across the regions of the EU-27 in terms of technology creation. Some regions in the terminal year of the analysis exhibit percentages lower, relative to that in the initial period. Only 33 % of the

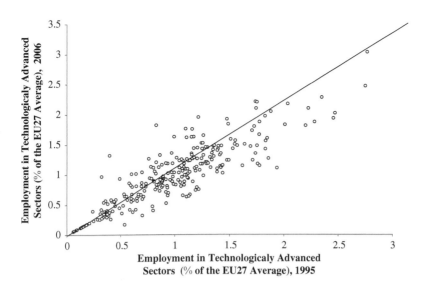

Fig. 7.2 Technology-adoption, 268 NUTS-2 regions, 1995–2006

EU-27 regions fell into that category while the remaining regions have experience a relative increase in the terminal year. The relatively high percentage in the latter category can be taken as an indication that the EU regions tend to become more similar in terms of technology-creation. A more thorough examination of the regions involved in both categories indicates that about 26 % of the regions that increased their ability to create technology belong to countries in New Member-States. Predominantly are regions located in Poland, Czech Republic and Romania (about 5 % in each country). In the EU-15 the highest percentage of the regions in this category is found in advanced countries, such as Germany, France and the UK (18 %, 7 %, and 7 %, respectively) while considerably high percentages are found in Mediterranean countries, such as Greece, Italy and Spain (7 %, 9 % and 8 %, respectively). Conversely, regions with a relatively high level of technology-creation in 1995 and a relatively low level in 2006 are located principally in countries of the EU-15, with most of them in the UK (27 %), France (15 %) and Germany (10 %).

Using the IC_i variable, the descriptive analysis suggests a 'glimmer of hope' for the technologically lagged regions of the EU-27. On the other hand, less than 50 % of the EU-27 regions were able to increase their adoptive abilities throughout the examined period. The vast majority in this group refers to regions belonging to the EU-15 countries (16 % and 14 % of them located in Germany and the UK) while just 22 % are located on the New Member-States. An almost equal percentage of regions in the New Member-States experienced a reduction in their adoptive abilities within the examined period. In general, Fig. 7.2 suggests that only as small proportion of advanced technologies can be adopted by the lagging regions of the EU.

Although this analysis can be considered as a simple descriptive approach, nevertheless, some interesting aspects of the ongoing process of regional convergence in EU-27 can be exposed. While technology-creation tends to be uniform across the regions of an enlarged Europe, nevertheless, this cannot be said for the process of technology adoption. Any beneficiary effects from an increasing ability of technology-creation are cancelled-out by a relatively low ability of lagging regions to adopt technology.

The presence of technologically dynamic sectors in a regional economy, encapsulated by Eq. 7.12, represents the level of technological development, but also, indicates a capacity for technology adoption, since these are taken to be the most technologically dynamic and advanced sectors. However, the potential for such technology diffusion increases as the technological gap increases, defined as the distance between a region's technological level and that of the most advanced technological region. Consequently, in this context a variable that approximates the technological gap for region i at time t can be defined as follows:

$$TG_{i,t} = ADP_{L,t} - ADP_{i,t} \qquad (7.13)$$

where the subscript L refers to the leading region, defined as the region with the highest percentage of employment in high-tech manufacturing and knowledge-intensive high-technology services during the initial year of the analysis.[19]

Embodied in this variable is the idea of both a gap and the capacity to adopt and implement technological innovations. As shown by a simple model in Chap. 4, the presence of a technological gap alone is not sufficient to promote significant technology diffusion. There has to be an appropriate level of capability to adopt technology. Thus, the bigger the gap the greater the potential for technology adoption, but the lower the capacity to actually achieve this.

7.3.3 Agglomeration Effects

Although the ability of an economy to catch up may substantially depend on its capacity to absorb, imitate and adopt innovations developed in neighbouring regions, it must also be recognised that *intra*-regional spatial interaction may contribute to growth trends in that the spatial concentration of economic activity

---

[19] This is region UKJ1 (Berkshire, Bucks and Oxfordshire). The choice is made for two reasons. First, this region has retained its leading position throughout the examined period. In 1995 the share of employment in high-tech manufacturing and knowledge-intensive high-technology services ('innovative employment') in the total labour force of this region was 9.77 % and 11.44 % in 2006. Second, this region is an illustrative example of local empowerment can create possibilities of invention to overcome local difficulties, and enhance the likelihood of increased localisation of the geographic scope of spillovers between knowledge creation and production (Smith 2000, p. 88).

within any region has the potential to produce agglomeration economies and a virtuous cycle of growth, as well as some diseconomies associated with concentration. As discussed in Chap. 3, the spatial concentration of economic activity can lead to enhanced competitiveness, by generating benefits that are internalised within regions, but which have the characteristics of externalities to individual firms. Typically separated into two categories, localisation effects derive from the concentration of similar economic activities, whilst diversity effects flow from the spatial concentration of a variety of economic activities.

However, an important point in the present context is that if there are significant regional agglomeration effects, where the benefits of specialisation, concentration and diversity outweigh the costs, then this is not compatible with convergence occurring across all regions. The presence of such agglomeration economies is more consistent with divergent growth trends, or with limited convergence between some, rather than all, regions.

From an empirical point of view, although agglomeration externalities are considered to be a non-tangible concept, nevertheless a traditional approach is to use total population in an area[20] (e.g. Baumol 1967; Schaefer 1977; Segal 1976; Sveikauskas et al. 1988; Mullen and Williams 1990). However, it should be noted that population has been argued to be a poor proxy for (external) agglomeration effects.[21] Carlino (1978) summarises the argument as follows:

> [...] while population scale might serve as a reasonable proxy for household and social agglomeration economies, population scale is a worthless surrogate for business agglomeration economies. The latter tend to be related to industry size (localisation economies) and/or inter-industry size (urbanisation economies). Therefore, proxies which capture these influences are more appropriate. (p. 75)

Thus, the extent of these external effects depends upon the number and variety of activities within a region rather than its population size. Any empirical approach to external economies should also make a distinction between the differential effects stemming from the concentration of particular activities and the overall concentration of economic activity in a location.

As outlined in Henderson (1996, 1997), if externalities arise primarily from a build-up of knowledge among only local firms in the same industry in a specific area, then they are referred to as localisation externalities. An increase in an industry's concentration will facilitate knowledge spillovers and, as a consequence, regions are likely to specialise in this specific activity, which, in turn allows for full exploitation of scale economies. A critical question, which then arises, is how to measure such localisation externalities.

---

[20] Richardson (1973c) notes that the relevant empirical work relies heavily on demographic data and, consequently, growth is associated with an increase in a locality's population.

[21] This has been surrounded by considerable controversy. See for example Alonso-Villar et al. (2004), Baldwin (1999), Bertinelli and Black (2004), Braunerhjelm and Borgman (2004), Carlino (1980, 1982, 1987), Ricci (1999), Mion (2004), Moomaw (1988, 1998).

Ciccone and Hall (1995) argue that a concentration measure is required to represent the degree of local specialisation or intensity of one activity, on the assumption that intensity facilitates communication. In the relevant empirical literature[22] the concentration of an activity in an area can be measured either by a location quotient or by localisation coefficients based on employment shares of particular sectors or industries. According to Richardson (1978a) a location quotient is:

> [...] a measure comparing the relative importance of an industry in an area with its relative importance in the nation. (p. 89)

A location quotient is measured as follows:

$$LQ_i = \frac{X_i^r / X^r}{X_i^n / X^n} \tag{7.14}$$

where X refers to a given variable, usually employment or output of a particular industry i while r and n denote region and nation, respectively.[23] If $LQ_i > 1$ it is assumed that there is export activity, because the specific region has a higher concentration of a particular industry than in the nation as a whole.

In the present context, however, the concentration measure (LOC) to be used in the empirical analysis is based on the alternative measure, the distribution of employment across industry sectors (Henderson 1997), which is calculated as follows:

$$LOC_{i,t} = \frac{e_{i,t}^j}{\sum e_{i,t}^j} \tag{7.15}$$

where $e_{i,t}^j$ refers to the labour employed in sector j in region i.

This choice is made primarily for two reasons. First, localisation externalities refer mainly to regional specialisation, of which employment share of a particular sector is a standard measure, irrespective of whether a region or an activity is considered as small or large. Second, in other relevant empirical studies (e.g. Henderson 1997; 2003a; Henderson et al. 2001a) employment shares of particular industrial sectors are widely accepted as representing this kind of externality.[24] Thus, a set of localisation coefficients in the form of sectoral employment shares using data for the various sectors is calculated for each region. The highest localisation coefficient is selected for each region to indicate the extent to which a

---

[22] See for example Isard (1956), Leigh (1970), Mayer and Pleeter (1975), Norcliffe (1983), McDonald (1989), among others.

[23] A location quotient is used as a proxy for trade flows across regions. See for example Isserman (1977), Ford et al. (2009).

[24] Empirical tests were conducted also using location quotients and results were very similar.

particular sector is dominant in a region. Preliminary inspection of the $LOC_{i,t}$ coefficient indicates the activities related to processing stages of agricultural, fishing or forestry products tend to locate close to the source of the raw material.[25] The most specialised regions in retail trade, construction hotels and restaurants are found in countries traditionally associated with tourism, mainly in Greece, Portugal and Spain. In northern Europe the most specialised regions in this sector are the regions NL31, FI20 and UKI1. Regions specialised in manufacturing and high technological activities are located in the United Kingdom, Germany and Belgium.[26]

The second type of spatial externality to be considered refers to the diversity of activities in a given area. Diversity is said to enhance knowledge accumulation as producers in any one industry can draw upon a greater range of ideas from other industries, through interacting socially and commercially. There are several approaches[27] to the measurement of diversity, but the Hirschman-Herfindahl index (hereafter HH) is a standard measure and one of the most frequently used in recent empirical literature (e.g. Rigby and Essletzbichler 2002; Lucio et al. 2002; Ketenci and McCann 2009; Goschin et al. 2009). This index is defined as follows:

$$HH_{i,t}^{j} = \sum_{j \neq l} (\varpi_{i,t}^{j})^{2} \tag{7.16}$$

where ϖ is the share of each sector j in region i.

This index is often used to measure concentration at the industry level, using mainly market shares in its calculation. Nevertheless, this index can be used to measure diversity of economic activities across regional economies as well, using employment shares instead of market shares, since similar principles may be applied.

In an extreme case, a diverse regional economy could be one in which all sectors are represented with equal employment shares. A less diverse economy would be one where fewer sectors are present, in which case some sectors would have above average shares of employment. Therefore, a low value of the HH ratio indicates a high degree of diversity while a more concentrated, less diverse environment in a region is associated with a higher HH index.

In this study the HH ratio, which approximates the DVR_i variable, is constructed using data for sectors in each region, excluding only the sector in which a specific region is specialised (l). Thus, in order to obtain a clearer picture of diversity in a

---

[25] Typical examples are the regions FR52 and PL33, highly specialised in food/beverage processing and mining and quarrying, respectively. Highly specialised regions in activities related to wood, pulp and paper products can be found in the Baltic and Nordic forested areas.

[26] Regions UKD2, BE21, BE31, DEE1, DE71, DEA3, DEE2 and DEB3, for example, can be characterised as highly specialised in chemical products, DE26 in machinery equipments, DE21 in R&D and UKJ1 in computer activities.

[27] For example, the number of establishments per worker in an area (region, city, etc.) can be considered as a proxy. Nevertheless, in several studies (e.g. Glaeser et al. 1992; de Vor and de Groot 2010) this proxy approximates competition. For a more detailed review see Wagner (2000).

region all other sectors of economic activities are included. The logic of this approach is to produce a measure of the diversity of the economic environment surrounding and interacting with the key sector in each region. Preliminary examination of the degree of diversity in regional economic activities shows that several 'central' regions of the European Union in which the capital cities and large urban centres are located, such as UKI2, UKI2, FR10 and LU) are characterised by highly diverse environments.

Nevertheless, it is worth noting that several low productivity regions, located mainly in Eastern European countries (CZ01 and CZ02, for example) have a degree of diversity considerably higher than that of regions with relatively high productivity. This may be considered as a possible source of convergence. Nevertheless, such an argument should be established empirically.

Before proceeding to the more formal empirical analysis, it is necessary to consider further the time dimension of the variables representing localisation and diversity. Henderson (1997), in his industry-specific model, argues for the use of lagged values of these variables, in order to represent the role of 'history' or initial conditions, and the 'stock of trade secrets' in generating growth in a given location. Moreover, introducing these variables measured at the initial time not only has the potential to capture the long-run effects on growth, as implied by the model in Sect. 7.4.1, but also from an econometric point of view, helps in avoiding the problem of endogeneity. Subsequent empirical analysis, therefore, presents the results from the estimation of a model of regional convergence, conditioned upon technological and agglomeration effects.

7.3.4   Technology and Agglomeration in Regional Convergence

Having examined the variables to be used in the empirical analysis, the next step forward in testing for technological conditional convergence across the 268 NUTS-2 regions of the EU-27 is to combine these variables within a single regression. Consequently, the model to be estimated is defined as follows:

$$g_i = a + b_1 y_{i,0} + b_2 \ln(IC_{i,0}) + b_3 \ln(TG_{i,0}) + b_4 \ln(LOC_{i,0}) + b_5 \ln(DVR_{i,0}) + \varepsilon_i$$

$$(7.17)$$

Technology creation is represented by $IC_{i,0}$ whilst technology diffusion is examined by means of the 'technological gap' variable ($TG_{i,0}$), defined in Eq. 7.13. Employment shares in each NUTS-2 region approximate localisation effects, measured by Eq. 7.15, while diversity effects are reflected by Eq. 7.16. The values of these variables for each region are calculated for the initial year, as required by the model developed in Sect. 7.4.1.

Equation 7.17, thus, incorporates the potential impact of both internally generated technological change and technology adoption upon a region's growth.

Broadly speaking, it is anticipated that $b_2 > 0$, since regions with high initial levels of propensity to innovate are normally associated with high levels of growth and vice versa. However, it is not automatically the case that this condition promotes convergence. In other words, if low productivity regions have a high initial level of intentional technology creation, then this will have positive impacts on convergence, by enhancing their growth rates. On the other hand, if such regions have a low propensity to innovate, then no significant impacts on growth are anticipated and, hence, it may be difficult to converge with technologically 'rich' regions. The latter case is the more likely.

In the case of the $TG_{i,0}$ variable, this variable reflects two distinct features, namely the level of 'technological distance' from the leading region and the degree to which existing (initial) conditions in a region allow adoption of technology. A high initial technological gap combined with a high rate of growth may indicate, ceteris paribus, that less advanced regions are able to adopt technology, which is transformed into high growth rates and, subsequently, convergence with the technologically regions.[28] It may be argued, therefore, that the condition $b_3 > 0$ promotes convergence. On the other hand, a high initial value for $TG_{i,0}$ may indicate that although there is significant potential for technology adoption, initial infrastructure conditions are not appropriate to technology adoption and, therefore, there are no significant impacts on growth. In other words, if $b_3 < 0$, then convergence between technologically lagging and technologically advanced regions is not feasible. Turning to agglomeration effects, if localisation effects are present, then $b_4 > 0$ is expected, that is, a higher degree of specialisation is associated with higher growth. On the other hand, the impact of the diversity variable is ambiguous. Thus, as with the $TG_{i,0}$ variable, the $DVR_{i,0}$ variable may interpreted in two ways. If greater diversity leads to higher growth, then the coefficient attached to this variable should be negative, since greater diversity is associated with a lower value of the HH ratio. If, on the other hand, low diversity, i.e. a high initial HH ratio, leads to high rates of growth, then it is expected that $b_5 > 0$. Assuming that rich (poor) regions are associated with a high (low) degree of diversity, then a sign $b_5 > 0$ indicates that negative externalities are present in highly diversified areas, lowering rates of growth, which is not the case for the poorer less diversified economies. In this light, therefore, $b_5 > 0$ may act as a source of convergence.

While both convergence and divergence patterns due to technology and agglomeration externalities are possible from a theoretical point of view, their actual impact on growth and convergence is an empirical issue, depending on the specific context and particular time that is examined. Therefore, the remainder of this section considers the results of estimating Eq. 7.17 in the context of the 268 NUTS-2 regions of Europe (Table 7.3).

---

[28] At the firm level Griffith et al. (2009) present evidence that establishments further behind the industry frontier experience faster rates of productivity growth.

Table 7.3 Technological and spatial externalities in regional convergence

OLS, Sample: 268 NUTS-2 regions estimated equation:

$g_i = a + b_1 y_{i,0} + b_2 \ln(IC_{i,0}) + b_3 \ln(TG_{i,0}) + b_4 \ln(LOC_{i,0}) + b_5 \ln(DVR_{i,0}) + \varepsilon_i$

a	b_1	b_2	b_3	b_4	b_5	*Implied* β
0.872**	−0.037**	−0.039**	−0.075**	−0.028	0.097**	0.0031**
AIC	−322.778	SBC	−301.232	LIK	167.389	
Test statistics for heteroscedasticity [p-value]						
White		68.2959	[0.000]			
Breusch-Pagan		37.2482	[0.000]			
Koenker		23.7594	[0.000]			

Notes: ** indicates statistical significance at 95 % level of confidence while * indicates significance at 90 % level. AIC, SBC and LIK denote the *Akaike* and the *Schwartz-Bayesian* information criteria and Log-Likelihood, respectively.

Table 7.4 Variance inflation factors

Variable	$y_{i,0}$	$IC_{i,0}$	$TG_{i,0}$	$LOC_{i,0}$	$DVR_{i,0}$
VIF	1.934	2.413	1.684	2.210	2.391

However, before taking further step, an essential question seems to arise at this point that requires some attention. A potential problem with the model is related with the presence of multicollinearity. A measure to detect multicollinearity is by using variance inflation factors (*VIF*).[29] The average *VIF* value is 2.126, indicating that the model does not suffer from multicollinearity. The obtained *VIF* values of each independent variable are set out in Table 7.4.

Estimation of Eq. 7.17 yields a lower rate of convergence of 0.31 % per year, compared to the model of absolute convergence (Table 7.1). However, it should be noted that conditional convergence models (such as Eq. 7.17) typically lead to a slower rate of convergence, as pointed out in Chap. 2. The estimated values of b_2 and b_3 are negative, as perhaps anticipated and both statistically significant at the 95 % level. The coefficient on the propensity to innovate is negative, suggesting that regions with a high propensity to innovate, normally high productivity regions, grow slower than technologically lagging regions. This might act as source of convergence, provided that the poor regions are able to absorb technology. However, this does not seem to be the case. A negative sign is also estimated for the variable representing technology adoption. The existence of a high technology gap and associated low capability for technology adoption is thus inhibiting growth and convergence.

---

[29] More specifically, for any regression equation with k independent variables, it is possible to calculate a *VIF* for every dependent variable running an OLS regression for each variable as a function of all the other explanatory variables. Then a *VIF* is calculated for each $\hat{\beta}_i$: $VIF(\hat{\beta}_i)$ $= \frac{1}{1-R_i^2}$, $\forall i = 1, \ldots, k$, where R_i^2 is the multiple correlation coefficient. As a rule of thumb, if $VIF(\hat{\beta}_i) > 5$, or $VIF(\hat{\beta}_i) > 10$ according to Neter et al. (1990), then multicollinearity is high.

At this point in the analysis there is therefore substantial evidence of the impact of technology in explaining regional growth. While the obtained results indicate that the process of intentional technology creation does promote a process of regional convergence, nevertheless, the estimated negative sign of the $TG_{i,0}$ variable suggests a diverging effect. While $b_2 > 0$ can be conceived as a convergence effect, nevertheless the impact of the technology adoption variable works in the opposite direction. Regions with low productivity levels, typically associated with high technological gaps, are in a difficult position to adopt and assimilate technology. This inability is reflected in relatively low growth rates. On average, regions with high technological gaps at the start of the period grow slower than regions with low gaps, ceteris paribus.[30] In this context, it might be argued that unfavourable conditions, reflected in a high initial technological gap, prevailing to the less productive regions of EU-27 constitutes an obstacle to the catch-up process in an enlarged Europe.

In summary, the evidence presented thus far clearly supports the arguments put forward in Chap. 4, that technology adoption is a route by which lagging regions might be able to converge with leading regions, but that this is a process which is likely to be difficult, especially during the early stages of development when conditions in the lagging regions are least supportive.[31] Thus, a high technology gap presents an obstacle to convergence because of the implied poor infrastructure and weak adoptive capacity. These factors work to sustain initial differences across regions, and suggest the possibility of club convergence towards different equilibria following the predictions of the model examined in Chap. 4.

The results of this model identify the estimated coefficient of $LOC_{i,0}$ to be statistically insignificant and negative. It was anticipated that $b_4 > 0$, since localisation externalities, approximated by the $LOC_{i,0}$ variable, are predicted to promote regional growth, given that a high degree of specialisation, normally, leads to faster productivity growth. As the $LOC_{i,0}$ coefficient is statistically insignificant it could be further argued that the concentration effects are not consistent across the

---

[30] Gripaios et al. (2000) using actual percentages of employment in similar sectors for the UK counties, estimate a negative coefficient. In this case a negative coefficient can be interpreted as a source of convergence, if employment in these sectors is located mainly in rich regions. In this case, a high percentage of employment in such sectors is associated with low rates of growth, thus, promoting convergence between rich and poor regions. Experimenting with the proxy by Gripaios et al. (2000) the resulting coefficient was positive, which can be considered an indication of diverging tendencies (Alexiadis 2010a). However, the technological gap variable is chosen because of its ability to embody two concepts, namely the extent of the potential for technology adoption and the appropriateness of infrastructure conditions to take advantage of this potential.

[31] The null hypothesis associated with the Ramsey RESET test is accepted indicating that the particular model is well specified. Furthermore, the probability associated with the F-statistic for overall significance of the regression rejects the null hypothesis of zero coefficients.

European regions. Highly specialised regions do not experience any advantage in growth terms.[32] This is possible if the dominant economic activity in a region is related to low value added activities (e.g. commodity production). In actual fact, according to the obtained results, a relatively high initial degree of specialisation induces *negative* effects in the process of regional growth.

On the other hand, regional diversity, as measured by the *HH* index, does contribute to an explanation of regional growth, since the coefficient (b_5) on the $DVR_{i,0}$ variable is statistically significant. The econometric estimates yield a positive sign for the variable approximating the degree of diversification externalities. The interpretation of this outcome runs as follows. High (low) productivity regions are, normally, associated with a high (low) degree of diversity. Hence, $b_5 > 0$ can be taken as an indication that high productivity regions, associated with highly diversified areas, exhibit relatively lower rates of growth.[33] It may be argued, therefore, that the majority of benefits from moving to a more diversified economy have already been experienced, resulting to relatively slow rates of growth in highly diversified regions. However, this does not seem to be the case for the low-productivity regions, with less diversified environments. In this light, therefore, $b_5 > 0$ may act as a source of convergence. It is worth noting that the estimated value of b_5 implies that a 1 % increase to the degree of diversification induces an increase in the growth rate about 0.1 %. The inference is that an increasing degree of diversity of their economic environments in low-productivity regions will put them into a fast path of convergence towards regions with high-productivity.

Nonetheless, irrespective of the introduction of the four conditional variables, the obtained rate of convergence remains relatively low. Accordingly, it will take a long time for the less productive regions of the EU-27 to catch-up with the regions exhibiting relatively high levels of labour productivity. Given the structure of the model, encapsulated by Eq. 7.17, it seems that overall conditions, captured in terms of the variables describing technological and spatial externalities, differ considerably across the NUTS-2 regions of EU-27. Moreover, the White, Breusch-Pagan and Koenker tests indicate the presence of heteroscedasticity, despite the introduction of variables representing spatial externalities.

The final step in this section, therefore, involves the introduction of the set of variables representing technology and agglomeration externalities into a spatial econometric model. As previously, the three models take the following forms:

---

[32] The variable employed to approximate localisation in this study does not distinguish between dynamic and non-dynamic sectors. That is, it does not distinguish between the different sectors in which regions are specialised, some of which grow faster than others. Dynamic sectors could be defined as promoting exports; in which case a location quotient would be a more suitable proxy. However, using such a proxy gives similar results in econometric terms.

[33] This outcome can be interpreted also as evidence that negative externalities are present in highly diversified regions.

Table 7.5 Regional convergence: geography, technology and externalities

I. Spatial-Error model: $g_i = a + b_1 y_{i,0} + b_2 \ln IC_{i,0} + b_3 \ln TG_{i,0} + b_4 \ln LOC_{i,0} + b_5 \ln DVR_{i,0} + (\mathbf{I} - \zeta\mathbf{W})^{-1} u_i$, ML sample 268 EU-27 NUTS-2 regions

a	b_1	b_2	b_3	b_4	b_5	ζ	Implied β
0.8527**	−0.0447**	−0.0364**	−0.0596**	−0.0486	0.1049**	0.6551**	0.0038**
AIC	−528.277	SBC	−503.140	LIK	271.138		

II. Spatial-Lag model: $g_i = a + b_1 y_{i,0} + b_2 \ln IC_{i,0} + b_3 \ln TG_{i,0} + b_4 \ln LOC_{i,0} + b_5 \ln DVR_{i,0} + \rho(\mathbf{W}g_i) + \varepsilon_i$, ML, sample 268 EU-27 NUTS-2 regions

a	b_1	b_2	b_3	b_4	b_5	ρ	Implied β
0.7964**	−0.0265**	−0.0418*	−0.0638*	−0.0402	0.1073*	0.1496**	0.0022**
AIC	−322.778	SBC	−301.232	LIK	167.389		

III. Spatial cross-regressive model:

$g_i = a + b_1 y_{i,0} + b_2 \ln IC_{i,0} + b_3 \ln TG_{i,0} + b_4 \ln LOC_{i,0} + b_5 \ln DVR_{i,0} + c(\mathbf{W}y_{i,0}) + \varepsilon_i$, OLS, sample 268 EU-27 NUTS-2 regions

a	b_1	b_2	b_3	b_4	b_5	c	Implied β
0.8132**	−0.0370**	−0.0391**	−0.0793	−0.0060	0.0558*	0.5969*	0.0031**
AIC	−526.058	SBC	−500.921	LIK	270.029		

Notes: ** indicates statistical significance at 95 % level of confidence while * indicates significance at 90 % level. AIC, SBC and LIK denote the *Akaike*, the *Schwartz-Bayesian* information criteria and Log-Likelihood, respectively.

$$\mathbf{g}_i = a + b_1 y_{i,0} + b_2 \ln IC_{i,0} + b_3 \ln TG_{i,0} + b_4 \ln LOC_{i,0} + b_5 \ln DVR_{i,0}$$
$$+ (\mathbf{I} - \zeta\mathbf{W})^{-1} u_i \qquad (7.18)$$

$$\mathbf{g}_i = a + b_1 y_{i,0} + b_2 \ln IC_{i,0} + b_3 \ln TG_{i,0} + b_4 \ln LOC_{i,0} + b_5 \ln DVR_{i,0}$$
$$+ \rho(\mathbf{W}g_i) + \varepsilon_i \qquad (7.19)$$

$$\mathbf{g}_i = a + b_1 y_{i,0} + b_2 \ln IC_{i,0} + b_3 \ln TG_{i,0} + b_4 \ln LOC_{i,0} + b_5 \ln DVR_{i,0} + c$$
$$\times (\mathbf{W}y_{i,0}) + \varepsilon_i \qquad (7.20)$$

Estimating these models produces the results on Table 7.5.

In all three spatial specifications, the explanatory variables have the same signs as previously while the variable representing localisation externalities in a region is always statistically insignificant. According to the selection criteria, the spatial error specification is to be preferred. This model implies a relatively higher rate of convergence. This can be taken as evidence that the combined effect of technology and spatial externalities promotes convergence.

It is obvious that for all model specifications, examined in this section, the average rate of convergence is very low. Strictly speaking, there is no compelling evidence of regional absolute convergence or divergence across the NUTS-2 regions of EU-27. Although low productivity regions, on average, grow faster than high productivity regions, having conditioned for factors that affect regional growth yields an even lower rate of convergence, suggesting that established differences across the EU-27 regions have been maintained throughout the period under examination. This should not be surprising, bearing in mind that conditional convergence '[...] does not imply the existence of a spontaneous tendency towards the reduction of inequality' (de la Fuente 1997, p. 24).

What should be the verdict then on regional convergence in an enlarged Europe? Clearly, the European regions, as a *whole*, exhibit extremely very slow convergence tendencies. As pointed out in Sect. 7.4.2, any beneficiary effects from an increasing ability of technology-creation in low productivity regions are cancelled-out by their relatively low ability to adopt technology. This implies that (overall) infrastructure conditions in these regions are less supportive. This brings an alternative hypothesis into consideration. The European regions follow a pattern of convergence into different groups that exhibit dissimilar rates of convergence due to variations in the infrastructure conditions. The idea of regional clusters leads to the alternative hypothesis of club convergence. The next section, therefore, tests the hypothesis of 'club convergence' across the NUTS-2 regions of the EU-27 in a way which combines technology creation and diffusion with agglomeration externalities in an explicit spatial context.

7.4 Convergence Clubs Across the EU-27 Regions

The empirical analysis is moving towards a more thorough examination of the hypothesis of regional club convergence in Europe. However, prior to this, consideration must be given to the choice of an appropriate methodology to detect convergence clubs.

7.4.1 Choosing a Method for Detecting Convergence Clubs

As pointed out in Chap. 5, there are several different approaches for identifying convergence clubs. Economic theory offers little guidance in detecting both the number and composition of such clubs within a given cross-section of regional economies, as Corrado et al. (2005) claim. As a result, choosing a methodology that is appropriate or suitable in the present context is not necessarily a straightforward task, particularly when data is limited. Nevertheless, existing methodologies can be classified into two broad categories, namely methods that are based on time-series data[34] and those that rely on cross-section data. However, a potential pitfall in these methodologies is that they rely exclusively upon a single variable, namely GVA per-worker, which may be unsatisfactory in terms of policy implications. From a policy perspective, identification of convergence clubs alone is not enough, since

---

[34] Some evidence using time-series data is provided in Appendix III.

successful implementation of economic policies at the regional level requires information on the specific factors that determine the pattern of regional growth. Thus, for example, Corrado et al. (2005) develop an approach that identifies both the number and the composition of convergence clubs using pair-wise stationarity tests on time-series data, but for a variety of conditioning variables. Using these variables, Corrado et al. (2005) test for regional 'convergence-clusters' across the EU regions against a number of hypothetical, a priori determined clusters. However, an application of this methodology across all the regions of the 27 countries of the EU is entirely feasible, since it requires an extensive time-series data for variables such as R&D labour and so forth; a requirement that it is difficult to fulfil, especially for the new member-states. Using cross-section methodologies, on the other hand, can overcome the problem of small data sets for particular conditional variables.

Durlauf and Johnson (1995), for example, apply a 'tree-regression' method using cross-section data sets. Here,[35] a conditional convergence equation is estimated for the entire data set and then the same equation is estimated excluding those economies that do not fulfil certain criteria, defined ex-ante. However, application of such a methodology seems to be biased in identifying a predetermined convergence club. Moreover, applying a 'tree-regression' method in a regional context (e.g. Siano and D'Uva 2006; D'Uva and Siano 2007) fails to take into account the spatial dimension of the growth and convergence process (Fischer and Stirböck 2006).

Apart from the above methodologies, there are two traditional cross-section approaches to convergence club detection, examined in Chap. 5 and which are found in Baumol and Wolff (1988) and Chatterji (1992). The latter defines convergence in terms of the narrowing of gaps between a leading region and other regions and has been applied in Chap. 7. Such an approach does not seem entirely appropriate in the case of EU-27, as the group of leading regions is an exceptional case. Thus, a predominant focus on gaps compared to the leading region reveals very little about underlying growth and convergence trends across the remaining regions. Fischer and Stirböck (2006) propose a methodology that overcomes several of the shortcomings of the previous methodologies and involves two broad stages. In a first stage "spatial regimes in the data in the sense that groups (clubs) obey distinct growth regressions" (p. 695) are identified. The hypothesis of β-convergence within the clubs in conjunction with spatial dependence is then examined in a second stage. It is possible, however, to introduce these

---

[35] The existing observations are ordered in increasing order based on a control variable and then the split that minimises the residual variance is identified. Durlauf and Johnson (1995) propose two methods. The first identifies the number of splitting in an arbitrary way, based exclusively on one variable (usually per-capita income). The second implements a branching approach. The entire sample is divided into two sub-samples based on the variable that produces the best fit and this procedure is repeated for each of the resulting sub-samples, until the degrees of freedom become too small or the split into sub-samples becomes insignificant.

Table 7.6 Convergence clubs: Baumol and Wolff's specification

Estimated equation: $g_i = a + b_1 y_{i,0} + b_2 y_{i,0}^2$, 2SLS sample: 268 EU-27 NUTS-2 regions

a	b_1	b_2	R^2	[ser]	Implied y^*
0.0567	0.3233**	−0.0704**	0.17261	[0.1361]	2.2926**
Ramsey reset test: 0.4344 [0.6480]			F-statistic: F(2,265) 27.5374 [0.000]		
LIK	155.034	AIC	−304.068	SBC	−293.306
Test statistics for heteroscedasticity [p-value]					
White		14.4754 [0.006]			
Breusch-Pagan		14.5225 [0.000]			
Koenker		9.9954 [0.007]			

Notes: ** indicates statistical significance at 95 % level of confidence [ser] and [p-value] denote the standard error of the regression and the probability associated with each test, respectively. AIC, SBC and LIK denote the *Akaike*, the *Schwartz-Bayesian* information criteria and Log-likelihood, respectively.

considerations in the Baumol and Wolff's framework (1988). The reason is that in this methodology a bias from a leading region, although still present to some degree, is much reduced, and can be systematically investigated. More importantly, perhaps, the logic and structure of the model is such that additional variables, which represent initial conditions, can be accommodated, with a view to improving the explanation of growth patterns.

Subsequent empirical analysis is, therefore, based upon application of Baumol and Wolff's (1988) specification. Furthermore, using the Baumol and Wolff (1988) specification it is possible to distinguish between different clubs due to dissimilarities in the rate of β-convergence, which is an essential feature in the methodology for identifying convergence clubs, developed by Fischer and Stirböck (2006).

7.4.2 Detecting Convergence Clubs Across the EU-27

Baumol and Wolff's model is defined by the following equation:

$$g_i = a + b_1 y_{i,0} + b_2 y_{i,0}^2 + \varepsilon_i \qquad (7.21)$$

As pointed out in Chap. 5, a pattern of club convergence is established if $b_1 > 0$ and $b_2 < 0$ (Table 7.6). Members of a convergence club are identified as those economies which exhibit an inverse relation between the growth rate and initial level of GVA per-worker and exceed a threshold value of initial GVA per-worker, which is calculated as:

$$y^* = \frac{-b_1}{2b_2} \qquad (7.22)$$

Statistical significance for the critical coefficients b_1 and b_2 is detected while the estimated threshold values of initial GVA per-worker are all highly significant. Based on these results, it may be argued that there is some evidence for the presence of a convergence club. The simple specification of club convergence by Baumol and Wolff (1988), essentially, draws a line between regions that converge or diverge, as the notion of β-convergence requires. According to the analysis in Chap. 6, the convergence club includes, almost exclusively regions for the EU-15 countries. On the other hand, the diverging club refers to regions located to new member-states. Stated alternatively, it might be argued that converging regions are located around high productivity regions and vice versa. This suggests that a club convergence pattern may depend to a great extent on geographical factors. Furthermore, the three diagnostic tests accept the hypothesis of heteroscedasticity for the 10 % level while the Breusch-Pagan clearly indicates that heteroscedasticity is present in the model. Therefore, the next step in the assessment of club convergence across the regions of the EU-27 is to test for spatial interaction using the three spatial econometric models.

7.4.3 'Convergence Clubs': Does Geography Matter?

Chapter 5 has considered three spatial econometric models, i.e. the spatial-error, the spatial-lag and the cross-regressive models. Introducing these forms of spatial dependence into the convergence club model leads to:

$$\mathbf{g_i} = a + b_1 y_{i,0} + b_2 y_{i,0}^2 + (\mathbf{I} - \zeta \mathbf{W})^{-1} u_t \tag{7.23}$$

$$\mathbf{g_i} = a + b_1 y_{i,0} + b_2 y_{i,0}^2 + \rho(\mathbf{W} g_i) + \varepsilon_i \tag{7.24}$$

$$\mathbf{g_i} = a + b_1 y_{i,0} + b_2 y_{i,0}^2 + c(\mathbf{W} y_{i,0}) + \varepsilon_i \tag{7.25}$$

In this context an interesting issue arises. Is it possible to calculate the threshold value for initial GVA per-worker (y^*) as in the non-spatial model? Obviously, for the spatial-error model the calculation of y^* is performed in exactly the same way, since the new variable does not include the growth rate or the initial level of GVA per-worker. On the other hand, the spatial-lag model includes the dependent variable as one of the explanatory variables yielding a value for $y_{i,0}^*$ identical to the non-spatial model. Conversely, the spatial cross-regressive model does not provide a unique threshold value for the determination of a convergence-club.

Hence, in the subsequent analysis detection of convergence club is undertaken using the spatial-error and spatial-lag models of club convergence, given by Eqs. 7.23 and 7.24. Estimation of these two extended models gives the results shown in Table 7.7.

Table 7.7 Convergence clubs: spatial specifications

I. Spatial-Error model $\mathbf{g}_i = a + b_1 y_{i,0} + b_2 y_{i,0}^2 + (\mathbf{I} - \zeta\mathbf{W})^{-1} u_i$ ML, Sample 268 NUTS-2 Regions			
a	b_1	b_2	ζ
0.1405*	0.4195**	−0.0856**	0.6073**
AIC −253.3563	SBC −521.0075	LIK	271.6782
*Implied y**	2.45**		
II. Spatial-Lag model $\mathbf{g}_i = a + b_1 y_{i,0} + b_2 y_{i,0}^2 + \rho(\mathbf{Wg}_i) + \varepsilon_i$ ML, Sample 268 NUTS-2 Regions			
a	b_1	b_2	ρ
0.1914*	0.2251**	−0.0536**	0.6646**
AIC −532.8878	SBC −518.5388	LIK	270.4439
*Implied y**	2.10**		
0.1405*	0.4195**	−0.0856**	0.6073**
AIC −253.3563	SBC −521.0075	LIK	271.6782

Notes: ** indicates statistical significance at 95 % level of confidence while * indicates significance at 90 % level. AIC, SBC and LIK denote the *Akaike*, the *Schwartz-Bayesian* information criteria and Log-Likelihood, respectively.

All coefficients are statistically significant and of the expected sign, indicating that the convergence club is characterised by spatial interaction. Nevertheless, from the perspective of model selection the spatial-error model would appear to provide a better fit to the data, as indicated by the calculated values of the LIK criterion. This model yields a higher value of y^* compared to the non-spatial specification, implying that the 'convergence club' is restricted when spatial factors are taken into consideration. In fact, this threshold value obtained from the spatial-error specification indicates that six regions (regions CZ05, CZ06, CZ08, RO32, SI00 and SK02) are excluded from the convergence club implied by Eq. 7.21. The geographical pattern of the two regional groupings, implied by the spatial-error specification, (Fig. 7.3) enhances the argument put forward in Chap. 7, that convergence is a property that characterises almost exclusively the regions of the 'advanced' member-states of the EU.

7.5 Convergence-Clubs: Geography, Agglomeration and Technology

This section takes the empirical analysis forward by examining the impact of geography, technology and agglomeration externalities in shaping a pattern of club convergence. Thus, two alternative forms of spatial dependence are investigated and, in each case, the estimated equation takes account of the potential impact of localisation and diversity externalities, innovation propensity and technology diffusion. All variables are measured at the starting point of the time period under investigation, to capture the contribution of the 'history' of a given location to growth, as implied by the model in Sect. 7.4.1. Thus, the two estimating equations are as follows:

Fig. 7.3 Convergence clubs, spatial error specification

$$\mathbf{g_i} = a + b_1 y_{i,0} + b_2 y_{i,0}^2 + b_3 \ln IC_{i,0} + b_4 \ln TG_{i,0} + b_5 \ln LOC_{i,0}$$
$$+ b_6 \ln DVR_{i,0} + (\mathbf{I} - \zeta \mathbf{W})^{-1} u_i \qquad (7.26)$$

$$\mathbf{g_i} = a + b_1 y_{i,0} + b_2 y_{i,0}^2 + b_3 \ln IC_{i,0} + b_4 \ln TG_{i,0} + b_5 \ln LOC_{i,0}$$
$$+ b_6 \ln DVR_{i,0} + \rho(\mathbf{W} g_i) + \varepsilon_i \qquad (7.27)$$

Equations 7.26 and 7.27 attribute the pattern of club convergence not only to conditions related to the initial level of GVA per-worker, that is to say initial economic conditions, but also to certain structural characteristics.[36] Furthermore, the spatial error model is able to capture the effects from changes in the explanatory variables in surrounding regions through the term $(\mathbf{I} - \zeta\mathbf{W})^{-1}$, which is essentially a 'spatial multiplier effect', (Anselin 2004). As shown in previous sections, the spatial specifications are superior to non-spatial models. Thus, subsequent analysis concentrates on the spatial specifications. It may be argued that the models presented above imply that the threshold value, which distinguishes the convergence club, is determined not only by initial levels of GVA per-worker. Instead the process of determining the convergence club is more complex and involves the joint effect of a series of distinct factors that affect the growth rate in a region, namely the intentional creation and adoption of technology and agglomeration externalities.

By conditioning for these factors it is likely to be the case that membership of the convergence club will change. In other words, if the overall impact of these conditioning factors on growth is to work towards poor regions catching-up to rich regions (for example, by absorbing new technologies developed in the rich regions), then the members of the club exhibiting underlying convergence are likely to be smaller in number. It may therefore be argued that the threshold value implied from the extended model (y_{EX}^*), described by Eqs. 7.26 and 7.27, is expected to exceed that implied by the simple Baumol and Wolff specification (y_{BW}^*), i.e. $y_{EX}^* > y_{BW}^*$. Table 7.8 presents the obtained results.

The non-spatial specification of the extended club convergence model is overall significant, as indicated by the F-test. Moreover, according to the Ramsey RESET test suggests that a specification of club convergence conditioned upon the impact of technology and dynamic externalities is adequate for the EU-27 regions. Nevertheless, heteroscedasticity is present, as indicated by the three diagnostic tests. Attention, therefore, is turned to the spatial specification.

For the two models, the coefficients b_1 and b_2 have the appropriate signs but individually highly significant coefficients (at 95 % level) are detected only using the spatial-error model. This outcome is perhaps not unexpected in that convergence is now conditional upon the spatial interaction between regions and initial structural characteristics. The threshold value of GVA per-worker (y^*), which is a combination of the two estimated coefficients, is found to be statistically significant, however.

Turning to the impact of the other explanatory variables, statistically significant coefficients for the innovation and technology gap variables at the 95 % level are found only in the spatial-error model. Here, the innovation variable ($IC_{i,0}$) indicates a negative relationship with growth for the overall period, which can be interpreted as a source of convergence, in the sense that benefits from a high initial technological level have already taken place. As a result, regions with high initial $IC_{i,0}$ grow

---

[36] Stated in alternative terms, Eq. 7.26 and 7.27 imply that low-level equilibria arise not because the ratio between the poor and the rich regions is below some critical value, but due to the fact that the poor regions have not managed to cross a threshold level in their initial technological and agglomerative conditions.

Table 7.8 Convergence clubs: geography, technology and externalities

Estimated equation: $g_i = a + b_1 y_{i,0} + b_2 y_{i,0}^2 + b_3 \ln IC_{i,0} + b_4 \ln TG_{i,0} + b_5 \ln LOC_{i,0} + b_6 \ln DVR_{i,0} + \varepsilon_i$; OLS, sample 268 NUTS-2 regions

a	b_1	b_2	b_3	b_4	b_5	b_6
0.5421**	0.1974*	−0.0434**	−0.0320**	−0.0744**	−0.0290	0.0889**

Implied y*   2.27**   Ramsey Reset Test: 0.2693 [0.7640]   F-Statistic: F(6,261) 15.1721 [0.000]

AIC   −323.6304   SBC   −294.9324   LIK   169.8158

Test statistics for heteroscedasticity [p-value]

White	85.8453 [0.000]
Breusch-Pagan	33.8623 [0.000]
Koenker	22.2434 [0.001]

I. Spatial-Error model: $g_i = a + b_1 y_{i,0} + b_2 y_{i,0}^2 + b_3 \ln IC_{i,0} + b_4 \ln TG_{i,0} + b_5 \ln LOC_{i,0} + b_6 \ln DVR_{i,0} + (I - \zeta W)^{-1} u_i$, ML, Sample 268 NUTS-2 Regions

a	b_1	b_2	b_3	b_4	b_5	b_6	ζ
0.3494**	0.2871**	−0.0567**	−0.0347**	−0.0604**	−0.0423	0.1030**	0.1879**

Implied y*   2.54**

AIC   −524.0985   SBC   −495.4005   LIK   270.9237

II. Spatial-Lag model: $g_i = a + b_1 y_{i,0} + b_2 y_{i,0}^2 + b_3 \ln IC_{i,0} + b_4 \ln TG_{i,0} + b_5 \ln LOC_{i,0} + b_6 \ln DVR_{i,0} + \rho(W g_i) + \varepsilon_i$; 2SLS, Sample 268 NUTS-2 Regions

a	b_1	b_2	b_3	b_4	b_5	b_6	ρ
0.5626**	0.1844**	−0.0417*	−0.0310*	−0.0614*	−0.0521	0.1104	0.6154**

Implied y*   2.20*

AIC   −530.0985   SBC   −512.1623   LIK   270.0495

Notes: ** indicates statistical significance at 95 % level of confidence while * indicates significance at 90 % level. AIC, SBC and LIK denote the *Akaike*, the *Schwartz-Bayesian* information criteria and Log-Likelihood, respectively.

Table 7.9 'Movements-matrix', employment in technological advanced sectors

	n [1995]	ADP, 2006					n [2006]
ADP, 1995	51	[0–0.5]	**0.1493**	0.0299	0.0075	0.0000	0.0037	49
	34	[0.5–0.75]	0.0261	**0.0597**	0.0299	0.0112	0.0000	34
	51	[0.75–1]	0.0075	0.0187	**0.0970**	0.0522	0.0149	51
	69	[1–1.3]	0.0000	0.0187	0.0560	**0.1194**	0.0634	68
	63	[1.3–]	0.0000	0.0000	0.0000	0.0000	**0.0000**	66
	268		[0–0.5]	[0.5–0.75]	[0.75–1]	[1–1.3]	[1.3–]	268

Table 7.10 'Movements-matrix', technological gaps

	n [1995]	Technological gap, 2006			n [2006]
Technological Gap, 1995	214	[0–0.5]	**0.7603**	0.0412	0.0000	232
	46	[0.5–0.75]	0.1086	**0.0637**	0.0000	33
	7	[0.75–1]	0.0000	0.0187	**0.0075**	2
	267		[0–0.5]	[0.5–0.75]	[0.75–1]	267

slowly, which can create a catch-up potential. However, the negative and significant value for b_4 suggests that, in the long-run, regions with high technological gaps at the start of the period grow slower than regions with low gaps, ceteris paribus.

Bearing in mind that a high initial technological gap may also signify inappropriate conditions for technology adoption, then a large gap may not promote convergence. Since $b_4 < 0$ in all the equations above this suggests that for technologically poor regions this problem exists. Alternatively, $b_4 < 0$ indicates that regions with high technological gaps do not have the potential to adopt technology. This constitutes a substantial barrier to the diffusion of technology across the regions of the EU-27. These findings enhance the argument put forward by Fischer and Stirböck (2006) that "technology does not instantaneously flow across regions and countries in Europe" (pp. 710–711). It is possible to provide further evidence using a 'movements-matrix' for the *ADP* variable.

Table 7.9 shows that over 40 % of the EU-27 NUTS-2 regions have remained to the same range of distribution. About 21 % of the technologically lagging regions[37] have not changed their low position while over 22 % of the technologically advanced regions remained in the same range of distribution. Fewer upward movements took place, suggesting that the technological differences across the EU-27 regions remained virtually unchanged during the period 1995–2006. This argument receives further support by examining the 'movements-matrix' using the *TG* variable (Table 7.10).

The results in Table 7.10 illustrate several points. The gap with the leading region has remained the same range (less than 50 %) for 76 % of the EU-27 regions. For the period under examination, only 10 % of the EU-27 regions were able to

---

[37] 'Technologically lagging' regions are defined as regions with employment shares in technological advanced sectors less than 75 % of the EU-27 average.

Table 7.11 'Movements-matrix', patents per-capita

	n [1995]	Patents per-capita, 2006					n [2006]
Patents	127	[0–0.5]	**0.4328**	0.0336	0.0075	0.0000	0.0000	126
per-capita,	25	[0.5–0.75]	0.0187	**0.0187**	0.0373	0.0112	0.0075	20
1995	15	[0.75–1]	0.0112	0.0112	**0.0075**	0.0075	0.0187	26
	22	[1–1.3]	0.0075	0.0037	0.0187	**0.0261**	0.0261	23
	79	[1.3–]	0.0000	0.0000	0.0000	0.0000	**0.0000**	73
	268		[0–0.5]	[0.5–0.75]	[0.75–1]	[1–1.3]	[1.3–]	268

reduce their technological gaps. These regions had a gap in 1995 within the range between 50 % and 75 % while in 2006 they moved to a gap less than 50 %. Only 2 % of the EU-27 regions were able to reduce their gap with the leader, i.e. regions that were above 75 % in 1995 and moved to the range between 50 % and 75 % in 2006. It might be argued, therefore, that the process of technological diffusion across the regions of the EU-27 is a slow one. For example, regions with a technological gap above 75 % retained this relatively low position throughout the period 1995–2006.

Clearly, a catch-up with the technologically advanced regions is a difficult process. More than 43 % of the EU-27 regions have a relatively low level of technology creation or innovative capacity,[38] approximated by patents per-capita, as indicated in Table 7.11.

In the model examined in this section, the variables approximating both the creation and adoption of technology are statistically significant. Overall, the joint interaction of intentional creation and adoption of technology is of critical significance for regional growth. However, its ability to promote regional convergence in an enlarged Europe is ambiguous. To be more specific, the econometric results suggest that while creation of technology does contribute to an advancement of regional convergence, the inability of poor regions to assimilate technology constitutes a serious obstacle in the catching-up process. As a result, the process of regional convergence, in terms of labour productivity, occurs at a very slow pace. It seems that any efforts or policies to promote regional convergence across Europe through technology creation were not particular successful. Although lagging regions were able to create technological innovations, which put them in a convergence path, as suggested by the negative sign on the $IC_{i,0}$ variable, nevertheless, their limited ability to incorporate these technological improvements in their production structure prevents the convergence to take place. As argued in Chap. 3, a highly diverse environment in a region encourages adoption of technology. Therefore, if the degree of diversity increases in lagging regions, then this will induce technology adoption and growth, which is equivalent to a decrease of the technological gap with the leader and, subsequently will lead to a catch-up.

---

[38] The European Commission (1999) argues that a low innovative capacity, combined with an 'unfavourable' sectoral structure and disparities in transport and telecommunications infrastructure, reduces competitiveness. Similar factors were identified by Fatás (1997), Beine and Hecq (1998), Paci and Pigliaru (1999a,b), Martin (1998), Dyson (2000), Marginson and Sisson (2002).

Turning, thus, to the effects stemming from spatial agglomeration, namely localisation and diversity effects, the results indicate that the former do not appear to be influential in explaining the regional pattern of growth over the whole period. The evidence, such as it is, suggests that localisation effects are not significant and that regions with a higher degree of specialisation do not experience any advantage in growth terms. It had been anticipated that b_5 would be positive, since localisation externalities, approximated by the $LOC_{i,0}$ variable, are predicted to promote regional growth. The fact that the $LOC_{i,0}$ variable is insignificant may be because specialisation does not lead to faster growth. But this result may also stem from the way that specialisation effects are measured, as the extent of specialisation in one particular sector. Specialisation or increasing returns to scale is a complex phenomenon and difficult to capture in terms of a simple variable. In particular the $LOC_{i,0}$ variable does not distinguish between dynamic and non-dynamic sectors, that is does not distinguish between the different sectors in which regions are specialised, some of which grow faster than others. Dynamic sectors can be defined in terms of advanced technology or in terms of sectors that promote export activities in a region. In the former case, two related variables are already included in the model while in the latter a location quotient would be a more suitable proxy. However, using such a proxy gives similar results in econometric terms. On the other hand, if dynamic sectors are defined in terms of scale economies, then another model is required, which of course is beyond the scope of this research. The negative sign attached to the $LOC_{i,0}$ variable should not be very surprising if one considers that most highly specialised regions are those with low initial level of productivity and low rates of growth. As noted earlier, it is certainly the case that regions with the highest localisation coefficients are located in the east and south parts of the EU. Those regions are specialised in sectors characterised by the absence of scale economies or other favourable growth characteristics. Very few regions appear to be highly specialised in sectors with dynamic characteristics. Nonetheless, given that several regions have relatively high localisation coefficients, it may be argued that this variable may explain the growth performance of, at least, some regions, although not the group as a whole.

On the other hand, regional diversity, as measured by the HH index, does contribute to an explanation of regional growth, with the coefficient (b_6) on the $DVR_{i,0}$ variable statistically significant in the spatial-error model, at the 95 % level. The positive sign indicates that regions with a high degree of spatial concentration of diverse activities (with a lower value of the HH index) at the start of the period exhibit slower rates of growth, ceteris paribus. Thus, this can be interpreted as a source of convergence, since regions with high degree of diversity are, on average, high productivity regions.[39] It may be argued, therefore, that the majority of

---

[39] Such findings are in accordance with Fothergill and Gudgin (1982) who, in an examination of the growth performance of the UK regions over the period 1952–1979, find that those regions with heavy concentration in urban areas suffer from slow growth. They also detect divergence in terms of the growth rates of regional manufacturing employment.

benefits from moving to a more diversified economy have already experienced, resulting to relative slow rates of growth in highly diversified regions.

The results in Table 7.8 suggest that there is evidence of a convergence club, in all the examined specifications, since the coefficients that signify the presence of a convergence club (b_1 and b_2) are significant. Moreover, it is established that technology creation/diffusion and diversity in economic activities are important factors in regional growth. In particular, the results imply that regions with low initial technological gaps and high initial levels of diversity exhibit a lower growth rate, relative to regions with high initial technological gaps and less diverse environments. This process may promote convergence, but, its effects on convergence take time and that may explain the observed slow rate of regional convergence across the regions of the EU-27 and, consequently, the established pattern of club convergence.

Overall, the spatial models confirm, yet again, the existence of the convergence club across the NUTS-2 regions of the EU-27. Selecting the most appropriate from the two spatial models, it is apparent from Table 7.8 that the spatial-error specification appears to provide a better fit to the data compared to the spatial-lag model. In particular, according to the SBC criterion, the spatial-error model is clearly preferred, and this is confirmed using the LIK statistic. The spatial-error model scores the highest value of the LIK statistic compared to the spatial-lag model, suggesting that this particular model provides a better explanation of the pattern of regional growth in Europe. This conclusion is also enhanced by the robust version of the Lagrange Multiplier test. In particular, this test is significant for the spatial error model (p-value: 0.000) and insignificant for the spatial lag model (p-value: 0.4327). Following the decision rule by Anselin and Florax (1995), the most appropriate model is the spatial error model. Furthermore, the hypothesis of normality is accepted for Eq. 7.26 at the usual levels of significance (p-value: 0.2201) while spatial Breusch-Pagan test accepts the alternative hypothesis of homoscedasticity (p-value: 0.4021).

The conclusion from the empirical tests in this section is that the extended spatial-error model provides a better explanation of the pattern of club convergence, in the case of the 268 NUTS-2 regions of the EU-27. Therefore, the extended spatial-error model is used in examining convergence club membership in the next section.

7.5.1 Convergence Club Membership

Identification of the convergence club, which includes those regions exhibiting the property of β-convergence, is therefore based upon the threshold value (y^*) from the spatial-error model. The 'convergence-club' is seen to include 217 regions whose initial level of GVA per-worker exceeds this threshold value. For these regions the average growth rate over the period 1995–2006 is 0.73 % (Table 7.12).

The extended specification suggests that the convergence club grow relatively slow. Thus, it may be argued that an extended specification – a spatial conditional

Table 7.12 Average growth rates, extended convergence club specification

All regions	Convergence club	Non-members of the convergence club
0.94 %	0.73 %	1.88 %

club convergence model – identifies those regions that exhibit the property of β-convergence, after conditioning for certain structural characteristics. Estimating the model of absolute convergence using data for the regions in the convergence club suggests that these regions convergence at an average annual rate equal to 0.84 %. This rate is higher compare to that implied for all the EU-27 regions (0.65 % per annum). Conversely, the regions excluded from the convergence club exhibit diverging tendencies at a rate estimated to 1.6 % per annum.

Hence the argument of a 'Europe at different speeds' receives considerable support, based on the empirical analysis in this section. Furthermore, it follows that the property of β-convergence is restricted to a specific group of regions, provided that their initial levels in GVA per-worker are similar, or at least quite close. However, the extent to which these regions share similar characteristics with respect to technology and agglomeration externalities is considered in Sect. 7.5.2.

Figure 7.4 shows the spatial distribution of the convergence-club member regions.

Conditioning the convergence-club specification for technology, agglomeration externalities, excludes two regions from the initial convergence club. These are two regions located in the Czech Republic (CZ03 and CZ04). The enhanced specification implies that the convergence club includes all the regions of the EU-15 and only four regions from the new member-states (CY00, CZ01, CZ02 and MT00). It might be argued, therefore, that the geographically remote regions of the new member-states constitute a 'diverging club'. Overall, the results reported in this section suggest that regional convergence dynamics and patterns of convergence across the regions of an enlarged Europe are complex and vary markedly across different groups of regions. Hence, the next issue to consider is the specific factors that lead some regions to follow a pattern of club convergence.

7.5.2 Which Factors Determine 'Convergence Club' Membership?

Section 7.5.1 has demonstrated that over the period 1995–2006 there is a group of regions that can be characterised as a convergence club. The core of this club includes the regions of the EU-15. Yet, a question remains – what accounts for a club convergence pattern? Baumol and Wolff's specification implies that a convergence club includes regions for which a negative relationship between the growth rate and initial levels of productivity (β-convergence) holds above a certain threshold level of GVA per-worker. However, this approach can be considered as narrow, in the sense that attributes club convergence to only one characteristic of this group.

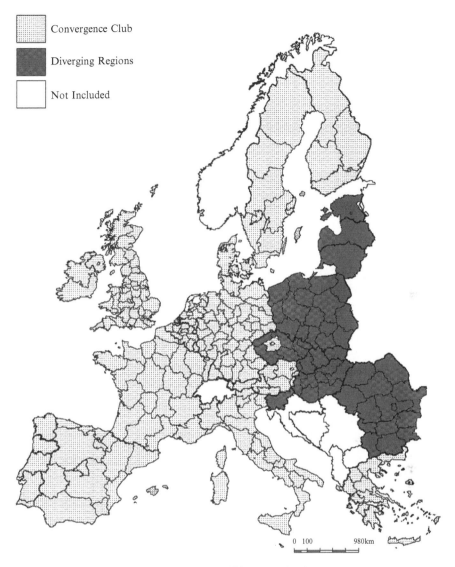

Fig. 7.4 Convergence clubs: geography, externalities and technology

Several empirical and theoretical approaches, discussed in Chap. 4, suggest a variety
of *initial* structural characteristics that account for a club convergence pattern. The
model in Sect. 7.4.1 provides a way to identify regions exhibiting β-convergence is
apparent by taking into account technology and agglomerative conditions. To assess
the extent to which members of the convergence club share initial similar
characteristics, Table 7.13 shows the average level of GVA per-worker, the number
of patents per-capita, the share of employment in technologically dynamic sectors,

Table 7.13 Structural characteristics of the convergence club

	$y_{i,0}$	$IC_{i,0}$	$ADP_{i,0}$	$LOC_{i,0}$	$HH_{i,0}$
Average of the convergence club	3.54	77.2	3.7 %	0.14	0.069
Average of the 'diverging club'	1.94	5.9	2.8 %	0.10	0.055
EU-27 Average	3.23	63.6	3.5 %	0.13	0.065

the localisation coefficient and the HH ratio for the convergence club for the first year of the analysis (1995).

An overall impression from Table 7.13 is that the average values of these key variables for the region-members of the convergence club are different from the averages for the non-members. Thus, it may be argued that regions in this group share similar structural characteristics. In the case of technology creation, for example, the regions of the convergence club, on average, exhibit a relatively high level of technology creation (above the EU-27 average). A similar situation appears for the variable representing technology adoption. The employment shares in the technologically dynamic sectors in the convergence club are above the EU-27 average. This can be considered as an indication that the ability to adopt technology is a powerful source of convergence for European regions; an argument that is supported further by the fact that in most empirical tests, the associated variable is always highly statistically significant. In a simple model of club convergence, discussed in Chap. 4, it is argued that a low initial technological gap reflects favourable initial conditions to adopt technology. Indeed, as shown in Table 7.13, the convergence club, on average, has an initial technological gap with the leader about 60 %, while the gap for regions excluded from the club exceeds 71 %. Thus, it may be argued that initial conditions in the convergence club are able to allow adoption and assimilation of advanced technology, which in turn leads to relatively higher growth rates and, subsequently, to convergence with the group of the leading regions. On the other hand, the regions excluded from the convergence-club, although innovative, nevertheless this does not enable them to catch-up with the club, given that initial infrastructure conditions do not allow an effective adoption of technological innovations.[40]

As Table 7.13 shows, the convergence club is characterised by a relatively high degree of specialisation, since on average the localisation coefficients are above the non-members' average. Given that the estimates of the relevant coefficient are statistically insignificant in the models tested, it may be argued that localisation effects have relatively small long-run impacts of regional growth in the EU-27.

---

[40] Huggins and Johnston (2009) identify a series of characteristics 'unfavourable' to regional competitiveness, such as a limited number of knowledge-intensive firms and organizations and a 'thin' institutional structure. Several other elements were proposed The relevant literature (e.g. Doloreux and Dionne 2008; Malecki 2007; Tödtling and Trippl 2005) put emphasis on the lack of an innovation-driven public sector, high dependence on Small-Medium Enterprises (SMEs) with low-growth trajectories (a typical characteristic of the regions in the Southern Member-States), fragmented connection to external sources of knowledge, etc.

Table 7.14 Convergence clubs, excluding the leading regions

$\mathbf{g}_i = a + b_1 y_{i,0} + b_2 y_{i,0}^2 + b_3 \ln IC_{i,0} + b_4 \ln TG_{i,0} + b_5 \ln LOC_{i,0} + b_6 \ln DVR_{i,0} + (\mathbf{I} - \zeta \mathbf{W})^{-1} u_i$ ML, Sample 261 NUTS-2 Regions

a	b_1	b_2	b_3	b_4	b_5	b_6	ζ
0.4252**	0.2429**	−0.0525**	−0.0302**	−0.0611**	−0.0450	0.0823**	0.6364**
Implied y^*	2.31**						

Notes: ** indicates statistical significance at 95 % level of confidence while * indicates significance at 90 % level.

Whilst it is true that non-club regions exhibit relatively faster growth rates, a higher degree of specialisation does not appear to be a significantly contributory factor and hence is not likely to promote catch-up. On the other hand, the effects from a diverse environment is a more important factor in regional growth, given that this variable in all cases is statistically significant, and according to Table 7.13, the average *HH* ratio of the non-members is lower, suggesting that regions excluded from the club are characterised by relatively more diversified environments.

This argument is supported further by the fact that the average localisation coefficient is lower than for the regions excluded from the club. It may be argued, therefore, that the property of β-convergence does not hold among regions with more specialised environments, and that a high degree of diversity in regional economic activities is a source of convergence, in the sense that regions with a high initial degree of diversity exhibit relatively slower rates of growth, ceteris paribus, allowing regions with less diversity to catch-up.

7.5.3   'Convergence', 'Interim' and 'Poor' Clubs

An interesting final question is: do the regions in the convergence club actually converge to the leading region? The simple model of club convergence in Chap. 4 shows that if regions share similar characteristics with a leader, then this may eventually lead to convergence with the leading region. Indeed, as their economies become more similar to that of the leaders, convergence towards the leader appears to be feasible in the long-run. On the other hand, regions outside of this club, which do not exhibit significant similarities with the leader or the convergence club do not exhibit any tendency for convergence. The model also suggests that in certain circumstances a convergence club can develop, which excludes the leading regions – with the latter continuing to maintain its relative advantage. Estimating the extended club convergence specification, but excluding the leading regions,[41] might reveal a different pattern (Table 7.14). Given that previous

---

[41] These are: LU, BE10, DE60, FR10, NL11, BE21 and DE71. The choice was made on the basis that GVA per-worker in these regions exceeds 4 (in natural logarithms). Moreover, the time-series tests in Appendix III imply absence of convergence towards these regions.

Table 7.15 Average growth rates in initial, interim and poor club

All regions[a]	Initial club	Interim club	Poor club
0.95%	0.73%	1.76%	1.91%

[a]Excluding the leading regions.

analysis has shown the spatial-error model to be the superior model, compared to other specifications, subsequent analysis is based on this particular model.

If the leading regions can be considered as a club of its own,[42] then estimating the extended specification allows the remaining regions to be classified into three distinct groups. The first includes all those regions that are included in the initial club (apart from the leading regions), obtained from estimating the extended specification using data for all regions. The second includes the new regions in the club, which are identified when the leading regions are excluded, i.e. an interim club. The third group contains those regions that are excluded from both clubs, i.e. a 'poor' and diverging club. Table 7.15 shows the growth rates of each group.

Table 7.15 suggests that there are considerable differences in the growth rates of each club. Nevertheless, it is noticeable that regions in the interim club tend to grow faster on average than the regions in the initial club. Thus, the regions in the interim club are in a process of catching-up with the initial club. On the other hand, despite the relatively faster rate of growth, the regions in the poor club fail to catch-up with the interim and initial club. It may be argued that due to initial differences, convergence among groups is difficult. Essentially, Baumol and Wolff's (1988) specification of convergence clubs identifies which regions follow a pattern of β-convergence, i.e. a negative relation between growth rates an initial level of GVA per-worker. Thus, the extended specification (Eq. 7.26), examined in this chapter, identifies which regions exhibit the property of β-convergence and share similar characteristics regarding technology and agglomeration externalities. Thus, this relation also holds for the regions in the interim club. This is shown in Fig. 7.5, which indicates that the property of β-convergence is not apparent for the poor club. Indeed, regions below the threshold value (2.3) tend to exhibit a positive association between growth and initial GVA per-worker. For regions above this threshold (the interim club), a negative relationship is more apparent. From this perspective, it may be argued, that the interim club is in a process of convergence with the initial club.

The interim club includes nine regions, the majority of which are located in Czech Republic (CZ03, CZ04, CZ05, CZ06 and CZ08). The remaining four regions are located in Slovakia (SK02), Slovenia (SI00), Hungary (HU10) and Romania (RO32). Most regions in the interim club are located in close proximity and around the leading region of Czech Republic.[43] It might be argued, that spatial proximity to advanced regions constitutes a factor that determines the pattern of regional

---

[42] Excluding these regions yields a rate of absolute convergence about 1 %.

[43] Interestingly, the value of the initial level of productivity implied by the spatial-lag version of the extended club convergence model excludes regions CZ04 and CZ06 from the interim club.

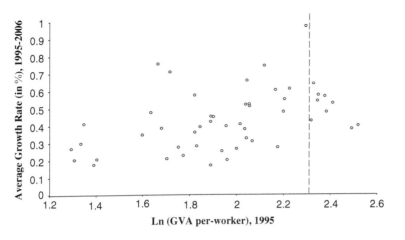

Fig. 7.5 β-convergence in the poor and interim clubs

convergence in Europe. Despite improvements in communication and information technology, the geographical distance still is factor that constraints spillovers which might be beneficial in order to promote regional convergence in an enlarged Europe; an argument that seems to receive support given that the diverging areas are located mainly in the Eastern periphery of EU-27 (Fig. 7.6).

In this context, an interesting question is the extent to which the *initial* structural characteristics of the regions in the interim club are closer to those of the regions in the initial club. Table 7.16 shows the structural characteristics of the interim club, in comparison to the other groupings.

Table 7.16 indicates that the regions in the interim club are closer to the initial club, rather than to the poor club in terms of initial level of GVA per-worker. It is important to note that the share of employment in technologically dynamic sectors is above that of the EU-27 and the initial club averages. This fact may be interpreted as an indication that the interim club is in the process of converging with the initial club, mainly to its ability to adopt technology. The conditions prevailing in the interim club enable an effective adoption of technology. If it is assumed that a relatively high diverse environment promotes technology adoption, then such an environment should be found in the regions of the interim club. Indeed, this club is not characterised by a high degree of localisation, as opposed to the initial club (Table 7.16). Instead, the degree of diversity in the interim club is close to the leading regions, enhancing the argument that the regions in this group are in the process of convergence with the convergence club. This conclusion corresponds in a sense to the argument that club convergence is an 'intermediate' state prior to overall convergence (Corrado et al. 2005). In summary, estimation of the extended convergence club model, excluding the leading regions, reveals a new distinct group of regions, which is described as an interim convergence club. On the other hand, convergence is not present for the regions excluded from both clubs, due to their unfavourable initial characteristics. A scatterplot of the level of labour productivity in 1995 against the growth rate for the regions of the initial club is

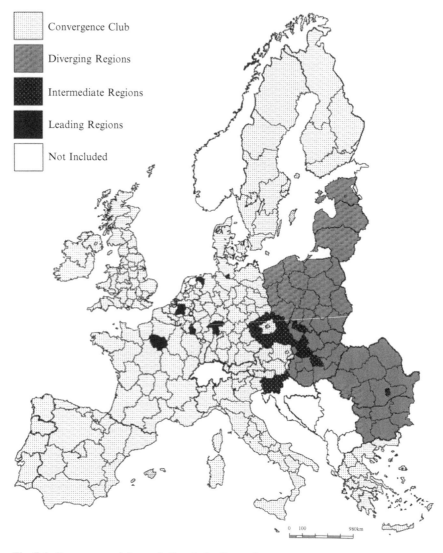

Fig. 7.6 Convergence clubs, excluding the leading regions

Table 7.16 Structural characteristics of the regional groupings

	$y_{i,0}$	$IC_{i,0}$	$ADP_{i,0}$	$LOC_{i,0}$	$HH_{i,0}$
Average of the 'interim' Club	2.39	6.19	3.79 %	0.105	0.081
Average of the 'poor' club	1.85	5.94	2.69 %	0.104	0.050
Average of the 'initial' club	3.52	74.44	3.64 %	0.141	0.067
Leading Regions	4.09	161.53	4.88 %	0.198	0.094
EU-27 Average	3.23	63.65	3.53 %	0.131	0.065

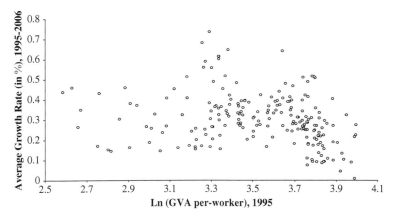

Fig. 7.7 β-convergence in the initial club, excluding the leading regions

Table 7.17 Intra-club variation

$g_i = a + b_1 y_{i,0} + b_2 y_{i,0}^2 + b_3 \ln IC_{i,0} + b_4 \ln TG_{i,0} + b_5 \ln LOC_{i,0} + b_6 \ln DVR_{i,0} + (\mathbf{I} - \zeta\mathbf{W})^{-1} u_i$

Maximum Likelihood, Sample 216 NUTS-2 Regions

a	b_1	b_2	b_3	b_4	b_5	b_6	ζ
1.0267**	1.0502**	−0.1565**	−0.0362**	−0.0436**	−0.0982	0.1250**	0.3065**
Implied y^*	3.36**						

Notes: ** indicates statistical significance at 95 % level of confidence while * indicates significance at 90 % level.

shown on Fig. 7.7. The 'initial' convergence club includes several regions which exhibit a positive relation between the level of labour productivity in 1995 and the growth rate over the examined period. This suggests an *intra*-club variation. This hypothesis is examined using the spatial error model of the extended club-convergence specification using data only for the regions in the initial club (Table 7.17).

A pattern of club convergence can also be detected *within* the initial club, since the property of β-convergence is more evident for the regions with a level of labour productivity in excess of 3.36 (Fig. 7.8). It might be argued that these regions constitute an 'advanced' convergence club, as opposed to regions with an initial level of labour productivity less than 3.36, which form a 'diverging' group. Estimating the spatial error model of the extended club-convergence specification excluding the leading regions (Table 7.18) indicates that an 'interim' club can also be detected. This club includes regions with a level of initial labour productivity in the range [3.29–3.36] (Fig. 7.9).

The property of convergence is not apparent across all the regions in the initial club, but is restricted to a selected group for which its members have a level of labour productivity in 1995 in excess of 3.36 (Fig. 7.10).

Estimating an absolute convergence model for only these regions yields an average rate of convergence equal to 3.4 %. On the other hand, for the 43 diverging regions of the initial club, a negative relation is estimated implying that these

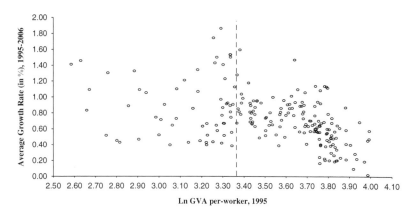

Fig. 7.8 'Diverging' and 'Advanced' regions in the initial club

Table 7.18 Intra-club variation, excluding the leading regions

$$\mathbf{g}_i = a + b_1 y_{i,0} + b_2 y_{i,0}^2 + b_3 \ln IC_{i,0} + b_4 \ln TG_{i,0} + b_5 \ln LOC_{i,0} + b_6 \ln DVR_{i,0} + (\mathbf{I} - \zeta \mathbf{W})^{-1} u_i$$

Maximum likelihood, Sample 209 NUTS-2 Regions

a	b_1	b_2	b_3	b_4	b_5	b_6	ζ
1.0301**	1.6240**	−0.2464**	−0.0336**	−0.0423**	−0.0779*	0.1342**	0.2862**

Implied y^* 3.29**

Notes: ** indicates statistical significance at 95 % level of confidence while * indicates significance at 90 % level.

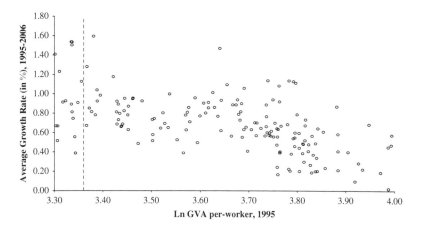

Fig. 7.9 'Interim' regions in the initial club

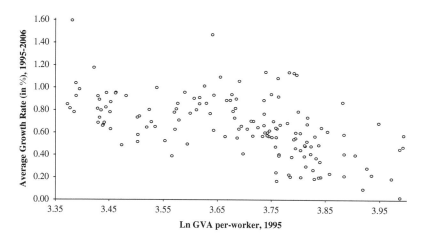

Fig. 7.10 β-convergence in the 'Advanced' club

regions falling behind from the 'advanced' club at an average annual rate almost 0.45 %. Thus, the property of β-convergence is limited amongst the regions of the 'core' or 'advanced' regions of the EU-15; a set of regions which can be considered as the 'true' convergence club.

Figure 7.11 shows the geographical location of the groups detected in this section.

Figure 7.11 suggests an East-West divide and a core-periphery pattern (North-South). The North-West 'advanced' convergence club includes 148 regions, located in the geographical 'core' of Europe. Such an outcome should not be surprising if one considers that the regions in this club appear to be homogenous in several respects.[44] On the other hand, the regions located in the southern cohesion countries

---

[44] This similarity between the 'northern' regions of the EU-15 is pointed out by several studies. Neven and Gouyette (1995), for example, prove that the 'northern' regions are more homogenous in terms of output per-head than the 'southern' regions. This pattern is attributed, mainly, to two factors. First, the regions of the 'northern' countries exhibited a better degree of adjustment to policy changes during the mid 1980s (i.e. implementation of the internal market programme) and second the response of population of the southern regions to wages and unemployment differences is slow, relative to the 'northern' regions. Cardoso (1993) uses the Dutch regions during the period 1984–1988, as an example of how migration contributes to a fall in regional inequalities and concludes that human resource management and spatial mobility (e.g. spatial redistribution of civil servants) are more effective in promoting regional development than financial transfers. Similarly, Boldrin and Canova (1995) argue that regional and structural policies in the EU are of a redistributive character and have limited success in fostering economic growth. On the premise that tests for regional convergence can be considered as an indirect evaluation of the effectiveness of regional policy, this argument receives further support given the relatively low rates of regional convergence reported in this study.

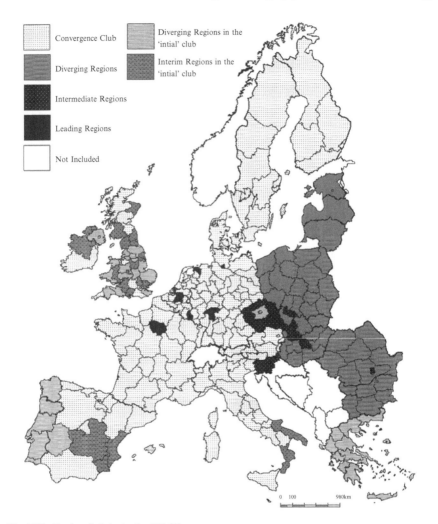

Fig. 7.11 Regional clubs in the EU-27

Table 7.19 Structural characteristics of the regional groupings in the initial club

	$y_{i,0}$	$IC_{i,0}$	$ADP_{i,0}$	$LOC_{i,0}$	$HH_{i,0}$
Average of the 'diverging' regions in the 'initial' club	3.06	33.30	2.37 %	0.15	0.075
Average of the 'interim' regions in the 'initial' club	3.33	44.83	3.91 %	0.14	0.067
Average of the 'advanced' club	3.68	90.30	3.98 %	0.13	0.064
Leading regions	4.09	161.51	4.88 %	0.19	0.094
EU-15 average	3.55	78.64	3.68 %	0.14	0.067
EU-27 average	3.23	63.65	3.53 %	0.13	0.065

(Greece and Portugal) are excluded.[45] These regions, the geographic periphery of the EU-15, are characterised by a low level of development and, according to the econometric results diverge from this 'advanced' club. The majority of the regions of the 'advanced interim' club, which is in the process of convergence with the 'advanced' club are in the UK with fewer located in the south periphery of the EU, mainly in Spain and Italy. In all estimations the sign of the variable describing technology creation suggests a converging effect in the sense that regions with relatively low levels of innovation grow faster. However, the variable approximating technology adoption remains negative. It seems that the process of technology adoption is slow and difficult even across the advanced regions of Europe. Unfavourable initial conditions, captured in terms of a relatively large technological gap, constitute a significant barrier to a process towards convergence across the European regions. Technology adoption is constrained to a selected group of regions, which share similar structural characteristics. Table 7.19 shows the initial structural characteristics with respect labour productivity, technological conditions and agglomeration externalities for the four regional clubs of EU-15.

As indicated by the values on Table 7.19 the group of the leading regions can be considered as a single club, since the average values suggest that these regions are outliers in almost every respect. At the other extreme, the 'poor' club falls behind not only from the leaders but from the other two clubs. Clearly this is a diverging group, which is closer to the poor club identified for the EU-27 regions. On the other hand, the 'interim' club of the EU-15 regions moves closer to the 'advanced' club, especially in terms of technology adoption and diversification effects. To be more

---

[45] Rodríguez-Pose (1999a) reports an analogous pattern. This pattern can be attributed to specific characteristics of these countries. Puga (2002) points out that the industrial structures of the UK, France, Italy and Germany are relatively similar, but different from Greece and Portugal. In these countries, for example, several regions are characterised by a very large agricultural sector. Consequently a substantial amount of funds were transferred to these countries. Between 2000 and 2006, for example, cohesion programmes boosted Greece's GDP by 2.8 % and Portugal's by 2 %. In Portugal there was a successful use of these funds. On the other hand, in Greece (a country with unfavourable investment climate due to unstable macroeconomic policies, characterized by the presence of a substantial 'black' economy, about 29–35 % of total employment), there are several difficulties by authorities to implement European regional development programmes and regional policies lack an overall strategy, a programming approach and co-ordination.

precise, the average percentage of employment in technologically advanced sectors is almost similar to that of the 'advanced' club.

This fact suggests that the regions of the 'interim' club, irrespective of a relative low ability to create technology, are able to adopt technology in an efficient manner, which allows them to be in a catch-up process with the 'advanced' club. Moreover, regions in the 'interim' club seem to be characterised by relatively diverse environments, a factor that, as argued in Chap. 3, promotes technology adoption and, consequently, leads to a path of convergence. Therefore, it might be argued that these two factors, in the long-run, will enable the 'interim' regions to join the 'advanced' club.

7.6 Conclusions

Using Baumol and Wolff's (1988) specification of convergence clubs as the main vehicle of analysis, this chapter has extended the model to provide an analysis of economic convergence within the regions of an enlarged Europe which addresses the question of club-convergence and investigates the role of spatial interaction, agglomeration, innovation and technology spillovers in the growth pattern of the European regions.

Application of this extended model has shown that spatial interaction, innovation potential and technology diffusion are significant determinants of a region's growth rate, whilst agglomeration economies in the form of localisation effects are not. On the other hand, agglomeration, as expressed in terms of diversity effects, does appear to be a significant factor in regional growth. The regions of the club are located mainly in the 'core' members of the European Union (EU-15). Fewer regions from the 'new' members-states of the EU-27 can be found in this club. The location pattern of the convergence club suggests that there are strong links and spatial interaction among the high-income regions of Europe, which in turn leads them to a common growth path.

The results also show that the members of the convergence club, which includes the leading regions, share similar structural characteristics on average. Further cross-section tests, which exclude the leading regions, have shown that there is a group of regions that has the potential to converge with the more advanced regions. As the model in Chap. 4 indicates, convergence towards the leader requires certain conditions be met.

Thus, regional characteristics must be similar to those of the leader. As this chapter has shown, overall conditions differ markedly across the regions of the EU-27, with the set of the leading regions an exceptional case. As a result, building conditions similar to those of the leading regions is not an easy task. Nevertheless, an overall impression from the empirical analysis in this chapter is that some regions actually do have the potential to catch-up with the convergence club.

Chapter 8
Conclusions

This study is placed within a wide literature that is concerned with whether levels of per-capita income or labour productivity across economies converge or diverge in the long-run and using the NUTS-2 regions of EU-27 as an empirical context. It has addressed the issue of regional convergence using a data set that covers the period 1995–2006. An attempt is made to provide a detailed and thorough view of the issue of convergence across the regions of the EU-27 by considering various empirical approaches.

The theoretical background to the many issues involved and upon which the empirical work is based, forms the early chapters. It has been shown that the notion of convergence embodied in neoclassical models, is used extensively in empirical applications, since its structure offers a series of testable predictions regarding regional convergence. The alternative Keynesian approach postulates that regions are unlikely to converge and a pattern of cumulative causation occurs across regions, with advanced regions growing at the expense of less-advanced regions. It is in the context of this discussion that the role of agglomeration economies in regional growth is first examined. Furthermore, several models in the tradition of Endogenous Growth theory and New Economic Geography have been shown to permit a wider set of possibilities with regard to convergence behaviour by implying that convergence might be an exclusive property of a selected set of regions. In other words, while overall or global convergence is not apparent, it is possible that a group of regions exhibits a tendency to converge towards steady-state equilibrium – local or club convergence.

The notion of club convergence, from both theoretical and empirical points of view, has been examined in some detail. In an attempt to provide a further explanation, an existing model has been extended, which attributes club convergence to existing differences with respect to the degree of technology adoption across regions. Although this model remains in the tradition of the standard neoclassical model, at least from an empirical point of view, nevertheless several of its elements are rooted in models of Endogenous Growth. From this perspective, convergence amongst regions is feasible only if they share similar structural characteristics, regarding the creation and adoption of technology.

S. Alexiadis, *Convergence Clubs and Spatial Externalities*,
Advances in Spatial Science, DOI 10.1007/978-3-642-31626-5_8,
© Springer-Verlag Berlin Heidelberg 2013

This model argues that even in the case where technology creation is limited to one region, the remaining regions may converge towards the leader provided that they are able to adopt and assimilate technology. The higher the technological distance from the leader, the greater the incentive to adopt technology. However, this model has also shown that a high technological gap may indicate and reflect inappropriate conditions for the adoption of technology, which prevent or constrain convergence with the more technologically advanced regions. Hence, a technological catch-up is feasible only amongst those regions whose conditions are similar or close to those of the technologically advanced regions. In this way club convergence is a probable outcome.

Having discussed and developed the theoretical context, a range of empirical tests for convergence have been applied in the context of an enlarged Europe, for the period 1995 to 2006. More specifically, in a first stage, regional convergence is approximated using the standard neoclassical model of β-convergence, using cross-section data. The results suggest that in terms of absolute convergence the EU regions converge at an average rate about 0.66 % per annum. This slow rate of convergence is confirmed by using alternative empirical specifications, so as to include spatial interaction and conditioning variables for technology creation and adoption and externalities from spatial agglomeration. In a sense, these results are consistent with the findings of previous studies, which claim that regional convergence in Europe occurs very slowly.

The final stage of the empirical analysis has involved the development of an alternative test of club convergence, using concepts introduced in the model of Chapter 4 and employing cross-section data. The full model provides a test for a single convergence club, which incorporates the impact of spatial interaction, agglomeration externalities and technology.

The spatial econometric techniques, employed show that the convergence club follows a certain geographical pattern, in that the regions-members of the club are located mainly in the advanced members of the EU.

The econometric results also clearly suggest the importance of technology creation and adoption in determining the patterns of club convergence across the NUTS-2 regions of the EU-27. It is established that region-members of the convergence club share several similarities in terms of technology creation and adoption, but there are indications that the remaining regions do have the potential to adopt technology. Such findings are in accordance with a wide range of theoretical and empirical models of Endogenous Growth that place emphasis on these factors for understanding regional growth. In this sense, both the theoretical and the empirical perspectives in this study fit within an established context in a coherent manner.

Apart from technological factors, this study has shown that agglomeration externalities are also of significance in determining regional growth, but as the relevant results indicate, the effects from diversity of economic activity are more powerful, compared to localisation effects, in explaining the patterns of regional growth. As the empirical application of the extended club convergence model has shown, region-members of the convergence club exhibit a relatively high degree of diversity together with relatively high levels of technology creation and adoption.

From this perspective, it may be argued that this is an indication that technology creation and adoption is more efficient in diverse rather than in localised environments, so that regions with a relatively diverse environment are able to adopt the latest technological improvements and converge towards leading regions. A highly diverse environment in a region creates favourable conditions for adopting technological innovations. On the other hand, regions with an economy specialised in traditional activities are in a disadvantageous position and this constrains their possibilities for high rates of economic growth. Thus, such unfavourable conditions lock regions into positions of low productivity and growth. Indeed, given the econometric results reported in this study, it may be argued that it is difficult to overcome the problem of regional disparities in the short or medium-run, due to substantial initial differences across regions. The message from this model, there-fore, is quite clear. Only regions with diverse environments that exhibit dynamic externalities reflected in high adoptive abilities are able to converge with the leading regions, constituting a convergence club.

Modifying the extended club convergence model has revealed the existence of a further group of regions. In particular, by excluding the leading region from the analysis, two further groups of regions have emerged; one that includes regions in the process of converging with the convergence club, described as an interim club, and the other containing regions that diverge from both groups. Further inspection of these groups has shown that that the interim club is quite close to the first convergence club (the initial club) in terms of technology and agglomeration.

Thus, from an empirical perspective, this study has contributed to a thorough understanding of the process of regional convergence in the EU-27 by considering a range of methodologies and including factors that have not received attention in the existing literature. This study has identified a series of critical factors that lead regional economies to formulate a convergence club, suggesting thus some impor-tant policy implications.

Turning, therefore, to the policy implications, the empirical results reported in this study imply that the observed pattern of club convergence is rooted in the fact that most high technology activities are unevenly distributed across the regions of the EU-27. In the lagging, and remote geographically regions of the EU, the adoption process is not immediate and these regions generally access innovations at a later stage. This time-lag will remain significant, as regional disparities and the centre-periphery pattern in the EU persist. It may be argued that this constrains any possibilities for convergence, or catching-up with the leading regions. Furthermore, several regions, especially those located in the Eastern and the south part of Europe lack those conditions that will allow them to achieve such convergence.

Such, convergence towards the leaders seems to be a long and difficult process, the only vehicle for such convergence appears to be the development of an appropriate infrastructure on behalf of regions falling behind, so as to allow rapid adoption of new technology. The key to the development of an appropriate infra-structure depends to a great extent on diversification. In a diverse environment, there are more incentives to create (or to discover new products and solutions to problems in the production process) and apply innovations, factors that certainly play a critical part in promoting convergence for lagging regions.

These points, if taken into account by policy makers, require a need to rethink regional policies along the lines of more innovative and region-specific development strategies. Given that economic growth is driven to a large extent by technological progress, it is of critical importance for effective regional policy to identify those activities whose rate of innovation and technology adoption is fast. Increasing returns are present in almost every activity, especially those related to knowledge and technology (adoption and creation). This should be taken into account by policy makers when they design regional policies and development projects. In this light, a primary aim of regional economic policy in the context of an enlarged Europe should be the promotion of high technology activities, and R&D, including universities, scientific and research institutions, creating and sustaining knowledge networks. Moreover, in order to enhance regional growth and convergence, regional policy in the EU-27 should aim at reorientation of these activities. To be more specific, high technological and activities that create knowledge should be directed if possible towards regions with unfavourable infrastructure conditions, as to stimulate the production structure in those regions towards activities that implement high technology.

This implies that regional assistance, to a substantial extent, should be diverted towards those regions that do not belong to the initial convergence or to the interim club. In terms of the extended model of club convergence, it may be argued that regions in the initial club do not need any assistance, since they have the potential and are in the process of converging with the leading region. Moreover, assistance should be club selective, in that regions in the interim club receive lower levels of assistance relative to regions of the poor club. The reason for this is that regions in the former group already have, to some degree, the characteristics which allow them to converge with the initial club. The greater part of effort and assistance should therefore be oriented towards the regions that fail to converge even with the interim club, in order to improve their underlying infrastructure conditions and shift their characteristics closer to those of the convergence club. Finally, the examination of regional characteristics in terms of technology creation and adoption, localisation and diversity of economic activities enables the identification of a region's relative advantages or disadvantages signifying, thus, in which particular areas regional policy should divert its efforts.

While this study has been concerned with examining club convergence, focusing upon the role of technology, agglomeration and spatial interaction, there is no intention of implying that this approach represents the only route to understanding regional growth and convergence. While the empirical results are significant for the case of the European regions in their own right, nevertheless, they must be placed in perspective. However, the model developed in this study is flexible enough to be extended by adding variables to approximate specificities of particular places. More importantly, it can be applied to other regional contexts, e.g. the US states, perspective members of the EU. Empirical studies in those contexts, especially in countries with immense regional inequalities, may perhaps reveal different or more interesting features for regional growth and convergence.

Indeed, there is a little pretence that the foregoing analysis provides an exhaustive account of all the factors that affect the process of regional convergence, but this work does provide an approach to club convergence, and suggests possible avenues for future research in different contexts and examining different factors that shape the pattern of club convergence.

Appendix I: An Empirical Expression for Testing Absolute Convergence

Consider a 'conventional' Cobb-Douglas production function:[1]

$$Y_i = K_i^{\alpha}(A_i L_i)^{1-\alpha}, \text{ where } i \text{ denotes a region and } 0 < \alpha < 1 \qquad (AI.1)$$

Equation AI.1 can be expressed in terms of effective units of labour by dividing Eq. AI.1 with $A_i L_i$:

$$\frac{Y_i}{A_i L_i} = \frac{K^{\alpha}}{(A_i L_i)^{\alpha}} \qquad (AI.2)$$

Defining $Q_i = \frac{Y_i}{A_i L_i}$ and $k_i = \frac{K_i}{A_i L_i}$ Eq. AI.2 can be written as follows:

$$Q_i = k_i^{\alpha} \qquad (AI.3)$$

Labour force grows in accordance to the following relation:

$$L_i = L_0 e^{\eta t} \text{ and } \frac{\dot{L}_i}{L_i} = n \qquad (AI.4)$$

Total investment less depreciation approximates the growth rate of capital stock, $\dot{K}_i = \frac{dK_i}{dt}$:

$$\dot{K}_i = sY_i - \delta K_i \qquad (AI.5)$$

Dividing Eq. AI.5 with K_i and using Eq. AI.1 yields:

$$\frac{\dot{K}_i}{K_i} = s_i k_i^{\alpha-1} - \delta \qquad (AI.6)$$

---

[1] The sum of the coefficients in equation (A1) is equal to 1.

S. Alexiadis, *Convergence Clubs and Spatial Externalities*,
Advances in Spatial Science, DOI 10.1007/978-3-642-31626-5,
© Springer-Verlag Berlin Heidelberg 2013

Given that $k_i = \frac{K_i}{A_i L_i} \Rightarrow \log k_i = \log K_i - \log A_i - \log L_i$ and defining $g_{Q_i} = \frac{\dot{Q}_i}{Q_i}$, $g_{A_i} = \frac{\dot{A}_i}{A_i}$ and $g_{k_i} = \frac{\dot{k}_i}{k_i}$, where $\dot{Q}_i = \frac{dQ_i}{dt}$, $\dot{A}_i = \frac{dA_i}{dt}$ and $\dot{k}_i = \frac{dk_i}{dt}$, then capital stock per effective worker grows as follows:

$$g_{k_i} = g_{K_i} - g_{A_i} - n \tag{AI.7}$$

Using Eq. AI.6 it is possible to transform Eq. AI.7 as follows:

$$g_k = \frac{\dot{k}_i}{k_i} = sk_i^{\alpha-1} - (n + g_{A_i} + \delta) \tag{AI.8}$$

Multiplying both sides of Eq. AI.8 by k_i yields:

$$\dot{k}_i = sk_i^{\alpha} - k_i(n + g_{A_i} + \delta) \tag{AI.9}$$

Taking a first order Taylor approximation of Eq. AI.9 around the steady-state value of k_i yields:[2]

$$\dot{k}_i \cong \frac{\partial \dot{k}_i}{\partial k_i}(k_i - k^*) \Rightarrow \dot{k}_i \cong [\alpha sk_i^{a-1} - (n + g_{A_i} + \delta)](k_i - k^*) \tag{AI.10}$$

In the steady-state $\dot{k}_i/k_i = 0$. Setting Eq. AI.8 equal to zero, and solving for s yields:

$$s = \frac{(n + g_{A_i} + \delta)}{k_i^{-(1-\alpha)}} \tag{AI.11}$$

Substituting Eq. AI.11 into Eq. AI.10 and after some manipulations yields:

$$\dot{k}_i = -(1 - \alpha)(n + g_{A_i} + \delta)(k_i - k^*) \tag{AI.12}$$

Given that the gap between actual and steady-state level of k_i can be written, in logarithmic terms, as $\log k_i - \log k^* = \log\left(\frac{k_i}{k^*}\right)$ and $\log \dot{k}_i = \frac{d\log k_i}{dt}$, Eq. AI.12 can be written as follows:

---

[2] Taylor's theorem states that a function $f(x)$ can be approximated around a point x^* with a polynomial of degree n as follows: $f(x) = f(x^*) + \frac{df}{dx}\big|_{x^*} \cdot (x - x^*) + \cdots + \frac{df^n}{dx^n}\big|_{x^*} \cdot (x - x^*) \cdot \frac{1}{n!}$, where is $\frac{df^n}{dx^n}\big|_{x^*}$ the nth derivative of f with respect to x evaluated at the point x^* and $n!$ is the factorial of $n(n! = n \cdot [n - 1] \cdots 2 \cdot 1)$. For a more detailed analysis of this method see Ferguson and Lim (1998).

$\frac{d \log k_i}{dt} \simeq -\beta \log \left(\frac{k_i}{k^*}\right)$, where

$$\beta = (1 - \alpha)(n + g_{A_i} + \delta) \tag{AI.13}$$

Output per-worker, in effective terms (Q_i), grows as follows:

$$\frac{\dot{Q}_i}{Q_i} = \alpha \frac{\dot{k}_i}{k_i} \text{ implying that } \frac{\dot{k}_i}{k_i} = \frac{\dot{Q}_i/Q_i}{\alpha} \tag{AI.14}$$

Given that $\log Q_i = \alpha \log k_i$ and in the steady-state $\log Q_i^* = \alpha \log k_i^*$, then

$$\log Q_i - \log Q_i^* = \alpha(\log k_i - \log k^*) \Rightarrow \log \left(\frac{Q_i}{Q^*}\right) = \alpha \log \left(\frac{k_i}{k^*}\right) \tag{AI.15}$$

Equation AI.15 implies that

$$\log \left(\frac{k_i}{k^*}\right) = \frac{\log(Q_i/Q^*)}{\alpha} \tag{AI.16}$$

Using Eqs. AI.14 and AI.15, Eq. AI.13 can be written as follows:

$$\frac{\dot{Q}_i}{Q_i} = -\beta \log \left(\frac{Q_i}{Q^*}\right) \tag{AI.17}$$

Equation AI.17 can be written as follows:

$$\frac{\dot{Q}_i}{Q_i} = -\beta(\log Q_i - \log Q^*) \Rightarrow \frac{d \log Q_i}{dt} + \beta \log Q_i = \beta \log Q^* \tag{AI.18}$$

Equation AI.18 is a differential equation in $\log Q_{i,t}$. A general solution (GS) of a differential equation is given by a complementary function (CF) and a particular solution (PS), defined as follows:[3]

$$CF = \bar{A}e^{-\beta t} \tag{AI.19}$$

where $\bar{A}$ is an arbitrary constant, estimated by initial conditions.

$$PS = \log Q^* \tag{AI.20}$$

---

[3] See Allen (1956) for a more detailed description.

Given that $GS = CF + PS$, then

$$Q_{i,t} = \bar{A}e^{-\beta t} + \log Q^* \tag{AI.21}$$

Setting $t = 0$ in Eq. AI.21 yields:

$$\bar{A} = Q_{i,0} - \log Q^* \tag{AI.22}$$

Inserting Eqs. AI.22 into AI.21 and rearranging terms yields:

$$\log Q_{i,t} = (1 - e^{-\beta t}) \log Q^* + e^{-\beta t} \log Q_{i,0} \tag{AI.23}$$

Equation AI.23 is a general solution of Eq. AI.18. Subtracting $\log Q_{i,0}$ from both sides yields:

$$g_{i,T} = c + b \log Q_{i,0} \tag{AI.24}$$

where $g_{i,T} = \log Q_{i,t} - Q_{i,0}$ is the growth rate of Q_i over a given time period $T = t - 0$, $c = (1 - e^{-\beta})Q^*$ and $b = -(1 - e^{\beta})$.

Appendix II: Regional Convergence: Conditioning for Technology and Spatial Externalities

Consider a Cobb-Douglas production function, augmented with a set of factors related to technology creation (IC_i) and (ADP_i) and spatial agglomeration (E_i):

$$Y_i = K_i^{\alpha}(E_i A_i L_i)^{1-\alpha}, \text{ where } A_i = IC_i ADP_i \text{ and } E_i = LOC_i DVR_i \qquad (\text{AII.1})$$

Equation AII.1 can be written as follows:

$$\tilde{Q}_{i,} = k_i^{\alpha}, \text{ where } \tilde{Q}_{i,} = \frac{Y_i}{A_i L_i E_i} \text{ and } k_i = \frac{K_i}{A_i L_i E_i} \qquad (\text{AII.2})$$

As shown in Chap. 2, $\tilde{Q}_{i,}$ converges towards its steady-state value, $\tilde{Q}^*$, as follows:

$$\frac{\dot{\tilde{Q}}_i}{\tilde{Q}_i} \cong -\beta \log\left(\frac{\tilde{Q}_i}{\tilde{Q}_i^*}\right) \qquad (\text{AII.3})$$

Equation AII.3 can be written equivalently as follows:

$$\frac{\dot{\tilde{Q}}_i}{\tilde{Q}_i} = -\beta(\log \tilde{Q}_i - \log \tilde{Q}^*) \text{ implying that } \frac{d\log \tilde{Q}_i}{dt} + \beta \log \tilde{Q}_i = \beta \log \tilde{Q}^* \qquad (\text{AII.4})$$

Equation AII.4 is a differential equation in $\log \tilde{Q}_{i,t}$ with the following general solution:

$$\log \tilde{Q}_{i,t} = (1 - e^{-\beta t}) \log \tilde{Q}^* + e^{-\beta t} \log \tilde{Q}_{i,0} \qquad (\text{AII.5})$$

Given that $\log \tilde{Q}_i = \log \left(\frac{Y}{L}\right)_i - (\log IC_i + \log ADP_i) - (\log LOC_i + \log DVR_i)$, then

$$\log \left(\frac{Y}{L}\right)_{i,t} = (1 - e^{-\beta t}) \log \tilde{Q}^* +$$

$$+ e^{-\beta t} \left(\log \left(\frac{Y}{L}\right)_{i,0} - \log IC_{i,0} - \log ADP_{i,0} - \log LOC_{i,0} - \log DVR_{i,0} \right) +$$

$$+ \log IC_{i,t} + \log ADP_{i,t} + \log LOC_{i,t} + \log DVR_{i,t} \qquad (AII.6)$$

Subtracting $\log \left(\frac{Y}{L}\right)_{i,0}$ from both sides of Eq. AII.6 yields:

$$g_{i,T} = c + b_1 \left(\frac{Y}{L}\right)_{i,0} + b_2 \log IC_{i,0} + b_3 \log ADP_{i,0} + b_4 \log LOC_{i,0} + b_5 \log DVR_{i,0}$$

$$\qquad (AII.7)$$

where $g_{i,T} = \log \left(\frac{Y}{L}\right)_{i,t} - \log \left(\frac{Y}{L}\right)_{i,0}$, $T = t - 0$, $b_1 = -(1 - e^{-\beta t})$, $c = (1 - e^{-\beta t}) \log \tilde{Q}^* + (\log IC_{i,t} + \log ADP_{i,t} + \log LOC_{i,t} + \log DVR_{i,t})$ and $b_2, b_3, b_4, b_5 = -e^{-\beta t}$.

Appendix III: Club Convergence: Time-series Evidence

Testing for time-series convergence in the context of the European regions is not an easy task, mainly, due to data availability. EUROSTAT provides time-series with a length of time suitable for the relevant application (1977–2006) only for 110 regions of EU-12. Nevertheless, this dataset is able to offer, at least, some indications of the prevailing tendencies across the territorial divisions of Europe. As noted in Chap. 5, one way to test for stochastic convergence is by bivariate ADF tests. The ability of these (conventional) tests to identify convergence clubs might be regarded as somewhat limited, given that they detect convergence between *pairs* of economies. The issue is further compounded by the lack of knowledge about a common convergence point, i.e. the 'steady-state' equilibrium to which economies are assumed to converging. In recognition of the above, Nahar and Inder (2002) have developed a methodology that tests whether different groups converge towards a common steady-state.

In an empirical setting, two proxies are suggested to represent the steady-state. The first is average output per worker of all economies included in the set and the second is the output per-worker of the leading economy. Convergence is now defined accordingly, as either a declining deviation from average output per worker or as declining differences in output per-worker compared to the leader. In this context, it should be noted that both steady-state proxies do not remain constant through time. In other words, it is assumed that in every period of time economies tend (or aim) to converge towards the average GVA per-worker or GVA per-worker in the leading economy, of the current time period rather than a given (fixed) point in time. Hence, the two steady state proxies vary over time and this adds a 'dynamic' aspect to this notion of convergence. To summarise the discussion in Chap. 5, the first empirical test developed by Nahar and Inder (2002) is expressed in terms of the following regression equation:

$$\phi_{i,t} = \theta_0 + \theta_1 t + \theta_2 t^2 + \ldots + \theta_{k-1} t^{k-1} + \theta_k t^k + u_{i,t} \qquad \text{(AIII.1)}$$

where $\phi_{i,t}$ is the ith region's squared deviation from average GVA per-worker and θ_i's are parameters.

The condition for convergence requires that the squared deviations decline through time, that is to say, the average slope of Eq. AIII.1 is negative. Equation AIII.1 is estimated by OLS for various values of k. The specific choice of the polynomial order is then made using the Akaike and the Schwartz-Bayesian information criteria (hereafter AIC and SBC, respectively). Estimation of Eq. AIII.2 leads to the average slope estimates for each NUTS-2 region shown in Table AIII.1. The interpretation of these results is as follows. A region is deemed to be converging to the common steady-state, which is the average level of GVA per-worker, when the slope estimate is both statistically significant and negative in sign.

Evidence of statistically significant convergence towards the EU-12 average, at 95% level, is found in 35 cases, while convergence at 90% level is identified for three regions. These regions (34% of the EU-12 regions) can be considered as a convergence club. Most regions in this club are in 'Northern-advanced' countries of EU (Germany, France, UK and Netherlands). In the Netherlands, due to active regional policies aimed at stimulating employment in peripheral regions and reducing congestion in 'core' regions there was an outstanding reduction in regional inequalities (Cardoso, 1993). Twelve 'Southern' regions converge towards the EU average (I_4, I_8, I_9, I_{14}, I_{18}, E_1, E_3, E_9, E_{10}, E_{11}, E_{17} and P_3). Almost 20% of the regions in the sample appear to diverge from EU average. Positive deviation, (above average), is identified for 10 regions while negative deviation, (below average) for 8 regions, located mainly in the south part of Europe. In the UK the relatively good economic performance at the national level was not reflected equally among the regions. Indeed, three British regions (UK_2, UK_3 and UK_{10}) appear to diverge from EU average. In this case, however, the estimated average rate of divergence is close to zero and any conclusions are questionable.

Based, therefore, based on the results in Table AIII.1, three different regional groupings can be identified, shown in Fig. AIII.1.

Figure AIII.1 shows that most regions in the convergence-club (66%) are located in a 'zone' of three countries, Spain-France-Germany. Closer inspection of Fig. AIII.1 indicates that most regions-members are located around the capital regions of each country; an obvious pattern in the UK, Spain, France and Belgium. This pattern suggests that regional growth and convergence in Europe is spatially dependent. In Italy, spatial dependence is evident for regions that converge towards average, which are located on the northern part of the country; a well known 'growth pole' in Europe. Five Greek regions (about 5% of the EU-12 regions) follow negative deviation from EU average, two regions located in the north part of the country, one in the south and two island-regions. A similar pattern is indicated for the UK with the region around London converging towards the average and three northern-regions to diverge, although at very small rates.

Figure AIII.1 indicates that the convergence-club follows a locational pattern in favour of the central parts of EU. Regions located around leading-regions converge towards the European average while southern-regions diverge, suggesting a 'core-periphery' pattern.

An alternative approach, proposed by Nahar and Inder (2002) is to examine the convergence process of the NUTS-2 regions relative to the leading economy.

Table AIII.1 Average slope estimates (average steady-state proxy)

Code	Region	Polynomial order	Average slope	Code	Region	Polynomial order	Average slope
B_1	Bruxelles	3	0.00051	F_{12}	Pays de la Loire	2	-0.00023
B_2	Vlaams-Gewest	3	0.00114**	F_{13}	Bretagne	4	0.01524
B_3	Région-Wallonne	3	0.00132**	F_{14}	Poitou-Charentes	4	0.03013
D_1	Baden-Württemberg	2	-0.00105*	F_{15}	Aquitaine	2	-0.00098*
D_2	Bayern	2	-0.00006	F_{16}	Midi-Pyrénées	4	-0.00997
D_3	Berlin	2	-0.00270*	F_{17}	Limousin	2	-0.00020*
D_4	Bremen	3	-0.00229*	F_{18}	Rhône-Alpes	2	-0.00145*
D_5	Hamburg	3	0.00567	F_{19}	Auvergne	4	-0.00533
D_6	Hessen	2	0.00170**	F_{20}	Languedoc-Roussillon	2	-0.00062*
D_7	Niedersachsen	2	-0.00071*	F_{21}	Alpes-Côte d'Azur	2	-0.00193*
D_8	Nordrhein-Westfalen	3	-0.02209*	F_{22}	Corse	3	0.00008
D_9	Rheinland-Pfalz	4	0.01152	I_1	Piemonte	4	-0.02231
D_{10}	Saarland	4	-0.01549	I_2	Valle d'Aosta	4	-0.01271
D_{11}	Schleswig-Holstein	2	-0.00191*	I_3	Liguria	3	0.00151**
G_1	Anatoliki Makedonia, Thraki	4	0.01232	I_4	Lombardia	2	-0.00095*
G_2	Kentriki Makedonia	4	0.02668	I_5	Provincia Autonoma Trento	2	0.00002
G_3	Thessalia	4	0.07023	I_6	Veneto	3	-0.00018
G_4	Ipeiros	4	0.01449	I_7	Friuli-Venezia Giulia	2	0.00205**
G_5	Dytiki Makedonia	4	0.06624**	I_8	Emilia-Romagna	3	-0.00068*
G_6	Ionia Nisia	4	0.04164	I_9	Toscana	3	-0.00058*
G_7	Dytiki Ellada	3	-0.00401	I_{10}	Umbria	3	-0.00020
G_8	Sterea Ellada	2	-0.00046	I_{11}	Marche	3	0.00013
G_9	Peloponnisos	4	0.00552	I_{12}	Lazio	2	0.00051
G_{10}	Attiki	2	0.00310**	I_{13}	Campania	4	-0.02760
G_{11}	Voreio Aigaio	4	0.03520	I_{14}	Abruzzo	2	-0.00203*
G_{12}	Notio Aigaio	4	0.03056	I_{15}	Molise	4	0.04089
G_{13}	Kriti	4	-0.00932	I_{16}	Puglia	4	0.00814

(continued)

Table AIII.1 (continued)

Code	Region	Polynomial order	Average slope	Code	Region	Polynomial order	Average slope
E_1	Galicia	3	−0.00272*	I_{17}	Basilicata	3	−0.00023
E_2	Principado de Asturias	2	−0.00012	I_{18}	Calabria	3	−0.00079
E_3	Cantabria	2	−0.00025*	I_{19}	Sicilia	2	0.00001
E_4	País Vasco	2	−0.00033	I_{20}	Sardegna	2	−0.00001
E_5	Comunidad Foral de Navarra	2	0.00007	UK_1	North East	3	−0.00088*
E_6	La Rioja	2	−0.00027	UK_2	Yorkshire & The Humber	2	0.00065**
E_7	Aragón	4	0.05253	UK_3	East Midlands	2	0.00061**
E_8	Comunidad de Madrid	4	0.01775	UK_4	East Anglia	3	0.00026
E_9	Castilla y León	2	−0.00043*	UK_5	South East	3	0.00010
E_{10}	Castilla-la Mancha	2	−0.00055*	UK_6	South West	3	0.00021
E_{11}	Extremadura	3	−0.00557*	UK_7	London	2	−0.00038
E_{12}	Cataluña	2	0.00033**	UK_8	West Midlands	4	−0.03447*
E_{13}	Comunidad Valenciana	2	0.00026**	UK_9	North West	3	0.00023
E_{14}	Illes Balears	2	−0.00023	UK_{10}	Wales	3	0.00029
E_{15}	Andalucía	3	0.00023**	UK_{11}	Scotland	4	−0.02877
E_{16}	Región de Murcia	4	−0.01206	UK_{12}	Northern Ireland	3	0.00015
E_{17}	Canarias (ES)	2	−0.00097*	N_1	Noord-Nederland	2	−0.00855*
F_1	Île de France	3	0.00348***	N_2	Oost-Nederland	4	−0.01834
F_2	Champagne-Ardenne	3	−0.00278*	N_3	West-Nederland	2	−0.00768*
F_3	Picardie	3	−0.00259*	N_4	Zuid-Nederland	3	−0.00432*
F_4	Haute-Normandie	2	−0.00011	P_1	Norte	4	−0.03204
F_5	Centre	2	−0.00040*	P_2	Centro (PT)	3	0.01571**
F_6	Basse-Normandie	2	0.00049	P_3	Lisboa	2	−0.00186*
F_7	Bourgogne	2	−0.00051*	P_4	Alentejo	2	0.00892
F_8	Nord-Pas-de-Calais	3	−0.00088*	P_5	Algarve	2	−0.00277
F_9	Lorraine	4	0.01587	DK	Denmark	3	0.00011
F_{10}	Alsace	2	−0.00203*	IE	Ireland	3	−0.00333*
F_{11}	Franche-Comté	2	−0.00170*	LU	Luxembourg	4	0.02966

Note: * indicates that the average slope is statistically significant at 95 % level and of the correct sign to indicate convergence. ** indicate divergence from the average. The final choice on the polynomial order was made based on the Akaike and the Schwartz Bayesian information criterion

Fig. AIII.1 Convergence towards the average, EU-12 NUTS-2 regions

In choosing the leading region, two candidates were considered, Île de France (F_1) and Hamburg (D_5). Both regions have the highest GVA per-worker in 1977, but D_5 exhibits a relatively constant path above the EU-12 average and, therefore, was chosen. Thus, the associated test approximates the steady-state by GVA per worker of that region, which is the leading region throughout, and takes the following form:

$$(y_{i,t} - y_{D_{5,t}}) = \theta_0 + \theta_1 t + \theta_2 t^2 + \ldots + \theta_{k-1} t^{k-1} + \theta_k t^k + u_t \qquad \text{(AIII.2)}$$

where $y_{i,t} - y_{D_5,t}$, is the difference or 'gap' between a region's GVA per-worker $(y_{i,t})$ and the leading region (D_5) $(y_{D_5,t})$ at time t. As shown in Chap. 5, Sect. 5.6.4, convergence towards the steady-state for any region is indicated by a positive slope coefficient, the value of which represents the average rate of convergence. Equation AI.2 is estimated for several values of k and the final choice of the polynomial order is based on the computed values of the AIC and SBC.

Table AIII.2 reports the average slope estimates. Given that Eq. AI.2 can be interpreted as indicating the average rate of convergence towards the leading region, a negative sign for the estimated average slopes suggests that the gap of any region with the leading region has increased.

About 22% of the EU-12 regions converge towards the leading region, half of them in Mediterranean countries, while 15% of the EU-12 regions falling behind the leading region.

Figure AIII.2 suggests a 'core-periphery' dichotomy across the European regions, when an alternative proxy for the steady-state equilibrium is considered, namely GVA per-worker of the leading region. Most of the regions that converge towards the European leader are located in central areas of Europe near Belgium. In this context, some remarks by Krugman (1991a) are highly pertinent:

> It has often been noted that night-time satellite photos of Europe reveal little of political boundaries but clearly suggest a *centre-periphery pattern* whose hub is somewhere in or near Belgium. (p. 484) [Emphasis added]

Several central-capital regions (e.g. London, Madrid and Paris) converge towards the leader. On the other hand, Italian and Greek Southern-Mediterranean regions seem to diverge from the European leader. It is worthy of note that regions G_3 and G_5 diverge not only from the leading region but also from the EU-12 average.

Table AIII.2 Average slope estimates (leading region steady-state proxy)

Code	Region	Polynomial order	Average slope	Code	Region	Polynomial order	Average slope
B_1	Bruxelles	2	0.00485*	F_{13}	Bretagne	2	-0.00127
B_2	Vlaams-Gewest	2	0.00479*	F_{14}	Poitou-Charentes	2	0.00037
B_3	Région-Wallonne	2	0.00670*	F_{15}	Aquitaine	2	-0.00205
D_1	Baden-Württemberg	4	0.00468	F_{16}	Midi-Pyrénées	4	-0.03605
D_2	Bayern	4	-0.00531	F_{17}	Limousin	4	0.03404
D_3	Berlin	2	-0.01335**	F_{18}	Rhône-Alpes	2	-0.00241
D_4	Bremen	4	-0.00431	F_{19}	Auvergne	2	0.00127
D_6	Hessen	2	0.00572*	F_{20}	Languedoc-Roussillon	2	-0.00346
D_7	Niedersachsen	4	-0.00435	F_{21}	Alpes-Côte d'Azur	2	-0.00144
D_8	Nordrhein-Westfalen	3	0.00582*	F_{22}	Corse	2	0.00252
D_9	Rheinland-Pfalz	2	0.00272	I_1	Piemonte	4	-0.02162
D_{10}	Saarland	3	0.00124*	I_2	Valle d'Aosta	4	0.02438
D_{11}	Schleswig-Holstein	2	-0.00491**	I_3	Liguria	2	0.00544*
G_1	Anatoliki Makedonia, Thraki	2	0.00196	I_4	Lombardia	4	-0.00125
G_2	Kentriki Makedonia	4	0.06363	I_5	Provincia Autonoma Trento	4	-0.00496
G_3	Thessalia	3	-0.00394**	I_6	Veneto	4	-0.00650
G_4	Ipeiros	4	0.05259	I_7	Friuli-Venezia Giulia	2	-0.00846**
G_5	Dytiki Makedonia	2	-0.02795**	I_8	Emilia-Romagna	3	0.00230
G_6	Ionia Nisia	4	-0.04059	I_9	Toscana	4	-0.00481
G_7	Dytiki Ellada	4	-0.00205	I_{10}	Umbria	3	0.00167
G_8	Sterea Ellada	4	0.02116	I_{11}	Marche	3	0.00448*
G_9	Peloponnisos	4	0.07643	I_{12}	Lazio	3	0.02123*
G_{10}	Attiki	4	0.08505	I_{13}	Campania	4	-0.00820
G_{11}	Voreio Aigaio	2	-0.00767**	I_{14}	Abruzzo	2	-0.00449**
G_{12}	Notio Aigaio	3	-0.00756**	I_{15}	Molise	4	0.00344
G_{13}	Kriti	3	-0.01579**	I_{16}	Puglia	3	0.00935*
E_1	Galicia	2	-0.00045	I_{17}	Basilicata	3	-0.00189

(continued)

Table AIII.2 (continued)

Code	Region	Polynomial order	Average slope	Code	Region	Polynomial order	Average slope
E_2	Principado de Asturias	2	0.00414*	I_{18}	Calabria	3	−0.00201**
E_3	Cantabria	4	−0.02825	I_{19}	Sicilia	3	−0.00478**
E_4	País Vasco	2	0.00173	I_{20}	Sardegna	4	−0.00391
E_5	Comunidad Foral de Navarra	2	0.00229	UK_1	North East	2	−0.00223**
E_6	La Rioja	2	0.00150	UK_2	Yorkshire & The Humber	2	−0.00090
E_7	Aragón	2	0.00684**	UK_3	East Midlands	2	0.00015
E_8	Comunidad de Madrid	3	0.00360*	UK_4	East Anglia	2	0.00106
E_9	Castilla y León	4	0.02722	UK_5	South East	3	0.00380*
E_{10}	Castilla-la Mancha	4	0.12680	UK_6	South West	3	0.00059
E_{11}	Extremadura	4	0.00874	UK_7	London	2	0.01752*
E_{12}	Cataluña	2	0.00412*	UK_8	West Midlands	2	−0.00032
E_{13}	Comunidad Valenciana	2	−0.00054	UK_9	North West	2	−0.00044
E_{14}	Illes Balears	2	0.00236	UK_{10}	Wales	2	0.00090
E_{15}	Andalucía	4	0.00551	UK_{11}	Scotland	2	0.00066
E_{16}	Región de Murcia	2	0.00337*	UK_{12}	Northern Ireland	2	0.00026
E_{17}	Canarias (ES)	3	0.00048	N_1	Noord-Nederland	2	−0.01470**
F_1	Île de France	2	0.00702*	N_2	Oost-Nederland	2	−0.01903**
F_2	Champagne-Ardenne	4	0.02250	N_3	West-Nederland	2	−0.01583**
F_3	Picardie	4	0.02609	N_4	Zuid-Nederland	2	−0.01549**
F_4	Haute-Normandie	2	0.00257	P_1	Norte	4	−0.06306
F_5	Centre	2	−0.00009	P_2	Centro (PT)	3	0.01571*
F_6	Basse-Normandie	2	0.00531*	P_3	Lisboa	2	−0.00595**
F_7	Bourgogne	2	−0.00058	P_4	Alentejo	2	−0.00684
F_8	Nord - Pas-de-Calais	4	0.00204	P_5	Algarve	2	0.00617
F_9	Lorraine	3	0.00597*	DK	Denmark	2	0.00261*
F_{10}	Alsace	4	0.00126	IE	Ireland	2	0.02558*
F_{11}	Franche-Comté	3	−0.00246	LU	Luxembourg	3	0.02715*
F_{12}	Pays de la Loire	2	0.00092				

Note: * indicates that the average slope is statistically significant at 95 % level and of the correct sign to indicate convergence. ** indicate divergence from the leader. The final choice on the polynomial order was made based on the Akaike and the Schwartz-Bayesian information criterion

Fig. AIII.2 Convergence towards the leading region

Appendix IV: The Regions used in the Empirical Analysis

BE10 Région de Bruxelles	DE94 Weser-Ems
BE21 Prov. Antwerpen	DEA1 Düsseldorf
BE22 Limburg	DEA2 Köln
BE23 Oost-Vlaanderen	DEA3 Münster
BE24 Vlaams Brabant	DEA4 Detmold
BE25 West-Vlaanderen	DEA5 Arnsberg
BE31 Brabant Wallon	DEB1 Koblenz
BE32 Hainaut	DEB2 Trier
BE33 Liège	DEB3 Rheinhessen-Pfalz
BE34 Luxembourg (B)	DEC0 Saarland
BE35 Namur	DED1 Chemnitz
BG11 Severozapaden	DED2 Dresden
BG12 Severen tsentralen	DED3 Leipzig
BG13 Severoiztochen	DEE1 Dessau
BG14 Yugoiztochen	DEE2 Halle
BG21 Yugozapaden	DEE3 Magdeburg
BG22 Yuzhen tsentralen	DEF0 Schleswig-Holstein
CZ01 Praha	DEG0 Thüringen
CZ02 Strední Cechy	EE00 Estonia
CZ03 Jihoz´pad	IE01 Border, Midlands and Western
CZ04 Severozápad	IE02 Southern and Eastern
CZ05 Severovýchod	GR11 Anatoliki Macedonia, Thraki
CZ06 Jihovýchod	GR12 Kentriki Macedonia
CZ07 Strední Morava	GR13 Dytiki Macedonia
CZ08 Moravskoslezsko	GR14 Thessalia
CY00 Cyprus	GR21 Ipeiros
DK Denmark	GR22 Ionia Nisia
DE11 Stuttgart	GR23 Dytiki Ellada
DE12 Karlsruhe	GR24 Sterea Ellada
DE13 Freiburg	GR25 Peloponnisos
DE14 Tübingen	GR30 Attiki
DE21 Oberbayern	GR41 Voreio Aigaio

(continued)

DE22 Niederbayem	GR42 Notio Aigaio
DE23 Oberpfalz	GR43 Kriti
DE24 Oberfranken	ES11 Galicia
DE25 Mittelfranken	ES12 Principado de Asturias
DE26 Unterfranken	ES13 Cantabria
DE27 Schwaben	ES21 Pais Vasco
DE30 Berlin	ES22 Comunidad Foral de Navarra
DE41 Brandenburg – Nordost	ES23 La Rioja
DE42 Brandenburg – Südwest	ES24 Aragón
DE50 Bremen	ES30 Comunidad de Madrid
DE60 Hamburg	ES41 Castilla y León
DE71 Darmstadt	ES42 Castilla-la Mancha
DE72 Gießen	ES43 Extremadura
DE73 Kassel	ES51 Cataluña
DE80 Mecklenburg-Vorpommern	ES52 Comunidad Valenciana
DE91 Braunschweig	ES61 Andalucia
DE92 Hannover	ES62 Región de Murcia
DE93 Lüneburg	ES63 Ciudad Autónoma de Ceuta
ES64 Ciudad Autónoma de Melilla	HU10 Közép-Magyarország
ES70 Canarias	HU21 Közép-Dunántúl
FR10 Île de France	HU22 Nyugat-Dunántúl
FR21 Champagne-Ardenne	HU23 Dél-Dunántúl
FR22 Picardie	HU31 Észak-Magyarország
FR23 Haute-Normandie	HU32 Észak-Alföld
FR24 Centre	HU33 Dél-Alföld
FR25 Basse-Normandie	MT00 Malta
FR26 Bourgogne	NL11 Groningen
FR30 Nord – Pas-de-Calais	NL12 Friesland
FR41 Lorraine	NL13 Drenthe
FR42 Alsace	NL21 Overijssel
FR43 Franche-Comté	NL22 Gelderland
FR51 Pays de la Loire	NL23 Flevoland
FR52 Bretagne	NL31 Utrecht
FR53 Poitou-Charentes	NL32 Noord-Holland
FR61 Aquitaine	NL33 Zuid-Holland
FR62 Midi-Pyrénées	NL34 Zeeland
FR63 Limousin	NL41 Noord-Brabant
FR71 Rhône-Alpes	NL42 Limburg
FR72 Auvergne	AT11 Burgenland
FR81 Languedoc-Roussillon	AT12 Niederösterreich
FR82 Provence-Alpes-Côte d'Azur	AT13 Wien
FR83 Corse	AT21 Kärnten
FR91 Guadeloupe	AT22 Steiermark
FR92 Martinique	AT31 Oberösterreich
FR93 Guyane	AT32 Salzburg
FR94 Reunion	AT33 Tirol
ITC1 Piemonte	AT34 Vorarlberg
ITC2 Valle d'Aosta/Vallée d'Aoste	PL11 Lódzkie

(continued)

ITC3 Liguria	PL12 Mazowieckie
ITC4 Lombardia	PL21 Malopolskie
ITD1 Provincia Autonoma Bolzano-Bozen	PL22 Slaskie
ITD2 Provincia Autonoma Trento	PL31 Lubelskie
ITD3 Veneto	PL32 Podkarpackie
ITD4 Friuli-Venezia Giulia	PL33 Swietokrzyskie
ITD5 Emilia-Romagna	PL34 Podlaskie
ITE1 Toscana	PL41 Wielkopolskie
ITE2 Umbria	PL42 Zachodniopomorskie
ITE3 Marche	PL43 Lubuskie
ITE4 Lazio	PL51 Dolnoslaskie
ITF1 Abruzzo	PL52 Opolskie
ITF2 Molise	PL61 Kujawsko-Pomorskie
ITF3 Campania	PL62 Warminsko-Mazurskie
ITF4 Puglia	PL63 Pomorskie
ITG1 Sicilia	PT16 Centro
ITG2 Sardegna	PT17 Lisboa
LV00 Latvia	PT18 Alentejo
LT00 Lithuania	PT20 Região Autónoma dos Açores
LU00 Luxembourg (Grand-Duché)	PT30 Região Autónoma da Madeira
RO11 Nord-Vest	UKD5 Merseyside
RO12 Centru	UKE1 East Riding and North Lincolnshire
RO21 Nord-Est	UKE2 North Yorkshire
RO22 Sud-Est	UKE3 South Yorkshire
RO31 Sud – Muntenia	UKE4 West Yorkshire
RO32 Bucuresti – Ilfov	UKF1 Derbyshire and Nottinghamshire
RO41 Sud-Vest Oltenia	UKF2 Leicestershire, Rutland and Northants
RO42 Vest	UKF3 Lincolnshire
SI00 Slovenia	UKG1 Herefordshire, Worcestershire and Warks
SK01 Bratislavský kraj	UKG2 Shropshire and Staffordshire
SK02 Západné Slovensko	UKG3 West Midlands
SK03 Stredné Slovensko	UKH1 East Anglia
SK04 Východné Slovensko	UKH2 Bedfordshire, Hertfordshire
FI13 Itä-Suomi	UKH3 Essex
FI18 Etelä-Suomi	UKI1 Inner London
FI19 Länsi-Suomi	UKI2 Outer London
FI20 Åland	UKJ1 Berkshire, Bucks and Oxfordshire
FI1A Pohjois-Suomi	UKJ2 Surrey, East and West Sussex
SE01 Stockholm	UKJ3 Hampshire and Isle of Wight
SE02 Östra Mellansverige	UKJ4 Kent
SE04 Sydsverige	UKK1 Gloucestershire, Wiltshire & North Somerset
SE06 Norra Mellansverige	UKK2 Dorset and Somerset
SE07 Mellersta Norrland	UKK3 Cornwall and Isles of Scilly
SE08 Övre Norrland	UKK4 Devon
SE09 Småland med öarna	UKL1 West Wales and The Valleys
SE0A Västsverige	UKL2 East Wales
UKC1 Tees Valley and Durham	UKM1 North Eastern Scotland
UKC2 Northumberland, Tyne and Wear	UKM2 Eastern Scotland

(continued)

UKD1 Cumbria	UKM3 South Western Scotland
UKD2 Cheshire	UKM4 Highlands and Islands
UKD3 Greater Manchester	UKN0 Northern Ireland
UKD4 Lancashire	

References

Åberg Y (1973) Regional productivity differences in Swedish manufacturing. Reg Urban Econ 3 (2):131–156

Abler D, Das J (1998) The determinants of the speed of convergence: the case of India. Appl Econ 30(12):1595–1602

Abramovitz M (1956) Resource and output trends in the United States since 1870. Am Econ Rev 46(1):5–23

Abramovitz M (1986) Catching up, forging ahead and falling behind. J Econ Hist 46(2):385–406

Abramovitz M (1993) The search for the sources of growth: areas of ignorance, old and new. J Econ Hist 53(2):217–243

Abramovitz M (1994) Catch-up and convergence in the post-war growth boom and after. In: Baumol W, Nelson R, Wolff E (eds) Convergence of productivity – cross-national studies and historical evidence. Oxford University Press, New York, pp 86–125

Abreu M, de Groot H, Florax R (2005) Space and growth: a survey of empirical evidence and methods. Rég Dév 21:12–43

Acosta P (2010) The 'flypaper effect' in presence of spatial interdependence: evidence from Argentinean municipalities. Ann Reg Sci 44(3):453–466

Acs Z, Audretsch D (1987) Innovation in large and small firms. Econ Lett 23(1):109–112

Acs Z, Audretsch D, Feldman M (1994) R&D spillovers and recipient firms size. Rev Econ Stat 76 (2):336–340

Aghion P, Bolton P (1996) A trickle-down theory of growth and development with debt-overhang. Rev Econ Stud 64(2):151–172

Aghion P, Howitt P (1992) A model of growth through creative destruction. Econometrica 61 (2):323–351

Aghion P, Caroli E, Garcia-Penelosa C (1999) Inequality and economic growth: the perspective of the new growth theory. J Econ Lit 37(4):1615–1660

Albelo C (1999) Complementarity between physical and human capital and speed of convergence. Econ Lett 64(3):357–361

Alderman N, Fischer M (1992) Innovation and technological change: an Australian comparison. Environ Plann A 24(2):273–288

Alesina A, Rodrik D (1994) Distributive politics and economic growth. Q J Econ 109(2):465–490

Alexiadis S (2010a) Regional convergence clubs and dynamic externalities. Ital J Reg Sci 9 (1):41–64

Alexiadis S (2010b) The nexus between regional growth and technology adoption. A case for club convergence? Theor Pract Res Econ Fields 1(1):4–11

Alexiadis S (2010c) Interregional differences in adoptive abilities: an alternative framework. Reg Sci Inquire 1(2):41–52

Alexiadis S (2011) Does technological heterogeneity promote regional convergence? Implications for regional policy and entrepreneurship'. Ann Innovation Enterp 2(1):1–7

Alexiadis S, Alexandrakis A (2008) "Threshold conditions" and regional convergence in European agriculture. Int J Econ Sci Appl Res 1(2):13–37

Alexiadis S, Eleftheriou K (2010) A note on the morphology of regional unemployment in Greece. Econ Bull 30(4):2779–2786

Alexiadis S, Korres G (2009) Technology adoption and spatial interaction: evidence from the European regions. In: Markowski T, Turała M, Żuber P (eds) Innovation and space – European and national approach. Polish Academy of Sciences, Poland, pp 24–42

Alexiadis S, Korres G (2010) Adoption of technology and regional convergence in Europe. Eur Spat Res Policy 17(2):94–105

Alexiadis S, Tomkins J (2004) Convergence clubs in the regions of Greece. Appl Econ Lett 11 (6):387–391

Alexiadis S, Tsagdis D (2006a) Examining the location factors of R&D labour in the regions of Greece. Ann Reg Sci 40(1):43–54

Alexiadis S, Tsagdis D (2006b) Reassessing the validity of Verdoorn's law under conditions of spatial dependence: a case study of the Greek regions. J Post Keynes Econ 29(1):149–175

Alexiadis S, Tsagdis D (2010) Is cumulative growth in manufacturing productivity slowing down in the EU-12 regions? Camb J Econ 34(6):1001–1017

Allen R (1956) Mathematical economics. Macmillan, London

Alonso W (1968) Industrial location and regional policy in economic development. Center for Planning and Development Research, University of California

Alonso-Villar O, Chammoro-Rivas J, Gonzáles-Cerdeira X (2004) Agglomeration economies in manufacturing industry: the case of Spain. Appl Econ 36(18):2103–2116

Álvarez-Garcia S, Prieto-Rodriguez J, Salas R (2004) The evolution of income inequality in the European Union during the period 1993–1996. Appl Econ 36(13):1399–1408

Ames E, Rosenberg N (1963) Changing technological leadership and industrial growth. Econ J 73 (289):13–31

Andersen E (1996) Evolutionary economics: post-schumpeterian contributions. Pinter, London

Andersen T, Moene K (eds) (1995) Endogenous growth. Blackwell, Oxford

Andonelli C (1990) Induced adoption and externalities in the regional diffusion of innovation technology. Reg Stud 24(1):31–40

Andrade E, Márcio L, Madalozzo R, Pereira P (2004) Convergence clubs among Brazilian municipalities. Econ Lett 83(2):179–184

Anselin L (1988) Spatial econometrics: methods and models. Kluwer, Dordrecht

Anselin L (2004) Spatial externalities, spatial multipliers and spatial econometrics. Int Reg Sci Rev 26(2):153–166

Anselin L, Bera A (1998) Spatial dependence in linear regression models with an introduction to spatial econometrics. In: Ullah A, Giles D (eds) Handbook of applied economic statistics. Marcel Dekker, New York, pp 237–289

Anselin L, Florax R (1995) Small sample properties of tests for spatial dependence in regression models: some further results. In: Anselin L, Florax R (eds) New directions in spatial econometrics. Springer, Berlin, pp 21–75

Anselin L, Moreno R (2003) Properties of tests for spatial error components. Reg Sci Urban Econ 33(5):595–618

Anselin L, Bera A, Florax R, Yoon M (1996) Simple diagnostic tests for spatial dependence. Reg Sci Urban Econ 26(1):77–104

Arauzo-Carod J (2009) Locational determinants of high-tech manufacturing activities: a preliminary analysis. Lett Spat Resource Sci 2(1):23–29

Arbia G (2006) Spatial econometrics: statistical foundations and applications to regional convergence. Springer, Berlin

Arbia G, Paelinck J (2003) Spatial econometric modelling of regional convergence in continuous time. Int Reg Sci Rev 26(3):342–362

Arbia G, le Gallo J, Piras G (2008) Does evidence on regional economic convergence depend on the estimation strategy? Outcomes from analysis of a set of NUTS-2 EU regions. Spat Econ Anal 3(2):209–224

Argyrous G (2001) Setterfield on cumulative causation and interrelatedness: a comment. Camb J Econ 25(1):103–106

Armstrong H (1995a) Trends and disparities in regional GDP per-capita in the European Union, United States and Australia. European Commission Report 94/00/74/017. Commission of European Communities, Brussels

Armstrong H (1995b) An appraisal of the evidence from cross-sectional analysis of the regional growth process within the European Union. In: Armstrong H, Vickerman R (eds) Convergence and divergence among European regions. Pion, London, pp 40–65

Armstrong H, Taylor J (1985) Regional economics and policy. Allen and Unwin, London

Armstrong H, Taylor J (2000) Regional economics and policy. Allen and Unwin, London

Armstrong H, Taylor J (eds) (2001) The economics of regional policy. Elgar, Cheltenham/ Northampton

Arrow K (1962) The economic implications of learning-by-doing. Rev Econ Stud 29(3):155–173

Arthur B (1989) Competing technologies, increasing returns and lock-in by historical events. Econ J 99(394):116–131

Arthur B (1990) Silicon Valley locational clusters: when do increasing returns imply monopoly? Math Soc Sci 19(3):235–251

Arthur B (1994) Increasing returns and path dependence in the economy. Michigan University Press, Michigan

Atesoglu H (1993) Manufacturing and economic growth in the United States. Appl Econ 25 (1):67–69

Attfield C, Cannon E, Demery D, Duck N (2000) Economic growth and geographic proximity. Econ Lett 68(1):109–112

Audretsch D (1998) Agglomeration and the location of innovative activity. Oxf Rev Econ Policy 14(2):18–29

Audretsch D, Feldman M (1996a) R&D spillovers and the geography of innovation and production. Am Econ Rev 86(3):630–640

Audretsch D, Feldman M (1996b) Innovative clusters and the industry life cycle. Rev Ind Organisation 11(2):253–273

Audretsch D, Feldman M (2004) Knowledge spillovers and the geography of innovation. In: Henderson V, Thisse J (eds) Handbook of regional and urban economics. pp 2713–2739

Audretsch D, Vivarelli M (1996) Firms size and R&D spillovers: evidence from Italy. Small Bus Econ 8(3):249–258

Austin J, Schmidt J (1998) Convergence amid divergence in a region. Growth Change 29(1):67–89

Azariadis C, Drazen A (1990) Threshold externalities in economic development. Q J Econ 105 (2):501–526

Baddeley M, Martin R, Tayler P (1998) European regional unemployment disparities: convergence or persistence? Eur Urban Reg Stud 5(3):195–215

Badinger H, Müller W, Tondl G (2004) Regional convergence in the European Union, 1985–1999: a spatial dynamic panel analysis. Reg Stud 38(3):241–253

Bairam E (1987) The Verdoorn's law, returns to scale and industrial growth: a review of the literature. Aust Econ Pap 26:20–41

Bairam E (1991) Economic growth and Kaldor's law: the case of Turkey, 1925–1978. Appl Econ 23(8):277–280

Baland J, Francois P (1996) Innovation, monopolies and poverty trap. J Dev Econ 49(1):151–178

Baldwin R (1999) Agglomeration and endogenous capital. Eur Econ Rev 43(2):253–280

Baldwin J, Beskstead D, Brown M, Rigby D (2008) Agglomeration and the geography of localized economies in Canada. Reg Stud 42(1):117–132

Barde S (2010) Knowledge spillovers, black holes and the equilibrium location of vertically linked industries. J Econ Geogr 10(1):27–53

Barro R (1991) Economic growth in a cross-section of countries. Q J Econ 106(2):407–443

Barro R (1997) Determinants of economic growth. MIT Press, Cambridge

Barro R, Lee J (1993) International comparisons of educational attainment. J Monet Econ 32 (3):363–394

Barro R, Sala-i-Martin X (1991) Convergence across states and regions. Brooking Pap Econ Act 1:107–182

Barro R, Sala-i-Martin X (1992a) Convergence. J Pol Econ 100(2):223–251

Barro R, Sala-i-Martin X (1992b) Regional growth and migration: a Japanese-US comparison. J Jpn Int Econ 6(4):312–346

Barro R, Sala-i-Martin X (1995) Economic growth, 2nd edn. MIT Press, Cambridge

Barro R, Sala-i-Martin X (1997) Technology diffusion, convergence and growth. J Econ Growth 2 (1):1–25

Barro R, Mankiw G, Sala-i-Martin X (1995) Capital mobility in neoclassical models of growth. Am Econ Rev 85(5):103–115

Bartelsman E, Caballero R, Lyons R (1994) Customer and supplier driven externalities. Am Econ Rev 84(4):1075–1084

Basile R (2008) Regional economic growth in Europe: a semi parametric spatial dependence approach. Pap Reg Sci 87(4):527–544

Bassino J-P (2006) Inequality in Japan (1892–1941): physical stature, income and health. Econ Hum Biol 4(1):62–88

Baumol W (1967) Macroeconomics of unbalanced growth: the anatomy of urban crisis. Am Econ Rev 57(3):415–426

Baumol W (1986) Productivity growth, convergence and welfare: what the long-run data show. Am Econ Rev 76(5):1072–1085

Baumol W (1988) Is entrepreneurship always productive? J Dev Plann 18:85–93

Baumol W, Wolff E (1988) Productivity growth, convergence and welfare: a reply. Am Econ Rev 78(5):1155–1159

Baumont C, Ertur C, le Gallo J (2003) Spatial convergence clubs and the European growth process, 1980–1995. In: Fingleton B (ed) European regional growth. Springer, Berlin, pp 131–158

Beardsell M, Henderson V (1999) Spatial evolution of the computer industry in the USA. Eur Econ Rev 43(2):431–456

Beaudry C, Schiffauerova A (2010) Who's right, Marshall or Jacobs? The localization versus urbanization debate. Res Policy 38(2):318–337

Becker G (1964) Human capital: a theoretical and empirical analysis, with special reference to education. National Bureau of Economic Research, New York

Becker G, Murphy K, Tamura R (1990) Human capital, fertility and economic growth. J Pol Econ 98(5):S12–S37

Beine M, Hecq A (1998) Co-dependence and convergence in the EC economies. J Policy Model 20 (4):403–426

Bellini E, Ottaviano G, Pinelli D, Prarolo G (2008) Cultural diversity and economic performance: evidence from European regions. Hamburg Institute of International Economics Research Paper, No. 3–14

Benabou R (1993) Workings of a city: location, education and production. Q J Econ 108 (3):619–652

Benabou R (1994) Human capital, inequality and growth: a local perspective. Eur Econ Rev 38 (3–4):817–826

Benabou R (1996) Equity and efficiency in human capital investment: the local connection. Rev Econ Stud 63(2):237–264

Ben-David D (1993) Equalising exchange, trade liberalisation and income convergence. Q J Econ 108(3):653–679

Ben-David D (1996) Trade and convergence among countries. J Int Econ 40(3–4):279–298

Ben-David D (1998) Convergence clubs and subsistence economies. J Dev Econ 55(1):155–171

Ben-David D, Papell D (2000) Some evidence on the continuity of the growth process among the G7 countries. Econ Inq 38(2):320–330

Benhabib J, Spiegel M (1994) The role of human capital in economic development: evidence from aggregate cross-country data. J Monet Econ 34(2):143–173

Bennett R, Hordijk L (1986) Regional econometric and dynamic models. In: Mills E, Nijkamp P (eds) Handbook of regional and urban economics. North Holland, Amsterdam, pp 407–441

Bennett R, Glennerster H, Nevison D (1995) Regional rates of return to education and training in Britain. Reg Stud 29(3):279–295

Benos N, Karagiannis S (2008) Convergence and economic performance in Greece: evidence at the regional and prefecture level. Rev Urban Reg Dev Stud 20(1):52–69

Bentzen J (2005) Testing for catching-up periods in time-series convergence. Econ Lett 88 (3):323–328

Bergsman J, Greenston P, Healy R (1972) The agglomeration process in urban growth. Urban Stud 9(3):263–288

Bernard A, Durlauf S (1995) Convergence of international output. J Appl Econom 10(2):97–108

Bernard A, Jones C (1996a) Technology and convergence. Econ J 106(437):1037–1044

Bernard A, Jones C (1996b) Productivity across industries and countries: time series theory and evidence. Rev Econ Stat 78(1):135–146

Bernard A, Jones C (1996c) Productivity and convergence across US States and industries. Empir Econ 21(1):113–135

Bernard A, Jones C (1996d) Comparing apples to oranges: productivity convergence measurement across industries and countries. Am Econ Rev 86(5):1216–1238

Bernat G (1996) Does manufacturing matter? A spatial econometric view of Kaldor's laws. J Reg Sci 36(3):463–477

Bertinelli L, Black D (2004) Urbanisation and growth. J Urban Econ 56(1):80–96

Bhattacharya M (2002) Industrial concentration and competition in Malaysian manufacturing. Appl Econ 34(17):2127–2134

Birnie J, Hitchens D (1998) Productivity and income per-capita convergence in a peripheral European economy: the Irish experience. Reg Stud 32(3):223–234

Bishop P, Gripaios P (2004) Earnings biases and convergence in the UK: a county level analysis. Appl Econ Lett 11(1):33–37

Bishop P, Gripaios P (2005) Patterns of persistence and mobility in GDP per-head across GB counties. Tijdschrift voor Economische en Sociale Geographie 96(5):522–540

Bishop P, Gripaios P (2006) Earnings convergence in UK counties: a distribution dynamics approach. Appl Econ Lett 13(1):29–33

Bivand R (1999) Dynamic externalities and regional manufacturing development in Poland. Tijdschrift voor Economische en Sociale Geografie 90(4):347–362

Black J (1962) The technical progress function and the production function. Economica 29 (114):166–170

Black D, Henderson V (1999) A theory of urban growth. J Pol Econ 107(2):252–284

Bliss C (1999) Galton's Fallacy and economic convergence. Oxf Econ Pap 51(1):4–14

Bliss C (2000) Galton's Fallacy and economic convergence: a reply to Cannon and Duck. Oxf Econ Pap 52(2):420–422

Blitch C (1983) Allyn Young on increasing returns. J Post Keynes Econ 5(3):359–371

Blomstrom M, Lipsey R, Zejan M (1996) Is fixed investment the key to economic growth? Q J Econ 111(1):269–276

Bode E (2004) The spatial pattern of localised R&D spillovers: an empirical investigation for Germany. J Econ Geogr 4(1):43–64

Bode E, Nunnenkamp P, Waldkirch A (2012) Spatial effects of foreign direct investment in US States. Can J Econ 45(1):16–40

Boldrin M, Canova F (2001) Inequality and convergence in Europe's regions: reconsidering European regional policies. Econ Policy 16(32):207–253

Boldrin M, Rustichini A (1994) Growth and indeterminacy in dynamic models with externalities. Econometrica 62(2):323–342

Boltho A, Holtham G (1992) The assessment: new approaches to economic growth. Oxf Rev Econ Policy 8(4):1–14

Boltho A, Carlin W, Scaramozzino P (1999) Will East Germany become a new Mezzogiorno? In: Adams J, Pigliaru F (eds) Economic growth and change: national and regional patterns of convergence and divergence. Edward Elgar, Cheltenham/Northampton, pp 323–348

Borts G (1960) The equalisation of returns and regional economic growth. Am Econ Rev 50 (3):319–347

Borts G, Stein J (1964) Economic growth in a free market. Columbia University Press, New York

Boschma R (2005) Proximity and innovation: a critical assessment. Reg Stud 39(1):61–74

Boschma R, Frenken K (2006) Why is economic geography not an evolutionary science? Towards an evolutionary economic geography. J Econ Geogr 6(3):273–302

Boschma R, Lambooy J (2002) Knowledge, market structure and economic coordination: dynamics of industrial districts. Growth Change 33(3):291–311

Boschma R, Wenting R (2007) The spatial evolution of the British automobile industry: does location matter? Ind Corp Change 16(2):213–238

Boudeville J (1966) Problems of regional economic planning. Edinburgh University Press, Edinburgh

Boulier B (1984) What lies behind Verdoorn's law? Oxf Econ Pap 36(2):259–267

Boyer R (1997) The convergence hypothesis revisited: globalisation but still a century of nations? In: Berger S, Dore R (eds) National diversity and global capitalism. Cornell University Press, Ithaca, pp 29–59

Boyle G, McCarthy T (1997) A simple measure of b-convergence. Oxf Bull Econ Stat 59 (2):257–264

Boyle G, McCarthy T (1999) Simple measures of convergence in per-capita GDP: a note on some further international evidence. Appl Econ Lett 6(6):343–347

Bracalente B, Perugini C (2010) The components of regional disparities in Europe. Ann Reg Sci 44 (3):621–645

Bradley S, Taylor J (1996) Human capital formation and local economic performance. Reg Stud 30(1):1–14

Brakman S, Garretsen H (2003) Rethinking of the new geographical economics. Reg Stud 37 (6–7):637–648

Braunerhjelm P, Borgman B (2004) Geographical concentration, entrepreneurship and regional growth: evidence from regional data in Sweden, 1975–99. Reg Stud 38(8):929–947

Breschi S (2000) The geography of innovation: a cross-sector analysis. Reg Stud 34(3):213–229

Breunig R (2001) An almost unbiased estimator of the coefficient of variation. Econ Lett 70 (1):15–19

Brezis E, Krugman P, Tsiddon D (1993) Leapfrogging and international competition: a theory of cycles in national technological leadership. Am Econ Rev 85(5):1211–1219

Brinkman R, Brinkman J (2001) The new growth theories: a cultural and social addendum. Int J Soc Econ 28(5):506–525

Brulhart M (1998) Economic geography, industry location and trade: the evidence. World Econ 21 (6):775–801

Button K (1976) Urban economics: theory and policy. McMillan, London

Button K, Pentecost E (1995) Testing for convergence of the EU regional economies. Econ Inq 33 (4):664–671

Button K, Pentecost E (1999) Regional economic performance within the European Union. Edward Elgar, Northampton

Calem P, Carlino G (1991) Urban agglomeration economies in the presence of technical change. J Urban Econ 29(1):82–95

Camagni R, Capello R (2009) Knowledge-base economy and knowledge creation: the role of space. In: Fratesi U, Senn L (eds) Growth and innovation of competitive regions: the role of internal and external connections. Springer, Berlin, pp 145–165

Camagni R, Capello R (2010) Macroeconomic and territorial policies for regional competitiveness: an EU perspective. Reg Sci Pol Pract 2(1):1–19

Cameron G, Proudman J, Redding S (2005) Technological convergence, R&D, trade and productivity growth. Eur Econ Rev 49(3):775–807

Canaleta C, Arzoz P, Gárate M (2004) Regional economic disparities and decentralisation. Urban Stud 41(1):71–94

Cannon E, Duck N (2000) Galton's fallacy and economic convergence. Oxf Econ Pap 52 (2):415–419

Canova F (2004) Testing for convergence clubs in income per-capita: a predictive density approach. Int Econ Rev 45(1):49–77

Capolupo R (1998) Convergence in recent growth theories: a survey. J Econ Stud 25(6):496–537

Cappelen A, Castellacci F, Fagerberg J, Verspagen B (2003) The impact of EU regional support on growth and convergence in the European Union. J Common Market Stud 41(4):612–644

Cardoso A (1993) Regional inequalities in Europe – have they really been decreasing? Appl Econ 25(8):1093–1100

Carlberg M (1981) A neoclassical model of interregional economic growth. Reg Sci Urban Econ 11(2):191–203

Carlino G (1978) Economies of scale in manufacturing location: theory and measure. Martinus Nijhoff, Leinden

Carlino G (1979) Increasing returns to scale in metropolitan manufacturing. J Reg Sci 19 (3):363–373

Carlino G (1980) Contrasts in agglomeration: New York and Pittsburgh reconsidered. Urban Stud 17(3):343–351

Carlino G (1982) Manufacturing agglomeration economies as returns to scale: a production function approach. Pap Reg Sci 50(1):95–108

Carlino G (1985) Declining city productivity and the growth of rural regions: a test of alternative explanations. J Urban Econ 18(1):11–27

Carlino G (1987) Comparisons of agglomeration: or what Chinitz really said: a reply. Urban Stud 24(1):75–76

Carlino G, de Fina R (1995) Regional income dynamics. J Urban Econ 37(1):88–106

Carlino G, Mills L (1993) Are U.S. regional incomes converging? A time series analysis. J Monet Econ 32(2):335–346

Carlino G, Mills L (1996a) Testing neoclassical convergence in regional incomes and earnings. Reg Sci Urban Econ 26(6):565–590

Carlino G, Mills L (1996b) Are US regional incomes converging? Reply. J Monet Econ 38 (3):599–601

Carlino G, Voith R (1992) Accounting for differences in aggregate state productivity. Reg Sci Urban Econ 22(4):597–617

Carlton D (1983) The location and employment choices of new firms: an econometric model with discrete and continuous endogenous variables. Rev Econ Stat 65(3):440–449

Carluer F (2005) Dynamics of Russian regional clubs: the time of divergence. Reg Stud 39 (6):713–726

Carree M, Klomp L (1997) Testing the convergence hypothesis: a comment. Rev Econ Stat 79 (4):683–686

Carree M, Klomp L, Thurik A (2000) Productivity convergence in OECD manufacturing industries. Econ Lett 66(3):337–345

Carrington A (2003) A divided Europe? Regional convergence and neighbourhood spillover effects. Kyklos 56(3):381–394

Carter A (1990) Know-how trading as economic exchange. Res Policy 18(3):155–163

Casetti E (1984) Verdoorn's law and the components of manufacturing productivity growth: a theoretical model and an analysis of US regional data. In: Anderson Å, Isard W, Puu T (eds) Regional and industrial theories: models and empirical evidence. Elsevier, Amsterdam, pp 295–308

Casetti E, Jones J (1987) Spatial aspects of the productivity slowdown: an analysis of U.S. manufacturing data. Ann AssocAm Geogr 77(1):76–88

Casetti E, Tanaka K (1992) The spatial dynamics of Japanese manufacturing productivity: an empirical analysis by expanded Verdoorn equations. Pap Reg Sci Assoc 71(1):1–13

Cashin P (1995) Testing for convergence across the seven colonies of Australasia: 1861–1991. Econ Record 71(213):132–144

Cashin P, Strappazzon L (1998) Disparities in Australian regional incomes: are they widening or narrowing? Austr Econ Review 31(1):3–26

Cass D (1965) Optimum growth in an aggregative model of capital accumulation. Rev Econ Stud 32(3):233–240

Castellacci F, Archibugi D (2008) The technology clubs: the distribution of knowledge across nations. Res Policy 38(10):1659–1673

Cesaratto S (1999) Savings and economic growth in neoclassical theory. Camb J Econ 23 (6):771–793

Cetorelli N (2002) Could Prometheus be bound again? A contribution to the convergence controversy. J Econ Dyn Conrol 27(1):29–50

Chapman K, Walker D (1988) Industrial location: principles and policies. Blackwell, London

Chatterji M (1992) Convergence clubs and endogenous growth. Oxf Rev Econ Policy 8(4):57–69

Chatterji M, Dewhurst H (1996) Convergence clubs and relative economic performance in Great Britain: 1977–1991. Reg Stud 30(1):31–40

Cheshire P, Carbonaro G (1995) Convergence-divergence in regional growth rates: an empty black box? In: Armstrong H, Vickerman R (eds) Convergence and divergence among European regions. Pion, London, pp 89–111

Cheshire P, Carbonaro G (1996) Urban economic growth in Europe: testing theory and policy prescriptions. Urban Stud 33(7):1111–1128

Cheshire P, Magrini S (2000) Endogenous processes in European regional growth: convergence and policy. Growth Change 31(4):455–479

Chinitz B (1961) Contrasts in agglomeration: New York and Pittsburgh. Am Econ Rev 51 (2):279–289

Chipman J (1970) External economies of scale and competitive equilibrium. Q J Econ 84 (3):347–385

Chiquiar D (2005) Why Mexico's regional income convergence broke down? J Dev Econ 77 (1):257–275

Chisholm M (1991) Regions in recession and resurgence. Allen and Unwin, London

Ciccone P, Hall R (1995) Productivity and density of economic activity. Am Econ Rev 86 (1):54–70

Cliff A, Ord J (1981) Spatial processes: models and applications. Pion, London

Coffey W, Bailly A (1996) Economic restructuring: a conceptual framework. In: Lever W, Bailly A (eds) The spatial impact of economic changes in Europe. Avebury, Aldershot, pp 13–37

Collins L, Walker D (eds) (1975) Locational dynamics of manufacturing activity. Wiley, London

Cooke P (2008) Regional innovation systems, clean technology and Jacobean cluster-platform policies. Reg Sci Pol Pract 1(1):23–45

Cornwall J (1976) Diffusion, convergence and Kaldor's laws. Econ J 86(342):307–314

Corrado L, Martin R, Weeks M (2005) Identifying and interpreting regional convergence clusters across Europe. Econ J 115(502):C133–C160

Coulombe S (2000) New evidence of convergence across Canadian provinces: the role of urbanisation. Reg Stud 38(8):713–725

Coulombe S, Lee F (1995) Convergence across Canadian Provinces, 1961 to 1991. Can J Econ 28 (4a):886–898

Coulombe S, Tremblay J (2001) Human capital and regional convergence in Canada. J Econ Stud 28(3):154–180

Cowell F (1995) Measuring inequality. London School of Economics

Crafts N (1995a) The Golden age of economic growth in Western Europe, 1950–1973. Econ Hist Review 48(3):429–447

Crafts N (1995b) Exogenous or endogenous growth? The industrial revolution Reconsidered. J Econ Hist 55(4):745–772

Crafts N (1996) Post-neoclassical endogenous growth theory: what are its policy implications? Oxf Rev Econ Policy 12(2):30–47

Crampton G, Evans A (1992) The economy of an agglomeration: the case of London. Urban Stud 29(2):259–271

Crikfield J, Panggabean M (1995) Growth and convergence in US cities. J Urban Econ 38 (2):138–165

Cuadrado-Roura J, Garcia-Greciano B, Raymond J (1999) Regional convergence in productivity and productive structure: the Spanish case. Int Reg Sci Rev 22(1):35–53

Cunado J, Gil-Alana L, de Gracia F (2003) Empirical evidence on real convergence in some OECD Countries. Appl Econ Lett 10(3):173–176

D'Uva M, Siano R (2007) Human capital and 'club convergence' in Italian regions. Econ Bull 18 (1):1–7

Dahmén E (1950) Entrepreneurial activity and the development of Swedish industry, 1919–1939. American Economic Association Translation Series

Dahmén E (1988) "Development blocks" in industrial economics. Scand Econ Hist Rev 36 (1):3–14

Dalgaard C, Hansen J (2005) Capital utilisation and the foundation of club convergence. Econ Lett 87(2):145–152

Dalgaard C, Vastrup J (2001) On the measurement of s-convergence. Econ Lett 70(2):283–287

Dall'erba S, Percoco M, Piras G (2008) The European regional growth process revisited. Spat Econ Anal 3(1):7–25

Das S, Finne H (2008) Innovation and co-location. Spat Econ Anal 3(2):159–194

Datta A (2003) Time-series tests of convergence and transitional dynamics. Econ Lett 81 (2):233–240

Davelaar E, Nijkamp P (1989) The role of metropolitan milieu as an incubation centre for technological innovation: a Dutch case study. Urban Stud 26(5):517–525

Davelaar E, Nijkamp P (1997) Spatial dispersion of technological innovation: a review. In: Bertuglia C, Lombardo S, Nijkamp P (eds) Innovative behaviour in space and time. Springer, Berlin, pp 17–40

David P (1985) Clio and the economics of QWERTY. Am Econ Rev 75(2):332–337

David P (1994) Why are institutions the carriers of history? Path dependence and the evolution of conventions, organisations and institutions. Struct Change Econ Dyn 5(2):205–220

Davis J, Henderson V (2003) Evidence on the political economy of the urbanisation process. J Urban Econ 53(1):98–125

Davis D, Weinstein D (1999) Economic geography and regional production structure: an empirical investigation. Eur Econ Rev 43(2):379–407

De la Fuente A (1997) The empirics of growth and convergence: a selective review. J Econ Dyn Conrol 21(1):23–73

De la Fuente A (2000) Convergence across countries and regions: theory and empirics. Eur Invest Bank Pap 5(2):25–45

De la Fuente A (2002) On the sources of convergence: a closer look at the Spanish regions. Eur Econ Rev 46(3):569–599

De la Fuente A, Vives X (1995) Infrastructure and education as instruments of regional policy: evidence from Spain. Econ Policy 10(20):11–51

De Long B (1988) Productivity growth, convergence and welfare: comment. Am Econ Rev 78 (5):1138–1154

De Vor F, de Groot H (2010) Agglomeration externalities and localized employment growth: the performance of industrial sites in Amsterdam. Ann Reg Sci 44(3):409–431

Dekle R (2002) Industrial concentration and regional growth: evidence from the prefectures. Rev Econ Stat 84(2):310–315

Dekle R, Eaton J (1999) Agglomeration and land rents: evidence from the prefectures. J Urban Econ 46(2):200–214

Den Haan W (1995) Convergence in stochastic growth models: the importance of understanding why income levels differ. J Monet Econ 35(1):65–82

Desdoigts A (1999) Patterns of economic development and the formation of clubs. J Econ Growth 4(3):305–330

Desmet K, Fafchamps M (2005) Changes in the spatial concentration of employment across US Counties: a sectoral analysis: 1972–2000. J Econ Geogr 5(3):261–284

Detragiache E (1998) Technology diffusion and international income convergence. J Dev Econ 56 (2):367–392

Dewhurst J (1998) Convergence and divergence in regional household incomes per-head in the United Kingdom, 1984–93. Appl Econ 30(1):31–35

Diamond P (1965) National debt in a neoclassical growth model. Am Econ Rev 55(5):1126–1150

Dicken P, Lloyd P (1990) Location in space: theoretical perspectives in economic geography. Harper and Row, New York

Dickey D, Fuller W (1979) Distribution of the estimators for autoregressive time series with a unit root. J Am Stat Assoc 74(366):427–431

Dickey D, Fuller W (1981) Likelihood ratio statistics for autoregressive time series with a unit root. Econometrica 49(4):1057–1072

Dixit A, Stiglitz J (1977) Monopolistic competition and optimum price diversity. Am Econ Rev 67 (3):297–308

Dixon R, Thirlwall A (1975) A model of regional growth differences on Kaldorian lines. Oxf Econ Pap 27(2):201–214

Dobkins L, Ioannidis Y (2001) Spatial interaction among US Cities: 1900–1990. Reg Sci Urban Econ 31(6):701–731

Dobson S, Ramlogan C (2002) Convergence and divergence in Latin America, 1970–1998. Appl Econ 34(4):465–470

Dollar D (1991) Convergence of South Korean productivity on West German levels, 1966–78. World Dev 19(2–3):263–273

Doloreux D, Dionne S (2008) Is regional innovation system development possible in peripheral regions? Some evidence from the case of La Pocatiére, Canada. Enterp Reg Dev 20 (3):259–283

Dosi G (1988) Sources, procedures and microeconomic effect of innovation. J Econ Lit 26 (3):1120–1171

Dosi G, Freeman C, Nelson R, Silverberg G, Soete L (1988) Technical change and economic theory. Pinter, London

Dosi G, Pavitt K, Soete L (1990) The economics of technical change and international trade. Harvester Wheatsheaf, London

Douglas-Carrol J (1955) Spatial interaction and the urban–metropolitan regional description. Pap Reg Sci 1:59–73

Dowrick S (1992) Technological catch-up and diverging incomes: patterns of economic growth 1960–1988. Econ J 102(412):600–610

Dowrick S, Gemmell N (1991) Industrialisation, catching-up and economic growth: a comparative study across the world's capitalist countries. Econ J 101(405):263–275

Dowrick S, Nguyen D (1989) OECD comparative economic growth 1950–85: catch-up and convergence. Am Econ Rev 79(5):1010–1030

Doyle E, O'Leary E (1999) The role of structural change in labour productivity convergence among European Union countries: 1970–1990. J Econ Stud 26(2):10–12

Drakopoulos S, Theodossiou I (1991) Kaldorian approach to Greek economic growth. Appl Econ 23(10):1683–1689

Drennan M, Lobo J (1999) A simple test for convergence of metropolitan income in the US. J Urban Econ 46(3):350–359

Drennan M, Lobo J, Strumsky D (2004) Unit-root tests of s income convergence across US metropolitan areas. J Econ Geogr 4(5):583–595

Drifflied N (2006) On the search for spillovers from foreign direct investment (FDI) with spatial dependency. Reg Stud 40(1):107–119

Drucker P (1989) The new realities: in government and politics/in economics and business/in society and world view. Harper & Row, New York

Dubin R (2003) Robustness of spatial autocorrelation specifications: some simple Monte Carlo evidence. J Reg Sci 43(2):221–248

Duffy N (1987) Returns to scale behaviour and manufacturing agglomeration economies in U.S. urban areas. J Reg Anal Policy 17(1):42–54

Dunford M (1993) Regional disparities in the European Community: evidence from the REGIO databank. Reg Stud 27(8):727–743

Dunford M (1996) Disparities in employment, productivity and output in the EU: the roles of labour market governance and welfare regimes. Reg Stud 30(4):339–357

Dunford M, Smith A (2000) Catching-up or falling behind? Economic performance and regional trajectories in the New Europe. Economic Geography 76(2):169–195

Durlauf N (1993) Nonergodic economic growth. Rev Econ Stud 60(2):349–367

Durlauf S (1994) Spillovers, stratification and inequality. Eur Econ Rev 38(3–4):836–845

Durlauf S (1996) On the convergence and divergence of growth rates. Econ J 106(437):1016–1018

Durlauf S, Johnson P (1995) Multiple regimes and cross-country growth behaviour. J Appl Econom 10(4):365–384

Durlauf S, Quah D (1999) The new empirics of economic growth. In: Taylor J, Woodford M (eds) Handbook of macroeconomics. Elsevier, New York, pp 235–308

Durlauf S, Kourtellos A, Minkin A (2001) The local Solow growth model. Eur Econ Rev 45 (4–6):928–940

Dyson K (2000) EMU as Europeanization: convergence, diversity and contingency. J Common Market Stud 38(4):645–666

Easterlin R (1958) Long term potential income changes: some suggested factors. Pap Reg Sci Assoc 2:313–325

Elhorst J (2010) Applied spatial econometrics: raising the bar. Spat Econ Anal 5(1):9–28

Ellison G, Glaeser E (1997) Geographic concentration in US manufacturing industries: a dartboard approach. J Pol Econ 105(5):889–927

Ellison G, Glaeser E (1999) The geographic concentration of industry: does natural advantage explain agglomeration? Am Econ Rev 89(2):311–316

Enders W (1995) Applied econometric time series. Wiley, Chichester

Engle R, Granger C (1987) Cointegration and error–correction: representation, estimation and testing. Econometrica 55(2):251–276

Ertur C, Koch W (2005) Une analyse exploratoire des disparite´s re´gionales dans l'Europe elargie. Région et Développement 21:65–92

Ertur C, Le Gallo J, Le Sage J (2007) Local versus global convergence in Europe: a Bayesian spatial economic approach. Review Reg Stud 37(1):82–108

Esteban J (2000) Regional convergence in Europe and the industry mix: a shift-share analysis. Reg Sci Urban Econ 30(3):353–364

Ethier W (1982) National and international returns to scale in the modern theory of international trade. Am Econ Rev 72(3):567–585

European Commission (1996) First report on economic and social cohesion. Office for Official Publications of the European Communities, Luxemburg

European Commission (1999) Sixth period report on the social and economic situation of the regions of the EU. Official Publication Office, Luxemburg

European Commission (2003) Second progress report on socio-economic cohesion. Official Publication Office, Luxemburg

European Commission (2004) Third report on social cohesion. Official Publication Office, Luxembourg

European Commission (2006a) The growth and jobs strategy and the reform of European cohesion policy. Fourth progress report on cohesion. EC, Brussels

European Commission (2006b) The demographic future of Europe – from challenge to opportunity. COM (2006) 571, Final, Brussels

European Commission (2007a) Growing regions, growing Europe. Fourth report on *economic* and social cohesion. EC, Brussels

European Commission (2007b) Cohesion policy 2007–2013. EC, Brussels

Evans A (1986) Comparisons of agglomeration: or what Chinitz really said. Urban Stud 23 (5):387–389

Evans P (1997) How fast do economies converge? Rev Econ Stat 79(2):219–225

Evans P, Karras G (1993) Do standards of living converge? Some cross-country evidence. Econ Lett 43(2):149–155

Evans P, Karras G (1996a) Convergence revisited. J Monet Econ 37(2):249–265

Evans P, Karras G (1996b) Do economies converge? Evidence from a panel of U.S. States. Rev Econ Stat 78(3):384–388

Ezcurra R (2009) Does income polarization affect economic growth? The case of the European regions. Reg Stud 43(2):267–285

Ezcurra R, Rapun M (2006) Regional disparities and national development revisited: the case of Western Europe. Eur Urban Reg Stud 13(4):355–369

Ezcurra R, Gil C, Pascual P (2005) Regional welfare disparities: the case of the European regions. Appl Econ 37(12):1423–1437

Fafchamps M, Shilpi F (2005) Cities and specialisation: evidence from South Asia. Econ J 115 (503):477–504

Fagerberg J (1987) A technology-gap approach to why growth rates differ. Res Policy 16 (2–4):87–99

Fagerberg J (1988) International competitiveness. Econ J 98(391):355–374

Fagerberg J (1994) Technology and international differences in growth rates. J Econ Lit 32 (3):1147–1175

Fagerberg J (1996) Technology and competitiveness. Oxf Rev Econ Policy 12(3):39–51

Fagerberg J, Verspagen B (1996) Heading for divergence? Regional growth in Europe reconsidered. J Common Market Stud 34(3):431–448

Fagerberg J, Verspagen B, Caniëls M (1997) Technology, growth and unemployment across European regions. Reg Stud 31(5):457–466

Faini R (1999) Trade unions and regional development. Eur Econ Rev 43(2):457–474

Faini R, Galli G, Gennari P, Rossi F (1997) An empirical puzzle: falling migration and growing unemployment differentials among Italian regions. Eur Econ Rev 41(3–5):571–579

Fan C, Casetti E (1994) The spatial and temporal dynamics of US regional income inequality, 1950–1989. Ann Reg Sci 28(2):177–196

Fase M, van den Heuvel P (1988) Productivity and growth: Verdoorn's law revisited. Econ Lett 28 (2):135–139

Fase M, Winder C (1999) Baumol's law and Verdoorn's regularity. De Economist 147(3):277–291

Fatás A (1997) EMU: countries or regions? Lessons from EMS experience. Eur Econ Rev 41 (3–5):743–751

Feldman M (1994) The geography of innovation. Kluwer, Boston

Feldman M, Kutay A (1997) Innovation and strategy in space: towards a new location theory of the firm. In: Bertuglia C, Lombardo S, Nijkamp P (eds) Innovative behaviour in space and time. Springer, Berlin, pp 239–250

Feldstein M, Horioka C (1980) Domestic saving and international capital flows. Econ J 90 (385):314–329

Ferguson B, Lim G (1998) Introduction to dynamic economic models. Manchester University Press, Manchester

Ferguson M, Ali K, Olfet M, Partridge M (2007) Voting with their feet: jobs versus amenities. Growth Change 38(4):567–594

Ferreira A (2000) Convergence in Brazil: recent trends and long-run prospects. Appl Econ 32 (4):479–489

Feve P, lePen Y (2000) On modelling convergence clubs. Appl Econ Lett 7(5):311–314

Fine B (2000) Endogenous growth theory: a critical assessment. Camb J Econ 24(2):245–265

Fingleton B (1997) Specification and testing of Markov chain models: an application to convergence in the European Union. Oxf Bull Econ Stat 59(3):385–403

Fingleton B (1999) Spurious spatial regression: some Monte Carlo results with spatial unit root and spatial cointegration. J Reg Sci 39(1):1–19

Fingleton B (2000) Spatial econometrics, economic geography, dynamics and equilibrium: a third way. Environ Plann A 32(8):1481–1498

Fingleton B (2001) Theoretical economic geography and spatial econometrics: dynamic perspectives. J Econ Geogr 1(2):201–225

Fingleton B, Fischer M (2010) Neoclassical theory versus new economic geography: competing expectations of cross-regional variation in economic development. Ann Reg Sci 44 (3):467–491

Fingleton B, McCombie J (1998) Increasing returns and economic growth: some evidence from the European Union regions. Oxf Econ Pap 50(1):89–105

Fisch O (1984) Regional income inequality and economic development. Reg Sci Urban Econ 14 (1):89–111

Fischer M, Stirböck C (2006) Pan-European regional income growth and club convergence. Ann Reg Sci 40(4):693–721

Fischer M, Stumpner P (2008) Income distribution and cross-region convergence in Europe: spatial filtering and novel stochastic Kernel representations. J Geogr Syst 10(2):109–139

Fisher W (1971) Econometric estimation with spatial dependence. Reg Urban Econ 1(1):19–40

Folloni G (2009) A model of local development. In: Fratesi U, Senn L (eds) Growth and innovation of competitive regions: the role of internal and external connections. Springer, Berlin, pp 45–58

Ford T, Logan B, Logan J (2009) NAFTA or nada? Trade's impact on US border retailers. Growth Change 40(2):260–286

Formby J, Smith W, Zheng B (1999) The coefficient of variation, stochastic dominance and inequality: a new interpretation. Econ Lett 62(3):319–323

Fothergill S, Gudgin G (1982) Unequal growth: urban and regional employment change in the United Kingdom. Heinemann, London

Frankel A (1962) The production function in allocation and growth: a synthesis. Am Econ Rev 52 (5):995–1022

Frenkel A, Shefer D (1997) Technological innovation and diffusion models: a review. In: Bertuglia C, Lombardo S, Nijkamp P (eds) Innovative behaviour in space and time. Springer, Berlin, pp 41–63

Friedman M (1992) Do old fallacies ever die? J Econ Lit 30(4):2129–2132

Friedmann J (1969) The future of urbanisation in Latin America. Stud Comp Int Dev 5:179–197

Friedmann J (1972) The spatial organisation of power in the development of urban systems. Dev Change 4(3):12–50

Frizado J, Smith B, Carroll M, Reid N (2009) Impact of polygon geometry on the identification of economic clusters. Lett Spat Resource Sci 2(1):31–44

Fujita M, Tabuchi T (1997) Regional growth in post-war Japan. Reg Sci Urban Econ 27 (6):643–670

Fujita M, Krugman P, Mori T (1999a) On the evolution of hierarchical urban systems. Eur Econ Rev 43(2):209–251

Fujita M, Krugman P, Venables A (1999b) The spatial economy: cities, regions and international trade. MIT Press, Cambridge

Funke M, Niebuhr A (2005) Regional geographic research and development spillovers and economic growth: evidence from West Germany. Reg Stud 39(1):143–153

Funke M, Strulik H (1999) Regional growth in West Germany: convergence or divergence. Econ Model 16(4):489–502

Furceri D (2005) b and s-convergence: a mathematical relation of causality. Econ Lett 89 (2):212–215

Gaile G (1980) The spread-backwash concept. Reg Stud 14(1):15–25

Galor O (1996) Convergence? Inferences form theoretical models. Econ J 106(437):1056–1069

Galor O, Tsiddon D (1991) Technological breakthroughs and development traps. Econ Lett 37 (1):11–17

Galor O, Tsiddon N (1997) The distribution of human capital and economic growth. J Econ Growth 2(1):93–124

Galor O, Zeira J (1993) Income distribution and macroeconomics. Rev Econ Stud 60(1):35–52

Gerschenkron A (1962) Economic backwardness in historical perspective. Bellknap Press, Cambridge

Gertler M (2003) Tacit knowledge and the economic geography of context. J Econ Geogr 3 (1):75–99

Gezici F, Hewings G (2004) Regional convergence and the economic performance of peripheral areas in Turkey. Rev Urban Reg Dev Stud 16(2):113–132

Gibson H, Thirlwall A (1993) Balance of payments theory and the United Kingdom experience. St. Martin's Press, London

Glaeser E (1999) Learning in cities. J Urban Econ 46(2):254–277

Glaeser E, Kallal H, Scheinkman J, Schleifer A (1992) Growth in cities. J Pol Econ 100 (6):1126–1152

Goddard J, Wilson J (2001) Cross sectional and panel estimation of convergence. Econ Lett 70 (3):327–333

Goetz S, Hu D (1996) Economic growth and human capital accumulation: simultaneity and expanded convergence tests. Econ Lett 51(3):355–362

Gomulka S (1971) Inventive activity, diffusion and the stages of economic growth, institute of economics. Aarhus, Denmark

Gomulka S (1983) Industrialisation and the rate of growth: Eastern Europe 1955–75. J Post Keynes Econ 5(3):388–396

Gomulka S (1986) Growth, innovation and reform in Eastern Europe. University of Wisconsin Press, Madison

Gomulka S (1990) The theory of technological change and economic growth. Routledge, London

Goodfriend M, McDermott J (1998) Industrial development and the convergence question. Am Econ Rev 88(5):1277–1289

Gordon I, McCann P (2005) Innovation, agglomeration and regional development. J Econ Geogr 5 (5):523–543

Goschin Z, Constantin D, Roman M, Ileanu B (2009) Specialisation and concentration in the Romanian economy. J Appl Quant Methods 4(1):95–111

Gouyette C, Perelman S (1997) Productivity convergence in OECD industries. Struct Change Econ Dyn 8(3):279–295

Graham D (2001) Productivity growth in British manufacturing: spatial variation in the role of scale economies, technological growth and industrial structure. Appl Econ 33(6):811–821

Gray D (2004) Persistent regional unemployment differentials revisited. Reg Stud 38(2):167–176

Gray D (2005) An examination of regional interaction and super-regions in Britain: an error-correction model approach. Reg Stud 39(5):619–632

Greasley D, Oxley L (1997) Time-series based tests of the convergence hypothesis: some positive results. Econ Lett 56(2):143–147

Griffith R, Redding S, van Reenen J (2003) R&D and absorptive capacity: theory and empirical evidence. Scand J Econ 105(1):99–118

Griffith R, Redding S, Simpson H (2009) Technological catch-up and geographical proximity. J Reg Sci 49(4):689–720

Griliches Z (1957) Hybrid corn: an exploration in the economics of technological change. Econometrica 25(4):501–522

Gripaios P, Bishop P, Keast S (2000) Differences in GDP per-head in GB counties: some suggested explanations. Appl Econ 32(9):1161–1167

Gross D (1997) Aggregate job matching and returns to scale in Germany. Econ Lett 56(2):243–248

Grossman G, Helpman E (1991a) Innovation and growth in the global economy. MIT Press, Cambridge

Grossman G, Helpman E (1991b) Endogenous product cycles. Econ J 101(408):1214–1229

Grossman G, Helpman E (1991c) Quality leaders in the theory of growth. Rev Econ Stud 58 (1):43–61

Grossman G, Helpman E (1994) Endogenous innovation in the theory of growth. J Econ Perspect 8 (1):32–44

Gruber S, Soci A (2010) Agglomeration, agriculture and the perspective of the periphery. Spat Econ Anal 5(1):43–72

Guerrero D, Seró M (1997) Spatial distribution of patents in Spain: determining factors and consequences on regional development. Reg Stud 31(4):381–390

Gugler K, Pfaffermayr M (2004) Convergence in structure and productivity in European manufacturing? Ger Econ Rev 5(1):61–79

Guthrie J (1955) Economies of scale and regional development. Pap Reg Sci 1:1–10

Hagerstrand T (1966) Aspects of the spatial structure of social communication and the diffusion of innovation. Pap Reg Sci Assoc 16(1):27–42

Hagerstrand T (1967) Innovation diffusion as a spatial process. Chicago University Press, Chicago (Translated by A. Pred)

Hahn F, Matthews R (1964) The theory of economic growth: a survey. Econ J 74(296):779–902

Hall P (1982) Enterprise zones: a justification. Int J Urban Reg Res 6(3):416–421

Hammond P, Rodriguez-Clare A (1995) On endogenising long-run growth. In: Andersen T, Moene K (eds) Endogenous growth. Blackwell, Oxford, pp 1–36

Hanna F (1959) State income differentials, 1919–54. Duke University Press, Durham

Hansen P, Knowles S (1998) Human capital and returns to scale. J Econ Stud 25(2):118–123

Hansen J, Zhang J (1996) A Kaldorian approach to regional economic growth in China. Appl Econ 28(6):679–685

Hanson G (1996) Agglomeration, dispersion and the pioneer firm. J Urban Econ 39(3):255–281

Hanson G (2001) Scale economies and the geographic concentration of industry. J Econ Geogr 1 (3):255–276

Harrington J, Barney W (1995) Industrial location: principles, practice and policy. Routledge, London

Harris C (1954) The market as a factor in the localisation of industry in the United States. Ann Assoc Am Geogr 44(4):315–348

Harrison B (1992) Industrial districts: old wine in new bottles? Reg Stud 26(5):469–483

Harvey J (1992) Urban and land economics, 3rd edn. Macmillan, London

Hayter R (1997) The dynamics of industrial location. Wiley, London

Henderson V (1974) The sizes and types of cities. Am Econ Rev 64(4):640–656

Henderson V (1982) The impact of government policies on urban concentration. J Urban Econ 12 (3):280–303

Henderson V (1983) Industrial bases and city sizes. Am Econ Rev 73(2):164–168

Henderson V (1994) Where does an industry locate? J Urban Econ 35(1):83–104

Henderson V (1996) Ways to think about urban concentration: neoclassical urban systems versus the new economic geography. Int Reg Sci Rev 19(1–2):31–36

Henderson V (1997) Externalities and industrial development. J Urban Econ 42(3):449–470

Henderson V (2003a) Marshall's scale economies. J Urban Econ 53(1):1–28

Henderson V (2003b) The urbanisation process and economic growth: the so-what question. J Econ Growth 8(1):47–71

Henderson V, Kuncoro A, Turner M (1995) Industrial development in cities. J Pol Econ 103 (5):1067–1090

Henderson V, Zmarak S, Venables A (2001a) Geography and development. J Econ Geogr 1 (1):81–105

Henderson V, Lee T, Lee V (2001b) Spatial externalities in Korea. J Urban Econ 49(3):479–504

Heston A, Summers R (1984) Improved international comparisons of real product and its composition, 1950–1980. Review Income Wealth 30(2):207–262

Heston A, Summers R (1988) A new set of international comparisons of real product and price levels: estimates for 130 countries, 1950–1980. Review Income Wealth 34(1):1–26

Hierro M, Maza A (2010) Per-capita income convergence and internal migration in Spain: are foreign-born migrants playing and important role? Pap Reg Sci 89(1):89–107

Hildreth A (1989) The ambiguity of Verdoorn's Law: a case study of the British regions. J Post Keynes Econ 11(2):279–294

Hirschman A (1957) Investment policies and 'dualism' in underdeveloped countries. Am Econ Rev 47(5):550–570

Hirschman A (1958) Strategy of economic development. Yale University Press, New Haven

Hirschman A (1962) Economic development, research and development, policy making: some converging views. Behav Sci 7(2):211–224

Hobijin B, Frances P (2000) Asymptotically perfect and relative convergence of productivity. J Appl Econ 15(1):59–81

Hobijin B, Frances P (2001) Are living standards converging? Struct Change Econ Dyn 12 (2):171–200

Hofer H, Wörgötter A (1997) Regional per-capita income convergence in Austria. Reg Stud 31 (1):1–12

Hoover E (1936) Location theory and the shoe and leather industry. Harvard University Press, Cambridge

Hoover E (1948) Location of economic activity. McGraw-Hill, New York

Hordijk L (1974) Spatial correlation in the disturbances of a linear interregional model. Reg Urban Econ 4(2):117–140

Hossain F, Chung P (1999) Long-run implications of neoclassical growth models: empirical evidence from Australia, New Zealand, South Korea and Taiwan. Appl Econ 31(9):1073–1082

Howitt P, Mayer-Foulkes D (2005) R&D, implementation and stagnation: a Schumpeterian theory of convergence clubs. J Money Credit Bank 37(1):147–177

Huggins R, Johnston A (2009) Knowledge networks in an uncompetitive region: SME innovation and growth. Growth Change 40(2):227–259

Hurst C, Thisse J, Vanhoudt P (2000) What diagnosis for Europe's ailing regions? Eur Invest Bank Pap 5(1):9–29

Inkster I (2002) Politicising the Gerschenkron schema: technology transfer, late development and the state in historical perspective. J Eur Econ Hist 31(1):45–87

Isard W (1954) Location theory and trade theory: short-run analysis. Q J Econ 68(2):305–320

Isard W (1956) Location and space economy. MIT Press, Cambridge

Islam N (1995) Growth empirics: a panel-data approach. Q J Econ 110(4):1127–1170

Islam N (2003) What have we learnt from the convergence debate? J Econ Surv 17(3):309–362

Isserman A (1977) The location quotient approach to estimating regional economic impacts. J Am Inst Plann 43:33–41

Jacobs J (1964) The death and life of great American cities. Pelican Books, London

Jacobs J (1969) The economies of cities. Random House, New York

Jacobs J (1984) Cities and the wealth of nations: principles of economic life. Random House, New York

Jacobs J (1993) The city unbound: qualitative approaches to the city. Urban Stud 30(4–5):827–848

Jaffe A, Trujtenberg M, Henderson R (1993) Geographic localisation of knowledge spillovers as evidenced by patent citations. Q J Econ 108(3):577–598

Je Su J (2003) Convergence clubs among 15 OECD countries. Appl Econ Lett 10(2):113–118

Johnson H (1966) The neo-classical one-sector growth model: a geometrical exposition and extension to the monetary economy. Economica 33(131):265–287

Johnson P (2000) A non-parametric analysis of income convergence across the US States. Econ Lett 69(2):219–223

Johnson P, Takeyama L (2001) Initial conditions and economic growth in the US States. Eur Econ Rev 45(4–6):919–927

Jones C (1995a) R&D-based models of economic growth. J Pol Econ 103(4):759–784

Jones C (1995b) Time-series tests of endogenous growth models. Q J Econ 110(2):495–525

Jones C (1998) Introduction to economic growth. W. Norton, New York

Jones L, Manuelli R (1990a) Convex model of equilibrium growth: theory and policy implications. J Pol Econ 98(5):1008–1038

Jones L, Manuelli R (1990b) The sources of growth. J Econ Dyn Conrol 21(1):75–114

Kakamu K, Fukushige M (2006) Productivity convergence of manufacturing industries in Japanese MEA. Appl Econ Lett 13(10):649–653

Kaldor N (1957) A model of economic growth. Econ J 67(268):591–624

Kaldor N (1967) Strategic factors in economic development. Ithaca, New York

Kaldor N (1970) The case for regional policies. Scott J Pol Econ 17(3):337–348

Kaldor N (1972) The irrelevance of equilibrium economics. Econ J 82(328):1237–1255

Kaldor N (1975) Economic growth and the Verdoorn's law – a comment on Mr. Rowthorn's article. Econ J 85(340):891–896

Kanbur R, Venables A (2007) Spatial disparities and economic development. In: Held D, Kaya A (eds) Global inequality. Polity Press, London, pp 204–215

Kane R (2001) Investigating convergence of the U.S. regions: a time-series analysis. J Reg Anal Policy 31(1):1–22

Kang S, Lee M (2005) Q-convergence with interquartile ranges. J Econ Dyn Contol 29 (10):1785–1806

Kangasharju A (1998) b-convergence in Finland: regional differences in the speed of convergence. Appl Econ 30(5):679–687

Kangasharju A (1999) Relative economic performance in Finland: regional convergence, 1934–1993. Reg Stud 33(3):207–217

Kawashima T (1975) Urban agglomeration economies in manufacturing industries. Pap Reg Sci 34(1):157–175

Ke S, Bergman E (1995) Regional and technological determinants of company productivity growth in the late 1980s. Reg Stud 29(1):59–71

Keeble D, Lawson C, Moore B, Wilkinson F (1999) Collective learning processes, networking and 'institutional thickness' in the Cambridge region. Reg Stud 33(4):319–332

Kelejian H, Prucha I (2002) 2SLS and OLS in a spatial autoregressive model with equal spatial weights. Reg Sci Urban Econ 32(6):691–707

Keller W (1996) Absorptive capacity: on the creation and acquisition of technology in development. J Dev Econ 49(1):199–227

Keller W (2000) From Socialist to Mezzogiorno? Lessons on the role of technical change from East Germany's post-World War II growth performance. J Dev Econ 63(2):485–514

Kelly M, Hageman A (1999) Marshallian externalities in innovation. J Econ Growth 4(1):39–54

Kendrick J (1956) Productivity trends: capital and labour. Rev Econ Stat 38(3):248–257

Kenny C, Williams D (2001) What do we know about economic growth? Or why don't we know very much? World Dev 29(1):1–22

Ketenci N, McCann P (2009) Regional restructuring and manufacturing firm performance in a Central-Asian transitions economy: observations from Kazakhstan. Lett Spat Resour Sci 2 (1):11–21

King R, Rebelo S (1990) Public policy and economic growth: developing neoclassical implications. J Pol Econ 98(5):S126–S150

King R, Rebelo S (1993) Transitional dynamics and economic growth in the neoclassical model. Am Econ Rev 83(4):908–931

Kirdar M, Saracoğlu D (2008) Migration and regional convergence: an empirical investigation for Turkey. Pap Reg Sci 87(4):545–566

Klenow P, Rodriguez-Clare A (1997) Economic growth: a review essay. J Monet Econ 40 (3):597–617

Knight F (1921) Risk, uncertainty and profit. Harper and Row, New York

Knight F (1944) Diminishing returns for investment. J of Pol Econ 52(1):26–47

Knight M, Loayza N, Villanueva D (1993) Testing the neoclassical theory of economic growth. IMF Staff Pap 40(3):512–541

Kocherlakota N, Yi K (1995) Can convergence regressions distinguish between exogenous and endogenous growth models? Econ Lett 49(2):211–215

Kocherlakota N, Yi K (1996) A simple time-series test of endogenous vs. exogenous growth models: an application to the United States. Rev Econ Stat 78(1):126–134

Kocherlakota N, Yi K (1997) Is there endogenous long-run growth? Evidence from the US and the UK. J Money Credit Bank 29(2):235–262

Koopmans T (1965) On the concept of optimal economic growth. In: The Econometric Approach to Development Planning, Pontif. Acad. Sc. Scripta Varia 28, pp 225–300; reissued North-Holland Publ. (1966)

Kristensen T (1974) Development in rich and poor countries. Praeger, New York

Krugman P (1979) A model of innovation, technology transfer and trade. J Pol Econ 87(2):253–266

Krugman P (1980) Scale economies, product differentiation and the pattern of trade. Am Econ Rev 70(5):950–959

Krugman P (1981) Trade, accumulation and uneven development. J Dev Econ 8(2):149–161

Krugman P (1991a) Increasing returns and economic geography. J Pol Econ 99(3):483–499

Krugman P (1991b) History and industrial location: the case of the manufacturing belt. Am Econ Rev 81(2):80–83

Krugman P (1991c) Geography and trade. MIT Press, Cambridge

Krugman P (1991d) History versus expectations. Q J Econ 106(2):651–667

Krugman P (1995) Development, geography and economic theory. MIT Press, Cambridge

Krugman P (1996a) The self-organising economy. Blackwell, Cambridge

Krugman P (1996b) Urban concentration: the role of increasing returns and transport costs. Int Reg Sci Rev 19(1–2):5–30

Krugman P (1998) What's new about the new economic geography? Oxf Rev Econ Policy 14(2):7–17

Krugman P, Venables A (1995a) Globalisation and the inequality of nations. Q J Econ 110(4):857–880

Krugman P, Venables A (1995b) Integration, specialisation and adjustment. Eur Econ Rev 40(3–5):959–967

Kuznets S (1955) Economic growth and income inequality. Am Econ Rev 45(1):1–28

Kuznets S (1964) Modern economic growth. Yale University Press, New Haven

Lall S, Yilmaz S (2001) Regional economic convergence: do policy instruments make a difference? Ann Reg Sci 35(1):153–166

Lampard E (1955) The history of cities in the economically advanced areas. Econ Dev Cult Change 3(2):81–136

Lampard E (1963) Urbanisation and social change: on broadening the scope and relevance of urban history. In: Handlin O, Burchard J (eds) The historian and the city. MIT Press, Cambridge, pp 225–247

Lasuen J (1969) On growth poles. Urban Stud 6(2):137–161

Lawson C (1999) Towards a competence theory of the region. Camb J Econ 23(2):151–166

Lawson C, Lorenz E (1999) Collective learning, tacit knowledge and regional innovative capacity. Reg Stud 33(4):305–317

Le Gallo J, Dall'erba S (2008) Spatial and sectoral productivity convergence between European regions, 1975–200. Pap Reg Sci 87(4):505–525

Lee J, Mossi D (1996) On improvements of Phillips-Perron unit-Root tests using optimal bandwidth estimates. Appl Econ Lett 3(3):197–200

Lee M, Longmire R, Mátyás L, Harris M (1998) Growth convergence: some panel data evidence. Appl Econ 30(7):907–912

Leibenstein H (1957) Economic backwardness and economic growth. Wiley, New York

Leigh R (1970) The use of location quotients in urban economic base studies. Land Econ 48 (2):202–206

Leonida L, Petraglia C, Murillo-Zamoranos L (2003) Total factor productivity and the convergence hypothesis in the Italian regions. Appl Econ 36(19):2187–2193

LeSage J, Fischer M (2009) Spatial growth regressions: model specification, estimation and interpretation. Spat Econ Anal 3(3):275–304

Leser C (1948) Industrial specialisation in Scotland and in regions of England and Wales. Bull Econ Res 1(1):19–30

Lever W, Bailly A (eds) (1996) The spatial impact of economic changes in Europe. Aldershot, Avebury

Levhari D (1966a) Extensions of Arrow's learning-by-doing. Rev Econ Stud 33(2):117–132

Levhari D (1966b) Further implications of 'learning-by-doing'. Rev Econ Stud 33(1):31–39

Levine R, Renelt D (1992) A Sensitivity analysis of cross-country growth regressions. Am Econ Rev 82(4):942–963

Lichtenberg F (1994) Testing the convergence hypothesis. Rev Econ Stat 76(3):576–579

Linden M (2002) Trend model testing of growth convergence in OECD countries, 1946–1997. Appl Econ 34(2):133–142

Loewy M, Papell D (1996) Are U.S. regional incomes converging? Some further evidence. J Monet Econ 38(3):587–598

Lopez J (1997) The power of the ADF tests. Econ Lett 57(1):5–10

Lopez-Bazo E, Vaya E, Artis M (2004) Regional externalities and growth: evidence from European regions. J Reg Sci 44(1):43–73

Lösch A (1938) The nature of economic regions. South Econ J 5(1):71–78

Lösch A (1954) The economics of location. Yale University Press, New Haven

Lucas R (1988) On the mechanisms of economic development. J Monet Econ 22(1):3–42

Lucio J, Herce J, Goicolea A (2002) The effects of externalities on productivity growth in Spanish industry. Reg Sci Urban Econ 32(2):241–258

Machlup F (1962) The production and distribution of knowledge in the United States. Princeton University Press, New York

Maddison A (1982) Phases of capitalist development. Oxford University Press, Oxford/New York

Magrini S (1999) The evolution of income disparities among the regions of the European Union. Reg Sci Urban Econ 29(2):257–281

Malecki E (1983) Technology and regional development: a survey. Int Reg Sci Rev 8(2):89–125

Malecki E (1991) Technology and economic development: the dynamics of local, regional and national change. Longman, London

Malecki E (2004) Jockeying for position: what it means and why it matters to regional development policy when places compete. Reg Stud 38(9):1101–1120

Malecki E (2007) Cities and regions competing in the global economy: knowledge and local development policies. Environ Plann C Gov Policy 25(5):638–654

Mallick R, Carayannis E (1994) Regional economic convergence in Mexico: an analysis by industry. Growth Change 25(3):325–334

Mancha-Novarro T, Garrido-Yserte R (2008) Regional policy in the European Union: the cohesion-competitiveness dilemma. Reg Sci Pol Pract 1(1):47–66

Mankiw N (1995) The growth of nations. Brooking Pap Econ Act 1:276–326

Mankiw N, Romer D, Weil N (1992) A contribution to the empirics of economic growth. Q J Econ 107(2):407–438

Mansfield E (1968) The economics of technical change. W. Norton, New York

Marchante A, Ortega B (2006) Quality of life and economic convergence across Spanish regions, 1980–2001. Reg Stud 40(5):471–484

Marcus M (1965) Agglomeration economies: a suggested approach. Land Econ 41(3):279–284

Marginson P, Sisson K (2002) European integration and industrial relations: a case of convergence and divergence? J Common Market Stud 40(4):671–692

Marjit S, Beladi H (1998) Product versus process patents: a theoretical approach. J Policy Model 20(2):193–199

Markusen A (1985) Profit cycles, oligopoly and regional development. MIT Press, Cambridge

Markusen A (1996) Sticky places in slippery space: a typology of industrial districts. Econ Geogr 72(3):293–313

Markusen J, Venables A (1999) Foreign direct investment as a catalyst for industrial development. Eur Econ Rev 43(2):335–356

Marquis M, Reffett K (1995) New technology spillovers into the payment system. Econ J 104 (426):1123–1138

Marshall A (1890) Principles of economics. Macmillan, London

Marshall A (1892) Economics of industry. Macmillan, London

Marshall A (1920) Industry and trade. Macmillan, London

Martin R (1997) Regional unemployment disparities and their dynamics. Reg Stud 31(3):237–252

Martin P (1998) Can regional policies affect growth and geography in Europe? World Econ 21 (7):757–774

Martin R (1999) The new geographical turn in economics: some critical reflections. Camb J Econ 23(1):65–91

Martin R (2001) EMU versus the regions? Regional convergence and divergence in Euroland. J Econ Geogr 1(1):51–80

Martin P (2005) The geography of inequalities in Europe. Swed Econ Policy Rev 12(1):83–108

Martin P, Ottaviano P (1999) Growing locations: industry location in a model of endogenous growth. Eur Econ Rev 43(2):281–302

Martin P, Ottaviano P (2001) Growth and agglomeration. Int Econ Rev 42(4):947–968

Martin R, Sunley P (1996) Paul Krugman's geographical economics and its implications for regional development theory: a critical assessment. Econ Geogr 72(3):259–292

Martin R, Sunley P (1998) Slow convergence? New endogenous growth theory and regional development. Econ Geogr 74(3):201–227

Martin R, Sunley P (2006) Path dependence and regional economic evolution. J Econ Geogr 6 (4):395–437

Martin R, Tyler P (2000) Regional employment evolutions in the European Union: a preliminary analysis. Reg Stud 34(7):601–616

Maskell P, Malmberg A (1999) Localised learning and industrial competitiveness. Camb J Econ 23(2):167–185

Mauro L (2004) The macroeconomics of Italy: a regional perspective. J Policy Model 26 (8–9):927–944

Mauro L, Podrecca E (1994) The case of Italian regions: convergence or dualism? Econ Notes 24 (3):447–472

Maurseth P (2001) Convergence, geography and technology. Struct Change Econ Dyn 12 (3):247–276

Mayer W, Pleeter S (1975) A theoretical justification for the use of location quotients. Reg Sci Urban Econ 5(3):343–355

Maza A, Villaverde J (2004) Regional disparities in the EU: mobility and polarisation. Appl Econ Lett 11(8):517–522

McCann P (1995) Rethinking the economics of location and agglomeration. Urban Stud 32 (3):563–577

McCombie J (1981) What still remains of Kaldor's laws? Econ J 91(361):206–216

McCombie J (1982a) How important is the spatial diffusion of innovations in explaining regional growth rate disparities? Urban Stud 19(4):377–382

McCombie J (1982b) Economic growth, Kaldor's laws and the static-dynamic paradox. Appl Econ 14(3):279–294

McCombie J (1983) Kaldor's laws in retrospect. J Post Keynes Econ 5(3):414–429

McCombie J (1985) Increasing returns and the manufacturing industries: some empirical issues. Manchester School 53(1):55–75

McCombie J (1986) On some interpretations of the relationship between productivity and output growth. Appl Econ 18(11):1215–1225

McCombie J (1988a) A synoptic view of regional growth and unemployment Part I: the neoclassical view. Urban Stud 25(4):267–281

McCombie J (1988b) A synoptic view of regional growth and unemployment Part II: the post Keynesian theory. Urban Stud 25(5):399–417

McCombie J, deRidder J (1983) Increasing returns, productivity and output growth: the case of the United States. J Post Keynes Econ 5(3):373–387

McCombie J, deRidder J (1984) The Verdoorn's law controversy: some new evidence using US data. Oxf Econ Pap 36(2):268–284

McCombie J, Thirlwall A (1994) Economic growth and balance of payment constraint. St. Martins Press, London

McCombie J, Thirlwall A (1997) The dynamic Harrod foreign trade multiplier and the demand-oriented approach to economic growth: an evaluation. Int Rev Appl Econ 11(1):5–26

McDonald J (1989) On the estimation of localisation economies. Econ Lett 29(3):275–277

McGuinness S, Sheehan M (1998) Regional convergence in the UK, 1970–1995. Appl Econ Lett 5 (10):653–658

Meade J (1952) External economies and diseconomies in a competitive situation. Econ J 62 (245):54–67

Meade J (1961) A neo-classical theory of economic growth. Allen and Unwin, London

Michelis M, Monfort P (2008) Some reflections concerning GDP, regional convergence and European cohesion policy. Reg Sci Pol Pract 1(1):14–22

Miguélez E, Moreno R, Artís M (2011) Does social capital reinforce technological inputs in the creation of knowledge? Evidence from the Spanish regions. Reg Stud 45(8):1019–1038

Mila T, Marimon R (1999) Regional integration and public investment in Spain. In: Adams J, Pigliaru F (eds) Economic growth and change: national and regional patterns of convergence and divergence. Edward Elgar, Northampton/Cheltenham, pp 349–416

Miller S (1996) A note on cross-country growth regressions. Appl Econ 28(8):1019–1026

Mills E (1967) An aggregative model of resource allocation in a metropolitan area. Am Econ Rev 57(2):197–201

Mion G (2004) Spatial externalities and empirical analysis: the case of Italy. J Urban Econ 56 (1):97–118

Mishan E (1971) The post-war review on externalities. J Econ Lit 9(1):1–28

Mitra A (1999) Agglomeration economies as manifested in technical efficiency at the firm level. J Urban Econ 45(3):490–500

Moomaw R (1982) Productive efficiency and region. South Econ J 48(2):344–358

Moomaw R (1983) Spatial productivity variations in manufacturing: a critical survey of cross-sectional analyses. Int Reg Sci Rev 8(1):1–22

Moomaw R (1988) Agglomeration economies: localisation or urbanisation? Urban Stud 25 (2):150–161

Moomaw R (1998) Agglomeration economies: are they exaggerated by industrial aggregation? Reg Sci Urban Econ 28(2):199–211

Mora T (2004) Role of mobility in evolution of disparities: European regions evidence. Appl Econ Lett 11(5):325–328

Mora T (2005) Evidencing European regional convergence clubs with optimal grouping criteria. Appl Econ Lett 12(15):937–940

Mora T, López-Tamayo J, Sariñach J (2005) Are wages and productivity converging simultaneously in Euro-Area countries? Appl Econ 37(17):2001–2008

Morgan K (2004) The exaggerated death of geography: learning proximity and territorial innovation systems. J Econ Geogr 4(1):3–21

Moses L (1958) Location and the theory of production. Q J Econ 72(2):259–272

Moses L, Williamson H (1967) The location of economic activity in cities. Am Econ Rev 57 (2):211–222

Moucque D (2000) A survey of socio-economic disparities between the regions of the EU. Eur Invest Bank Pap 5(2):13–24

Moulaer F, Seria F (2003) Territorial innovation models: a critical survey. Reg Stud 37 (3):289–302

Mukkala K (2004) Agglomeration economies in the Finnish manufacturing sector. Appl Econ 36 (21):2419–2427

Mulas-Granados C, Sanz I (2008) The dispersion of technology and income in Europe: evolution and mutual relationship across regions. Res Policy 37(5):836–848

Mulder P, de Groot H (2007) Sectoral-energy and labour – productivity convergence. Environ Resour Econ 36(1):85–112

Mullen J, Williams M (1990) Explaining TFP differentials in urban manufacturing. J Urban Econ 28(1):103–123

Mulligan G (1984) Agglomeration and central place theory: a review of the literature. Int Reg Sci Rev 9(1):1–42

Mulligan G (2008) A new shortcut method for estimating economic base multipliers. Reg Sci Pol Pract 1(1):67–84

Muscatelli A, Tirelli P (2001) Unemployment and growth: some empirical evidence from structural time series models. Appl Econ 33(8):1083–1088

Muth R (1965) Migration: chicken or egg? South Econ J 38(1):295–306

Myrdal G (1944) An American dilemma. Harper & Bros, New York

Myrdal G (1957) Economic theory and underdeveloped regions. Duckworth, London

Nahar S, Inder B (2002) Testing convergence in economic growth for OECD countries. Appl Econ 34(16):2011–2022

Nakamura R (1985) Agglomeration economies in urban manufacturing industries: a case of Japanese cities. J Urban Econ 17(1):108–124

Neary J (2001) Of hype and hyperbolas: introducing the new economic geography. J Econ Lit 39 (2):536–561

Nelson R (1956) A theory of low-level equilibrium trap in underdeveloped economies. Am Econ Rev 46(5):894–908

Nelson R (1960) Growth models and the escape from the equilibrium trap: the case of Japan. Econ Dev Cult Change 8(4):378–388

Nelson R (1981) Research on productivity growth and productivity differences: dead ends and new departures. J Econ Lit 19(3):1029–1064

Nelson R, Phelps E (1966) Investment in humans, technological diffusion and economic growth. Am Econ Rev 56(2):69–75

Nelson R, Winter S (1974) Neoclassical vs. evolutionary theories of economic growth: critique and prospectus. Econ J 84(336):886–905

Nelson R, Winter S (1982) An evolutionary theory of economic change. The Bellknap Press, Cambridge

Neter J, Wasserman W, Kunter M (1990) Applied linear statistical models, 3rd edn. Irwin, Boston

Netzer D (1992) The economy of the New York metropolitan region, then and now. Urban Stud 29 (2):251–258

Neven D, Gouyette C (1995) Regional convergence in the European community. J Common Market Stud 33(1):47–65

Nicholson R (1956) The regional location of industry. Econ J 66(263):467–481

Nijkamp P, Abreu M (2009) Regional development theory. In: Kitchin R, Thrift N (eds) International encyclopaedia of human geography, vol 9. Elsevier, Oxford/Boston, pp 202–207

Nonaka I, Takeuchi H (1995) The knowledge-creating company. Oxford University Press, New York

Norcliffe G (1983) Using location quotients to estimate the economic base and trade flows. Reg Stud 17(3):161–168

North D (1955) Location theory and regional economic growth. J Pol Econ 63(3):243–258

Norton R (1992) Agglomeration and competitiveness: from Marshal to Chinitz. Urban Stud 29 (2):155–170

Novales A, Fernández E, Ruíz J (2010) Economic growth: theory and numerical solutions. Springer, Berlin

Novell J, Viladecans-Marsal E (1999) Kaldor's laws and the spatial dependence: evidence for the European regions. Reg Stud 33(5):443–451

O'Leary E (1997) The convergence performance of Ireland among EU Countries: 1960 to 1990. J Econ Stud 24(1–2):43–58

O'Leary E (2001) Convergence of living standards among Irish regions: the roles of productivity, profit outflows and demography, 1960–1996. Reg Stud 35(3):197–205

Oakey R (1984) Innovation and regional growth in small high technology firms: evidence from Britain and the USA. Reg Stud 18(3):237–251

Oakey R, Thwaites A, Nash P (1980) The regional distribution of innovative manufacturing establishments in Britain. Reg Stud 14(3):235–253

Oates W, Howrey E, Baumol W (1971) The analysis of public policy in dynamic urban models. J Pol Econ 79(1):142–153

Obstfeld M, Peri G (1998) Regional non-adjustment and fiscal policy. Econ Policy 13 (26):205–259

Oerlemans L, Meeus M (2005) Do organisational and spatial proximity impact on firm performance? Reg Stud 39(1):89–104

Ohlin B (1933) Interregional and international trade. Harvard University Press, Cambridge

Ottaviano G, Peri G (2005) Cities and cultures. J Urban Econ 58(2):304–337

Ottaviano G, Peri G (2006) The economic value of cultural diversity: evidence from the US cities. J Econ Geogr 6(1):9–44

Ottaviano G, Puga D (1998) Agglomeration in the global economy: a survey of the new economic geography. World Econ 21(6):707–731

Ottaviano G, Thisse J (2001) On economic geography in economic theory: increasing returns and pecuniary externalities. J Econ Geogr 1(2):153–179

Oxley L, Greasley D (1995) A time-series perspective on convergence: Australia, UK and USA since 1870. Econ Record 71(214):259–269

Oxley L, Greasley D (1999) A Nordic convergence club. Appl Econ Lett 6(3):157–160

Pace K (1997) Performing large spatial regressions and autoregressions. Econ Lett 54(3):283–291

Paci R (1997) More similar and less equal: economic growth in the European regions. Weltwirtsch Arch 133(4):609–634

Paci R, Pigliaru F (1997) Structural change and convergence: an Italian regional perspective. Struct Change Econ Dyn 8(3):297–318

Paci R, Pigliaru F (1999a) Is dualism a source of convergence in Europe? Appl Econ 31 (11):1423–1436

Paci R, Pigliaru F (1999b) European regional growth: do sectors matter? In: Adams J, Pigliaru F (eds) Economic growth and change: national and regional patterns of convergence and divergence. Edward Elgar, Cheltenham/Northampton, pp 213–235

Paci R, Usai S (2000a) Technological enclaves and industrial districts. An analysis of the regional distribution of innovative activity in Europe. Reg Stud 34(2):97–114

Paci R, Usai S (2000b) Externalities, knowledge spillovers and the spatial distribution of innovation. Geo J 49(4):381–390

Pack H (1994) Endogenous growth theory: intellectual appeal and empirical shortcomings. J Econ Perspect 8(1):55–72

Paelnick J (1978) Spatial econometrics. Econ Lett 1(1):59–63

Parente S, Prescott E (1994) Barriers to technology adoption and development. J Pol Econ 102 (2):298–321

Parente S, Prescott E (1999) Monopoly rights: a barrier to riches. Am Econ Rev 89(5):1216–1233

Parikh A (1978) Differences in growth rates and Kaldor's laws. Economica 45(177):83–91

Parr J (1999a) Growth-pole strategies in regional economic planning: a retrospective view. Part 1: origins and advocacy. Urban Stud 36(7):1195–1215

Parr J (1999b) Growth-pole strategies in regional economic planning: a retrospective view. Part 2: implementation and outcome. Urban Stud 36(8):1247–1268

Partridge M (2005) Does income distribution affect US state economic growth? J Reg Sci 45 (2):363–394

Pascal A, McCall J (1980) Agglomeration economies, search costs and industrial location. J Urban Econ 8(3):383–388

Pascual A, Westermann F (2002) Productivity convergence in European manufacturing. Rev Int Econ 10(2):313–323

Pekkala S (2000) Aggregate economic fluctuations and regional convergence: the Finnish case 1988–1995. Appl Econ 32(2):211–219

Peri G, Urban D (2006) Catching-up to foreign technology? Evidence on the Veblen-Gerschenkron effect of foreign investment. Reg Sci Urban Econ 36(1):72–98

Perroux F (1950) Economic space, theory and applications. Q J Econ 64(1):89–104

Perroux F (1955) Note sur la notion de pôle de croissance. Econ Appliq 7:307–320

Persson J (1997) Convergence across the Swedish counties, 1911–1993. Eur Econ Rev 41 (9):1835–1852

Persson T, Tabellini G (1994) Is inequality harmful growth? Theory and evidence. Am Econ Rev 84(3):600–621

Pesaran H, Smith R (1995) Estimating long-run relationships from dynamic heterogeneous panels. J Econ 68(1):79–113

Petracos G, Artelaris P (2009) European regional convergence revisited: a weighted least squares approach. Growth Change 40(2):314–331

Phelps E (1966) Models of technical progress and the golden rule of research. Rev Econ Stud 33 (2):133–145

Phelps N (1992) External economies, agglomeration and flexible accumulation. Trans Inst Br Geogr 17(1):35–46

Piergiovanni R, Santarelli E (2001) Patents and the geographic localisation of R&D spillovers in French manufacturing. Reg Stud 35(8):697–702

Pigliaru F (2003) Detecting technological catch-up in economic convergence. Metroeconomica 54 (2–3):161–178

Pike A, Rodríguez-Pose A, Tomaney J (2006) Local and regional development. Routledge, London

Pinch S, Henry N (1999) Paul Krugman's geographical economics, industrial clustering and the British motor sport industry. Reg Stud 33(9):815–827

Pinch S, Henry N, Tallman S (2003) From industrial districts to "knowledge clusters": a model of knowledge dissemination and competitive advantage in industrial agglomerations. J Econ Geogr 3(4):373–388

Plummer P, Taylor M (2001a) Theories of local economic growth: Part 1: Concepts, models and measurements. Environ Plann A 33(2):219–236

Plummer P, Taylor M (2001b) Theories of local economic growth: Part 2: Model specification and empirical validation. Environ Plann A 33(3):385–398

Ponds R, van Oort F, Frenken K (2010) Innovation, spillovers and university–industry collaboration: an extended knowledge production function approach. J Econ Geogr 10(2):231–255

Porter M (1990) The competitive advantage of nations. Macmillan, London

Porter M (1994) The role of location in competition. J Econ Bus 1(1):35–39

Porter M (2003) The economic performance of regions. Reg Stud 37(6–7):549–578

Prebisch R (1962) The economic development of Latin America and its principal problems. Econ Bull Lat Am 7:1–22

Proietti T (2005) Convergence in Italian regional per-capita GDP. Appl Econ 37(5):497–506

Puga D (1999) The rise and fall of regional inequalities. Eur Econ Rev 43(2):303–334

Puga D (2002) European regional policies in the light of recent location theories. J Econ Geogr 2 (4):373–406

Puga D, Venables A (1999) Agglomeration and economic development: import substitution versus trade liberalisation. Econ J 109(455):292–311

Qiu T, Hudson J (2010) Private returns to education in urban China. Econ Change Restruct 43 (2):131–150

Quah D (1993a) Galton's fallacy and tests of the convergence hypothesis. Scand J Econ 95 (4):427–443

Quah D (1993b) Empirical cross-section dynamics in economic growth. Eur Econ Rev 37 (2–3):426–434

Quah D (1996a) Regional convergence clusters in Europe. Eur Econ Rev 40(3–5):951–958

Quah D (1996b) Empirics for economic growth and convergence. Eur Econ Rev 40(6):1353–1376

Quah D (1996c) Twin peaks: growth and convergence in models of distribution dynamics. Econ J 106(437):1045–1055

Quah D (1996d) Aggregate and regional disaggregate fluctuations. Empirical Econ 21(1):137–159

Quah D (1997) Empirics for growth and distribution: polarisation, stratification and convergence clubs. J Econ Growth 2(1):27–59

Quigley J (1998) Urban diversity and economic growth. J Econ Perspect 12(2):127–138

Ramsey F (1928) A mathematical theory of saving. Econ J 38(152):543–559

Rauch J (1993) Productivity gains from geographic concentration of human capital: evidence from the cities. J Urban Econ 34(3):380–400

Ravallion M, Jalan J (1996) Growth divergence due to spatial externalities. Econ Lett 53 (2):227–232

Rebelo S (1991) Long-run policy analysis and long-run growth. J Pol Econ 99(3):500–521

Rey S, Dev B (2006) Sigma convergence in the presence of spatial effects. Pap Reg Sci 85 (2):217–234

Rey S, Janikas M (2005) Regional convergence, inequality and space. J Econ Geogr 5(2):155–176

Rey S, Montouri B (1999) US regional income convergence: a spatial econometric perspective. Reg Stud 33(2):143–156

Ricci L (1999) Economic geography and comparative advantage: agglomeration versus specialisation. Eur Econ Rev 43(2):357–377

Rice P, Venables A (2003) Equilibrium regional disparities: theory and British evidence. Reg Stud 37(6–7):675–686

Richardson H (1969) Regional economics. Praeger, New York

Richardson H (1973a) Regional growth theory. Macmillan, London

Richardson H (1973b) Elements of regional economics. Penguin, London

Richardson H (1973c) Urban economics. Penguin, London

Richardson H (1974) Agglomeration potential: a generalisation of the income potential concept. J Reg Sci 14(3):325–336

Richardson H (1976) Growth pole spillovers: the dynamics of backwash and spread. Reg Stud 10:1–9

Richardson H (1978a) Regional and urban economics. Penguin, London

Richardson H (1978b) The state of regional economics: a survey article. Int Reg Sci Rev 3(1):1–48

Richardson H (1985) Input–output and economic base multipliers: looking backward and forward. J Reg Sci 25(4):607–661

Rietveld P (1991) A note on interregional versus intraregional inequality. Reg Sci Urban Econ 21 (4):627–637

Rigby D, Essletzbichler J (2002) Agglomeration economies and productivity differences in US cities. J Econ Geogr 2(4):407–432

Rivas A (2008) Les leyes des descarrolo economico endogeno de Kaldor. Revista de Economica Institucional 10(18):129–147

Robert-Nicoud F (2005) The structure of simple new economic geography models (or, on identical twins). J Econ Geogr 5(2):201–234

Roberts C (1979) Interregional per-capita income differentials and convergence: 1880–1950. J Econ Hist 39(1):101–112

Roberts M (2004) The growth performances of the GB counties: some new empirical evidence for 1977–1993. Reg Stud 38(2):149–165

Robinson E (1931) The structure of competitive industry. University of Chicago Press, Chicago

Rodríguez-Pose A (1999a) Convergence or divergence? Types of regional responses to socio-economic change in Western Europe. Tijdschrift voor Economische en Sociale Geographie 90 (4):363–378

Rodríguez-Pose A (1999b) Innovation prone and innovation averse societies: economic performance in Europe. Growth Change 30(1):75–105

Rodríguez-Pose A, Fratesi U (2004) Between development and social policies: the impact of European structural funds in Objective-1 regions. Reg Stud 38(1):97–113

Rogers A (1955) Some aspects of industrial diversification in the United States. Pap Reg Sci 1:31–46

Romans J (1965) Capital exports and growth among U.S. regions. Wesleyan University Press, Middletown

Romer P (1986) Increasing returns and long-run growth. J Pol Econ 94(5):1002–1037

Romer P (1987a) Growth based on increasing returns due to specialisation. Am Econ Rev 77 (2):56–62

Romer P (1987b) Crazy explanations for the productivity slowdown. NBER macroeconomics annual. MIT Press, Cambridge

Romer P (1990a) Endogenous technological change. J Pol Econ 98(5):S71–S102

Romer P (1990b) Are non-convexities important for understanding growth? Am Econ Rev 80 (2):97–103

Romer P (1993) Ideas gaps and object gaps in economic development. J Monet Econ 32 (3):543–573

Romer P (1994) The origins of endogenous growth. J Econ Perspect 8(1):3–22

Romer D (1996) Advanced macroeconomics. McGraw-Hill, New York

Rosenberg N (1982) Inside the black box: technology and economics. Cambridge University Press, Cambridge

Rosenstein-Rodan P (1943) Problems of industrialisation of Eastern and South-Eastern Europe. Econ J 53(210–211):202–211

Rosenthal S, Strange W (2001) The determinants of agglomeration. J Urban Econ 50(2):191–229

Rostow W (1960) The stages of economic growth: a non-communist manifesto. Cambridge University Press, Cambridge

Rowthorn R (1975a) What remains of Kaldor's laws? Econ J 85(337):10–19

Rowthorn R (1975b) A reply to Lord Kaldor's comment. Econ J 85(340):897–901

Rowthorn R (2008) Returns to scale and the economic impact of migration. Spat Econ Anal 3 (2):151–158

Rowthorn R (2009) Returns to scale and the economic impact of migration: some new considerations. Spat Econ Anal 4(3):329–341

Saaverda L (2003) Tests for spatial lag dependence based on method of moments estimation. Reg Sci Urban Econ 33(1):27–58

Saito H, Gopinath M (2011) Knowledge spillovers, absorptive capacity and skill intensity of Chilean manufacturing plants. J Reg Sci 51(1):83–101

Sala-i-Martin X (1994) Cross-sectional regressions and the empirics of economic growth. Eur Econ Rev 38(3–4):739–747

Sala-i-Martin X (1996a) Regional cohesion: evidence and theories of regional growth and convergence. Eur Econ Rev 40(6):1325–1352

Sala-i-Martin X (1996b) The classical approach to convergence analysis. Econ J 106 (437):1019–1036

Salardi P (2009) Brazilian poverty between and within groups: decomposition by geographical, group-specific poverty lines. Rev Urban Reg Dev Stud 21(1):50–71

Salinas-Jiménez M (2003) Technological change, efficiency gains and capital accumulation in labour productivity growth and convergence: an application to the Spanish regions. Appl Econ 35(17):1839–1851

Savvides A, Stegnos T (2000) Income inequality and economic development: evidence from the threshold regression model. Econ Lett 69(2):207–212

Schaefer G (1977) The urban hierarchy and the urban area production function: a synthesis. Urban Stud 14(3):315–326

Schaefer G (1978) Returns to scale and income distribution in urban areas in Saskatchewan. J Reg Sci 18(3):357–371

Schmutzler A (1999) The new economic geography. J Econ Surv 13(4):355–379

Schultz T (1961) Investment in human capital. Am Econ Rev 51(1):1–17

Schultz T (1981) Investing in people: the economics of population quality. University of California Press, Berkley

Schumpeter J (1934) The theory of economic development. Harvard University Press, Cambridge

Scitovsky T (1954) Two concepts of external economies. J Pol Econ 62(2):143–151

Scott A (1988) New industrial spaces. Pion, London

Scott M (1989) A new view of economic growth. Basil Blackwell, Oxford

Scott M (1990) A new theory of endogenous economic growth. Oxf Rev Econ Policy 8(4):29–42

Scott M (1992) Policy implications of 'a new view of economic growth. Econ J 102(412):622–632

Seers D (1962) A model of comparative rates of growth in the world economy. Econ J 72 (285):45–78

Segal D (1976) Are there returns to scale in city size? Rev Econ Stat 58(3):339–350

Setterfield M (1997) History versus equilibrium and the theory of economic growth. Camb J Econ 21(3):365–378

Setterfield M (1998) History versus equilibrium: Nicholas Kaldor on historical time and economic theory. Camb J Econ 22(5):521–537

Setterfield M (2001) Cumulative causation, interrelatedness and the theory of economic growth: a reply to Argyrous and Toner. Camb J Econ 25(1):107–112

Shanks M (1967) The innovators: the economics of technology. Penguin, London

Shaw G (1992) Policy implications of endogenous growth theory. Econ J 102(412):611–621

Shefer D (1973) Localisation economies in SMSAs: a production function analysis. J Reg Sci 13 (1):55–64

Shefer D, Frenkel A (1999) Agglomeration and industrial innovation in space: an empirical analysis. In: Rietveld P, Shefer D (eds) Regional development in an age of structural economic change. Ashgate, Aldershot, pp 53–71

Shefer D, Rietveld P (1999) Structural economic change and regional development. In: Rietveld P, Shefer D (eds) Regional development in an age of structural economic change. Ashgate, Aldershot, pp 255–267

Shucksmith M, Cameron S, Merridew T, Pichler F (2009) Urban–rural differences in quality of life across the European Union. Reg Stud 43(10):1275–1289

Siano R, D'Uva M (2006) Club Convergence in European Union. Appl Econ Lett 13(9):569–574

Simmie J (2003) Innovation and urban regions as national and international nodes for the transfer and sharing of knowledge. Reg Stud 37(6–7):607–620

Simmie J (2005) Innovation and space: a critical review of the literature. Reg Stud 39(6):789–804

Simon H (1972) From substantive to procedural rationality. In: McGuire C, Rander R (eds) Decision and organization. North Holland, Amsterdam

Siriopoulos C, Asteriou D (1998) Testing for convergence across the Greek regions. Reg Stud 32 (6):537–546

Skott P (1999) Economic development and institutional change: some observations on the convergence literature. J Econ Behav Org 39(3):235–247

Skott P, Auerbach P (1995) Cumulative causation and the new theories of economic growth. J Post Keynes Econ 17(3):381–402

Smith A (1776) An inquiry into the nature and causes of the wealth of nations (1982 edition). Penguin, London

Smith H (2000) Innovation systems and 'local difficulties': the Oxfordshire experience. In: Z. Acs (ed) Regional innovation, knowledge and global change. Pinter, London, pp 72–88

Soete L (1981) A general test of technological-Gap trade theory. Weltwirtsch Arch 117 (4):638–660

Solow R (1956) A contribution to the theory of economic growth. Q J Econ 70(1):65–94

Solow R (1957) Technical change and the aggregate production function. Rev Econ Stat 39 (3):312–320

Solow R (1994) Perspectives on growth theory. J Econ Perspect 8(1):50–85

Soroka L (1994) Manufacturing productivity and city size in Canada, 1975 and 1985: does population matter? Urban Stud 31(6):895–911

Soukiazis E, Castro V (2005) How the Maastricht criteria and growth pact affected real convergence in the European Union: a panel-data analysis. J Policy Model 27(3):385–399

Steinnes D (1980) Aggregation, gerrymandering and spatial econometrics. Reg Sci Urban Econ 10 (4):561–569

Stern N (1991) The determinants of growth. Econ J 101(404):122–133

Stigler G (1951) The division of labour is limited by the extent of the market. J Pol Econ 59 (3):185–193

Stokey N (1991) Human capital, product quality and growth. Q J Econ 106(2):587–607

Stoneman P (1979) Kaldor's Law and British economic growth: 1800–1970. Appl Econ 11 (3):309–319

Storper M (1992) The limits to globalisation: technology districts and international trade. Econ Geogr 68(1):60–93

Storper M (1993) Regional worlds of production: learning and innovation in the technology districts of France, Italy and the USA. Reg Stud 27(5):433–455

Strauss J (2000) Is there a permanent component in US real GDP? Econ Lett 66(2):137–142

Streeten P (1998) The cheerful pessimist: Gunnar Myrdal the dissenter (1898–1987). World Dev 26(3):539–550

Sveikauskas L (1975) The productivity of cities. Q J Econ 89(3):393–413

Sveikauskas L (1979) Interurban differences in the innovative nature of production. J Urban Econ 6(2):216–227

Sveikauskas L, Cowdy J, Funk M (1988) Urban productivity: city size or industry size? J Reg Sci 28(2):185–202

Swan T (1956) Economic growth and capital accumulation. Econ Record 32(2):334–361

Tamura R (1991) Income convergence in an endogenous growth model. J Pol Econ 99(3):522–540

Targetti F, Foti A (1997) Growth and productivity: a model of cumulative growth and catching-up. Camb J Econ 21(1):27–43

Tavernier E, Temel T (1997) National and regional analysis of convergence in real wages in the U. S. agricultural sector. J Reg Anal Policy 27(1):63–74

Taylor M (2009) Understanding local growth: regional science, globalization and recession. Reg Sci Pol Pract 1(2):129–140

Teixeira A, Fortuna N (2010) Human capital, R&D, trade, and long-run productivity. Testing the technological absorption hypothesis for the Portuguese economy, 1960–2001. Res Policy 39 (3):335–350

Temple J (1999) The new growth evidence. J Econ Lit 37(1):112–156

Thirlwall A (1980a) Regional problems are balance of payments problems. Reg Stud 14 (5):419–425

Thirlwall A (1980b) Rowthorn's interpretation of Verdoorn's law. Econ J 90(358):386–388

Thirlwall A (1983a) Introduction to a symposium on Kaldor's growth laws. J Post Keynes Econ 5 (3):341–344

Thirlwall A (1983b) A plain man's guide to Kaldor's growth laws. J Post Keynes Econ 5 (3):345–358

Thisse J (2000) Agglomeration and regional imbalance: Why? And is it bad? Eur Invest Bank Pap 5(1):47–67

Tiebout C (1956a) Exports and regional growth. J Pol Econ 64(2):160–164

Tiebout C (1956b) The urban economic base reconsidered. Land Econ 31(1):95–99

Tiebout C (1961) Intra-urban location problems: an evaluation. Am Econ Rev 51(2):271–278

Tödtling F, Trippl M (2005) One size fits all? Towards a differential regional innovation policy approach. Res Policy 34(8):1203–1219

Tondl G (1998) EU regional policy in the southern periphery: lessons for the future. S Eur Soc Politics 3(1):93–129

Tondl G (1999) The changing pattern of regional convergence in Europe. Jahrbuch fur Regionalwissenschaft 9(1):1–33

Toner P (2001) 'History versus equilibrium' and the theory of economic growth. Camb J Econ 25 (1):97–102

Tortosa-Ausina E, Perez F, Mas M, Goerlich F (2005) Growth and convergence: profiles in the Spanish providences (1965–1997). J Reg Sci 45:147–182

Tselios V (2009) Growth and convergence in income per capita and income inequality in the regions of the EU. Spat Econ Anal 4(3):343–370

Tsionas E (2000a) Regional growth and convergence: evidence from the United States. Reg Stud 34(3):231–238

Tsionas E (2000b) Real convergence in Europe: how robust are econometric inferences? Appl Econ 32(11):1475–1482

Tsionas E (2001) Regional convergence and common, stochastic long-run trends: a re-examination of the US regional data. Reg Stud 35(8):689–696

Tsionas E (2002) Another look at regional convergence in Greece. Reg Stud 36(6):603–609

Uzawa H (1962) On a two-sector model of economic growth I. Rev Econ Stud 29(1):40–47

Uzawa H (1963) On a two-sector model of economic growth II. Rev Econ Stud 30(2):105–118

Uzawa H (1965) Optimal technological change in an aggregate model of economic growth. Int Econ Rev 6(1):18–31

Vaciago G (1975) Increasing returns and growth in advanced economies: a re-evaluation. Oxf Econ Pap 27(2):232–239

Varga A, Schalk H (2004) Knowledge spillovers, agglomeration and macroeconomic growth: an empirical approach. Reg Stud 38(8):977–989

Veblen T (1915) Imperial Germany and the industrial revolution. Macmillan, New York

Venables A (1996a) Equilibrium locations of vertically linked industries. Int Econ Rev 37 (2):341–359

Venables A (1996b) Trade policy, cumulative causation and industrial development. J Dev Econ 49(1):179–197

Verdoorn P (1949) Fattori che regolano lo sviluppo della productivita del lovoro. L' Industria 1:3–10

Verspagen B (1991) A new theoretical approach to catching up and falling behind. Struct Change Econ Dyn 2(2):359–380

Verspagen B (1992) Endogenous innovation in neoclassical growth models: a survey. J Macroecon 14(4):631–662

Verspagen B (1995) Convergence in the global economy: a broad historical perspective. Struct Change Econ Dyn 6(2):143–165

Verspagen B (1999) European regional clubs: do they exist and where are they heading? On economic and technological differences between European regions. In: Adams J, Pigliaru F (eds) Economic growth and change: national and regional patterns of convergence and divergence. Edward Elgar, Cheltenham/Northampton, pp 238–256

Viladecans-Marsal E (2004) Agglomeration and industrial location: city-level evidence. J Econ Geogr 4(5):565–582

Villaverde J (2005) Provincial convergence in Spain: a spatial econometric approach. Appl Econ Lett 12(11):697–700

Von Neumann J (1945) A model of general equilibrium. Rev Econ Stud 13(1):1–9

Wagner J (2000) Regional economic diversity: action, concept, or state of confusion. J Reg Anal Policy 30(2):1–22

Walters B (1995) Engendering macroeconomics: a reconsideration of growth theory. World Dev 23(11):1869–1880

Webber M (1972) Impact of uncertainty on location. MIT Press, Cambridge

Webber D (2002) Labour's reward across regions of the EU: a distributional dynamic approach. Appl Econ 34(3):385–394

Weber A (1929) Theory of the location of industries. University of Chicago Press, Chicago

Weiss L (1972) The geographic size of markets in manufacturing. Rev Econ Stat 54(3):245–257

Weiss L, Gooding E (1968) Estimation of differential employment multipliers in a small regional economy. Land Econ 44(2):235–244

Whiteman J (1987) Productivity and growth in Australian manufacturing industry. J Post Keynes Econ 9(4):576–592

Williamson J (1965) Regional inequalities and the process of national development. Econ Dev Cult Change 13(4):3–45

Williamson X (1975) Regional growth: predictive power of export base theory. Growth Change 6 (1):3–10

Winnick L (1961) Economic questions in urban redevelopment. Am Econ Rev 51(2):290–298

Wolfe S (1968) Productivity and growth in manufacturing industry: some reflections on professor Kaldor's inaugural lecture. Economica 35(138):117–126

Wulwick N (1991) Did the Verdoorn's law hang on Japan? East Econ J 17(1):15–20

Yamamoto D (2008) Scales of regional income disparities in the USA, 1955–2003. J Econ Geogr 8 (1):211–215

Yamarik S (2000) Can tax policy help explain state-level macroeconomic growth? Econ Lett 68 (2):211–215

Yao S (1999) Economic growth, income inequality and poverty in China under economic reforms. J Dev Stud 59(2):463–496

Young A (1928) Increasing returns and economic progress. Econ J 38(152):527–542

Zhang Z, Yao S (2001) Regional inequalities in contemporary China measured by GDP and consumption. Econ Issues 6(2):13–29

Printed by Publishers' Graphics LLC